Sustainable Development Issues and Perspectives

Sustainable Development
Issues and Perspectives

Edited by

R.N. Pati
Odile Schwarz-Herion

D.K. Printworld (P) Ltd.
New Delhi-110015

Cataloging in Publication Data — DK
[Courtesy: D.K. Agencies (P) Ltd. <docinfo@dkagencies.com>]

Sustainable Development : issues and perspectives /
edited by R.N. Pati, Odile Schwarz-Herion.
xii, 572 p. 23 cm.
Contributed articles.
With special reference to India.
Includes bibliographical references.
Includes index.
ISBN 8124604371

1. Sustainable development. 2. Sustainable development — India. 3. Traditional medicine. 4. Traditional medicine — India. 5. Environmental policy. 6. Poverty — Prevention. 7. Sustainable agriculture. 8. Indigenous peoples — civil rights. I. Pati, R.N. (Rabindra Nath), 1954- II. Schwarz-Herion, Odile.

DDC 333.709 54 22

ISBN 81-246-0437-1
First published in India in 2007

Publication of this volume has partially been sponsored by
IK Foundation of India
AEI Research and Consultancy Mahamaya Bhawan, HIG-101,
Kanan Vihar, Phase-1, P.O. Patia, BHUBANESWAR – 751 031 (Orissa)
Tel.: 91-674-2741025; E-mail: <ikfoundationofindia@hotmail.com>

Published and printed by:
D.K. Printworld (P) Ltd.
Regd. Office: 'Srikunj', F-52, Bali Nagar
Ramesh Nagar Metro Station
New Delhi – 110 015
Phones: (011) 2545 3975; 2546 6019; *Fax*: (011) 2546 5926
E-mail: dkprintworld@vsnl.net
Website: www.dkprintworld.com

Foreword

SUSTAINABLE DEVELOPMENT is gaining more and more importance in society, economy and politics due to the increasing public awareness about urgent environmental problems, such as global warming, drinking water supply and biodiversity. These issues are going hand in hand with other problems of the time like population explosion and increasing globalisation, which is creating a real challenge for mankind to combine traditional knowledge of indigenous people of the developing countries with that of global knowledge in a democratic way to reach a win-win situation on a global base.

The idea for the book at hand was created by its editor, Prof. Rabindra Nath Pati, Senior Social Anthropologist of the IK Foundation of India. Prof. Pati is an internationally renowned Social Anthropologist who received his PhD in Social Anthropology from Utkal University. As an eminent expert and scientist, he was honoured with the prestigious Rajiv Gandhi Sadbhavana Award for the Best Social Scientist of the Indian Federal State Orissa in 2003. Prof. Pati has gained international reputation by action research regarding documentation of indigenous knowledge and course of protection of Intellectual Property Rights of indigenous innovators as well as by numerous publications. He has directed a large number of research and development projects in Orissa with the support from various international development agencies such as Norwegian Agency for Development Cooperation (NORAD), Danish International Development Agency (DANIDA), and the World Bank. His research findings have significantly contributed to the policy makers in many different sectors, including developing cultural approach towards HIV/AIDS, women empowerment, besides biodiversity conservation.

The IK Foundation of India is operating since 2002 in the State of Chhattisgarh under the leadership of Prof. Pati. It is a premier policy research institute, engaged in action research, focusing on indigenous knowledge and sustainable development. The institute is offering its research and consultancy service for various international, national, and government agencies. Priority areas of research are ethno-pharmacology, ethno-forestry, ethno-architecture, pheno-menology of indigenous objects and material culture. Furthermore, the institute takes steps for protecting the Intellectual Property Rights of indigenous innovators along with encouraging the grass-roots innovators. The IK Foundation also acts as a potential export house for exporting Indian tribal arts and crafts. It plays a vital role in disseminating and communicating traditional knowledge and expertise by means of training, research, production of films, TV serials, videos, and exchange visits among international scholars.

This book is the first volume of a planned Sustainability series of books, published from New Delhi. Containing 27 chapters, written by renowned Sustainability experts from all over the world, coming from diverse universities, research institutes and private enterprises, the book covers a large variety of issues in the fields of Sustainable Development. The issues covered in the book include forest protection in favour of plant-based medicine in rural regions of India over developing strategies to implement the Agenda 21 slogan **Think globally, act locally** up to integrated environmental production measures to combine environmental protection with cost reduction in industrial enterprises.

Compiling articles by Sustainability experts of different backgrounds from all over the world, *Sustainable Development: Issues and Perspectives* is a valuable source of knowledge in the field of Sustainable Development, giving significant impulses not only to professors and researchers in different sectors but also to practitioners in industry, and politics as well as to NGOs. Treating the challenging and complex issues in a clear and illustrative manner, it is equally an inspiring and enjoyable reading for all the interested people who want to become familiar with relevant issues in Sustainable Development. The excerpts of the book might also serve as teaching material at high schools worldwide for geography, history, politics, chemistry and biology lessons to give young students a general idea of the most important challenges of Sustainable Development and globalization as well as some insight into the mentality, the knowledge, and the lifestyle of indigenous people all over the world.

(Prof. Dr Werner F. Schulz)
Lehrstuhl für Umweltmanagement
(Chair of Environmental Management)
Universität Hohenheim
70593 – STUTTGART (Germany)
Ph: (0711) 459-24051, Fax: 459-23474

Contents

Part II
Environmental Governance and Sustainable Development

Part V
Indigenous Rights and Sustainable Development

Introduction

R.N. Pati and *O. Schwarz-Herion*

In remote regions of the world, the modern technology tends to bypass the indigenous communities and the local knowledge systems. A very little attempt has been made by development actors across the globe to learn from the local knowledge system and practices of these indigenous communities. More emphasis is given on empowerment process of indigenous people and alleviation of poverty through the process of sustainable development. The researches have validated that the true empowerment of poor people lies within the framework of synergy between local knowledge system and modern technology and helping them managing their own development in the larger context of globalization. Sustainable development intervention around the globe focuses on empowerment of poor people as the main thrust area of development. The empowerment always emerges from within the community. The poorest of the poor and vulnerable communities are provided space and opportunity through development process so that indigenous knowledge can be combined with global knowledge in a democratic and self-determined way for achievement of sustainable development. The modern technology and scientific approaches to knowledge generation have brought radical changes in the field of agriculture, medicine, communication, arms and ammunitions and space research. But there are many unsolved problems like hunger, HIV/AIDS, illiteracy, terrorism, unethical competition, etc. which the modern technology has failed to overcome. The globalization forces have drastically affected the local communities and promoted unequal distribution of wealth and opportunities in many regions of the developing countries. Systematic use of indigenous knowledge in the development forces has solutions for overcoming many unsolved problems which modern technology and scientific approach to knowledge have failed to solve. The research studies in different regions of the world have shown that the indigenous knowledge has empowered the local community to solve their local problems by exploring local resources and local knowledge system apart from contributing significantly towards promotion of solidarity and elimination of negative impacts of globalization.

The Local Health Tradition (LHT) in different indigenous communities of Asia, Africa and Australia has been sustained through traditional medicinal practices of herbalists, bone setters, traditional birth attendants, spiritualists, faith healers and psyche healers. The traditional medicinal practices explore indigenous knowledge, belief and customs for elimination of imbalances in psychological, physical or social well-being. The Governments of these nations have recognized the importance of traditional medicine practices and revival of medicinal plant sector for generating additional income and employment opportunities. A good number of researchers have noted potential visible differences with major philosophies of medicinal plants' commercialization and emphasized upon the regulation of the medicinal plant stock in countries like India and China. There is an urgent need for exploring the immense potential of medicinal plant system or indigenous systems of medicine in these countries for global market and appropriate international co-operation. This has not been appropriately explored.

The sustainable development is correlated with sustenance of local health tradition in indigenous communities. Some of the Indian researchers have explored the best practices of local healers of indigenous forest communities on identification, harvest and application of medicinal potencies for treatment of various diseases and correlated with local health tradition. The knowledge on habitat of plants is treated as very important in sustaining local health tradition. Transmission of knowledge on traditional medicinal plants is found to be acquired in a sequential manner. The transmission of traditional medicinal plant knowledge promotes conservation of rare medicinal plants and creates demand for new legal framework and systematic national programme for preventing the commercial exploitation of indigenous knowledge and resources.

The issues of sustainable development differ from country to country. The traditional healers have been considered as the dependable source of health care providers in a country like Ghana for centuries. The findings of explorative research studies have indicated the use of herbs, animals and mineral-based medicines along with spiritual therapies. The underutilization of the services of traditional practitioners poses a serious threat towards promoting a bridge between the medical establishment and large number of rural and poor people depending on the traditional practitioners in this country. It is believed that the integration of traditional medicines and practitioners into modern health care system will ensure better utilizations of new hospitals and clinics established in underserved areas and benefit everybody. The traditional healers need to be utilized as facilitators for prevention of diseases and dissemination of public health message in the community apart from making timely referral of patients to the hospitals. Renewal and revival of this local health tradition would pave ways for sustainable development and achievement of Millennium Development Goals (MDGs) in Ghana.

Some scientists have critically examined the sustainability of public health interventions in the context of sustainable development. Their explorative research studies have highlighted various dimensions of participatory learning approach and the framework adopted in the sustainability of health care resources. The insights drawn from such research work have provided meaningful guidelines and insights to development factors for application of the principle of sustainable development in public health.

Sustainable development as well as the MDGs cannot be achieved without safeguarding the intellectual and cultural property rights of the indigenous communities and their ownership over common productive resources. The in-depth study focused on the issues of intellectual and cultural property rights of tribal healers of Bastar in Chhattisgarh of India highlights the contradiction between government's perception and rules of revenues and forest department over ownership and property rights on forest resources. The Biological Diversities Act, 2002 enacted by Government of India has not been implemented appropriately in sharing the benefits with the stakeholders at the grassroots. The forces of globalization have adversely affected the cultural and biological diversities and hijacked the tangible and intangible assets of age-old indigenous knowledge and local health tradition. The biological resources in the indigenous territories of Chhattisgarh are at stake. The tribes like "Gond" and "Halba" sustain the preservation of biological resources through cultural practices. There is an urgent need for synthesization, reduction, standardization, and miniaturization of cultural knowledge and practices for mass reproduction and distribution based on scientific research and integration of local knowledge in mainstream of scientific exploitation. The situation of indigenous territory of Chhattisgarh can be compared with forest regions of any Indian State as well as forest territories of Africa and Australia.

Sustainable management of resources ensures sustainable development. Some of the scientists have focused on the vertical dimension of social integration and grassroot activities for sustainability management. Top-down transfer of political ideas and bottom-up transfer of local impacts are treated as two serious problems for global sustainability management on a vertical scale. The scientists have critically examined the variables like homogeneity of positions, internal communication, and social responsibility in the context of vertical dimensions of social integration. It is emphasized that the civil society organizations need to aggregate the interest of local people in a fair and democratic way. Efforts need to be made for bringing their will into the networks and social responsibility from civil society organizations towards achieving common goal of their members through process of top-down communication. The researchers have critically examined various dimensions of empowerment of civil society organizations and sustainability management. The findings of such innovative research have added new dimensions to the understanding of sustainable development.

Sustainable development is also linked with balancing between eco-health and social health. Recycling of solid waste leads to promotion of eco-health. The recycling of solid waste is a viable mechanism of preserving natural resources, reduction of pollution and saving of energy. The role of municipal councils in this direction has been appreciated by the people of a country like Malayasia. The researchers have critically examined different dimensions of the recycling process such as awareness generation, community participation, type of facility provided and types of material recycled in the national programme of solid waste recycling. It is emphasized that appropriate legislative measures enacted and enforced by municipal council for active public participation and elimination of harmful effects of solid waste recycling process on the environment is a key to success of the programme. This experiment needs to be replicated in other developing countries of the world.

A good number of research studies presented in this book have prioritized on the essence of sustainable governance, one of the greatest challenges in the global-ization era. These papers have examined the concept of sustainability in the context of social, economic and environmental consideration in decision-making processes. Some of the authors have focused on analytical tools such as Sustainability Analysis Framework (SAF) which has been divided into two parts, i.e. (a) Sustainability Analysis Framework (SAF), and (b) Sustainability Review Matrix (SRM).

In a country like India, various legislations have been enacted to enforce bureaucratic mechanisms for environmental governance in forest regions of the country. The issues of environmental governance are deep-rooted in cultural, social and natural life-support systems in forest regions of the country. These issues are correlated with the basic livelihood issues of these regions. The forces of globalization have paved ways for multinational companies for commercially exploiting the bio-wealth of these regions violating local traditional rules and hijacking intellectual and cultural property rights. The community-based mechanism of biodiversity conservation has been disrupted due to inappropriate legislative measures and poor protection of local health traditions. The protection of intellectual property rights is closely interlinked with indigenous knowledge and community efforts for sustainable development. The forest policy enacted by State and National Government of India emphasizes on *in situ* and *ex situ* conservation, domestication, non-destructive harvest and propagation of medicinal plants involving indigenous herbalists, shamans and community-based organizations. It is observed that the effects of globalization and militant infestation in forest regions of the country have sabotaged the efforts of local administration in gearing up innovative environmental governance initiatives.

The developed countries like Switzerland also face environmental threats in terms of disposal of industrial pollutants. The scientists and policy makers are more concerned for disposal of waste water through appropriate research on industrial engineering sector. The findings of such research studies provide meaningful guidelines for replication of the experiment in other parts of the globe ensuing environmental governance. Different researches have indicated that indigenous knowledge provides the knowledge base for determining food production and labour division between gender and age groups towards population survival. In many remote regions of the world, poverty alleviation measures need to be streamlined through uncovering the socio-political, religious, economic and environmental implication of indigenous knowledge system relating to sustainable development. There is an urgent need for promoting strong awareness for appreciation of indigenous knowledge and sustainable development in different parts of the globe. The experts have emphasized more on documentation, preservation, research and dissemination of indigenous knowledge which would promote development. This process is socially acceptable, biophysically permissible and economically viable. The policy makers, scientists and development practitioners need to work together to devise the consistent and sustainable approach to poverty alleviation, food security, and environmental governance. The MDGs have emphasized on appropriate exploration of indigenous knowledge for achievement of sustainable development. The indigenous knowledge system shall be appropriately utilized only when shared, challenged and applied for betterment of mankind.

Addressing issues of food security is another dimension of sustainable development. Food security is a burning issue for growing population in developing countries. The new farming technologies, crops and fertilizers have been introduced in indigenous communities for raising agriculture productivity. The land reclamation, soil erosion and wind management are major threats for promoting agriculture productivity in these communities. The low productivity of agriculture crops is one of the major threats causing low income and food insecurity in rural areas of India and Africa. The forces of globalization have geared up agricultural development worldwide which caused replacement of native plant species and reduction in diversity of seed stock in Africa and Indian subcontinent. The commercialization of medicinal herbs in tropical rainforest has replaced indigenous plants drastically. Such replacement has threatened varieties of food crops in the indigenous territories. The reduced diversity of seed stock leads to insurgencies in food security in the regions of Africa and other developing countries. In developed nations of the world, the high technology and genetic modifications of vegetables have brought radical change in agro industry. Such revolution in agro sector has drastically influenced the life support system of people in developing countries and led to disruption of genetic diversity in the stock of seeds. The organic farming and indigenous agriculture have been adversely affected. The introduction of agro chemicals in rural regions of developing countries like India and Africa has made farmers abandon the traditional techniques of controlling pests, insects and diseases. The subsidy-linked marketing of agro chemicals and chemical pesticides has promoted market of big players and disrupted the base of traditional organic farming. It is observed that after withdrawal of subsidies by Government on agricultural inputs, the cost of agro chemicals in many developing countries has gone high. Such technological transformation in agro sector has eroded the indigenous knowledge on organic farming from farming communities. The farmers' knowledge on indigenous crop rotation, weed management and organic farming disappeared. The increased use of agro chemicals in indigenous communities led to adverse effects on human health and environment. The disappearance of traditional knowledge on use of botanical pesticides has led to reduction of natural crop protection practices. The inappropriate farming methods and use of highly mechanized cultivations have caused soil erosion and drying up of rivers and streams in many developing countries of the world. These issues are serious threats to sustainable development which need to be addressed by social activists, policy makers and local governments.

This book contains research-based articles by different scientists of the world focusing on various issues of sustainable government.

In **Part I** of this book, the issues of sustainable development as correlated with local health tradition has been critically assessed through five research-based articles. Chapter One critically highlights the sensitive areas of research relating to medicinal plant species. This chapter focuses on various promotional schemes sponsored by National Medicinal Plant Board (NMPB), Government of India. The development of agro-techniques, scientific validation of traditional knowledge, bio-technology, exchange and trade of herbal products would go a long way ensuring the sustainability of medicinal plants in different forest regions of India. Chapter Two critically analyses different dimensions of transmission of traditional plant knowledge. The foundational skills covering interest towards plants, identification and harvesting of plants, processing for making final herbal products, rare plants are given top priority in the process of transmission of traditional medicinal plant knowledge among indigenous farmers. The author has cited success stories of community-based conservation of medicinal plants experimented by two Indian NGOs. This chapter provides valuable insights for undertaking explorative action research on commercialization of herbal medicine and conservation of biodiversity. Chapter Three focuses on traditional medicinal practices incorporating use of herbs, animal and mineral based medicines prevalent in Ghana. The author focuses on various sensitive areas for promoting synergy between traditional medical practices and existing medical system in Ghana. Chapter Four critically highlights various aspects of integration between ecological sustainability and public health practices. The author examines the applicability of the principles of sustainable development in the area of sustainable future. Chapter Five examines in depth various issues of globalisation and their adverse impact on environmental governance. The author has empirically validated the violation of intellectual property rights of tribal healers in forest villages of Chhattisgarh through commercialization of medicinal herbs and hijacking of patent right on rare medicinal herbs by multinational companies. The author critically examines different aspects of promoting synergy between indigenous model of health care and conservation of biodiversity basing upon validation of micro level empirical observation.

Part II covers issues of linking environmental governance with sustainable development based on findings of research studies conducted in different regions of the world. The MDGs emphasizes on eradication of poverty and achievement of sustainable development. In Chapter six, first of this Part, the scientist deals with the question to which extent grass-roots activities can be utilized for sustainable management on a local base. The challenge consists in promoting the idea of sustainable development on a global base while implementing particular ecological and social problems on a local base. One of the main problems is that concentrating too much on a small locally oriented group can lead to some kind of "corral-mentality", causing group pressure and dissociating small groups from each other. These problems might be solved by forming slack, non-hierarchical networks. This kind of networks would ensure that certain shared ideas (above all the three columns of sustainability) are supported by all local groups and that a balance between the interests of single groups on the one hand and networks on the other hand is created. Additionally, support by national State authorities, professional organizations, and by NGOS might be helpful in overcoming difficulties concerning communication and management of sustainable development. Chapter seven treats solid waste recycling in Malaysia, based on two case studies which were performed in households in the States of Terenggau and Perak. The outcome of these case studies, based on detailed questionnaires shows that the problem does not consist in the awareness that waste recycling is important but rather in the lack of conveniently accessible facilities, provided for recycling as well as in some misinformation about the actual availability of existing facilities. Chapter eight covers knowledge communication as essence of sustainable governance. Although the ecological problems, such as missing eco-balance, population explosion, or global warming are well-known, responsible people in politics and economy go on to hide their head in the sand, behaving like an ostrich. Since these problems cannot be solved by means of technology alone, a process of rethinking, has to be initiated by calculated information with the help of appropriate tools. The Government of the Australian Federal State of New South Wales (NSW) has designed such a tool to integrate sustainable development, including social, economic, and ecological factors. This tool, called Sustainability Analysis Framework (SAF), has already been introduced in 38 State agencies of NSW. SAF lays down the agency-specific assessment tool "Sustainability review matrix" (SRM) which had been implemented in "Sustainability Issues Practice Tables" and then has been spread by the educating public administrators. Chapter nine deals with the issues of forest villages in Chhattisgarh, India. This nascent Indian Federal State is famous for its big forest stand and its abundance of bio-wealth that forms a real treasure for the State, mainly due to the knowledge of tribal women in forest villages as primary users of natural resources. However, Chhattisgarh is facing two serious dangers: First, the growing deforestation by international industrial groups due to globalisation, damaging this sensitive eco-system, and therefore accelerating global warming, and second the bio-piracy, including smuggling out valuable local medicinal herbs in huge quantities, not only by hijacking the intellectual property of the tribal herbalists but also by exploiting the tribal herbalists without compensating them. Therefore, it is an urgent need to promote a meaningful and effective alliance between tribal women as bearers of indigenous knowledge, herbalists and shamans on the one hand and scientists, researchers, and agricultural development practitioners on the other hand to scale down bio-piracy, and to preserve the very rich indigenous knowledge in order to create sufficient living conditions for the indigenous people. Chapter 10 refers to several case studies which prove in an impressive way that environmental protection measures can generate added value in the process industry. Using instructive and convincing examples, the scientist demonstrates that improving current manufacturing processes in an intelligent and creative way can help to meet regulatory emission limits, improve product quality, increase production capacity, and reduce production cost at the same time. Sometimes, an improvement concerning emission values can be achieved merely by suitable training and motivating the staff or by minor technical measures. In this way, environmental protection regulations can lead to — besides their primary targets — an outcome of economic values. Chapter 11 deals with different types of relationships between firms, communities and government, including possible obstacles. The different processes are described with reference to the respective type of organization. In this connection, the scientist distinguishes between horizontal and vertical relationships of firms, communities and governments. In sum, he states that connectivity to an interorganizational network and competence at managing collaborations have become key drivers of a new logic of organization. The different problems of collaboration are shown in some instructive figures. In Chapter 12, the scientist describes co-operations and conflicts between a mining company and communities in the centre of Mexico. Furthermore, the article deals with New Social Movement and the three levels of government. This case study reveals the evident lack of sensitivity that some foreign investors (mining companies) show towards the historic heritage (e.g. churches from the seventeenth and eighteenth centuries) as well as the cultural interests and the health of the involved habitants by contaminating drinking water reserves in environmentally protected areas. Especially alarming is the fact that the mining companies violated Federal and State laws of Mexico with tacit consent of the government. Chapter 13 refers to the central role of higher education for a nation's cultural tradition as well as for social change, citing Romania and Tibet as examples. Concerning Romania which is orientating to the requirements for a country which will soon join the European Union, offers some chances on the one hand but involves the danger that national tradition and indigenous knowledge get lost by this assimilation process on the other hand. In Tibet, the communist indoctrination is less of a problem than the assimilation to the Chinese culture, which results in the destruction of the Tibetan civilization, religion, mentalities, traditions and cultures.

Part III of the book covers research-based articles on this dimension. The scientists emphasize on sustainable agriculture as a key to achievement of sustainable development. First Chapter of this part (Chapter 14), covers the improvement of treadle pumps and their possible contribution towards poverty alleviation, especially in arid and semi-arid rural areas of developing countries. The treadle pump is one of the most exciting innovations in manual irrigation, employing the user's body-weight and lack muscles to lift water from surface water resources. In spite of its advantages there is still some potential for improvement: aside from the physical, economic, and mechanical conditions, other parameters to be optimized are portability, reliability, and ease of manufacturing and repair. The issue of Chapter 15 is managing complexities in sustainable development. The complexity of the phenomenon itself is one factor, which is responsible for the difficulties of implementing sustainable development in enterprises. Designing a complexity framework for sustainable development might help to meet the next stage in sustainable development: delivering the desired results. Chapter 16 presents viable alternatives for sustainability, describing economic reforms in the forest villages in Chhattisgarh, which are well known for their unique treasures of biodiversity. The scientist claims that globalization has led to exploitation of indigenous people as it has happened in forest tribes of the Bastar region in Chhattisgarh: commercial exploitation of indigenous arts and crafts without any compensation, illegally felling of trees, ruthless exploitation of mineral resources, overexploitation of biological resources as well as bio-piracy by removing plants of enormous medical and commercial value, etc. Meanwhile, the Government of India has drafted some rules which are supposed to help solving this problem. A study performed by two anthropologists and one ethnobotanist has examined the relations between cultural factors and the economic transformation of tribal communities. The study revealed that women empowerment as a key issue for empowering the community concerning preservation of indigenous knowledge about plans should come out of the indigenous communities rather than from outside. Self help groups (SHGs) of tribal women have proved themselves to be very effective. Community biodiversity registry, initiated by SHGs network in partnership with NGOs and community, has not only empowered the women but equally the community as a whole by infusing the force for challenging the patent claim on knowledge of medicinal herbs. In Chapter 17, the scientist critically analyzes the historical background and the meaning of the term "sustainable development". Introduced by the Brundtland Commission in its report "Our Common Future" and further promoted by the World Bank and UN Environmental Programs, this term has been steadily developed and extended. The scientist stresses the holistic and integrated approach of sustainable development, considering man as part of nature and ecosystem. The need to preserve the rich animal and plant world, problems due to increasing population along with increasing consumption of limited resources makes it necessary to plan in advance and to involve all actors into the process: government, private enterprises and individuals.

The research findings of different scholars exploring different dimensions of sustainable agriculture as correlated with sustainable development have been presented in **Part IV** of this book. The indigenous communities perceive sustainable development entirely from a different angle than the perception of policy makers, planners and administrators. There exist a wide gap between macro level planning and perception and micro level understanding of the issues on sustainable development. A synergy between macro and micro level understanding, planning and implementation of sustainable development can be achieved through understanding of local knowledge system and involving community appropriately in the programme from the beginning. Chapter 18, being the first chapter of this Part, describes the globalization of the potato as an ancient indigenous crop. Since the potato had been cultivated in the Andean high plateau of Peru, it has been imported to Europe in the mid-1500s. Today, the CIP (International Potato Centre) has listed 5000 cultivars. Indigenous people have already cultivated potatoes containing different nutrients using their indigenous knowledge and additionally have developed different ways of cooking and of conservation, e.g. freeze drying. Chapter 19 deals with indigenous people of Guatemala, forming a large percentage of the population and possessing large knowledge in the traditional sustainable form of agriculture. Since the Ladinos (the successors of the Spanish conquerors) own by far the largest part of land and hold all-important positions, the indigenous people are more or less excluded from politics. Therefore, the Ladinos endanger sustainable tradition of indigenous knowledge in Guatemala. Chapter 20 describes life and culture of Polynesian people and gives an insight into their ancient life and original culture as well as into the way it has changed due to the invasion of Western culture. Polynesian people were used to eat healthy food which was prepared in a time-consuming way and which they served and ate in large quantity at special occasions. Due to the influence of Western eating culture, the traditional food has been replaced by fast food which is easy to prepare but rich in sugar and fat which Polynesian people now eat in huge quantities on a nearly daily basis. As a consequence, many Polynesian people suffer from obesity with its typical consequences such as cancer and diabetes. Chapter 21 promotes the necessity of the indigenous knowledge practices in sustainable agriculture production in villages of Benue State Nigeria. Because of the economic crisis, the Nigerian State could no longer afford the expenses for modern agriculture and thus started to reconsider a return to indigenous practices in agriculture. Nevertheless, wars, conflicts, natural disasters and HIV/AIDS make it difficult to revive indigenous knowledge. A study performed in the Otukpo local government in the Benue State verified and documented proven indigenous knowledge in crop production, environmental protection and animal disease control, and thus helped to make agriculture self-sustaining by application of this knowledge.

Part V of the book covers research articles on indigenous rights and sustainable development. The first Chapter of this part (Chapter 22), describes indigenous movements in Mexico since 1975 in order to actively participate in the democratization process. There are five indigenous organizations in Mexico, involving ethical components. These environmental and indigenous movements focus on agriculture and the quest for sustainable alternatives. Chapter 23 treats sustainable development from the view of indigenous people. While indigenous people aim at living in accordance with nature, people from modern civilized cultures tend to consider nature as an adversary which has to be fought. The scientist holds a wrong translation of Genesis 2 from the original Greek version of the bible into the Latin "Vulgata" and into other languages partly responsible for the attitude of Western people towards nature. In this chapter the scientist focuses on the quotation and the analyses of some crucial points of the "Indigenous Plan of Implementation on Sustainable Development", presented to the UN World Summit in Johannesburg in 2002. This plan, reflecting indigenous peoples' mind regarding sustainable development, lists a range of issues which are also treated in this book, e.g. the problem of deforestation in indigenous communities, serious losses of biodiversity, the importance of women empowerment for the preservation of commercially viable indigenous knowledge, bio-piracy, or the risk of ground pollution and drinking water contamination by mining. Chapter 24 focuses on the situation of indigenous people in Mexico. The largest part of the Mexican population is poor; 30 per cent of them are indigenous people whose voice is not taken into account. Additionally, there are other problems concerning forest, disorders by not curbing irregular settlements, and the lack of self-organization. Currently, solutions for this problem are sought to improve the living standards of indigenous communities, for instance, with different types of eco-tourism without destroying the environment, leading to protection and preservation of existing forest resources. In Chapter 25, the significance of indigenous locality within the framework of global sustainable development is treated. In this connection indigenous locality aims at a balance between economic, ecological and social needs by means of a compromise between global pressures and local systems which contribute significantly to the preservation of intact ecosystems and biodiversity by indigenous knowledge. The scientist gives evidence that locality can work as a lever of economic growth and furthermore of global sustainability. Chapter 26 gives an insight into the traditional way of life in Monkey River Village, a small village located along the southern coast of Belize in the Caribbean Sea and how it is changing over the time. Four interviews with different women who have grown up in this village and are working in different jobs there, helps to understand the mentality of the indigenous people towards gender roles, the importance of education as well as the career chances for future generations. Changing their traditionally gender-based and education-reluctant mentality is only slowly progressing even though the educational infrastructure has significantly improved and girls and boys are encouraged by committed teachers to finish their education. While education becomes more and more important in a changing world, it also creates new problems: if the educational level increases, the population of the village decreases, since well-educated young people are moving to locations with better job options. Having this in mind, higher education in Monkey River Village seems to be a two-edged sword. In Chapter 27, the political situation in Serbia is analyzed with view to sustainable development at the beginning of the Third Millennium. The scientist states that the biggest barrier to sustainable development in Serbia both on a national and on a local level is the failure of national governments to implement the international agreements signed by Serbia in the 1992 UN Summit and afterwards. According to the scientist, the achievement of sustainability in national development requires a strategic approach which is both long-term in its perspective and integrated in linking various development processes to solve complex issues. The scientist comes to the conclusion that regulations on municipalities and other types of territorial organizations, public administrations, property, local finances, and other fields will be indispensable to implement reforms in the field of sustainable development.

This book is a masterpiece highlighting different unexplored dimensions of sustainable development. It will provide meaningful insights and guidelines to scholars, policy-makers and administrators in developing legislative measures and interventions for achieving sustainable development as well as indicators of MDGs.

Abbreviations

CIP	—	International Potato Centre
LHT	—	Local Health Tradition
MDGs	—	Millennium Development Goals
NSW	—	New South Wales
SAF	—	Sustainability Analysis Framework
SHGs	—	Self Help Groups
SRM	—	Sustainability Review Matrix

Part I

Local Health Tradition and Sustainable Development

1

Medicinal Plants of India
Integrating Livelihood Options and Conservation Concerns

Chandra Prakash Kala* and *Bikram Singh Sajwan

Introduction

MEDICINAL plants play a central role in the treatment of existing and newborn diseases by providing raw material to the pharmaceutical industries and traditional herbal healers (Kala, 2005a). In addition, the cosmetic industries are increasingly using more natural ingredients, including extracts of medicinal plants, in their products (KIT, 2003; Kala, 2005b). Worldwide, about 52,885 species of plants are known for curing diseases (Schippmann, et al., 2002); of these >7500 species are found in India. The importance of Indian medicinal plants has been described in many outstanding historical works such as the *Rigveda, Charak Samhita, Sushrut Samhita* and *Ayurvedic Materia Medica*.

The use of plants for therapy in Indian culture is so important that the most knowledgeable person on herbal therapy has been considered an incarnation of Lord Vishnu, Dhanwantari (Kala, 2006a). Over the centuries of experiments, at present, medicinal plants are becoming a commodity with high added value. The World Health Organization (WHO) has estimated that the present demand for medicinal plants is about US $ 14 billion a year. The demand for medicinal plant-based raw materials is growing at the rate of 15 to 25 per cent annually, and according to the WHO estimates, the demand for medicinal plants is likely to increase to US $ 5 trillion in 2050 (Sharma, 2004).

The actual demand, however, will be even greater than the data suggested as a sizeable proportion of medicinal plant material is used for domestic consumption and a large part of the trade in medicinal plants is illegal and thus is unrecorded. The leading suppliers of the medicinal plants are China, Singapore, Brazil, India, and Egypt (Lange, 1997). The international demand is largely from the United States and the European Union, with Germany as the leading trade centre (KIT, 2003). According to a survey, in member states of European Union about 1400 herbal preparations are used for therapeutic purposes. There are about 7000 compounds and 47 modern pharmaceutical plant-based drugs already in the world market and the predicted 328 drugs (yet to be discovered) have a market potential of US $ 147 billion. In its first year, the sale of anti-cancer drug Taxol from *Taxus* species fetched more than US $ 2 billion (Crook and Clapp, 1998; Planning Commission, 2000; Teachnical Centre for Agriculture and Rural Cooperation (CTA) , 2002). Such popularity of plant-derived products in health care reflects their increasing acceptance across the world.

This increasing demand for plant-based drugs is however causing a heavy pressure on some selected high-value medicinal plant populations in the wild (Kala, 2004; Kala, 2005c; Kala et al., 2006). Moreover, many medicinal plant species have slow growth rates, low population densities and narrow geographic ranges (Kala, 2005d). On the other hand, the indigenous knowledge on the use of lesser-known medicinal plants is declining sharply. Realizing the importance of medicinal plants in recent years the Central and State Governments in India have shown interest in the medicinal plant sector, which they wish to strengthen in order to create additional income and employment opportunities (Sajwan and Kala, 2006). In view of the growing interest in plant-based drugs, it is imperative to study and understand the various aspects related to the medicinal plants sector across the country.

Traditional Harvesting Practices and Increasing Demand Pressure

Over years of observations, the indigenous communities of India have developed their own knowledge on the sustainable harvesting of medicinal plant species. They mostly collected mature plants. Underground plant parts (root and rhizomes) of perennials were generally gathered after two or three years of growth. Tubers and bulbs of the annual species were collected at the end of the flowering or fruiting. Young leaves of medicinal plants were gathered throughout the growing period to maximize the quality of active compounds. When the whole herb was required for medicine, the herb was collected at the beginning of the flowering stage. Fruits and seeds of medicinal plants were collected when mature. The bark was collected when trees and shrubs began to bud in spring and after leaves are shed in autumn (Kaul, 1997; Kala, 2002). It was perceived that the mistaken identity of plant during collection, particularly of plants with phenotypic similarity, might lead to accidental poisoning; therefore only the trained herbal healers used to collect the medicinal plants. After collection, proper care was taken to dry and process the material.

With the changing lifestyle and socio-economic values, tendency to over-harvest the valuable medicinal plants for immediate cash by selling to any prospective buyer has superseded the traditional values. Though laws have been enacted to prevent over-harvesting, illegal collection is continuing (Kala, 2002; 2003). With escalating competition to collect large quantities of medicinal plants, influential people even hire labourers from outside. These labourers have no training in traditional collection techniques. The ruthless and unscientific collection of many high-value medicinal plants is one of the causal factors for their rarity and imbalance in demand and supply. The potential erosion of genetic variability within each species must be studied to determine acceptable levels of rarity. The National Medicinal Plants Board of the Government of India has prioritized 32 medicinal plant species for research and development; of these many species are rare and endangered. Incorporating such important species for research and development is a step forward in increasing sustainability of the medicinal plant sector by safeguarding the raw material.

Traditional Knowledge and Bio-piracy

Will recording traditional knowledge prevent bio-piracy? Today, the conservationists and indigenous communities around the world are in search of the feasibility and applicability of this question. The lack of legal protection for the therapeutic properties of numerous medicinal plants has made indigenous knowledge vulnerable to bio-piracy, as illustrated by the cases of patents on *neem* and turmeric. The knowledge of traditional utility of plant is not patentable by indigenous practitioners since the criteria of patentability are: (a) novelty, (b) non-obviousness, and (c) industrial application. Being traditional is by definition not novel even though it is based on innovation, and the indigenous medical system is not industrial (Shiva, 1998).

There are reports, which have attracted the attention of developing nations, stating that patent monopolies on plant and plant products threaten to harm the developing nations in three major ways. First, by raising prices; second, by blocking local production when the patent owner so chooses; and third, for agricultural varieties, by unwelcoming farmers to continue breeding them as has been done for thousands of years. The problem of patenting the medicinal plants needs to be resolved on the bases of human respect, respect by communities of one another, respect by individual people within communities, and respect of different traditions.

In order to prevent the bio-piracy, to safeguard the sovereignty of traditional herbal knowledge, and to protect the traditional knowledge from being misused in patenting on non-original discoveries, the Government of India attempted to document this knowledge available in public domain. This innovative step has resulted in the documentation of 36,000 Ayurvedic formulations through collating the information from the existing literature in the digital form, which is called as Traditional Knowledge Digital Library (TKDL). This Digital Library has made an impact at an international level after realizing its utility in preventing misappropriation of the rich traditional knowledge and also making it a precious tool for encouraging advanced research.

Integration of Traditional and Modern Tools

In vitro plant tissue culture technology has been developed with the hope of obtaining desired products when medicinal plants are rare and difficult to acquire. However, the yield of desired material through *in vitro* technology is too low for commercial feasibility. In order to explore the potential, tissue culture is still going on. Globally, only a few products such as shikonin and ginseng are successfully manufactured on a large scale. Strategies and treatments, such as biotransformation, cell permeabilization, immobilization, elicitation and hairy root culture show promise for other products to reach commercial scale. In addition, protoplast fusion and somatic hybridization, media composition and selection of cell lines, and changing media composition can be adopted to improve the quality and quantity of bio-synthetic cell culture products (Lozoya, 1994; Khan and Khanum, 2000).

The culture conditions have also been reported to influence the amount of drugs obtained in culture. For example, the amount of ginseng produced doubled when the culture was rotated on a horizontal clinostat instead of being kept stationary (Zhao and Cai, 1998). Some researchers have proposed that cellular factories using recombinant DNA technologies may develop new therapeutics in the future. If such modern technologies are successfully applied to medicinal plants, they may help improve yields to meet commercial demand of required products. Therefore, there is an urgent need to integrate the modern tools with traditional herbal knowledge, as has been manifested by the creation of TKDL.

Community-based Conservation

There are hundreds of wildlife sanctuaries and national parks which have been set aside for the *in situ* conservation of biodiversity across the country. However, due to rising conflicts among conservationists on pro-park and pro-people views, the Protected Area networks are in a state of crisis (Wells, 1992). The Government of India has also enacted export restrictions on 29 plant species to prevent their further loss in wild. However, the sustainability of these species cannot be achieved merely by promulgating a ban on export or by fencing areas rich in medicinal plants.

The establishment of Medicinal Plants Conservation Areas (MPCA) in various States could be a step forward in conserving medicinal plants and also in mitigating the conflicts between conservationists and various user groups (Kala, 2000). The various agro-climatic zones could be selected for medicinal plants cultivation. The philosophy of joint forest management if applied on medicinal plants may be useful in mitigating the various conflicts. Giving ownership of natural resources to local people and encouraging profitable uses of those resources may provide a powerful incentive for both medicinal plant conservation and sustainable economic development of the local people (Child, 2002). Sustainable harvesting combined with cultivation can improve yields, and it may also reduce pressure in specified areas marked for biodiversity conservation (Kala, 2005d). It has been shown that under cultivation and in a consolidated area the plants give a better yield and assure the supply of quality planting material to the industries (Kaul, 1997; Kala, 2002; 2005b).

The MPCA may ensure the autonomous development of a rural community by enhancing the people's income. This way they can decide themselves how to use their assets and resources, for which market they wish to produce, and by which services they need to achieve their goals. It also enables them to restore resources depleted by overuse, assume the long-term supply of resources, regulate national and international trade by assuring a continuous supply of quality material, and ensure the conservation of not only the species concerned but also its associated species and ecosystems (Kaul, 1997; KIT, 2003; Kala, 2006b). The number of linkages in medicinal plants supply, process, drug formulation, trade, transport, and the retail industry can be used to generate employment. The available rural technologies for farming of some valuable medicinal plant species can be made useful for their large-scale cultivation. The promotion of community-based conservation through the establishment of MPCA and dissemination of awareness among the various stakeholders (e.g. herb cultivators, herb gatherers, herbal practitioners and traders) about sustainable harvesting techniques and processing through training can be a step forward in the conservation of medicinal plants.

The traditional beliefs of native communities with respect to the conservation of medicinal plants should also be taken into account. The practitioners of Ayurveda, used to worship many medicinal plant species before their harvest from nature (Kala, 2005a). Many medicinal plant species are medicinal as well as religious, and many medicinal plant species are worshipped as a symbol of local gods and goddesses (Table 1.1).

Table 1.1
Some important medicinal plant species of India conserved through religious philosophy

Species	*Religious Uses*	*Medicinal Uses*
Aegle marmelos (L.) Corr.	To worship the Lord Shiva and the Goddess Lakshmi	Digestive disorder, fever
Artemisia nilagirica (Cl.) Pamp	Sacred plant used in worshipping local deities	Asthma, skin ailment, headache, antiseptic
Betula utilis D. Don	Sacred plant	Cut, wounds, hysteria
Cannabis sativa L.	Associated with Lord Shiva	Delirium, eye disorder
Cedrus deodara (Roxb.) Loud.	Associated with gods and goddesses	Ulcer, rheumatic pain

Datura stramonium L.	Associated with Lord Shiva	Asthma, joint pain
Dendrocalamus strictus Nees	Used at various religious ceremonies performed right from the birth to death	Tonic, fever
Ficus benghalensis L.	Worship as symbol of Lord Shiva	Dysentery, scabies, tonic
Ficus religiosa L.	Worship as Lord Vishnu	Dysentery, cholera, scabies
Hedychium spicatum Ham. ex Smith	Used in the marriage ceremony	Stomach-ache, liver disorder
Juniperus communis L.	Its incense used for worshipping gods and goddesses	Kidney trouble
Musa balbisiana Cola	Used in the marriage ceremony	Indigestion
Nardostachys jatamansi (Don) DC.	Its incense used for worshipping gods and goddesses	Blood purification, cough
Ocimum sanctum L.	Worship as a local deity	Bronchitis, constipation
Origanum vulgare L.	Used in worshipping the Lord Badri Vishal or Vishnu	Diarrhoea, bronchitis
Pinus roxburghii Sarg.	Used in the marriage ceremony	Cut, wounds, bone fracture
Prunus cerasoides D. Don	Used on some special religious occasion	Body swelling
Saussurea obvallata (DC.) Edgew.	Worship as Lord Brahma	Cuts, aphrodisiac
Sesamum orientale L.	Worship as Lord Saturn	Aphrodisiac, bodyache
Zanthoxylum armatum DC.	Used in worshipping as Lord Shiva, Narsingh, Varuna	Toothache

Hence, there is a general fear in indigenous societies towards the over-exploitation of such medico-religious plant species. Generally, most of these medico-religious plant species are rare in nature like *Ficus benghalensis, Ficus religiosa, Saussurea obvallata* and *Zanthoxylum armatum.* Such a traditional belief in the society is a way of conserving the useful natural resource, which needs to be kept alive in order to sustain the medicinal plant's population.

Contribution of the National Medicinal Plants Board

In view of strengthening the medicinal plants sector in India, the National Medicinal Plants Board (NMPB) was set up in November 2000 by the Government of India. The prime objective of setting up NMPB is to establish an agency which would be responsible for co-ordination of all matters with respect to medicinal plants sector, including drawing up policies and strategies for *in situ* conservation, cultivation, harvesting, marketing, processing, drug development and any matter related to the medicinal plants (Rawat, 2003). The NMPB has two major schemes such as promotional and commercial. Promotional scheme mainly aims to facilitate research activities and to disseminate awareness about the importance of medicinal plants and medicinal plants sector as a whole. Commercial scheme aims to strengthen cultivation of medicinal plants on a large scale, value addition, harvesting, processing, storage, extraction, packaging and market mechanism.

Since its inception, the NMPB has successfully set up 35 State Medicinal Plants Boards for dealing with the various aspects of medicinal plants at the State level (Sajwan and Kala, 2006). From 2001 to March 2006, the NMPB has sanctioned 4,254 projects worth Rs. 17,593.78 Lakhs on the different aspects of the medicinal plants under both promotional and commercial schemes. Of the total projects sanctioned, 83 per cent projects were sanctioned under contractual farming scheme and the rest 17 per cent were sanctioned under promotional scheme. The allocation of funding was 50 per cent each to both the schemes. The NMPB schemes of funding projects have covered 32 States including Union Territories so far across the country. In comparison to contractual farming a higher number of States and Union Territories have been brought under promotional schemes.

The highest number of projects under both promotional and contractual farming schemes have been sanctioned to the States of central India, such as Rajasthan (808), and Madhya Pradesh (798), followed by south Indian State (Karnataka: 410), and western State of India (Maharastra: 237). In the promotional scheme itself, the highest number of projects (98) were sanctioned to a north Indian State, namely Uttaranchal, followed by south Indian States, Tamil Nadu (67) and Karnataka (51). Eight States and Union Territories such as Andaman and Nicobar, Bihar, Chandigarh, Goa, Lakshadweep, Meghalaya, Mizoram and Pondicherry are not yet covered under contractual farming scheme. Apart from Lakshadweep, all the States and Union Territories have been brought under promotional scheme of the NMPB.

So far, the NMPB has covered about 120 important medicinal plant species under various tasks of promotional schemes. Most of the projects were sanctioned for mixed-cropping of medicinal plants. Within prioritized species of medicinal plants, the highest number of projects have been sanctioned for cultivation and conservation of *Emblica officinalis*, followed by *Rauvolfia serpentina, Withania somnifera* and *Aegle marmelos*. Besides funding different research and development projects, currently the NMPB is engaged in a number of activities related to the medicinal plants, which includes the development of monographs on the good agricultural and collection practices, an e-portal on market information, database on supply and demand, supporting projects for raising quality planting material, development of resistant varieties of medicinal plant species and setting up of herbal gardens in schools.

The NMPB is co-ordinating with different Institutions and Universities for dissemination of information, capacity building and applications of research findings on various medicinal plant species. Since many important medicinal plant species have specific ecological requirements, long gestation period, low population size, high dependency on natural pollinators, unpredictable seed germination patterns and poor seed viability, the NMPB is giving equal importance to the *in situ* conservation of medicinal plants, and various government and non-government organizations have been supported in identifying suitable areas for meeting this objective. The major strategic role of NMPB is to generate livelihood options and employment, to reduce the dependency of medicinal plants stakeholders on the wild stock and to assure millions of people around the country and abroad about the quality standards that the Board seeks to ensure in the medicinal plants produced in the country.

Discussion

There are some inherent problems in the medicinal plants sector, including the proper identification of plant species that have multiple local names in the traditional medical systems. It is believed that medicinal plants collected from wild have greater medicinal benefits than those cultivated commercially as crops. Although there are many advantages of cultivation, the success rate of many species is low due to their specialized environmental requirements. Precariousness of market forces also creates a fear among medicinal plant growers: a medicinal plant, which has a powerful market today may not have the same market tomorrow, for example.

Although there are differences with major philosophies of medicinal plants commercialization and conservation, their overall aim attached with human welfare can be used for positive gains. Their perspectives can facilitate ways of allocating scarce resources among competing demands. There are opportunities to incorporate the conservation policies for medicinal plants within the framework of existing legal instruments such as, the Convention on Biological Diversity and Convention on International Trade of Endangered Species. To overcome the problems faced by farmers, the research should be farm-oriented rather than merely laboratory-based.

To ensure the long-term sustainability of medicinal plants as an essential commodity for health care, it is important to regulate and maintain the medicinal plant stock. Identification of traditional and modern tools used in the conservation of medicinal plants will be a step forward in strengthening the medicinal plant sector. The immediate need is to explore different tools for strengthening the medicinal plant sector including biotechnology, community conservation, bio-prospecting and ways to prevent bio-piracy. Attempts should be made by all stakeholders to encourage, recommend and promote the herbal medicines because such medicine is easily available at a price within the reach of the common people and is time-tested and considered to be much safer than the modern synthetic drugs.

Considering the high importance of Indian medicinal plants and Indian systems of medicines in the international market, there is an immense potential for international co-operation with countries that are endowed with rich plant resources and those having strong traditional systems of medicines. Like India, there are many countries, which have rich traditional knowledge, strong traditions and culturally acceptable herbal medical systems. Protecting medicinal plants and the indigenous knowledge associated with these valuable species is the major area of concern across the developing nations, which includes patenting products and indigenous knowledge. Besides, India may collaborate with countries involved in developing agro-techniques, scientific validation of traditional knowledge, biotechnology, techniques for mass propagation of medicinal plants, exchange and trade of herbal products, quality control, production of quality planting material and capacity building. Apart from these, there are many more areas, which need to be identified for development of the medicinal plants sector.

Abbrevations

CTA — Technical Centre for Agriculture and Rural Co-operation

KIT — The Royal Tropical Institute

MPCA — Medicinal Plants Conservation Areas

NMPB — National Medicinal Plants Board

TKDL — Traditional Knowledge Digital Library

WHO — World Health Organization

References

Child, B. (2002), The acceptable face of conservation, *Nature* 415, pp. 581-82.

Crook, C. and R.A. Clapp (1998), Is market-oriented forest conservation a contradiction in terms?, *Environmental Conservation* 25, pp. 131-45.

CTA (2002), Medicinal plants: Pluck not plunder, *Spore* 99, pp. 1-2.

Kala, C.P. (2000), Status and conservation of rare and endangered medicinal plant in the Indian trans-Himalaya, *Biological Conservation* 93, pp. 371-79.

——— (2002), *Medicinal Plants of Indian Trans-Himalaya,* Bishen Singh, Mahendra Pal Singh, Dehradun, India.

——— (2003), Commercial exploitation and conservation status of high value medicinal plants across the borderline of India and Nepal in Pithoragarh, *Indian Forester* 129, pp. 80-84.

——— (2004), Assessment of species rarity, *Current Science* 86, pp. 1058-59.

——— (2005a), Current status of medicinal plants used by traditional *Vaidyas* in Uttaranchal State of India, *Ethnobotany Research and Applications,* 3, pp. 267-78.

——— (2005b), Ethnomedicinal botany of the Apatani in the Eastern Himalayan region of India, *Journal of Ethnobiology and Ethnomedicine,* 1 (11), pp. 1-12.

——— (2005c), Health traditions of Buddhist community and role of amchis in trans-Himalayan region of India, *Current Science* 89, pp. 1331-38.

——— (2005d), Indigenous uses, population density and conservation of threatened medicinal plants in protected areas of the Indian Himalayas, *Conservation Biology* 19, pp. 368-78.

——— (2006a), Preserving Ayurvedic herbal formulations by Vaidyas: The traditional healers of the Uttaranchal Himalaya region in India, *Herbal Gram,* 70, pp. 42-50.

——— (2006b), Medicinal plants of the high altitude cold desert in India: Diversity, distribution and traditional uses, *International Journal of Biodiversity Science & Management,* 2 (1), pp. 43-56.

Kala, C.P., P.P. Dhyani and B.S. Sajwan (2006), Developing the medicinal plants sector in northern India: Challenges and opportunities, *Journal of Ethnobiology and Ethnomedicine,* 2, pp. 1-16.

Kaul, M.K. (1997), *Medicinal Plants of Kashmir and Ladakh,* New Delhi: Indus Publishing Company.

Khan, I.A. and A. Khanum (2000), *Role of Biotechnology in Medicinal and Aromatic Plants,* Hyderabad: Ukaaz Publications.

KIT (2003), *Cultivating a Healthy Enterprise*, Bulletin 350, Amsterdam, The Netherlands: Royal Tropical Institute.

Lange, D. (1997), Trade figures for botanical drugs worldwide, *Medicinal Plant Conservation Newsletter* 3, p. 17.

Lozoya, X. (1994), *Ethnobotany and the Search of New Drugs*, England: John Wiley and Sons.

Planning Commission (2000), *Report of the Task Force on Conservation and Sustainable Use of Medicinal Plants*, New Delhi: Government of India Press.

Rawat, R.B.S. (2003), National Medicinal Plants Board (Introduction and Schemes), *Indian Forester*, 129 (1), pp. 109-18.

Sajwan, B.S. and C.P. Kala (2006), Current strategies of National Medicinal Plants Board, Government of India, In *Current Trends in Medicinal Plants and Herbal Technology*, Pondicherry: Department of Plant Sciences, K.M. Centre for Post Graduate Studies, p. 15.

Schippmann, U., D.J. Leaman and A.B. Cunningham (2002), *Impact of Cultivation and Gathering of Medicinal Plants on Biodiversity: Global Trends and Issues*, Inter-Department Working Group on Biology Diversity for Food and Agriculture, FAO, Rome, Italy.

Sharma, A.B. (2004), Global medicinal plants demand may touch $ 5 trillion by 2050, *Indian Express*, March 29, 2004.

Shiva, V. (1998), Protecting our biological and intellectual heritage in the age of bio-piracy, In *Medicinal Plants: A Global Heritage*, Proceedings of the International Conference on Medicinal Plants for Survival, IDRC-CRDI, Bangalore, pp. 324-38.

Wells, M. (1992), Biodiversity conservation, affluence, and poverty: Mismatched costs and benefits and efforts to remedy them, *Ambio* 21, pp. 237-43.

Zhao, W. and W.M. Cai (1998), Influence of simulated micro gravity environmental factor on ginseng cell growth and ginseng saponin content, *Acta Physiologica Sinica* 24, pp. 159-64.

2

Transmission of Traditional Medicinal Plant Knowledge

Local Healers of Maharashtra, India

Shailesh Shukla

TRADITIONAL Medicinal Plant Knowledge (TMPK) helps meet the health needs of a large section of world's population, especially the economically disadvantaged and indigenous communities of developing countries like India. There are growing concerns over the erosion of TMPK. An important reason for such loss is the lack of its adequate transmission from older to younger generations. This paper presents description of crucial skills and their relative importance in TMPK transmission, privileging the perspective of 33 local healers in two economically poor tribal communities in Maharashtra, India. The study revealed that learning of TMPK happened through transmission of ten crucial skills, which also embodied personality traits, values, spiritual chanting and sustainability. Most of these skills were learnt in sequence during the age group of 14-20 years.

Transmission of TMPK is Important but is the Least Studied Field

The World Bank researchers (Nickel and Sennhauser, 2004), estimate that more than 80 per cent of the population of South

Asia uses plant-based medicines for maintaining and improving their health. The knowledge-based associated with the community-based or local uses of medicine, can be classified broadly into the following three categories (Hamilton, 2005): (i) Traditional Systems of Medicine, with a systematic codified body of knowledge either in the form of pharmacopoeias or ancient scriptures [Ayurvedic, Chinese or Tibetan medicine, Siddha, Unani (Arabic), etc.] WHO (2002) defines the Traditional Systems of Medicine (TSM) as "the diverse health practices, approaches, knowledge and beliefs incorporating mainly plants and plant products with or without spiritual therapies transmitted through generations by oral means to maintain well-being, as well as to treat, diagnose or prevent illness"; (ii) Traditional Medicinal Plant Knowledge or Folk Medicine (TMPK), which is transmitted by oral means and is mostly acquired through learning-by-doing approaches; and (iii) Shamanistic or Spiritual Medicine, with a strong religious/ spiritual element and can be practised only by highly specialized local experts called "shamans." The scope of this paper is limited to the TMPK, its practices and beliefs with respect to only plant-based medicines.

TMPK is most widely practised in countries like India (Shankar, 1999; Shukla and Gardner, 2006) and is being increasingly recognized by the governments and international agencies like UNESCO, OXFAM, and Ford Foundations. On the other hand, scholars (Gupta, 2003; Shankar, 2001) are expressing serious concerns on erosion of TMPK due to a variety of factors. One of the important factors that inhibit erosion is lack of transmission of TMPK from older to younger generations.

Ruddle (1993) aptly emphasizes the importance of understanding transmission: "During knowledge transmission over several generations, social institutions are generally crystallized. Routine or habitual ways of doing things gradually become the customary ways that things are done. For children, a community's customary ways eventually becomes the given-received social world, an analogue of the biological-physical world with which it overlaps" (Ruddle, 1993: 19). The transmission of traditional knowledge thus helps in institutionalizing ways of management of natural resources in the form of rules in use or conduct. In other words, understanding of transmission of TMPK can provide useful insights on the process of socialization of children in their own communities and the nature of social and cultural learning that younger people encounter before they become fully practising elders or adult members of the given community.

Process of Transmission : Glimpses from Literature

In their review on studies on transmission of knowledge, Battiste and Henderson (2000) commented that very few scholars have really tried to understand the transmission of indigenous knowledge within indigenous traditions. Berkes (1999) reconfirmed this observation, noting that the field of education has neglected this useful area of research within local knowledge systems.

The limited number of scattered studies concerning the inter-generational transmission of local knowledge systems such as Traditional Ecological Knowledge (TEK) largely focused on two major areas: (a) structure and/or processes of TEK transmission; and, (b) factors and changes affecting transmission. The studies on process of transmission highlight the — (i) skills, modes (processes) and methods, through which TEK is acquired between elders and younger generations; (ii) location or sites where teaching-learning of TEK occurs; and (iii) sources from which TEK is acquired; and (iv) Age at which various skills are acquired. The focus of this paper is limited to understanding skills of TMPK transmission and the age at which it is acquired.

Ruddle and Chesterfield (1977) summarized various studies on transmission of traditional knowledge in the context of subsistence-societies and suggested some features of the transmission processes as follows: (a) The training of various economic activities is age-specific; (b) The sequence for teaching particular task/skill complex is from simple to difficult/complex; (c) Tasks are location-specific and preferably taught at the sites at which they are to be used; (d) Specific time interval is allocated for teaching different tasks; and (e) The mechanisms for incentives (rewards) and disincentives (punishments) are associated with learning of certain task or task complexes.

This pioneering study also looked at the learning sequence for traditional food procurement techniques in the Orinoco Delta and provided an eight-step model of learning complex, viz.: (i) familiarization or identification of the skill to be learnt; (ii) observation of the elder/teacher performing the skill; (iii) assistance to learner with simple steps; (iv) helping the learner with the entire skill complex; (v) supervision of the actual performance of the skill complex; (vi) apprenticeship; (vii) independent implementation of the skill complex by the apprenticeship to the instructor; and (viii) working as a practitioner (equal partner) or peer to the teacher. However this framework, according to some scholars, is information-oriented and might pose a problem of "informant fatigue" in local communities. Ohmagari and Berkes (1997), therefore, reduced this eight-stage model to a shorter learning framework, while studying 93 bush skills among women of two sub-Arctic Cree Indian communities in Canada. The revised model proposed and used has three main stages: (i) skills learned by hands-on experience; (ii) learned by observing only; and (iii) not learned at all.

The traditional knowledge skills are generally acquired concurrently with learning of local language, usually by ages 12-14. For example, Zarger (2000) showed that among Q' eqchi' Maya of Belize, the acquisition of food resources and other subsistence skills occur between ages 4 and 14. Almost similar age range (2-14) was also reported in Guara Island of Venezuela in a study by Ruddle(1993), where in earlier phases children acquired familiarity of food items used in home and then gradually learnt more demanding tasks (such as fishing in a risky marsh land) as part of their subsistence skills. An age range of 13-15 years was reported as a key period for mastery of most of the bush skills among Cree communities of Canada (Ohmagari and Berkes, 1997).

In the Indian context, studies specifically looked at TMPK focused largely on documenting ethno-medicinal knowledge of local communities (Patil and Patil, 2005; Sharma and Majumdar, 2003) than transmission. Study by Chand and Shukla (2003), is an exception, which analyzed the transmission of traditional knowledge of medicinal plants among rural and tribal communities in western India and clearly identified three stages of apprenticeship which included: observation, imitation of practice and monitoring by mentor, which might be extended to requests for assistance in practice by elder healers. This study also suggests that learning about TMPK could start as early as 5-7 years of age and by the age of nine, most of the learners are well placed in the learning cycle, which might continue for several years.

Rationale and Research Questions

This paper attempts to contribute to a scanty body of literature on transmission by examining the structure of process of transmission of TMPK. However, to study the transmission of TEK is itself a large research area and therefore, this research paper focused on critical skills that are essential to acquire (or transmit) TMPK through the perspectives of the TMPK practitioners. The specific research questions that this paper addresses are:

1. What tasks or skills are considered crucial in transmission by TMPK practitioners;
2. What characteristics or features constitute these skills; and
3. What considerations of age and sequence are taken into account during transmission of these skills.

Transmission here refers to a transfer of skills from old healers to young healers (Ohmagari and Berkes, 1997). In other words, it is a process of acquisition of skills and values by younger healers in order to become mature healers who can independently practise TMPK. In this way, transmission is an inevitable part of the teaching process that the practising healer must go through to be recognized and accepted by local villagers as a full-fledged "local healer" or locally known as *vaidus*.[1] Some of the *vaidus* selected in this study will eventually acquire a mastery of skills, which will popularize them as general TMPK practitioners or *vaidus* who are local experts for treating specific diseases.

Selection of Research Sites, Participants and Research Methods

The field research was conducted in two villages of Maharashtra State,[2] selected in consultation with two NGOs

1. The term *vaidus* (Sanskrit : *vaidya*) is generic term commonly used to describe TSM and TMPK practitioners throughout Maharashtra and many parts of India.
2. The funding support from IDRC, Social Sciences and Humanities Research Council of Canada and University of Manitoba, Canada at various stages of my PhD research is gratefully acknowledged.

(Non-Governmental Organizations) viz. SRISTI (Society for Research and Initiatives for Sustainable Technologies and Institutions) and RCMPCC (Rural Commune's Medicinal Plant Conservation Center). Both SRISTI and RCMPCC have been internationally recognized for promoting community-based conservation in India, through use of traditional ecological knowledge. The following table describes the villages at (i) Amboli, located in southern Maharashtra State; and (ii) Baripada, located in northern Maharashtra State.

Table: 2.1
General description of villages selected for field research

Characteristics	*Amboli*	*Baripada*
Population	3647	786
Social groups	Two groups: *Marathas* and *Gurav* considered as higher castes. About ten per cent of lower castes include *dhangar, chamar, jadhav,* etc.	All tribals. But two main groups are *pawar* and *chaure.* A small proportion of Bhils also included.
Relationship among social caste/groups	Marathas and Gurav had a long standing history of religious conflict for old village temple. Social mobility between these groups strictly discouraged.	There is a good trade and social relationship among groups. Marriages can be possible among all community groups.
Altitude	690 m from sea level	About 350 m from sea level
Community-conserved Area	445.28 hectares	267.63 hectares
Landscape	Dry deciduous with patches of evergreen forests	Semi evergreen forests

Source: Self-compiled based on village records and information provided by local NGOs.

In this study, the traditional healers or *vaidus* were identified mainly on the basis of following criteria: (i) a person who is a resident of the village; (ii) a person who has demonstrated ability/skills to practise his/her knowledge of healers in and around village; and (iii) person, who has been recognized by local residents and/or neighbouring villages as general or specialized *vaidus*.

In total, 33 healers (N = 16 from Amboli and N = 17 from Baripada) were selected of which less than half were women. All healers from Baripada are from Scheduled Tribes or *ādivāsīs*, while majority (three-fourths) from Amboli are from Marāṭhā or higher-caste category. After selecting the healers, data on skills were obtained through informal interviews (Cohen, Manion and Morrison, 2000), based on healers' availability and willingness to participate in the study. The research question initially asked was "what skills are crucial to become a successful healer?" After pilot testing with five healers from both villages, it was realized that two important criteria were essential for being successful practising healers: (a) the personality traits, qualities or values that *vaidus* should possess; and (b) the set of skills that represented knowledge which are mostly observable and perceived by the elder healers as essential. The informal conversations with healers and participant observations of some practising healers yielded a list of more than 40 skills. The list was shared within the small groups of healers in each village and was further consolidated into a final set of the ten most important skills considered crucial to *vaidus*. These crucial skills were inclusive and consisted of a set of sub-skills or characteristics. Forest walks with healers (Martin, 1995) were organized to conduct semi-structured interviews (Cohen, Manion and Morrison, 2000) and obtain ranking of these ten crucial skills. These final ten skills were ranked, on the basis of three-point rating scale:

most important (ranked as No. 3), important (ranked as No. 2) and least important (ranked as No. 1). The averages of all ten crucial skills were calculated separately for all 33 healers, and skills were classified in descending order as shown in Table 2.2.

Identification of Plants

With a mean score of 2.76, identification of plants is the top-ranked skill to become a good healer as perceived by the *vaidus* from both the villages. Identification of plants is mostly learnt in the wild or forest areas or in some cases, in specially created areas such as home herbal gardens (Baripada) or village demonstration gardens (Amboli). Some healers have also suggested that seemingly alike plants should be identified based on a step-wise test. One should begin to look at the colour of the leaves. If the colours of two leaves are same then look for the shapes of leaves. If the shapes are same then crush the bark and smell. Most plants have distinct smell, but, even if one is confused with similar smells, then final criterion should be to check for the type, shape, size and smell of flowers and fruits. Most healers, however strongly believe that identification of poisonous plants must be taught. "Plants, for example like *Bhyunkuli* has potential to kill even human beings if eaten in a small quantity, therefore kids must know to recognize such plants in the wild" (personal interview, MC, Baripada). Even mere smelling or a little tasting of such plants could be dangerous. The correct identification is a key to avoid harmful effects of such plants when used in the treatment. Identification of rare plants is also considered an important sub-skill in order not to remove them inadvertently while picking other medicinal plants from the wild. Even though the mean age of acquiring the identification skills is close to 17 years, it is being learnt and taught throughout healers' lives.

Table 2.2
Crucial skills identified by local healers

Name of Skills	*Description of Skill / sub-set of skills*	*Mean Age*	**Importance** by Mean Rank (N=33) Highest Rank-3
Identification	a) Identification of rare plants b) Identification of Poisonous plants c) Distinguishing phenotypically similar plants	16.74	2.76
Knowledge of plant becoming rare	a) Name and location of rare plants species b) Marking location of rare plant species for other healers c) Regeneration/sustainable use/safer harvesting	20.57	2.52
Interest in plants	a) Developing sensitivity towards local biodiversity b) Showing a desire to learn about plants c) Curiosity to learn about plants	15.09	2.47

Harvesting of plants	a) Part and quantity to be removed b) Method of harvesting c) Time of removal (e.g. planetary movements) d) Special care/rules for harvesting to be taken e) Religious rituals to be performed during harvesting	18.57	2.39
Processing of plants	a) Part/parts and quantity to be used b) Method of preparation (mixture, decoction, etc.) c) Storage of raw material and/or final product	19.13	2.33
Consultation	a) Personal rapport with patients b) Instructions for repeat treatment c) Special care while dealing with serious illnesses, children and women d) Getting feedback through dialogue with patients	19.09	2.27
Habitat of plants	a) Knowledge of places/locations in and around villages b) Knowledge of geographical features as indicators of particular habitat	16.52	2.24

	c) Knowledge of use of landmarks/Special symbols/signals to relocate/indicate use/overuse of the plant		
Applications	a) Number, length and interval of dosages b) Quantities to be used in each dosage c) Religious ceremonies to be performed during application d) Knowledge of side effects/counter indications	19.04	2.21
Evaluation of treatment	a) Checking the efficacy of treatment through written record or dialogue with patients b) Network with other healers to assess relative importance of various treatments c) Checking effect of treatment through physical examination	19.61	2.18
Follow-up	a) Continuous contacts with patients through personal contacts/ consultations/informal meetings b) Referral to other healers	19.87	2.03

Knowledge of Rare and Locally Unavailable Plants

The knowledge of the rare and locally unavailable plants is one of the crucial skills, with the second highest mean score of 2.52. Name and location of rare medicinal plants is partially learnt during acquiring identification skills. During personal interviews, the healers indicated a variety of medicinal plants, which they thought were getting rare in their localities. "Since finding such a plant requires a good idea of identification and habitat, we teach about the local rare plants once the young learners can independently identify and use common medicinal plants" (personal interview, LP, Amboli). Some local healers have to travel long distances in search of certain plants. In Baripada for example, more than half of the healers walk more than twenty kilometres, on an average, to locate a locally rare but very useful plant of *ragat rohida*.

Marking of rare plants and their locations through landmarks or special specific identifiable symbols is practised by one-third of the healers from both sites. While the remaining two-thirds have not used such markings, they do acknowledge that marking the location of rare plants is an important skill. "I put a one rupee coin, *kanku* (red coloured powder) and a few grains of rice near a rare plant so that other healers might notice it as already used plants. Such markings also protects rare plants from over-extraction" (personal interview, RB, Baripada).

Nearly half the healers have cited wrongful and destructive methods of harvesting (by healers, villagers and outsiders) as a main cause of local village plants becoming rare. "We are almost on the verge of extinction of *Amruta* plant, because its anti-cancer properties were discovered by a few pharmaceutical companies and some of the plant collectors from outside the village have been indiscriminately chopping this valuable specie from our forest. As elders, we must teach younger healers to prevent such destructive actions though village-based monitoring and local regeneration" (personal interview, LGG, Amboli).

In Amboli, because of organized efforts by RCMPCC, forest nurseries within the village have been established. The local healers of Amboli, therefore, have indicated forest nurseries and Medicinal Plant Conservation Areas (Areas specifically earmarked for medicinal plant conservation by State Forest Department) as preferred sites for regeneration of local plants. In Baripada, more than one-third of the local healers set up loosely structured homes, herbal gardens in/around their homes/fields and their teachings and practices are therefore more geared towards individual conservation measures. The strategies for regeneration, therefore, were different but still constitute an important sub-set for the skills acquired in relation to the rare plants. The sensitivity and basic learning about rare plants though have started along with identification, the detailed and systematic knowledge of rare plants is generally acquired later at the average age of 20.

Interest in the Plants

The interest in the plants is considered as an important foundation skill by *vaidus* from both field sites. "One who does not like to play around with plants should not come into this profession" (personal interview, JY, Amboli). In fact, many healers mentioned lack of interest as one of the important factors in impeding transmission of TMPK to younger people. The sensitivity was developed at a younger age; partly while the supporting family is engaged in grazing cattle or in farming. Since most of the healers had opportunities to see and/or assist their parents or relatives with patients, the desire to learn was followed. "When a farmer from a neighbouring village had snakebite and visited my father. My father asked me to accompany him to the forest. I went with him to the forest to help him in removing the bark of two different plants. My father gave an oral dose of a medicinal pallet made from these two different barks and the patient was cured. This incident not only reinforced my faith in plant-based medicine but inspired me to learn it" (personal interview, DD, Amboli). In general, the interest started building up at the age of 14 years and if nurtured externally (through incidences like this), or by a mentor, it provided an entry point to become a *vaidus* by gradually learning other skills.

The mean rank of close to 2.5 indicates that "being interested in plants" is considered as one of the highly ranked skills by the *vaidus*.

Harvesting of the Plants

The harvesting of plants or their parts ranked slightly above the combined average rank score for all ten skills (2.34) and is considered as a crucial skill, both by local healers as well as formally-trained field botanists (RCMPCC, 1999). Therefore it is a highly-valued skill to practise as a good healer. In order to ensure long-term availability of the plants, the method and process of harvesting is very important.

Most healers indicated that no plant part should be removed until the plant is strong enough to withstand the loss. In general, a mature plant of more than 15 years old should be chosen for removal of the required parts. The right method of harvesting varies according to the growth of the plant and nature of the cure. However, as a general rule, the length of the removed bark should not be more than one foot and the cut should not penetrate more than 6". The time at which plant parts are harvested is important. Many healers, from Baripada, for instance, believed that Saturday night is an auspicious time for harvesting. Saturday night harvesting and Sunday treatments are the most common practices among the local healers of Baripada. "Plants harvested during the full-moon on Saturday nights are at their best in terms of vigour and effectiveness" (personal interview, RB, Baripada). In addition, knowledge of special care or practices related to safer harvesting is also considered important. Most of the healers have revealed that their shadow should not fall on the plants while harvesting. Similarly many healers would never remove the bark in a circular fashion in order to avoid a ring shape or complete removal from the stem. They believe that such a removal will permanently damage the xylem cells, which might lead to drying and death of the plants.

In addition to these special practices, religious or holy ceremonies are also performed while removing the useful parts of the plants by healers. "Whenever I remove part from a plant, I pray to the plants to bless us with their healing power" (personal interview, CSJ, Baripada). Many healers from Amboli and Baripada offered a handful of rice and prayer to plants before they remove them. "I worship medicinal plants by chanting *mantra*s and offering one rupee and twenty-five *paise*,[3] before I start removing any part from them" (personal interview, LP, Amboli). Most healers from Amboli, on the other hand, offered prayers while removal. During such prayers, they appreciate the effectiveness of the medicinal plants and express their gratitude. Knowledge of planetary movement is a specialized learning that healers of Baripada have acquired as part of their learning of ceremonial rituals.

3. *Paisa* is the smallest unit of Indian currency. One hundred paise is equal to one rupee.

The five sub-skills on harvesting of medicinal plants required a longer period to learn (more than three years) after the skills of identification and location of medicinal plants were acquired. The mean age at which the skills of harvesting were acquired was over eighteen (18.57) years.

Processing of the Plants

The processing of medicinal plants is rated as a crucial and important skill with an average score of 2.33 which is a little less than the average mean score (2.34) for all the ten skills required to become healers. The useful plant parts are given in raw form, but are mostly processed in a variety of forms. The most common forms reported by healers were crushed drugs, paste, fresh juice, (dried) powder, decoction, ash, *lehya* (semi-solid form derived by mixing powdered drug in a liquid base for ingestion), porridge, *lepa* (powder or paste in oil base for external application) and *dhoopa* (smoke for inhalation). The knowledge of useful parts and their proportions is essential to prepare the required formulations. Some healers use combinations of various plants in a variety of the forms to make complex products. For example a healer from Amboli mixes and crushes the dried barks of *Palasa, Biba surangi* and *Tamalpatra* in equal proportions. A small quantity of water is then added to make a ball which is given the smoke of a *googala* tree. While smoking, the flour of *raagi* plant is added and the final product thus obtained is used to treat a variety of wounds and bone injuries in cattle. "Some concoctions are given fresh while others are kept overnight for better effects" (personal interview, VMG, Amboli). The skill of storage is therefore also considered important. Most healers use earthen pots and avoid metal containers to store the concoction of liquid products overnight. A few healers like LP from Amboli, with the support from his educated sons, use well-labelled plastic bottles for dried herbal powder. LP has also printed handouts in the local language for his products. He has created a small processing unit in his home which has a small grinder and a power operated packing and sealing machine. Most healers have well-developed understanding about when to use fresh or stored plant parts. On an average, at the age of slightly above 19 years, the skills of processing are acquired.

Consultation with the Patients

Establishing personal rapport with patients was considered as one of foundational skill by local healers. Most local healers from both sites, either through planned or informal meetings, or during conversations at village gatherings, or on the farms or in the forest, developed personal relationships with the patients. However, in some cases, particularly with local healers from Amboli, there are better opportunities for outside exposure (through organizations like RCMPCC) and technologies (telephone, newspaper and television). While healers have opted to developing personal relationships by visiting their patients, they somehow have not shown the same enthusiasm for judging the effectiveness of earlier treatments.

The consultations also involve a set of repeat instructions, which overlap with the skills of evaluation. The repeat instructions are often prescribed during the second visit by the patients for change of dose, or change of treatments, or referral to another healer or dispensary.

The third set of skills is related to special care and handling of serious illnesses, or special groups like sick children, women, and old or disabled people. Patients suffering from serious illnesses such as cancer or infectious diseases are separately handled and given priority.

The final set of skills related to consultation is about establishing a specific dialogue with patients, in order to diagnose a disease. The local healers ask symptom-specific questions and check how the behaviour and well-being of patients are affected by existing ailments. These diseases-specific questions are sometimes supplemented by additional physical examination such as *nadi parikshan* for diagnosis. In case of external injuries (wounds or snakebites), physical examination is often conducted. "I start a funny discussion about joyful events and then suddenly twist the sprained bone, when patients have sprains or dislocation of bones and muscles" (personal interview, SA, Amboli).

Consultation skills are generally acquired at the age of 19 which is close to the time at which processing and application skills have been acquired. The consultation skills with 2.27 scores ranks higher than related skills such as application and evaluation but still lower than the average mean rank of all ten crucial skills.

Habitat of the Plants

The knowledge of habitat of the plants was also considered as a crucial skill, but considered less important than identification, with a mean rank of 2.24. Since the knowledge of habitat is also covered during teaching-learning of identification of plants, some healers felt that identification is a more inclusive category broad enough to include habitat. This may have caused the lower score for the habitat skills, which is complex in terms of its importance. The first sub-set of the skill is related to learning about the location of medicinal plants. Some of the healers from Amboli and Baripada also travel more than 20 km on foot in search of certain plants like *Narkya* or *Amruta* that are becoming locally unavailable, largely due to commercial exploitation by traders from outside. Knowledge of plant, animal, or geographical features that are closely linked to the preferred habitat of certain plants is also believed to be a useful skill. For example, the presence of black spider in certain patches of Amboli forest indicates the good habitat for the medicinal plants (personal interview, KG, Amboli). Similarly, medicinal trees like *Mahuda (Madhuka Indica)* thrive best when there is a rich source of underground water.

Such interrelationships among geographical features, medicinal plants, and animals provide clues in the better understanding of the preferred habitats of medicinal plants. The use of landmarks or other symbols that represent either location or status of that particular plant species is the third important skill that forms the habitat-skill complex. "I put a stone or tie a small flag on the branch of some medicinal plants, particularly if they are small and not commonly found" (personal interview, JG, Amboli). The plants that are becoming rare or locally extinct have been noted by special landmarks by healers so that they can be easily identified in the forest. In addition to rare plants, certain plant species that are used to cure serious health problems such as snakebites or scorpion bites have also been given special symbols (such as a presence of a big size neighbouring tree or tying a string on a branch of the plant or neighbouring tree in a way that can be recognized from a distance). The plant habitat skills are acquired at the mean age of 16.52 years, which is close to the mean age of 16.74, at which identification skills are learnt. The identification and habitat skills are therefore learnt at the same age.

Application of Medicines

The application of medicines is the next step in learning, after one has acquired good knowledge of plants, their habitat and processes of preparing herbal medicines.

The treatment is often prescribed by the healers in the form of dosages and frequencies at which herbal formulations need to be taken. "I always make separate doses wrapped in old waste newspaper. A number of these small packets help patients in remembering the right interval and quantity of medicine" (personal interview, BB, Baripada). Some healers prefer to administer medicine at their homes. The knowledge of combined or compound action (both synergistic and antidotal) of various herbs and other ingredients is also important. For example, to cure skin infections and blisters in humans dried roots of *Bharangi* are crushed and mixed with water to make turbid lotion. The same lotion can also be used to treat eczema and blisters and for first-aid after adding a small amount of a child's urine.

The timing of taking herbal medicines varies according to the nature of diseases. "As a general rule, herbs taken along with meals are the ones prescribed for stomach and digestive ailments, while herbs that are administered to cure kidney and reproductive problems are generally advised to be taken before meals" (personal interview, RB, Baripada). Many of the healers also perform religious processes while administering their medicines. The most common form of religious ritual is chanting of *mantra*s — the divine and sacred verses, often sung in local dialects. These *mantra*s are offered both to the patients as well as the medicines. Almost half of the healers interviewed from both sites believe that mere herbal medicine might not work and one-fifth of them have indicated that performing sacred rituals is inevitable for making the medicine work. "The medicinal uses of plants may be known but the training about religious rituals completes the making of full-fledged practising healers" (personal interview, JSC, Baripada).

The knowledge of *pathya,* or allowable dietary and life-style related restrictions is also important. While different healers prescribe different advice on *pathya*, the most common ones include: not to eat meat, not to eat black gram and not to eat chilly or spicy foods. In the case of snakebite, the patients are encouraged not to sleep overnight. Sometime the *pathya* is advised to be self-observed by patients. "I ask my patients to carefully observe the effect of food and drug interactions on their bodies. After the drug is orally taken, swelling may occur if sour tasting food is eaten. Such food therefore should not be eaten" (personal interview, SC, Baripada). The mean rank of 2.21 (for the skill complex of application) is lower than the average mean score of 2.34 (all ten crucial skills), which indicates that skill complex of application is not valued as highly crucial skills by local healers. At the average age of 19, the skills related to the application of medicinal plant are learnt.

Evaluation of Treatment

The effect of treatment is often assessed by local healers, mostly through verbal feedback from patients. In addition, the evaluation also included the knowledge of: (a) established networks with local healers; and (b) conducting a physical examination (such as *nadi parikshan* (checking pulsation through hand). More than one-third of the local healers have established contacts with at least five healers, while another one-third are closely connected with more than five healers in and around the villages. These healers maintain regular contacts through either informal (one-fourth) or planned visits (one-fifth). During such visits, almost one-third of the healers have either sought verification of their treatment or discussed the effectiveness of the same or related treatment for the same ailments. The skills related to evaluation also correspond closely to the application of skills. For instance, time required to recover takes into account the factors like length and interval of doses of the treatments. "My treatment for jaundice in humans should show its results in seven days. If a patient does not start improving after a week, I change my dose or the treatment. If that does not work, I refer my patients to go to a hospital in Ajra town" (personal interview, LP, Amboli). Most of the healers are well aware of the recovery period of their treatments. However, most of them would still look forward to automatic visits by their patients for judging the effectiveness of the prior treatment. Four healers have used *nadi parikshan* to check the effectiveness of previous treatments. Physical examinations of affected parts were carried out by most of the healers, in the case of external diseases. For internal diseases, however, almost one-third relied on directly asking patients about the symptoms of the disease. The skills of evaluation, with a rank of 2.18, seemed to achieve least importance amongst other ten crucial skills required to become a good healer. The skills of evaluation are also learnt in the later period of 19 years of age, just after processing and application skills have been learnt.

Follow-up of the Patients

The follow-up with patients is commonly practised at the end of treatment, which is considered as one of the crucial skills to become a practising healer. On an average, a healer treats close to 400 patients annually. In some cases (N = 5), the healers are reported to treat more than one thousand patients per year. With the exception of two cases, most of the healers engage in farming (close to half) and other businesses (the other half). Following up with patients is considered very demanding in terms of time. This constraint becomes more severe if patients are from outside the village. The follow-up is therefore limited to occasional personal visits by healers to patients. However, for the patients from the same village, local healers maintain regular interactions. Sometimes they also create situations, to compel patients to see local healers. "I ask my patients to accompany me to the temple to offer small religious rituals to express thanks to the God, once they are cured" (personal interview, JS, Baripada). The second skill, as part of the follow-up is referring to other healers or modern hospitals. This is considered useful because of ineffectiveness of earlier treatments by a particular healer or for the convenience of location. During follow-up, the advice on *pathya,* or diet restrictions, is the most commonly discussed topic by the local healers (slightly less than one-third), followed by general talk or examination for improvement (almost one-fifth). Interestingly, close to one-fifth of the healers have never made any attempt for follow-up with their patients, as it was covered during consultation. Consequently, follow-up is the lowest ranked skill (score = 2.03) in terms of importance by healers among the ten crucial skills. It is learned between nineteen and twenty years of age.

Conclusions

Transmission of traditional medicinal plant knowledge (TMPK) is skill and age-specific and includes an acquisition of a set of ten crucial skill complexes, normally between 14 to 21 years. Some of these skills are highly valued by older healers and embody spiritual learning (such as chanting *mantras*). Five of these (interest towards plants, identification and harvesting of plants, processing for making final herbal products, rare plants), were also known as foundational skills and were given more importance than the rest five human skills (habitat of the plants, application of medicine, evaluation of treatment, consultation and follow-up with patients). The learning of human skills entails understanding of interpersonal communication and relationships with patients. Many of these skills were mostly learnt in a sequential manner (interest, identification, habitat, harvesting, processing, application, evaluation, consultation and follow-up) and through family and other sources, which roughly corresponds to the earlier finding indicating transition of learners from simple to more complex and advanced tasks as established by the works of Ohmagari and Berkes (1997) and Ruddle and Chesterfield (1977).

The period of 14-20 years roughly corresponds to the age at which systematic learning of language takes place in the schools. While the interest might have developed in earlier years (5-7 years as indicated by another study in India on TMPK transmission by Shukla and Chand (2003), the children were not chosen as disciples unless they turned to 14 years by older healers.

More than half of these healers integrated religious or spiritual beliefs or *mantra*s in their herbal therapies. The spiritual beliefs therefore constituted an important and inseparable component of TMPK.

Certain closely-related skills were learnt simultaneously (such as identification and harvesting) and skills of rare plants were acquired life long. The amount of time between the successive skills indirectly indicates the time required to learn particular skills. For example, on an average, within a period of two years, one's interest can turn into acquisition of the very first skill of identification. A gap of more than two years between identification/habitat to harvesting implies that one would spend more time in learning these foundational skills of identification of plants and their locations.

Finally, the skill of rare plants was considered as essential and highly-ranked along with foundational skills, which corresponds to the dimension of sustainable use of plants. The sustainability of local medicinal plants was thus viewed as an integral part of one's professional learning to become a practising healer.

Abbrevations

NGOs	—	Non-Governmental Organizations
RCMPCC	—	Rural Commune's Medicinal Plant 'Conservation Center
SRISTI	—	Society for Research and Initiatives for Sustainable Technologies and Institutions
TEK	—	Traditional Ecological Knowledge
TMPK	—	Traditional Medicinal Plant Knowledge
TSM	—	Traditional Systems of Medicine
WHO	—	World Health Organization

References

Battiste, M. and J.Y. Henderson, *Protecting Indigenous Knowledge and Heritage: A Global Challenge*, Saskatoon: Purich Publishing, 2000.

Berkes, F., *Sacred Ecology: Traditional Ecological Knowledge and Resources Management*, Philadelphia: Taylor and Francis, 1999.

Chand, V.S. and S.R. Shukla, Biodiversity Contests: Indigenously-informed and transformed Environmental Education, *Applied Journal of Environmental Education and Communication,* 2003.2(3), pp. 229-36.

Cohen, L., L. Manion and K. Morrison, *Research Methods in Education* (5th ed.), New York: Routledge/Falmer, 2000.

Gupta, A.K., Rewarding Conservation of Biological and Genetic Resources and Associated Traditional Knowledge and Contemporary Grassroots Creativity, *Working Paper,* 6th Jan. 2003, Ahmedabad: Indian Institute of Management, 2003.

Hamilton, A., *Medicinal Plants and Conservation: Issues and Approaches.* Surrey, U.K.: International Plants Conservation Unit, WWF-UK, 2005.

Nickel, W. and E. Sennhauser, *Medicinal Plants: Local Heritage with Global Importance.* World Bank Group, South Asia, 2004. Available online <http://lnweb18.worldbank.org/sar/sa.nsf/0/fae63d87e2bd14038525687f0057e0d1?OpenDocument> (Accessed 21 August 2005).

Ohmagari, K. and F. Berkes, Transmission of Indigenous Knowledge and Bush Skills Among the Western James Bay Cree Women of Sub-Arctic Canada, *Human Ecology*, 25(2), pp. 197-222.

Patil, M.V. and D.A. Patil, Ethno-medicinal practices of Nasik District, Maharashtra, *Indian Journal of Traditional Knowledge*, 2005, 4(3), pp. 287-90.

Rural Commune's Medicinal Plant Conservation Center: *Village Biologist Concept Note*, Mimeo Pune: RCMPCC; 1999.

Shankar, D.S., *Agenda for Revitalization of Indian Medical Heritage* (2001), New Delhi: Voluntary Health Association of India (VHAI).

———, "Revitalizing local health traditions" In *Food for Thought : Ancient Visions and New Experiments of Rural People* (eds.), B. Haverkort and Wim Hiemstra. London: Zed Books; 1999, pp. 43-51.

Sharma, P.P. and A.M. Majumdar, Traditional knowledge on plants from Toranmaal plateau of Maharashtra, *Indian Journal of Traditional Knowledge* 2003, 2(3): pp. 292-96.

Shukla, S.R. and J.S. Gardner, Local Knowledge in Community-based approaches to medicinal plant conservation: Lessons from India, *Journal of Ethnobiology and Ethnomedicine* 2006, 2, Article 20, Available on-line <http://www.ethnobiomed.com/content/2/1/20> (Accessed August 8, 2006).

World Health Organization: *Traditional Medicines Strategy 2002-05*, Geneva: WHO, 2002.

Zarger, R.K., "Acquisition and Transmission of Subsistence Knowledge by Q'eqchi' Maya in Belize," In *Ethnobiology and Biocultural Diversity: Proceedings of the Seventh International Congress of Ethnobiology* (eds.), J. Stepp, R. Felice, S. Wyndham and Rebecca Zarger. Athens: International Society of Ethnobiology 2000, pp. 593-603.

3

Traditional Medicine
A Bridge to Better Health in Ghana

Mohammed Nadhir Ibn Muntaka
and
Grace Hampton

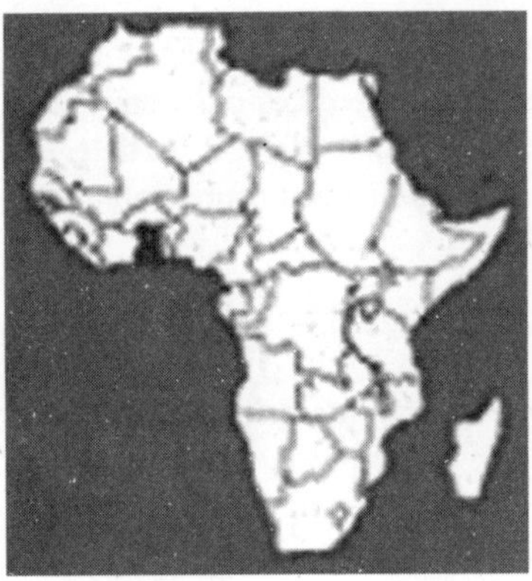

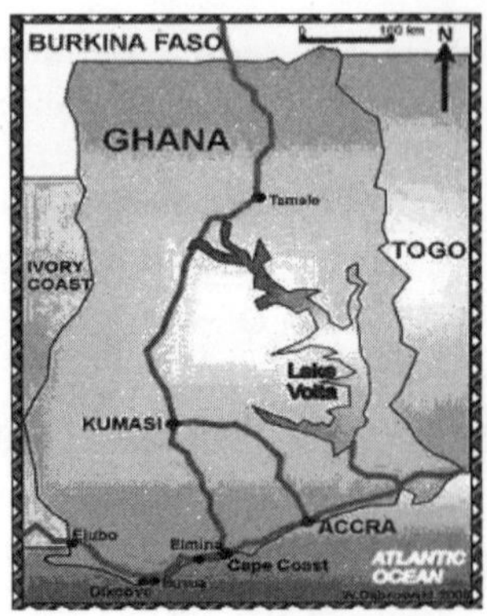

THE local people of Ghana have many ways and means of treating illnesses through the use of traditional medical practices. These practices incorporate the use of herbs, animal and mineral based medicines, spiritual therapies as a means of treating, diagnosing and in the prevention of illness. Ailments such as malaria, stomach disorders, fever, and boils are often treated by traditional medical practitioners with the use of herbs, leaves, roots and various salves. However, these traditional methods of delivering medical care is quite disorganized and on occasion patients are victimized by fraudulent individuals who may sell common sawdust as a healing potion to ill and unsuspecting people who are in need of medical care. However, the practice of traditional healing continues to play a very important role in the delivery of health care in Ghana. This paper contains a discussion of current Western and traditional medical practices and the medical delivery systems, the use of selected herbs by traditional practitioners in the healing of certain common illnesses and a recommendation for the full incorporation of traditional medicine into the existing medical system in Ghana.

Ghana: An Overview

Ghana, a former British colony, was known as the Gold Coast because of the vast amount of gold found in the country. Located in the western part of Africa, Ghana is bordered by Togo, Burkina Faso, Cote D'Ivoire, and the Atlantic Ocean, and encompasses a total of 239,460 square kilometres with 539 kilometres of coast line. The vegetation in Ghana varies from savanna in the northern two-thirds of the country to a tropical forest zone in the south. Gold, timber, industrial diamonds, bauxite, manganese, fish, rubber, hydropower, petroleum, silver, salt and limestone can be counted among Ghana's natural resources. Although well endowed with natural resources, the domestic economy continues to revolve around subsistence agriculture and employs 60 per cent of the work force of the country. The climate is tropical, warm and comparatively dry along the south-east coast, humid in the south-west, and hot and dry in the northern part of the country. Lake Volta, located in the south-east portion of the country, is the world's largest artificial lake and encompasses 4,880 kilometres of shoreline.

In 1957, Ghana was the first sub-Saharan country in Africa to attain political independence. The *World Factbook* estimates that the population of Ghana is 22,409,572 as of July 2006. There are approximately 73 persons per square mile in Ghana. Thirty-nine per cent of the population is under the age of 14, fifty-eight per cent are between the ages of 15-64 and 3 per cent are aged 65 or older. Life expectancy for men in Ghana is 58.07 years and 59.56 for women. The current Gross National Income per capita is $ 380 with much higher incomes found among professional and business people in large cities.

The educational system in Ghana consists of both public and private education from elementary through secondary school where the classes are taught in English. Sixty-three per cent of the males over the age of 15 in Ghana can read and write, with 46 per cent of the female possessing the same skills. There is a growing number of very well educated individuals who have been educated abroad or in one of the many well-established universities and technical institutions in Ghana and other parts of Africa that offer the bachelor, masters and doctorate degrees in all of the major disciplines.

Health Care Conditions In Ghana

Nuamah et al. in 2004 indicated that, "The health care delivery system in Ghana continues to face major challenges. These obstacles include the inadequacy and lack of quality of health facilities and health personnel, the limited supply of essential drugs, unsanitary environments, the underutilization of services due to insufficient

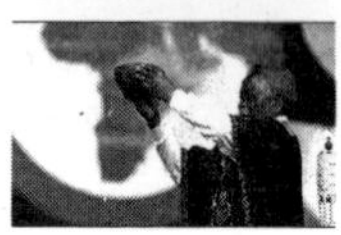

knowledge, poverty and the high costs for households." In 1985, Ghana initiated a user charge for health care services and a full cost recovery for drugs plan, popularly known as the "Cash and Carry" system. The major objective of the system was to establish and sustain the essential drug supply and to provide all public health facilities with adequate and safe drugs at affordable prices. Within the system, drugs are provided at cost to patients. While the legislation regulated the cost of drugs, other medical fees have not been adjusted since 1985. Prior to the introduction of the "Cash and Carry" system, private health care facilities in Ghana were operating on full cost recovery. Under the "Cash and Carry" system fees differ by type or level of facility, treatment location, age, nationality, and type of service provided. (Asenso-Okyere et al., 1999). Traditional and spiritual practitioners also operate on some form of cost recovery, although more informal, it seen by healers as a "thank you offering."

Ghana's "Cash and Carry" system was designed to ensure that the financial burden of health expenses did not fall upon the national government. While this cost-sharing measure increased the availability of medicines to many of the people of Ghana, for many of the poor, health care still remains very expensive and out of their reach. Consequently, new types of behaviours in health practices have emerged in the country. Due to the high cost of health care and drugs, many of the poor do not seek health care as quickly as needed, share their prescribed drugs with others, and often self-medicate themselves. (Asenso-Okyere et al., 1998). In addition, rising inflation has greatly exaggerated the situation. Researchers have found that a larger number of individuals have turned to the use of traditional methods of health care and the use of herbal medicines. (G.J.M. van den Boom, 1998)

Although this paper focuses primarily on the use of selected herbs in the treatment of common diseases, the spiritual component of healing still plays an important role in the health care system in Ghana. Prayer, calling upon the spirits to assist along with the use of natural medicines and herbs is still employed by many of the practitioners. Just as some Western medicine acknowledge the importance of prayer on the part of patients and their families, the spiritual aspect of healing is also important in Ghana. However, that aspect of healing is not covered in this paper.

The research findings of G.J.M. van den Boom and others indicate that about 50 per cent of Ghanaians, self-medicate when they fall sick, about 8 per cent do not seek treatment and consultation, and 6 per cent consult a traditional practitioner. About 36 per cent consult doctors, nurses, and medical assistants. Apparently, more people self-medicate by the use of drugs from the pharmacy, and traditional herbs because they do not have enough money to pay for their medical services. In table 3.1, In Table 3.1, the "Characteristics of the places of health care consultation" chart further indicates that 71 per cent of doctors see patients in public hospitals and clinics, while another 29 per cent of doctors see patients privately. Also, 30 per cent of midwives see their patients in public facilities, while 70 per cent of midwives work privately. The largest majority of traditional practitioners, 98 per cent, see their patients privately and only 2 per cent of these individuals work in the public hospitals. An analysis of where and by whom health care is delivered is clearly indicated by the above Table 3.1. A large proportion of people prefer to see traditional practitioners in a private setting. These figures also indicate that there is a widespread use of the services of traditional practitioners.

Table 3.1
Characteristics of places of health care consultation in per centage 1998/99*

Health care Providers	*Public*	*Private*	*Hospital facilities*	*Clinics*	*Others*
Doctors	71	29	67	32	2
Medical assistants	58	42	6	77	17
Pharmacists	4	96	0	95	5
Nurses	55	45	12	73	15
Midwives	30	70	17	39	43
Traditional Practitioner	2	98	0	4	96

*compiled by G.J.M. van den Boom, 1998-99

Major Forms of Health Care in Ghana

There are two major types of health care systems in Ghana today: orthodox and traditional. Within the orthodox system, providers have formal training in conventional health care practices as taught in universities. Traditional health care providers derive their skills from tradition and informal training. Under the traditional systems, traditional practitioners acquire their healing skills by spiritual means, others learn through their parents, grandparents, friends or relatives, and of course, while others learn through personal observations or by study with practising traditional healers. With few exceptions they do their work on their own or in the homes of their patients. The treatment provided by the traditional providers usually takes the form of plant preparation and prayers. It is not uncommon for the traditional health care provider to supplement traditional medication with modern medicines.

The Ghanaian government currently provides public health care services and facilities. These facilities can be grouped into four categories: (1) village or community health posts; (2) district clinics; (3) regional hospitals; and (4) teaching hospitals. The village health posts primarily provide preventive and primary health care services, while the hospitals are the main providers of conventional health care. The clinics provide a mixture of preventive and conventional care and use the regional hospitals for referrals. These hospitals are usually perceived to be the providers of the highest quality of medical treatment. The village posts are staffed by nurses and midwives. Clinics also have medical assistants. Urban clinics and hospitals usually have doctors, while medical specialists work only in the hospital setting. (Agyepong, 1999). Modern medicines are sold in pharmacies by licensed chemical sellers who sell over the counter medications and other non-prescription drugs to individuals. In 1999, it was estimated that there were about 1,100 pharmacists and about 6,000 licensed chemical sellers in the country (Nsowah-Nuamah et al., 2000).

Health Care Cost In Ghana

It is much more expensive for Ghanaians to visit a doctor than to consult a traditional practitioner. During 1998/99, a visit to a doctor in Ghana cost approximately 8,927 cedis or $ 4.35. A visit to a traditional health care provider was approximately $ 2.94 or 6097 cedis. For many low-income individuals and families, the difference in the cost of the visits was a substantial amount when the cost of medicine and transportation was factored into the equation.

Table 3.2
The Cost of treatment in Ghanaian Currency in 1998-99*

Treatment	*Consultation fee*	*Medicine*	*Cost of Transportation*	*Total cost*
Doctors	8927 ($ 4.35)	12299 ($ 5.99)	1835 (.89)	23061 ($ 11.23)
Traditional health care providers	6097 ($ 2.94)	8504 ($ 4.14)	1166 (.56)	15776 ($ 7.64)
Self medication	0	3708 ($ 1.80)	0	3708 ($ 1.80)

*In 1998 one American Dollar was equivalent to 2,050 Ghanaian cedis.

AIDS and the Herbal Medicine Debate in Ghana

It is important at this point to acknowledge the fact that HIV and AIDS is a major problem throughout Africa. In May 2006, the Joint United Nations Programme on HIV/AIDS reported that 320,000 in Ghana were living with HIV/AIDS. This figure represents 1.43 per cent of the population of Ghana. Of the reported cases, 180,000 are women between the ages of 15 and 49 and 70,000 cases were reported among men of the same age. Twenty-five thousand children under the age of 14 were living with the virus and 29,000 people died of AIDS during 2005 (UNAIDS 2006, Report on the Global Aids Epidemic).

In 2001, Mr Jacob Amoah and Dr George Acquah, from the Asante Manpong District Hospital in Ghana, claimed that a herbal preparation they concocted could reverse the health status of HIV/AIDS patients who suffered from a strain of the AIDS virus that was specific to Ghana. The research conducted in Obuasi, Ghana in October 2001, involved 30 randomly selected patients who were given the concoction prepared by the pharmacists over a period of six months. The pharmacists reported that "with the exception of two of the patients, one of whom died within six months from natural causes and the other from misapplication of the preparation, the remaining 28 had their status improved and had remained in that state to date." (Ghana News Association, September 15, 2003) However, the Director-General of the Ghana AIDS Commission (GAC), Professor Sakyi Amoah, speaking at a forum organized by the Ghana Federation of Traditional Medicine Practitioners Associations on September 4, 2003 expressed concern about the overenthusiasm of some herbalists who claim to have a herbal cure for the HIV/AIDS disease. He went on to say that the GAC has received several requests from some herbal practitioners to test the efficacy of their herbs on HIV/AIDS patients but had to turn down the requests due to the consequences involved. He concluded his remarks by stating that "GAC will not be made a dumping ground for all manner of herbal preparations simply because a herbalist claims to have preparations to cure HIV/AIDS." (Ghana News Association, September 15, 2003).

Both the World Health Organization (WHO) and the Ghana AIDS Commission have policies to promote the use of herbal medicines that have been proven to be safe. Both organizations have called for the mounting of a collaborative effort between herbal practitioners and AIDS research organizations to work collaboratively to find a cure for AIDS. Prof. Amoa indicated that the AIDS Commission was bringing together research institutions including the Noguchi Memorial Institute for Medical Research, the Centre for Scientific Research into Plant Medicine at Mampong-Adwapim and the Department of Herbal Medicine at the Kwame Nkrumah University of Science and Technology, Kumasi, to harness their complementary roles in herbal medicine research.

Common Diseases, Preventions and Cures Through the Use of Herbs

The most common diseases found in Ghana include malaria, cholera, typhoid, pulmonary tuberculosis, anthrax, whooping cough, tetanus, chicken pox, yellow fever, measles, and infectious hepatitis. Other diseases found in Ghana include guinea worm or various kinds of dysentery, river blindness or onchocerciasis, several kinds of pneumonia, dehydration, venereal diseases, and poliomyelitis. The Table 3.3 below contains a selected group of common diseases and herbs used to cure them, followed by a discussion of the disease and herbal treatment.

Table 3.3
Common Diseases and Herb used in Treatments

Disease	*Herb Treatment*
Malaria	*neem* Tree (along with other herbs)
Sores and wounds, bowel disorder, circulation problem, morning sickness, menstrual disorder, nausea and vomiting	Ginger
Fatigue, infertility, weak mind, body weakness, and sexual problems	Kola Nut
Fever	Mango (ginger and *neem* leaves are also used to cure fever)
Stomach disorder	Bitter leaf
Boils and indigestion	Nyame dua (ginger and bitter leaves are also used for boils and indigestion)
Colds, constipation, sore throat, gonorrhoea, sore eyes/conjunctivitis, jaundice, ringworm and parasitic skin diseases	Asifuaka

Discussion of Selected Diseases and Herbal Treatments

MALARIA

Malaria is the most common disease found in the tropical part of Africa. Malaria is caused by the anopheles mosquitoes, which breed on stagnant water or river. Symptoms of malaria include diarrhoea, fever and headache. Many people attempt to avoid malaria by wearing clothing that covers the arms and legs, applying a repellant on the body, or by the use of mosquito netting impregnated with insecticide while sleeping. A more traditional method of avoiding malaria is the practice of burning of dried orange or lemon peals in the area where mosquitoes are present.

Neem in the Treatment of Malaria

The leaves of *neem* tree are used by traditional practitioners to cure and relieve the symptoms of malaria. The leaves are boiled to make a tea that is ingested by individuals who have been infected with the malaria virus. The substances in the leaves of the *neem* tree have been proven to boost the immune system while helping the body fight infection. It also stimulates the production of T-cells to mount a head-on attack against infections. Unlike synthetic antibiotics, *neem* does not destroy beneficial bacteria and other micro-organisms needed to maintain optimum health. It also offers a non-toxic alternative to powerful and sometimes damaging prescription medicines. *Neem* leaves contain fibre, carbohydrates and at least ten amino acid proteins. They also contain calcium and other nourishing minerals. (Furlow, 1994) To minimize the effect of the fever that usually accompanies malaria infection, a mango tea is also used in tandem with *neem* tea.

Traditional practitioners suggest and believe that malaria can be prevented by drinking one cup of *neem* tea, at least one time per week. Researchers have found that the *neem* tea acts as an anti-bacterial agent for the liver, where the malaria parasite lives when it gets into the body.

SORES, WOUNDS, MORNING SICKNESS, AND MENSTRUAL PROBLEMS

Traditional practitioners use ginger to heal a wide range of ailments, from minor scrapes and bruses to circulation problems and vomiting. More recent medical research supports what traditional practitioners have believed for centuries. A study conducted with 120 pregnant women at the Royal hospital for Women in New South Wales, Australia found that ginger can be considered as a useful treatment option for women suffering from morning sickness with no negative side effects such as gestational age, congenital abnormalities, or the birthweight of the babies.

Ginger is a rhizome, or underground, horizontal stemmed plant that sends out roots and shoots from its node. It is primarily grown in India, and Malaysia, but is also grown in West Africa. Ginger is widely used in cooking, tea and the making of ginger ale. It helps free motion, cures morning sickness and is very good for digestion. It eases menstrual cramps, helpful for arthritis, is traditionally used in the orient for colds and flu and is excellent for reducing cholesterol, lowering blood pressure and preventing internal blood clots. It is also used in candies, beverages (ginger beer), preserves, and oriental cooking. In Great Britain it is used to make a hot tea to relieve night-time cold symptoms. Dried ground ginger tastes quite different from fresh ginger "root." However, large doses might cause stomach disorder.

FATIGUE, INFERTILITY, WEAK MIND, BODY WEAKNESS AND SEXUAL PROBLEMS

Traditional healers use the kola nut to cure and address a range of ailments. The kola nut is very accessible and inexpensive in West Africa; kola nuts primarily come from the African Cola *nitida* tree. They can be found in both the rural and urban communities in Ghana; they can also be found in Brazil and West Indies. These are the local names for kola nuts in three most commonly spoken local languages in the country. In Twi the word for the kola nut is *Bese,* in Housa, *Goro,* and in Dagbanle, *Gule.*

Cola is a relative of cacoa (the plant from which chocolate is made) and is best known for its use in cola soft drinks. The seeds are used after they are fermented, dried, and powdered. Ghanaians, particularly the local folks use kola nut for an array of purposes. Some people believe that it is an effective agent that arouses sexual desire amongst men. Others also believe that it helps to make women fertile. Meanwhile, a lot of people notice that it sharpens the mind, reduces fatigue, and provides energy to the body. It is noted that kola nut has two per cent of caffeine and the essential kola oil found in the nuts also acts as a stimulant to the body. For medical purposes, kola nut can be chewed or brewed. For chewing, it should be about two nuts, for brewing, it should be one tablespoon of ground nuts per cup, with a teaspoon of honey. Just as with coffee, kola nuts can also be habit-forming for human being. Excessive use of kola nuts can cause problems such as nervousness, insomnia and low sexual drive.

Users of Herbs

While many individuals in Ghana make use of herbs, traditional practitioners have more knowledge about herbs and the preparation of healing potions. The practitioners can be grouped into three main categories: herbalists who use preparations from leaves, roots, barks and parts of the plant in healing; Sufis who are locally known as Muslim Mallams and priests, who employ divination; and spiritualists using ritual manipulation in their healing. Also, the unlicensed druggists and traditional birth assistants are also part of the traditional system, as well as a range of other specialized traditional practitioners. Ghanaians often prefer self-medication rather than consult a health care provider. Some patients may go to a drug store or a drug peddler and without a prescription from authorized health personnel, buy drugs on the advice from the operators whose knowledge about disease treatment is sometimes questionable (UNICEF, 2002).

On the other hand some of the patients practise self-prescription, and buy drugs or herbs on self-advice to treat a particular disease. Usually, individuals identify the symptoms of their particular diseases and locate the cheapest form of treatment. They may gather herbs from a nearby garden or forest, or buy the herbs at a very low price from traditional healers. This is usually done for economic purposes; they prefer self-medication as a means of avoiding the payment of consultation fees and costs of transport to health care facilities (Asenso-Okyere et al., 1998). The Table 3.4 below identifies and describes the function of the three major groups of health care practitioners.

With such a variety of traditional practitioners applying their trade, this aspect of the health system in Ghana is particularly loose and very disorganized. There are quite a number of unlicensed individual traditional practitioners, predominantly in the urban markets and villages in Ghana. It is quite intriguing to note that some fraudulent practitioners sell common sawdust to patients in the name of traditional

Table 3.4
Description of major groups of traditional health care practitioners

Practitioner	*Duties/Activity*
Herbalists	Persons versed in knowledge of herbs and other natural products and their medical uses
Herbalists-cum-occultists	Combines herbal and spiritual healing
Neo-herbalist	Herbalists with some education who operate in urban areas
Sufis, priest and spiritualists	Persons attached to a mosque, church or shrine of a minor deity who practise healing
Traditional birth assistants	Usually old local women (occasionally men) with experience in child birth and care.
Other orthodox practitioners	Examples include chiropractors, or bone setters who specialize in fractures, using herbs and other natural products; traditional male circumcisers, locally called (wanzams) charlatans healing through various ways.
Unsupervised druggist or medicine peddlers	Persons selling modern medicine without any mediation of an orthodox practitioner.

healing without any knowledge of diseases, healing, or the side effects of the use of sawdust for medical conditions.

Summary, Conclusions and Recommendations

This paper focuses on the formal and traditional health care system in Ghana, the role of the traditional practitioner in the delivery of health care, and the herbs used to heal and cure selected illnesses. While the major purpose of this paper was to examine the use of herbs in the traditional healing process, as the research for background materials progressed, it became evident that the role of the traditional practitioners in the dispensing of herbal medicine and in the actual healing process plays an important role in the overall delivery of health care to the people of Ghana. The writers found that large number of Ghanaians, despite financial capabilities and educational background; seek the assistance of traditional medical practitioners and the use of herbs to cure illnesses. The information and data contained in this paper suggests that two viable health care systems exist side by side in Ghana. Although the government of Ghana has taken steps to improve the delivery of health care through plans such as the "cash and carry" system and the establishment of new hospitals and clinics in underserved areas, a more vigorous integration of the traditional practitioners into the health care system is needed.

The research presented in this paper indicates that the traditional practitioners are underutilized within the existing health care system in Ghana. These individuals are a valuable resource and can serve as a bridge between the medical establishment and the large number of rural and poor people who are in need of medical care. It is recommended that the government find ways to integrate the positive aspects of traditional medicine within the existing health systems. It will also be important to regulate the practice of traditional medicine in a manner that retains the herbal and natural method of healing employed by the traditional practitioner. It is important to assess the needs of traditional practitioners, establish training programmes that are built upon their innate skill and to find ways for doctors, nurses and other medical personnel to work in tandem with traditional practitioners.

4

Integrating the Concept of Sustainability into Public Health Practice

A Partnership, a Process, and a Practical Tool

G.K. Verrinder

Introduction

An open learning process was used to develop resources for the integration of the concept of ecological sustainability into public health practice. International experts, academicians, students and policy makers made up the learning group. The iterative process included web-based discussion forums, writers' workshops, and the introduction and evaluation of materials into public health courses in Australia and Canada. This led to a learning resource that promotes the adoption of an alternative paradigm for action for public health practice.

There is now general agreement on the continuing deterioration of the planet's natural resource cycles and on a response that conforms to sustainable development principles. There is less agreement on what the response should be in any particular place or profession. However, the Earth Charter (2000) supports the notion that education is one of the fundamental ways to transform society.

Public health as a profession urgently needs to reconsider its role in maintaining the health of human populations, in the light of current state of the world environment reports. Public

Health action in sustainable development will need to be revitalized in the twenty-first century; an approach that was first legitimized in the Ottawa Charter for Health Promotion (1986) (Hancock, 2000), but has declined in importance since then.

A learning resource was developed to address the overall question: Why do we have to worry about health risks from the environment? The resource also endeavours to offer answers to three questions regularly put to the researchers, teachers and administrators in sustainability and health who prepared this learning resource:

- why is sustainability of key importance for public health?,
- why does sustainability require a new approach for public health?, and
- what difference does sustainability make to my current practice?

Applying the principles of sustainable development is an accepted pathway worldwide to a sustainable future. In the *Sustainability and Health* project, the adequacy of the principles needed to be analysed as they apply to public health and re-examined in the light of social priorities, environmental change and the responsibilities of public health practice. We were of the view that a significant change in perspective and in the acquisition of knowledge and skills new to public health was required. This perspective guided the content of the learning resource *Sustainability and Health : Supporting Ecological Integrity in Public Health* (Brown et al., 2005).

Learning for Sustainability

Principle 14 of the Earth Charter states: *Integrate into formal education and lifelong learning the knowledge, values and skills needed for a sustainable way of life*. Further, part (a) states: *Provide all, especially children and youth, with educational opportunities that empower them to contribute actively to sustainable development* (p. 45).

Knowledge, Values and Skills for Sustainability

"Becoming a learning society is a public and political process . . . it is about recreating our democracy within and as part of the twenty-first century world" (Duke in Bradshaw, 1999, p. 18). The following eight lifelong learning goals can guide us in our roles in whatever place and whatever profession we are in. These are:

- understand complex systems that interact unpredictably;
- identify and integrate existing and emerging personal, local, national and global perspectives;
- prosper with difference, paradox and multiple sets of realities;
- see and make connections between the past, the present and the future;
- encourage sustainability in relationships and the environment;
- engage in a process of change, privately and publicly, civically and occupationally, throughout life;
- extend learning styles and repertoires; and
- develop insights through questioning, by asking "why?" and "what if?" as well as "what?" and "how?" (Bradshaw, 1999, p. 23).

Concepts that are common to all eight goals are multiplicity, connectedness, critical intelligence and transformation. These principles — indicators of quality future education — work together interdependently whatever be the topic, discipline or place. Bradshaw asserts that in practice, learners and teachers assemble alternative perspectives, explanations and possibilities (multiplicity); together they then make connections between these and beyond these (connectedness). They ask questions about these (critical intelligence). All the while, learners and teachers consolidate by determining and taking thoughtful action that makes a difference personally, locally, nationally and/or globally (transformation) (Bradshaw, 1999).

The Partnership

The collaborative process which forms a thread throughout the development of the *Sustainability and Health* learning resource was also used in the preparation of the resource itself. Being aware of a gap in public health understanding and practice in this critical arena, a research team applied for an Innovation Grant under the Australian Government's Public Health Education and Research Programme. Funding was granted for a three-year project to support the teaching of sustainability in public health training programmes across Australia. A basic discussion paper was compiled and a group of international experts were invited to form the project's advisory committee. The framework for learning resources was put together in an open learning process through interactive deliberations on a teaching/learning website. Forty academics and policy makers with environmental and public health expertise made up the learning group.

Learning Communities

The ideas of Kolb et al., (1974) strongly influenced the field of action research and these ideas are now used as a framework for lifelong learning in a number of professions. The work gave rise to the idea of the learning organization, an organization that is continually expanding its capacity to create its future (Senge, 1990, p. 14).

Learning communities are groups that come together to share their knowledges and that integrate the perspectives of community, specialists, government and industry. Everyone is both a teacher and a learner. Fundamental to learning communities is respecting people's different knowledges. This is very different from the traditional Western "didactic" lecture style, a "top-down" instructional approach whereby acknowledged experts pass on their (assumed) superior knowledge to be absorbed by the "empty vessels" waiting to be filled. Brazilian educationalist Paulo Friere was a strong critic of this approach, arguing that it represents nothing more than the oppression of the majority by a privileged minority (Friere, 1972). Friere's view of education is an essentially participatory process, an active partnership between teacher and learner, and one that is truly transformational and pivotal to human development, fitting well with the concept of the inter-generational and inter-cultural education that takes place in learning communities. The participatory learning approach involves respect for each other's learning, exchanging stories, listening to different groups and their values, and exploring open ways of learning. In this way learning communities can become empowered to identify their problems, critically assess their historical and social roots, envisage a healthier future for themselves and develop strategies to overcome barriers to sustainability (Wallerstien and Bernstein, 1998).

To work effectively, learning communities need to establish a culture, which openly and boldly encourages the challenges to be explored in a constructive and non-adversarial way. Learning communities are essentially solution-oriented and supportive of creative ideas. Their members respect and value the different knowledge constructs. They seek solutions that combine the lived experience of local community members, the specialist knowledge of professional experts, the strategic knowledge of government and the integrative knowledge of those whose role it is to work holistically across other groups (Brown, Nicholson, Stephenson, Bennett and Smith, 2001).

In a global information era we need to construct a new and holistic knowledge that combines the lived experience of local community members with specialized knowledge from research, professions and industry, and an understanding of the strategic processes of politics and administration. We need to be savvy as well as holistic.

Prior to putting the thinking into action, the teaching-learning process needs to move into designing action plans and reflecting on their implications, effects and the principles of what should be done. The cycle continues with the action being evaluated: what works, and if it has not worked what we can learn from the experience. This may involve examining the barriers to change in view of what was tried, and requires a continuing commitment to the process.

The Process

The *Sustainability and Health* process evolved from a virtual community of learners into a writers' workshop where the resource chapters and learning activities took further shape; subsequent working groups completed the first drafts. The learning materials were made available for testing with academics and students responsible for relevant public health courses in Australia and Canada providing extensive feedback, all of which has contributed to the final content.

The participatory learning approach involved respect for each other's learning, exchanging stories, listening to perspectives and exploring ways of learning. In this way the

Sustainability and Health learning community critically assessed issues, and developed strategies to overcome barriers to sustainability in public health.

The Practical Tool

The framework used in the *Sustainability and Health* learning resource is known as P4D4 (Brown, 1997), which was developed to guide local decision-making under conditions of system change toward sustainability. The four Ps of principles, people and place, potential, and practice, combine with the 4 Ds of describe, design, do and review and develop, to form a spiral learning process (Brown et al., 2005, p. 23). The framework is based on a combination of experiential learning principles (Kolb et al., 1974) and place-based change management (Brown et al., 2001). All learning is about change, and adult learning is best characterized as a form of personal inquiry into real world problems. This approach is well suited to responding to sustainability and health issues that require accepting the need for transformational change.

Our approach in the learning resource is that health and environment are interactive components of a dynamic system. We offer a range of ways to address changes in that system, including open learning, team building, strategic frameworks, knowledge synthesis, systems thinking, advocacy and leadership. These are key skills for the public health practitioner in any of the public health domains, but in *Sustainability and Health,* these are related to the need to work in both environment and health fields simultaneously.

We ask people to leave their bounded intellectual silos and reach out towards transdisciplinary and multi-stakeholder consensus. We respect and build on positivist scientific methods, especially as these methods have contributed to the advances in technological understanding. However, we take a social constructivist approach in our analysis and synthesis of the issues included in the learning resource. We hope the perspective we have taken will serve to bring about the change in thinking which, we feel, must occur for global ecological integrity to be a reality.

References

Bradshaw, D. (1999), *Transforming Lives Transforming Communities: A Conceptual Framework for Further Education*, Victoria, Melbourne: Adult, Community and Further Education Board.

Brown, V.A. (1997), *Managing for Local Sustainability: Policy, Problem Solving, Practice and Place*, Canberra: National Office of Local Government.

Brown, V.A., J. Grootjans, J. Ritchie, M. Townsend and G.K. Verrinder eds. (2005), *Sustainability and Health : Supporting Global Ecological Integrity in Public Health*, London: Earthscan.

Brown, V.A., R. Nicholson, P. Stephenson, K.J. Bennett and J. Smith (2001), *Grass Roots and Common Ground : Guidelines for Community-based Environmental Health Action*, New South Wales: Hawkesbury Regional Integrated Monitoring Centre, University of Western Sydney, Richmond.

Earth Charter Commission (2000), *The Earth Charter Initiative Handbook*, New York: Earth Charter Commission.

Friere, P. (1972), *Pedagogy of the Oppressed*, London: Penguin.

Hancock, T. (2000), Healthy Communities must also be sustainable Communities, *Public Health Reports*, vol. 115, pp. 151-56.

Kolb, D.A., I.M. Rubin and J.M. McIntyre (1974), *Organisational Psychology: An Experiential Approach*, New Jersey: Prentice Hall.

Senge, P. (1990), *The Fifth Discipline : The Art and Practice of the Learning Organisation*, London: Doubleday.

Verrinder, G.K. (2005), Innovating, Practitioners as innovators for sustainability and health, in V.A. Brown, J. Grootjans, J. Ritchie, M. Townsend, and G.K. Verrinder eds. (2005), *Sustainability and Health: Supporting Global Ecological Integrity in Public Health*, London: Earthscan.

Wallerstein and Bernstein (1998), Empowerment Education: Friere's ideas adapted to health education. *Health Education Quarterly*, vol. 15, no. 4, pp. 379-94.

5

Sui Generis Legislation and Valuing Biological Resources

Ethno-healing Practices among Tribes of Chhattisgarh

R.N. Pati

Introduction

CHHATTISGARH, a nascent tribal State of India was carved out of Madhya Pradesh on November 1, 2000. This State lies in eastern part of India between 17° 46' N and 24° 05' N latitude and 80° 15' E and 84° 20' E longitude. Forest covers 44 per cent of total geographic area of the State. Kurandi forest, Kurchel valley, Kanger Reserve, Bailadilla hills and Abhujmar constitute medicinal plant hotspots of the State. The issue of environmental governance is correlated with sustainable livelihood in forest villages in and around Abhujmar and Bailadilla. Medicinal plant hotspots in Bastar are numerous and complex. These issues are deep rooted in cultural, social and natural life support systems of communities living in this region.

The biological resources in these indigenous territories of Chhattisgarh consist of natural sources of agricultural, medicinal, ecological, veterinary and cosmological utility which ensure equilibrium between local environment and social health of the tribal communities inhabiting these forest villages. These biological resources influence the cultural practices, resources and local knowledge systems not only among Gond and Halba communities but also among other indigenous communities. The cultural practices both customary and non-customary, prevalent among Gond and Halba tribes of Chhattisgarh are not only inherited territorially but also continue to evolve under influence of individual innovations and local environment. The deficiencies in careful customization of these cultural practices restricts opportunities for innovation and reproduction of these practices. The circulation and reproduction of natural and social environment and local system of production are followed by these cultural practices which are potential substrata of local cultural resources. The process of globalization has threatened not only protection of intellectual property rights of these tribal innovators but also protection of cultural and biological resources of these indigenous territories. The reproduction of these cultural knowledge and practices for commercial application has not been appropriately explored. Because, they need to be synthesized, reduced, standardized and miniaturized for mass reproduction and distribution based on scientific research and integration of local knowledge in the mainstream of scientific exploration. These limitations have provided vast opportunities to big players for hijacking the intellectual property rights of the community over cultural and biological resources of this nascent State. The web of unique relationship between animal genetic resources and cultural practices (i.e. magic, rituals, medicine divisions, symptoms) prevalent among tribal communities of Chhattisgarh need to be explored through appropriate research initiative towards protection of the intellectual property rights of local communities and expanding access to rich biological resources in these indigenous territories.

A little attempt has been made to protect the intellectual property rights and medicine components of animal species administered by these herbalists, shamans and folk healers through awareness-generation and action-research interventions. The government and civil societies in these indigenous territories have not been adequately sensitized on these issues. Appropriate interventions on dissemination of knowledge on traditional medicine, expansion of scope of utilization of this system, identification and elimination of harmful traditional health care practices, enhancement of information sharing on traditional medicine, increasing collaboration between traditional healers and other health practitioners are required to be planned and co-ordinated.

The autonomy of any tribal community is not only manifested through the existence and operation of subsistence economy but also through ethno-medicinal practices adapted appropriately to their cultural framework. This healing system preserves the web of network of interrelationships of man with nature, flora and fauna. The administration of natural components and exploration of human interrelationships with invisible supernatural forces through magico-religious practices revolving around the stratum of folk medicine and traditional healing practices are prevalent among tribal communities in India. The community's confidence on rationality and effectiveness of traditional healing practices and the healers has been compounded by the traditional values and taboos regulating ethno-healing practices among tribal communities. The tribals foster their own traditional knowledge and belief prioritizing the origin and causes of indigenously recommended treatment for diseases which may be rejected as irrational, superstitious and non-scientific by modern medical practitioners. The modern medical practitioners very often fail to touch the raw cord in the heart of tribal patients. Any intervention without responding to sentiment, belief and health-seeking behaviour of tribal appropriately will certainly fail to bring them to centre of health planning in any part of our country. No doubt the *Baiga, Gayata,* the traditional healers among tribals of Chhattisgarh have adequate knowledge and answers to cure permanently many respiratory, reproductive and digestive ailments which modern medical practitioners have failed. The traditional healers with traditional wisdom and expertise on herbal as well as medicinal extracts from various organic components of animals are referred to as *Baiga* or *Sirha* or *Vadde* or *Baidya.* The traditional healers among tribal communities of Bastar have been graded as *Gayata* or *Pujari, Sirha* and *Gunia* on the strength of their expertise, therapeutic skill and job responsibilities. *Gayata* or *Pujari* and *Sirha* among Muria tribe of Bastar have acquired the art of inviting holy spirits from supernatural world as occultists upon themselves and get possessed through performing specific magico-religious rituals. They infuse healing forces awarded by the possessed supernatural spirits into the patient's body for eliminating ailments through healing touch. *Gunia* always works as assistant to *Sirha* in performing magico-religious rituals and worship of holy spirits in the forests. Spiritual component emphasizing on faith healing contributes significantly towards ensuring balances between mental health and physical health. *Perma* the elderly peer of the village takes lead in organizing ceremonies and rituals at community level. *Panjiya* is the astrologer who has expertise in forecasting the fate, crop yield, climate and well-being of persons and communities. These different types of folk healers have expertise and potentialities to serve as appropriate community-level health care providers, health counsellors, peer educators through their capacity-building interventions. This unexplored human resource base need to be fruitfully utilized for transforming the health scenario of the State. The biotechnology policy formulated by Government of Chhattisgarh has provisions for upgrading the capacity of people to exploit the natural, cultural and knowledge heritage of the State. These traditional healers upholding the existence of the thousands of years old culture of ethno-medicinal practices perpetuated through traditional wisdom provide vast opportunity to government and corporate bodies towards promotion of medical tourism in Chhattisgarh. These persons can be motivated to form Peer Group at village level to identify, plan and prioritize the cultivation of medicinal plants and get appropriately involved in the task of promoting bio-villages in the nascent State of Chhattisgarh.

The traditional healing practices of tribes are more or less based on the stimulation of self-healing efforts of the body guided by observance of laws of nature. The therapies under traditional healing practices among tribes have been influenced by the sets of interrelationship among human world, supernatural forces and nature. Nature is treated as the microcosm and universe as macrocosm crowned with spiritual and supernatural forces. Nature consists of minerals, vegetation and animal kingdom the ingredients of which have been derived from the universe. Human body contains all the ingredients, which both universe and nature possesses. The basic rationale of traditional healing therapies among tribals is deep-rooted in the understanding of human relationship with nature and universe. The ingredients from human world, animal kingdom, mineral resources and green vegetation along with unseen forces drawn from the supernatural world influence significantly these traditional healing therapies. The principles of these therapies are directed to generate forces for stimulating human happiness, community consciousness and harmony apart from igniting the process of self-healing within the human biological system. These days thousands of patients all over the world have developed a fascinating choice for a trial with treatment by folk healers for their chronic ailments and test the efficacy of alternative herbal or ethno-medical health care system practised by Indian traditional healers.

Research Design

The present paper is based on anthropological study of indigenous knowledge system of ethno-medicinal practices prevalent among Halba and Raj Gond, Muria tribal communities living in twelve forest-based mountain villages of Antagarh Block in Kanker district, Bastar region of Chhattisgarh. A team of two social anthropologists and one ethno-botanist camped in these villages for nine weeks during November-December 2002. The study focused on in-depth interview with 21 tribal herbalists (*Baiga*), 18 shamans (*Gayata*) and 35 community elites spread over these twelve forest villages adopted as samples under the study. The author administered Focus Group Discussion (FGD) with lineage elders, herbalists, herbal plant merchants, expectant mothers, Traditional Birth Attendants (TBAs) and shamans separately. More emphasis was given on analysis of data elicited from oral tradition, oral histories, and participant observation on rituals governing collection and use of biological resources. The village-based resource maps covering habitat of herbal species were developed involving these informants with administration of appropriate tools of Participatory Rural Appraisal (PRA). The field investigation was carried out with administration of both qualitative and quantitative tools such as interview guide, Focus Group Discussion, in-depth personal interviews and anthropological case studies. Some tribal herbalists were engaged as field guides to accompany the team for identifying the habitat of herbs in the forest.

Indigenous Model of Health Care and Conservation of Biodiversity

The indigenous model of cultivation of medicinal plants like ***Safed Moosali*** (*Chlorophytum-arundinaceum*) for expanding commercialization opportunities on experimental basis in some parts of the State has provided unexpected encouraging response to the farmers. The cultivation of medicinal plants like *Terminalia-arjuna* (***Arjuna***), *Melia-composita* (***Garood***), *Samilex perfolia* (***Phosar***), *Withania-Somnifera* (***Ashwagandha***), *Piper nigrum* (***Kālimirch***), *Madhuca-indica* (***Sarpagandha***), *Terminalia-belirica* (***Behada***), *Terminalia-Chebula* (***Harada***), *Plumbago-zeylanica* (***Chitawar***), *Curculigo archiolis* (***Kali Moosali***), *Azadiracle-indica* (***Neem***) holds a bright future for upholding economic prosperity of the State. The globalization process has facilitated the linkage with vast marketing network for commercialization of these rare herbs, which must be appropriately tapped. As many as 625 plant species including medicinal herbs have been traded from forests of Chhattisgarh. The results of such experimentation are urged to be disseminated through duplication in a larger scale operation, which will not only respond to community efforts in the eradication of poverty but also compound government efforts in transforming the State of Chhattisgarh into a herbal State of India with bigger strides. In the absence of enactment of a *sui generis* law for protection of traditional knowledge from being bio-pirated by multinational companies inspired by the growing trends of globalization and privatization, the rich cultural heritage shall fade away. Different multinational companies have been acquiring the traditional knowledge on ethno-medicines and commercializing these herbal medicines with their own patents. Lack of research and documentation of ethno-medicines and lack of rewards to efforts to integrate these folk healers in the country's mainstream of development have provided enough scope to bio-piracy of traditional knowledge and art-craft, and commercial use of the valuable rare herbs supporting the rich cultural heritage of Chhattisgarh. The issues of protection of Intellectual Property Rights (IPRs) of folk healers have not been appropriately addressed at Doha and incorporated in the TRIPS (Trade Related Intellectual Property Rights) agreement. The marketing of pure medicinal and aromatic plants along with provision of consultation by traditional healers capsuled in a package deal and handled by a federation of grass-root CBOs (Community Based Organisations) like Vana Suraksha Samiti or State level apex body of stakeholders' co-operative societies dealing with minor forest produce would pave a prosperous way for fruitful exploration of the ethno-medicine system in Chhattisgarh. Chhattisgarh State Minor Forest Produce (Trade and Development) Co-operative Federation Ltd. has been entrusted by the State Government to ensure IPRs of local health traditional practitioners. Unfortunately these initiatives have not been streamlined due to resource crunch, poor awareness of local bodies of their rights and responsibilities and inadequate institutional arrangements in place for keeping track of smuggling of medicinal plants out of the State.

The success stories of the experimentation initiated by the Tanga AIDS Working Group (TAWG) of Tanzania in addressing the problems of HIV/AIDS patients through appropriate collaboration with traditional healers provide examples of eye-opening interventions. Under this project, the traditional healers have been trained to work as HIV/ AIDS counsellors, peer educators, better health-care providers and condom distributors. The treatment of at least 2000 AIDS patients by traditional remedies have proved effective in elimination of skin problems, increase in appetite, improvement of quality of life and enhancement of longevity of life in these patients.

Issues of IPRs' : Need for Sui Generis Legislation

The Government of India had enacted Biological Diversity Act (BDA) in 2002, which seeks protection and regulation of the country's natural resources and traditional knowledge. This initiative has been stimulated by resolutions of International Convention on Biological Diversity (ICBD) to which India was one of the signatories. This Act has prescribed three-tier systems of regulation ranging from national level to grass root level. National Biodiversity Authority (NBA) has been created at apex level to co-ordinate the activities of State level Biodiversity Boards (SBB) and local level Biodiversity Management Committees (BMC). The Government of India have drafted the rules of Biodiversity Act (BA) in 2004, which entrusted NBA to take appropriate steps for creating database and documentation system for biological resources through biological registers and electronic data bank. The Ministry of Environment and Forest, Government of India, convened a series of workshops for preparing detailed manuals for People's Biodiversity Registry (PBR). It has been visualized that each Gram Panchayat of the country would be encouraged to promote Biodiversity Information System (BIS) and Peoples Biodiversity Registry. This would serve as a storehouse of all biodiversity-related information and would be used as a tool towards gaining access to forest produce. People will be sensitized to know biodiversity around them and curtail its use and plan ecological conservation accordingly. At the initial stage, Centre for Ecological Sciences (CES), Bangalore has been entrusted by the Government of India to prepare manuals for PBR to be launched at least in 300 Gram Panchayats of the country, which would promote Intellectual Property Rights (IPRs) regions and ensure conservation of bio-wealth.

The Government of India has taken a praiseworthy stand at international circle and denied IPRs on life forms at World Trade Organization (WTO) level. But, the flaws in domestic legislative provisions have not been prioritized and rectified so far. The Government of India has allowed IPRs on plant varieties. No policy has been enacted to empower the stakeholders for prevention of bio-piracy in terms of obtaining Prior Informed Consent (PIC) directly from the communities. Biodiversity Rules, 2004 enacted by the Government of India have entrusted power to NBA to grant permission to foreigners seeking access to biological resources and traditional knowledge without taking PIC from local Biodiversity Management Committee. The representation of community at the State and National Level Biodiversity Boards (NLBB) has been ignored. The role of local BMC has been confined to documentation of traditional knowledge and developing peoples biodiversity registry only. Besides, the provisions for equitable benefits-sharing by stakeholders from commercial use of bio-wealth and indigenous knowledge have not been well defined in the Biodiversity Rules. The district administration has been authorized to receive the benefit on behalf of the community. The principles of consent and benefit-sharing need to be revised and restructured incorporating rooms for empowerment of stakeholders as well as the local BMC in terms of granting Prior Informed Consent to users and availing benefits-sharing directly without involvement of any bureaucratic hurdles.

Conclusion

The challenges before us today are not to challenge the efficacy and rationality of traditional ethno-healing practices but the challenges to bridge the gap between traditional and modern bio-medicine, reclamation and exploring core essence of ethno-healing practices in terms of their contribution to humanity and science. The knowledge base of ethno-healing system may be significantly explored towards supplementing the existing modern bio-medical practices. The challenging tasks ahead of State Government today are exploration of indigenous knowledge system and promotion of an appropriate database, incorporation of field-tested concepts on indigenous knowledge into academic as well as development policies of the Government, promotion of national linkage between researchers and organizations involved in ethno-medicine initiatives, promotion of Indigenous Knowledge Resource Centre at State level for documentation, acquisition and dissemination of Indigenous Knowledge related information in the nascent State of Chhattisgarh. Without appropriate research initiatives towards documentation of traditional knowledge relating to medicinal plants preserved by elderly peers, the indigenous knowledge base is on the verge of erosion and elimination in the absence of promotional efforts by younger generations to acquire, promote and sustain this stream of knowledge gainfully. Some magico-religious practices prevalent among Abujhmaria and Baiga have tremendous impact on delaying child birth as experienced by some educated couples of the cities of Chhattisgarh. The Ministry of Culture, Government of India has set up National Mission for Manuscripts (NMM) and other appropriate

Missions to conserve country's intangible heritage, formulate appropriate policy and legislative framework. This will not only prevent erosion and unauthorized exploitation of traditions but also stimulate innovation and creativity as well as protection of transmission of traditional knowledge honouring the dignity and moral rights of innovators in this globalizing era.

The globalization has opened the spectrum of accessibility by overpowering multinational companies to procure, market and own Iintellectual Property Rights over herbal medicinal resources technology and processing of the natural ingredients of herbal medical system preserved by indigenous communities. In the absence of enactment of appropriate policy and legislation to protect the intellectual and cultural property rights of traditional folk healers and adequate exploration and documentation of intangible culture and oral tradition covering folklore, mythology, ritual, proverbs, etc. the tangible and intangible assets of age-old folk healing system have been taken over, owned and put for greater commercial use through process of privatization. These are highly sensitive issues which are to be dealt with by appropriate legislation and policy formulation with back-up support through appropriate research interventions in the growing State of Chhattisgarh.

The tribals sustain the preservation of rare medicinal plants in Common Productive Resources (CPR) in indigenous territories of this State. The contradictions between Government's perceptions and rules of revenue and forest department over ownership and property right on these common productive resources on one hand and tribal beliefs and practices concerning resource management on the other have posed serious threat not only to preservation of biodiversity resources but also to sustenance of ethno-medicinal practices. These issues have been taken for debate on various national and international forums. The "Principle of Self-determination" upholding home-rule and autonomy of tribal communities as recommended in the International Conference on Conflict Resolution, Peace Building, Sustainable Development and Indigenous People, 6-8 December, 2000, Manila (Philippines) may be explored as a guiding principle incorporated in the strategy for resolution of insurgencies and conflicts over tribal people's land and resources in this State. The deficiencies and vacuum in promoting capacities of tribal people to uphold and defend their rights are deep rooted in their inability to undertake research and documentation and dissemination of information world wide. They fail to promote appropriate global, regional and local networks. Collaboration in campaign and policy understanding on these issues of tribal people of this State is very poor.

There is an urgent need for promotion of appropriate public understanding in this regard through media advocacy with involvement of academicians, NGOs and civil society organizations of the State. There is an urgent need for Promotion of Tribal and Indigenous Peoples Global Network with a mission to promote and defend their rights and capacities to expose the abuses of their tradition. The agenda of public awareness must focus on issues of peace keeping in indigenous territories, social protection, partnerships, mobilization of resources, national and international co-operation for social protection, preservation and protection of bio-diversity resources with appropriate participation of tribals of the State.

India is treated as a treasure house of indigenous knowledge and numerous rare medicinal herbs. India preserves 7 per cent of world's biodiversity. National Biotech

Policy (NBP) of India is still at a rudimentary stage, which has not provided any consultation, sharing of success stories with stakeholders and civil society. No precautionary principle has been defined to initiate any precaution when the environment is exposed to threats. The rice exporters of India have bitter experience of the economic threat posed to them by Texas-based firm, Rice Tech, which could manage to hijack patent on Basamati Rice of India in 1997. Ultimately Rice Tech was forced to withdraw the claim for patent when challenged by the Government of India. Similarly, two US-based Indians have acquired patent for use of turmeric in wound healing. The Government of India has challenged this patent and forced it to revoke. There are numerous cases where Intellectual Property Rights of tribal innovators have been hijacked without their knowledge. There is an urgent need to promote national consensus regarding protection of IPRs on indigenous knowledge relating to medicinal and aromatic herbs. The issues of these rights need to be published and discussed by a broad audience of stakeholders. The policy needs to be based on informed public opinion and process of public engagement eliciting broad range of public opinions on these issues. The herbalists and folk healers upholding local health tradition need to be engaged with monetary and non-monetary incentives so that they would be encouraged to safeguard and share their knowledge for greater public cause. More focus is urged on research, documentation and publication of Local Health Tradition (LHT). Conservation Assessment and Management Plan (CAMP) workshops need to be organized for assessing commercially harvested medicinal plants in different forest regions of the State. The establishment of medicinal plants germ plasm banks would create a safety net for protection of intellectual property rights on use of the medicinal herbs. The civil society organizations have a major role in promoting a platform for debate and information-sharing between policy makers and stakeholders. The Government of India has promoted a network of four Gene Banks to conserve the rare endangered commercially important medicinal and aromatic plants on an experimental basis. The success stories of this experimentation need to be disseminated among stakeholders of different regions of the country.

Abbrevations

BA	—	Biodiversity Act
BDA	—	Biological Diversity Act
BIS	—	Biodiversity Information System
BMC	—	Biodiversity Management Committees
CAMP	—	Conservation Assessment and Management Plan
CBOs	—	Community Based Organisations
CES	—	Centre for Ecological Sciences
CPR	—	Common Productive Resources
FGD	—	Focus Group Discussion
ICBD	—	International Convention on Biological Diversity
IPRs	—	Intellectual Property Rights
LHT	—	Local Health Tradition
NBA	—	National Biodiversity Authority
NBP	—	National Biotech Policy
NMM	—	National Mission for Manuscripts
PBR	—	People's Biodiversity Registry
PIC	—	Prior Informed Consent
PRA	—	Participatory Rural Appraisal
SBB	—	State level Biodiversity Boards
TAWG	—	Tanga AIDS Working Group
TBAs	—	Traditional Birth Attendants

TRIPS — Trade Related Intellectual Property Rights

WTO — World Trade Organization

References

Abdul Hafeel, T.S. Suma (2000), "Monumental heritage" in Indian Health Traditions, 08 October 2000, *The Hindu*.

Census Summary : Tribals of Madhya Pradesh, Dec. 1995, Bhopal: Tribal Research Institute.

Chaudhari, Buddhadeb (1986), *Tribal Health Socio-Cultural Dimensions*, New Delhi: Inter-India Publications.

Dak, T.M. (1991), *Sociology of Health in India*, New Delhi: Rawat Publications.

India's National Magazine, *The Hindu*, vol. 22, Issues of 9 April 2003 and 6 May 2005.

Hughes, I. (1996), "Yolngu Rom : Indigenous Knowledge in North Australia," in P. Blunt and D. Warren (eds. 1996), *Indigenous Organizations and Development*, London: Intermediate Technology Publications.

Langton, M. (1999), "The Growing Co-operation between Indigenous and Mainstream Managers of Northern Australian Landscapes and the Challenge for Educators and Researchers," in P. Havemann (ed.), *Indigenous Peoples' Rights in Australia, Canada and New Zealand*, pp. 71-87, Auckland : Oxford University Press.

Miller, M. (1985), *Report of the Committee of Review of Aboriginal Employment and Training Programmes*, Canberra : AGPS.

Patel, G.P. and T.K. Vaishnav (1988), Report : Prohibition of Family Planning in Tribals of Madhya Pradesh, Bhopal: Tribal Research Institute.

Reeves, J. (1998), Report of the Review of the Aboriginal Land Rights (Northern Territory) Act 1976 — *Building on Land Rights for the Next Generation*, Canberra: Aboriginal and Torres Strait Islander Commission.

Report: Socio Anthropological Study, Keer Tribe, *TRI*, Bhopal, 1995-96.

Report: Socio Anthropological Study, Majhi Tribe, *TRI*, Bhopal, 1995-96.

Sathe, P.V. (1991), *Epidemiology and Management for Health Care for All*, Bombay: Popular Prakashan.

SEARO, Regional Health Paper no. 13: Concepts of Health Behaviour Research, WHO Regional Office, 1987.

Shukla, H.L. (1988), *Tribal Heritage of Madhya Pradesh*, Delhi: B.R. Publishing Corporation.

Singh, P. (1996), "The Role of Entrepreneurship in Economic Development," in *P.S. Lokanathon 72nd Birthday Commemorative Volume, Economic Development: Issues and Policies*, Bombay: Vora and Co.

Taylor, J. (1997), *The Opportunity Costs of Future Indigenous Labour Force Status*, CAEPR Discussion Paper no. 128, Canberra: Cantre for Aboriginal Economic Policy Research, Australian National University.

Tiwari, D.N. (1984), *Primitive Tribes of Madhya Pradesh*, New Delhi: Strategy for Development, Government of India, Ministry of Home Affairs, Tribal Development Division.

Tribal Health Bulletin, vol. I, no. 1, March 1992, Jabalpur, M.P.: RMRC.

Yunupingu, B. (1991), "A Plan for Ganma Research," in *Aboriginal Pedagogy: Aboriginal Teachers Speak Out*, Geelong: Deakin University Press.

Part II

Environmental Governance and Sustainable Development

6. Vertical Dimension of Social Integration : Grass-roots Activities for Managing Sustainability
   — *Wolfgang Meyer*

7. Solid Waste Recycling in Malaysia : Study of the Households in the States of Terengganu and Perak
   — *Abdelnaser Omran, Abdullah Mahmood*
   — *Hamidi Abdul Aziz*

8. Knowledge Communication : The Essence of Sustainable Governance
   — *Kendal Hodgman*

9. Linking Sustainable Development to Environmental Governance : Issues of Forest Villages in Chhattisgarh, India
   — *R.N. Pati*

10. Added Value in the Process Industry Through Integrated Environmental Engineering
    — *Markus Thüer*

6

Vertical Dimension of Social Integration

Grass-roots Activities for Managing Sustainability

Wolfgang Meyer

Introduction

THIS chapter is about a dream. It is dreamt in variations by people like Nelson Mandela, Martin Luther King or Mahatma Gandhi. This dream is about peacefully uniting all people on earth to live in respect for each other and all kind of species, jointly working for their own wealth and the wealth of the whole planet. To put it in scientific terms, this is the utopian idea of perfect *social integration*.

Some news can be found in the variation of this idea called "sustainable development." The most important one is the *ecological component*, emphasising the limits of natural resources and the possible disastrous results for the eco-system by following the path of modernity without any changes. While ignoring early warnings of wise men like the Suquamish Chief Sealth, leader of a small tribe of North American indigenous people in the nineteenth century, the environmental threat became popular in the late 1960s. Mass media spread the results of scientific research on topics like climate change all over the world and people formed social movements to give ecological issues a political voice. One outcome was the United Nations Conference on Human Environment 1972, where the United

Nations integrated ecology into their perception of global development. This was the starting point of the concept of "sustainable development," finally created in the late 1980s.

The second news was the *political results* of this process, leading to an agreement on joint action called the "Agenda 21" and being signed by almost all States in 1992 at the World Conference on Environment and Development in Rio de Janeiro. Moreover, representatives from civil society organizations got involved in this discussion very early and they also agreed on the concept of sustainable development as a basis for joint action. While Nelson Mandela, Martin Luther King and Mahatma Gandhi succeeded in forming powerful national movements, sustainable development is the first global attempt to realize the dream of perfect social integration. It is doing so by giving mankind a common goal: to save its planet and the natural resources needed for survival.

This chapter focuses on the contribution of *grass-roots activities* for sustainable development and therefore on the *vertical dimension of social integration.* Two serious problems must be solved for global sustainability management on a vertical scale: the *problem of consensus* on the meaning of sustainable development ("top-down" transfer of political ideas) and the *problem of impact aggregation* of grass-roots activities for global development ("bottom-up" transfer of local impacts). Some of the most important challenges for implementing institutions to support a sound performance at the grass-roots level are discussed here.

First, the relationship between social integration and sustainable development is briefly outlined, following the understanding of sustainable development as a three-dimensional social integration process for managing limited natural and human resources. On a second step, these management tasks are discussed by presenting the implications of non-hierarchical multi-actor policy networks, the "carriers of hope" for institutional solutions involving civil society on the local level. The third part focuses on internal communication processes within civil society organizations and their task to aggregate interests and to transfer social responsibility to individuals. Finally, a synopsis on the challenges for local sustainability management is presented.

The Vertical Dimension of Sustainability — Importance of Grass-roots Activities

The "Brundtland-Report" of the World Commission on Environment and Development published in 1987 defined sustainable development as a development "that meets the needs of the present without compromising the ability of future generations to meet their own needs" (World Commission, 1987: 8). Following this most cited definition, sustainable development should be the continuous *integration of needs* between different generations of human beings on a *time dimension*. Neither "needs" nor "time" are more precisely outlined in the report, leaving room for discussion on, for example, how long the duration of impacts has to be, how to handle changing needs, or how to decide on the weighting of human needs compared with natural needs. Nevertheless, nobody denies the time scale being one of the most important elements of sustainability.

Hence, the majority of sustainability discussion nowadays concentrates on another aspect of the concept, the integration of "the three pillars" (ecology, economy and social issues). Although the "Brundtland-Report" never used this metaphor, sustainability is widely seen as the task to balance environmental and economic interests for the wealth of human beings. This is for sure a popular view of scientists from the North-Western hemisphere: governments and researchers from Africa, Asia and South-America emphasize instead much more the "social pillar" and the task of combating poverty, still being the main North-South difference in the debates on environmental issues. Other people recommend adding a "fourth pillar" (sometimes even a fifth or a sixth one). The German government, for instance, accentuates education as an important element of sustainable development.

To include all these different views, the use of a horizontal "scale" instead of "pillars" should be preferred. Moreover, by bringing man back in the discussion, the question of balance is primarily linked to human interests referring to "the economy" or "the ecology" and not to the system functionalities themselves. The main topic is a *horizontal social integration* of combating economic, environmental and social interests (and interest groups) on the *target dimension*. The term "horizontal" does not imply any statement on need or target hierarchies, which may lead to different weightings of solutions. It just emphasizes the need for political measures to balance interests for managing sustainable development successfully. While sustainable development will not evolve itself in an endogenous process, some kind of *sustainability management* is necessary and, as far as we are all "stakeholders" regarding the fate of our planet, everybody should be involved.

The Agenda 21 and the other final documents of the famous World Summit in Rio de Janeiro 1992 clarify *who* is supposed *to do* this management of sustainable development (United Nations, 1992). The conference slogan "think globally — act locally" passed this task to the local level, recommending joint action of local people for solving local problems. In doing so, the activities at the grass-roots level should *accumulate* to global impacts and save our planet from the expected ecological catastrophes. Moreover, this is in need of a common understanding of sustainable development which should be represented in global policy and the documents of the United Nations.

This implies *communication procedures* for transferring social responsibility and commonly shared goals *top-down* to guide local action and for aggregating experiences and impacts of single activities *bottom-up* to prepare decisions and "good governance" in global policy. The task of all human activities is to contribute for *vertical social integration* on a *territorial scale* (for the problems of communication related to this task, see Meyer, 2006). Moreover, the above-mentioned social integration on the target- and the time-scale is primarily a task for the grass-roots level. While the global level (and especially the United Nations) will "think" about sustainability, the local level (and especially the grass-roots communities) has to "act" for sustainable development.

In summarizing this, sustainable development can be illustrated as a *utopian concept of total social integration* referring to at least three different dimensions (targets, territories and time) and of *adequate management rules to use limited resources on the grass-roots level* for fair and justice, environmental friendly and economically sound global development.

One of the most important tasks is to build up some kind of local governance which is able to fulfil these management requests. For sure, the solutions must be based on local traditions, norms and values, and it has to take the experience of indigenous people into account. Local problems are less complex than those on national or global level, making them easier, understandable and treatable. Especially the number of actors who have to be involved in sustainability management is smaller, making negotiations and solution-finding less difficult. If sustainability management is possible, the best opportunities can be probably found on the local level.

Managing Sustainable Development — Network Requirements

One of the most important aspects of managing sustainable development is the effort for involving civil society and its organizations into the process of decision making and local governance (e.g. in the local agenda, 2001). For sure, this is an attractive idea from a democratic point of view and nearly all grass-roots organizations agree on it. But the realization of this idea is difficult.

In most cases, the public sector and its state organizations have to be blamed for not sharing power and for not respecting participation rights. Some politicians reduce "participation" to "lobbyism" and they are following the money as they did all the time before. Others are afraid of losing their role as decision maker and they are combating the idea of involving civil society into decision making. And another group interprets stakeholder involvement as pure consultation, giving the civil society a fair opportunity to present their ideas and recommendations (as, for example, the EU did in their "white paper" on European governance, see: Commission of the EC 2001).

Without any doubt, the Agenda 21 is not very clear in defining the idea of participation and the expected role of civil society within the process of managing sustainable development. As far as the UN-documents are signed by nation States, one can critically assume that civil society should only be used for improving the impacts of government decisions. Hence, reserving decision making to the elected people in the political system will not help spreading the idea of sustainable development as a joint task for the whole society. Civil society is neither a State executive nor a supplement for State's tasks to improve common welfare. Moreover, civil society organizations are merely formations of political protest and they are uniting individual interests concerning specific political issues for acting as powerful political pressure groups. Especially strong multinational civil society organizations like Greenpeace, Friends of the Earth or Amnesty International are important observation posts for States' behaviour and they cannot agree in acting as States' executives.

Coming to the grass-roots level will change the perspective. Nearly all civil society groups at the grass-roots level are formed for solving local problems and not for influencing policies on a national or multinational level. In most cases, there are no widespread issues that allow building up national or multinational organizations. Associations of grass-roots movements are considerably weaker than national or multinational civil society organizations. In Germany, for instance, the "Bundesverband Bürgerinitiativen Umweltschutz" (BBU), the association of local environmental initiatives, never reached the same influence as the "Bund für Umwelt und Naturschutz Deutschland" (BUND) which is primarily aiming on national environmental policies. This does not mean that the BUND or other national-oriented civil society organizations are refusing to act on the grass-roots level. Contrarily, most multinational and national civil society organizations are strongly involved in local activities, but they are doing it because of their mission and not primarily because of local pressure or local roots. Even if these organizations are strongly decentralized (like the BUND), the initiative for engagement in this group is some way "top-down"-influenced: people join the BUND because the organization is famous and successful on the national level.

Grass-roots organizations are seldom interested in national policy — as far as it does not harm their own local tasks — and they sometimes do not even know how to act on this stage. People join them because they are local and because they are working on a specific local topic. Again they are merely formed because the authorities did not succeed in solving pressuring problems. But these problems are local ones and the authorities addressed are local authorities. Sometimes grass-roots organizations are even building a non-parliamentarian opposition against decisions of local authorities and some of them are illegal and persecuted. The spectrum of grass-roots organizations is varying extremely between regions and localities — not mentioning the cultural differences in political protest, public engagement of citizens, religious and traditional relations between State and society which are strongly differentiating, for instance, the Indian grass-roots movements from the European ones (for an overview on the Indian civil society, see, for example, Srivastava et al., 2004).

The World Conference on Environment and Development in Rio was quite right to emphasize the potential of the local level for problem solving and for managing sustainable development. Moreover, it is absolutely true that the opportunities for joint action are much better at the grass-roots than in global politics. The local agenda even highlighted that civil societies at the grass-roots have to be involved in managing sustainable development and, therefore, in local decision-making. The solution for sustainability management must be a *non-hierarchically ordered policy network including all stakeholder groups on the grass-roots level.*

From the viewpoint of *decision-making*, non-hierarchical networks have some visible advantages. They have the capability for producing more effective solutions because they are able to process more relevant information, to take a greater variety of values into account raising the acceptance of decisions by stakeholders, and to be more flexible in reaction on changing situations increasing the adaptability of solutions. As a result, policy networks proved to be able to create innovative answers on difficult questions in complex decision-making situations. Moreover, they are increasing the possibilities of executing these decisions and for transferring those into effective solutions (cf. Scharpf, 1993).

For doing so, they need to include all relevant interests in the decision-making process and to balance these interests during the negotiations. In other words: *policy networks have to beware their openness* to discuss innovative suggestions, to develop balanced and practicable solutions, and to force execution in a changing social environment. Social institutions for maintaining network activities have to guarantee this. While policy networks are implemented as durable institutions, they need to stay open for new members, new ideas and new ways of interactions for ensuring their durable capacity in solving local problems.

This argument focuses on the differentiation of network governance into "*governance of networks*" and "*governance through networks*". "Governance" is one of the scientific "catch-words" of the last decade and it is used in different contexts with a huge variety of meanings. Political scientists analyse the co-ordination problem between international, national and regional governments within democratic political systems by using the term "multi-level governance" (cf. Bache, 2004), while development aid policy claims for "good governance" in democratization processes by implementing a "spirit of democracy" in societies and supporting the formation of any kind of legitimated political steering (cf. Ginther, 1995). We suggested defining "governance" as the *institutionalized process of making and executing political decisions*, emphasizing three core elements: political *institutions, decision-making* and the *execution* of decisions (cf. Meyer and Elbe, 2007).

Obviously, such kind of governance is needed both for maintaining a policy network ("governance of networks") and for guaranteeing sustainable effects of network decisions within a given social environment ("governance through networks"). While "governance of networks" emphasizes the internal view of network management, "governance through networks" highlights the external perspective of network impacts.

There is an enormous amount of empirical literature on governance and most studies are interested in *governance through networks.* Renate Mayntz (2003), one of the most famous German social scientists working for more than thirty years on this issue, summarized her findings as follow:

- Governance through policy networks is in *need of a "strong" (nation) State to ensure the functionality of self-regulation*: "If self-regulation remains ineffective, the State can step in and regulate by direct intervention. . . . Self-regulation in the context of modern governance is always regulated self-regulation" (Mayntz, 2003: 4). Thus, policy networks often act "in the shadow of hierarchy" and powerful political authorities as "guardians of public welfare" are preconditions for effective self-regulation.
- A second precondition of effective governance in multi-actor constellations mentioned by Renate Mayntz is "the existence of *a strong, functionally differentiated, and*

well-organized civil society" (Mayntz, 2003: 5). Therefore, most important parts of civil society and policy-networks are corporate actors which are able to *integrate and aggregate the particular interests of citizens* and *to represent them for opinion-building within policy network* as well as *to produce common social responsibility* and *to organize collective action of its members in the sense of network decisions* (cf. Meyer, 2005).

- Finally, a *common identity* of corporate actors involved in network management is needed to (re)produce social responsibility not only in the network but also in the memberships of the participating civil society actors. Without at least a crude feeling of "belonging together," the willingness to co-operate and to waive claims on common resources will not exist. Therefore, extensive communication both between and within network actors for developing a shared "sense of community" and to enable social integration independently from nation State is needed.

These three preconditions of successful network governance — Strong state, strong civil society and a sense of community — cannot be found in all regions of the world. Even in the so-called "developed world" of the North, the influences of nation States, the establishment of civil society and the feeling to belong together vary extremely between regions and localities. Hence, it seems to be even easier to establish network governance in some areas of the Southern hemisphere due to community traditions and stronger relations between people at the local level. Especially in some Asian countries like China, India or Thailand the preconditions for network governance seem to be pretty good and it should be possible to establish good working policy networks for managing sustainable development on a local level here. Some indigenous communities in these regions may even offer interesting options for self-regulating policy networks which are not in need of a strong nation State.

Unfortunately, these preconditions are necessary but not sufficient for building up a successful working policy network on the local level. Four key problems of *"governance of networks"* have to be solved additionally (Meyer and Baltes, 2004):

- *Trust*: Collective action is only possible, if trust in the reliability of each member to act in a co-operative way can be guaranteed (cf. Knill, 2000: 119ff.). Therefore, network regulations have to avoid cheating (even the possibilities for it) and to produce trust between the network members. This is obviously difficult if organizations have combating interests and a long tradition of rivalry.
- *Durability*: To produce trust, to avoid cheating and to overcome "prisoner dilemma" situations, continuous (or, as a minimum, repeated) interaction between same actors is necessary (see the Considerations of Game theory, Ordeshook, 2003, especially on the importance of repeated interaction, Axelrod, 1984). Therefore, networks have to be stable constellations of actors at least to a certain extent and over a recognizable time period. Network regulations have to minimize fluctuations and make it difficult to leave the network (especially after pocketing benefits of common action).
- *Strategic Dependency*: Continuous interaction between formally independent and voluntary participating actors leads to "strategic dependency" (Streeck and Schmitter, 1996: 137f.). The scope of action for each actor in decision situation is reduced to co-operative alternatives because egoistic behaviour risks future

support of partners. Power imbalances have to be regulated by network rules to give all participants a fair opportunity in realizing their own interests (cf. Bachmann, 2000: 108ff.). This is obviously important for "weak" grass-roots organizations in co-operation with "strong" multinational companies or nation States.

- *Institutionalisation*: As mentioned above, especially for balancing power disparities between members' network rules have to be developed. Such an institutional framework regulates the modalities of participation, the process of decision-making, the distribution of commonly produced benefits and the possibility of access and exit to network (cf. Mayntz and Scharpf, 1995: 19ff.). While networks should not become closed organizations, network regulation has to guarantee a rational rules development that always balances both the internal efforts of co-operation and innovativeness with the external efforts of openness and effectiveness.

As a result, "governance of networks" need a *regulative regime* which is able to stabilize several contrary requests. While the main advantage of networks as a co-operation mechanism is its openness for new ideas and members, the *closing tendency* of the "iron law of oligarchy" (Michels, 1987) has to be prevented. This oligarchic tendency is a result of the production of trust by positive experiences of co-operation, because this "team-building" process reduces the willingness to involve others. In other words, *mistrust in others* is a result of *trust in companions*. Following the argumentation of Scharpf (1996: 518), such a dichotomy of "insiders" and "outsiders," companions and competitors, is needed as a radical cognitive simplification for reducing the complexity of co-operation situations. Regulative measures must be found to keep the network open while producing trust between its members.

Openness and closure are two main aspects of *social integration*. But social integration within one group is always associated with the threat of *social disintegration* in other ones. Building local policy networks may result in national disintegration; the involvement of local employers and employee groups may estrange them from unions or business associations; and single persons who are active in local policy networks may quit their engagement in other networks on national or multinational level. The durability of networks and their integrative function may lead to destabilizing other social institutions, and vice versa. Again regulative measures have to be found for solving these challenges.

While looking on strategic dependency, one can distinguish two contrary modes of self co-ordination (Scharpf, 1996: 512ff.). *Positive co-ordination* tries to maximize the common output of activities, and members are willing to invest personal resources to reach this goal. On the contrary, *negative co-ordination* emphasizes the minimal consensus to avoid individual disadvantages as a result of common activities. Moreover, positive co-ordination leads to *internal homogenization of interests with respect to shared network interests (collective egoism)* while negative co-ordination can be described as *internal heterogenization of interests with respect to individual actor interests* (*individual egoism*). Regulative measures have to balance collective and individual egoism in the most productive way.

Finally, each kind of group membership is to a certain extent a loss of individual freedom. This is also true for organizations and there are some important restrictions related with the participation in policy networks for grass-roots organizations which should be mentioned more in detail in the following part.

Internal Communication Processes — Organizing the Civil Society

If civil society organizations and interest groups are getting involved in political decision-making as members of policy networks, they have to manage a twofolded internal communication process in a professional way. *Bottom-up* communication refers to the problem of *representation of interests.* Due to democratic principles, each member of the electorate must have the same right and possibility to get his or her interests represented by delegates within the political system (cf. Dahl, 1998).

In organizations, delegates get elected by *members* of the organization. In opposite to State authorities or commercial enterprises, civil society organizations are highly dependent on active support of their members. Their prior task is the aggregation of individual interests on a specific topic and the representation of this common position in public activities or within a policy network. People join these organizations voluntarily because they support its political objectives. Participation in multi-actor policy networks with the aim of decision-making and problem-solving may influence members' support positively (e.g. the increasing opportunities to influence political decisions are a new incentive) or negatively (e.g. the organization may be held responsible for mismanagement of the network). Hence, if representatives of an organization are not able to push the commonly shared group position through network negotiations, members have the opportunity to leave the organization (exit) or to fight for a more radical position in negotiations (voice). At any rate, the "loyalty" of voluntary members in civil society organizations is not given but has to be (re-)produced all the time (cf. Hirschman, 1970).

By using policy networks for local governance, the burden of *social integration* is merely transferred from the political system on to civil society organizations. The participation in political decision-making increases the demand for *representative opinion-building within the organization.* To ensure equal opportunities and rights for representation, a professional communication management is needed. This is also demanded by the network which has to assure that participating organizations are reflecting the will of the majority of their clients — and not only the interests of a radical minority or a single regional subdivision. This puts the pressure for integrating all different positions within civil society on the organizations representing civil society in network negotiations.

Obviously, finding consensus is easier in homogenous small groups. Moreover, *homogeneity of positions* is important for powerful joint actions. The status of civil society organizations within a policy network is depending on its ability for *mass mobilisation,* not limited to their members but including as many as possible additional supporters. Increasing power means for civil society organizations increasing the number of supporters and therefore increasing the problems of communication management. The lesser the people support the group position, the more are the efforts are needed for communication.

Hence, internal communication is also "top-down" communication from delegates involved in political negotiations to the members of the organization they are representing. This is necessary to ensure internal support for the resulting decisions of these negotiations and the required collective action of the group. In other words, *corporate social responsibility* of the network must be transferred by communication tools within the participating organizations.

While members' interests differ more or less from the consensus reached in network negotiations, participating in policy networks leads to intra-organizational conflicts between *social and member responsibility*. The dependency of member support sharpens this problem in civil society organizations.

By reviewing scientific literature on "social responsibility," one has to state a remarkable lack of empirical research into civil society organizations. While a lot of material can be found on the question how social responsibility can be included in corporate governance processes within *commercial enterprises,* mainly multinational firms (cf. OECD, 2001; Bryane, 2003), these aspects are rarely mentioned for non-profit *interest organizations* (for an exception, see Take, 2002). Civil society organization's activities are directed towards some well-defined area of policy and they are only representing particular interests of their members in this specific area. They have to separate this interest from other ones and to protect it against other interest groups. Civil society organizations are "advocates of social responsibility" limited to one particular policy arena. This is also true for grass-roots organizations — with the addition that not only their issues but also their regional interests are limited.

Especially in grass-roots organizations, internal communication management is seldom mentioned as a specific challenge. As long as the groups are small, open discussions and basic democratic decision styles are dominating. While growing up and getting involved in policy networks, these "natural" interaction systems rapidly reach the limits of their functionality. The quality of performance is declining and endangers the further existence of the organization. Without any quality management including performance measurement and evaluation of internal communication processes, this risky development can easily be overseen by the boards. Several empirical studies on NGOs and the non-profit sector in various countries revealed the poor activities concerning performance measurement and professional communication management (see for example: Edwards and Hulme, 1997, 2002; Light, 2004; Duca, 1996). While most of these results are derived from huge multinational or national organizations, one can assume grass-roots initiatives being even less professional and engaged in monitoring and evaluating their own activities.

The problem is not a lack of interest but a lack of adequate measurement systems and instruments that are suitable for grass-roots organizations. Advanced quality management systems, derived from the industrial sector for commercial enterprises and following the ISO-standards, are too difficult to handle for small organizations — even small and medium-sized enterprises. For the non-profit sector and for grass-roots initiatives in particular nearly no professional support can be found. Two recently published books of CEval in German language on quality management and performance measurement in non-profit organizations are among the few exceptions (Stockmann, 2005; 2006).

Hence, professional communication in civil society organizations, especially on the grass-roots level, becomes one of the most important tasks for sustainability management. Only local interest groups are able to mobilize people for sustainable development and to spread the idea of global responsibility throughout the communities. Organizing civil society for sustainable development means overcoming several constraints, like individual egoism, misled preferences or poor circumstances for supporting sustainable development. Empowerment of grass-roots activities by civil society organizations will be one of the keys for successful sustainability management.

Conclusion

The described elements of vertical social integration and the associated difficulties are summarized in the following synopsis (Table 6.1). For sure, this table is not a complete overview (e.g. the important national level is missing) and some additional difficulties may be found (at least in practice). Moreover, by concentrating on civil society and grass-roots activities, other relevant actors — like companies — are out of focus here.

Nevertheless, this Table shows the scope of action necessary for implementing a sufficient institutional framework for sustainability management on the local level. Only the first topic "vertical global integration" needs support of other actors to assure aggregation of impacts and to develop a common understanding of sustainability (e.g. in a national sustainability strategy). Moreover, the formation of powerful and functional policy networks seems to be a difficult task without any support of national state authorities. For sure, this is not possible for civil society and its organizations alone; at least the most powerful stakeholders like local authorities, companies, churches, unions, associations, etc. must be involved in this foundation process. In Germany, a huge competition called "Regionen Aktiv" initiated by the Federal Ministry of Agriculture helped to develop local policy networks in selected German regions (cf. Meyer and Elbe, 2007).

The task for civil society organizations is concentrated especially on communication processes with their own members and other addressees of their activities. While being involved in policy networks for sustainability management, civil society organizations have to aggregate the interests of local people in a fair and democratic way, bringing their will into the network negotiations (bottom-up communication).

Table 6.1
Synopsis on vertical social integration for Sustainability Management

Topics	*Objectives*	*Difficulties*
Vertical Global Integration ("Think globally, act locally")	Bringing sustainable development into action	a) Single solutions on local level will not be aggregated for solving global problems (*bottom up-integration*) b) Common global ideas will not be shared by all relevant local stakeholders (*top down-integration*)
Policy Networks (non-hierarchical multi-actor decision-making)	Problem solving on local level	a) Lack of impacts derived by co-operation (*governance through networks*) b) Lack of maintaining co-operation of network partners (*governance of networks*)
Governance Through Networks (Execution of collective decisions)	Effective management of sustainable development	a) No incentives and pressure for co-operation from public authorities (*weak State*) b) No organization of interests by independent, free and open associations and clubs (*weak civil society*)

		c) No feeling to belong together (*weak identity*)
Governance of Networks (Production of proper solutions)	Functional network regulations	a) No trust between network partners (*openness vs. oligarchy*) b) Poor durability of network co-operation (*integration vs. disintegration*) c) Lack of strategic dependency (*positive vs. negative co-ordination*) d) Missing institutionalization of adequate rules (*individual vs. collective egoism*)
Communication Processes Within Organizations (Integration of members)	Organizing the civil society	a) Unbalanced aggregation of individual interests (*bottom-up communication*) b) Members are not sharing social responsibility (*top-down communication*)
Individual Behaviour (Sustainability awareness)	Contributing for sustainable development	a) No individual interest on global development (*egoism*) b) Individual needs for unsustainable products and services (*preferences*) c) Lack of opportunities for sustain-able sound behaviour (*framing*)

Moreover, they have to transfer the decisions of networks and the social responsibility for the common good to their members (top-down communication). This task may be easier for small grass-roots organizations, although more professional work is required even here. However, solutions for the described problems have to be found on the local level – best with some scientific support of University institutes and some financial empowerment by donor organizations or the nation State. This may offer the chance for realizing the dream of perfect social integration for sustainable development — and not let it linger as a "mission impossible."

Abbreviations

BBU — Bundesverband Bürgerinitiativen Umweltschutz

BUND — Bund für Umwelt und Naturschutz Deutschland

CEval — Centre for Evaluation

References

Axelrod, R. (1984), *The Evolution of Co-operation*, New York: Basic Books.

Bachmann, R. (1999), Die Ko-ordination und Steuerung inter-organizationaler Netzwerkbeziehungen über Vertrauen und Macht' in J. Sydow and A. Windeler (eds.), *Steuerung von Netzwerken, Konzepte und Praktiken*, Opladen/Wiesbaden: Westdeutscher Verlag, pp. 107-25.

Bache, I. (ed. 2004), *Multi-level Governance*, Oxford et al., Oxford University Press.

Bryane, M. (2003) "Corporate social responsibility in international development, An overview and critique," *Corporate Social Responsibility and Environmental Management* 10/3, pp. 115-28.

Commission of the European Communities (2001), *European Governance, A White paper*, Brussels: European Commission. (http://eur-lex.europa.eu/LexUriServ/site/en/com/2001/com2001_0428en01.pdf).

Dahl, R.A. (1998), *On Democracy*, New Haven/London: Yale University Press.

Duca, D.J. (1996), Nonprofit Boards, Roles, Responsibilities and Performance, Washington: Wiley.

Edwards, M. and D. Hulme, (eds. 1997), *Making a Difference: NGOs and Development in a Changing World*, London: Earthscan (3).

——— (eds. 2002), Non-Governmental Organizations — Performance and Accountability, *Beyond the Magic Bullet*, London: Earthscan (3).

Ginther, K. (ed. 1995), *Sustainable Development and Good Governance*, Dordrecht et al., Nijhoff.

Hirschman, A.O. (1970), *Exit, Voice and Loyalty*, Responses to Decline in Firms, Organizations, and States, Cambridge: Harvard University Press.

Knill, C. (2000), "Policy-Netzwerke, Analytisches Konzept und Erscheinungsform moderner Politiksteuerung" in J. Weyer (ed.), *Soziale Netzwerke, Konzepte und Methoden der sozialwissenschaftlichen Netzwerkforschung*, München/Wien: Oldenbourg, pp. 111-34.

Light, P.C. (2004), *Sustaining Non-profit Performance, The Case for Capacity Building and the Evidence to Support It*, Washington: Brooking Institution Press.

Mayntz, R. (2003), *From Government to Governance: Political Steering in Modern Societies*, Paper presented at the IOEW Summer Academy on IPP, Würzburg, September 7-11, 2003 (http://www.ioew.de/governance/english/veranstaltungen/Summer_Academies/SuA2Mayntz.pdf).

Mayntz, R. and F.W. Scharpf (1995), "Steuerung und Selbstorganization in staatsnahen Sektoren" in R. Mayntz and F.W. Scharpf (eds.), *Gesellschaftliche Selbstregelung und politische Steuerung*, Frankfurt/New York: Campus, pp. 9-38.

Meyer, W. (2005), "Regulation, Responsibility and Representation: Challenges for intra-Organizational communication," in I. Demirag (ed.) *Corporate Social Responsibility, Accountability and Governance: Global Perspectives*, Sheffield: Greenleaf Publishing, pp. 41-55.

——— (2006), *From Environmental to Sustainability Communication: Lessons learnt from the German Craft Sector* (Paper presented at the 13th International Conference of the Greening of Industry Network:

Partnerships for Sustainable Development, 02-05 July 2006, Cardiff, available at the GIN-homepage).

Meyer, W. and K. Baltes (2004), "Network Failures: How Realistic is Durable Co-operation in Global Governance?" in K. Jacob, M. Binder and A. Weiczorek (eds.), *Governance for Industrial Transformation, Proceedings of the 2003 Berlin Conference on the Human Dimensions of Global Environmental Change*, Berlin: Environmental Policy Research Centre, pp. 31-51.

Meyer, W. and S. Elbe (2007), "Initiating Network Governance by Competition, Experiences from 18 German Regions" in L. Cheshire, V. Higgins and G. Lawrence (eds.), *Rural Governance: International Perspectives*, Albindon: Routledge, pp. 81-97.

Michels, R. (1987), "Die oligarchischen Tendenzen der Gesellschaft, Ein Beitrag zum Problem der Demokratie [1908]" in R. Michels, *Masse, Führer, Intellektuelle, Politisch-soziologische Aufsätze 1906–1933* (Frankfurt/New York: Campus): pp. 133-81.

OECD (eds. 2001), *Corporate Social Responsibility: Partners for Progress*, Paris: OECD.

Ordeshook, Peter C. (2003), *Game Theory and Political Theory: An Introduction*, Boston: Birkhauser.

Scharpf, F.W. (1993), "Co-ordination in Hierarchies and Networks" In F. W. Scharpf (ed.), *Games and Hierarchies and Networks: Analytical and Theoretical Approaches to the Study of Governance Institutions*, Frankfurt/New York: Campus, pp. 125-65.

——— (1996) "Positive und negative Koordination in Verhandlungssystemen" in P. Kenis and V. Schneider (ed.), *Organisation und Netzwerk. Institutionelle Steuerung in Wirtschaft und Politik*, Frankfurt/New York: Campus, pp. 497-534.

Srivastava, S.S., R. Tandon, S.W. Sokolowski and L.M. Salamon (2004), "India" in L.M. Salamon, S.W. Sokolowskis and Associates (eds.), *Global Civil Society: Dimensions of the Non-profit Sector* (vol. 2), Bloomfield: Kumarian, pp. 157-69.

Stockmann, R. (2005), *Evaluation und Qualitätsentwicklung, Eine Grundlage für wirkungsorientiertes Qualitätsmanagement*, Münster: Waxmann.

———, (2006), *Handbuch zur Evaluation: Eine praktische Handlungsanleitung*, Münster: Waxmann.

Streeck, W. and P.C. Schmitter (1996), "Gemeinschaft, Markt, Staat — und Verbände?" In P. Kenis and V. Schneider (eds.), *Organisation und Netzwerk, Institutionelle Steuerung in Wirtschaft und Politik*, Frankfurt/New York: Campus, pp. 123-64.

Take, I. (2002), *NGOs im Wandel: Von der Graswurzel auf das diplomatische Parkett*, Wiesbaden: Westdeutscher Verlag.

United Nations (1992), *Agenda 21: United Nations Conference on Environment and Development Rio de Janeiro 1992*, United Nations: New York (http://www.un.org/esa/sustdev/agenda21.htm).

World Commission on Environment and Development (1987), *Our Common Future*, New York: Oxford University Press.

7

Solid Waste Recycling in Malaysia

Study of the Households in the States of Terengganu and Perak

Abdelnaser Omran,
Abdullah Mahmood and *Hamidi Abdul Aziz*

Introduction

RAPID economic growth has resulted in a large increase in refuse output in Malaysia. Landfill sites are now reaching capacity levels and the need to build new ones is putting pressure on Malaysia's limited land resources.

Malaysia, with a population of over 24 million in 2005 generates approximately 17,000 metric tonnes of domestic waste daily, making it one of the highest waste generators around (Noor, 2005). Waste generation on a per capita basis typically is reflective of the level of wealth and industrialization of a region in the country. At present, the per capita generation of solid waste in Malaysia varies from 0.45 to 1.44 kg/day depending on the economic status of an area, the national average being 0.5-0.8 kg/person/day [The Minitry of Housing and Local Government, Malaysia (MOHLG), 2005]. In general, the per capita generation rate is about 1 kg/day and may sometimes increase up to 1.7 kg/person/day in major cities (Kathirvale et al., 2003). Generally, Malaysian solid wastes contain very high organic waste and consequently high moisture content with bulk density of above 200 kg/m.[3] A recent study conducted in Kuala Lumpur revealed that the amount of organic wastes for residential area ranges from 62 to 72 per cent.

The management of municipal solid waste is currently one of Malaysia's most critical environmental issues. In response to this as well as to rising collection, infrastructure and operating costs, a waste minimization strategy was initiated by the Malaysian Government. The Government decided to adopt recycling as a long-term strategy for Solid Waste Management (SWM). A new law on SWM was introduced and a strategic plan in Peninsular Malaysia is being drafted for the same. In 1993, the Government of Malaysia, through the Ministry of Housing and Local Government, launched a national recycling campaign. However, despite the effort and money spent, the campaign received a lukewarm support from the people. Thus the Government decided to re-launch the campaign again in 2001. This time, more money was used to provide recycling facilities, for publicity and to educate the people on the importance of recycling. Community groups and NGOs were encouraged and given incentives to take part by spearheading recycling programmes and the collection of reusable material. The aim is to achieve a 22 per cent recycling by the year 2020.

However five years after the launch of the second campaign, the result is still the same (Abdelnaser et al., 2005). In 2005, the recycling quota amounted to a mere 5 per cent. This low achievement is largely due to lack of facilities and the attitude of the households towards recycling and environmental protection. As with other developing countries,

Table 7.1
1995 and 2025 Urban municipal solid waste generation in Asia

Country	*GNP per capita (1995 US $)*	*GNP per capita in 2025 (1995 US $)*	*Current Urban*	*2025 Urban*	*Current Urban MSW Generation (Kg/capita/day)*	*2025 Urban MSW Generation (Kg/capita/day)*
Low income	**490**	**1050**	**27.8**	**48.8**	**0.64**	**0.6-1.0**
Nepal	200	360	13.7	34.4	0.50	0.6
Bangladesh	240	440	18.3	40.0	0.49	0.6
Myanmar	240	580	26.2	47.3	0.45	0.6
Vietnam	240	580	20.8	39.0	0.55	0.7
Mongolia	310	560	60.9	76.5	0.60	0.9
India	340	620	26.8	45.2	0.46	0.7
Lao PDR	350	850	21.7	44.5	0.69	0.8
China	620	1500	30.3	54.5	0.79	0.9
Sri Lanka	700	1300	2.44	42.6	0.89	1.0

Middle income	**1410**	**3390**	**37.6**	**61.1**	**0.73**	**0.1-1.5**
Indonesia	980	2400	35.4	60.7	0.76	1.0
Philippines	1050	2500	54.2	74.3	0.52	0.8
Thailand	2740	6650	20.0	39.1	1.10	1.5
Malaysia	3890	9400	53.7	72.7	0.81	1.4
High Income	**30990**	**41140**	**79.5**	**88.2**	**1.64**	**1.4-4.5**
Korea Republic 07	9700	17600	81.3	93.7	1.59	1.4
Hong Kong	22990	31000	95.0	97.3	5.07	4.5
Singapore	26730	36300	100.0	100.0	1.10	1.1
Japan	39640	53500	77.6	84.9	1.47	1.3

Source: World Bank, *"What a Waste: Solid Waste Management in Asia,"* May 1999.

waste management in Malaysia is becoming an acute problem. As urbanization and economic development increases, larger quantities of waste materials requiring management will be generated in those countries. In Asia, the management of waste materials requires immediate attention especially in countries such as Malaysia, China and South Korea which have been categorized as emerging industrialized countries. According to a World Bank study, the urban areas of Asia produced about 760,000 tonnes of Municipal Solid Waste (MSW) or approximately 2.7 million/m^3/ per day (World Bank, 1999) in 1995. However, these were projected to increase to 1.8 million tonnes of waste per day, or 5.2 million tonnes of waste per day in 2025 (World Bank, 1999), refer Table 7.2.

In Malaysia, the most common waste management approach currently employed is landfill. There are now 168 disposal sites in Malaysia. Of these seven are sanitary landfills while the rest are open dumps. However, due to rapid development and lack of space for new sites about 80 per cent of these dumps have filled up and are expected to be closed in the next two years (2007-08). For Terengganu and Perak, the shortage of landfill sites is indeed a pressing problem. Thus, despite their relatively small population size, Solid Waste Management is fast becoming a critical issue.

Perak is the second largest State in Peninsular Malaysia. It is bordered on the north by Kedah and Thailand, on the east by Kelantan and Pahang, on the south by Selangor and to the west by the Strait of Malacca. Perak's population is approximately 2 million. Once Malaysia's most populous State, the decline in the cans industry caused an economic slowdown from which it has yet to recover, leading to a massive drain in manpower to higher-growth States such as Penang, Selangor and the Federal Territory of Kuala Lumpur. Modern Perak is divided into 10 administrative divisions. However, the Executive Council is the highest administrative body in the State. At the local Government level, the State has one local authority, namely the Municipal Council of Ipoh (MCI). The average throwaway in Perak is around 0.9-1.1 kg of waste/ person/day, which is higher than the national average (MOHLG, 2005).

Terengganu on the other hand is one of the three east coast States on Peninsular Malaysia. It has a land area of 12,995 square kilometres and 225 kilometres of picturesque coastline. Kuala Terengganu, its capital stands on the bank of the Terengganu River.

Terengganu's population, which stands at approximately 1 million people, consists of 90 per cent Malays, with the rest being made up of Chinese and Indians. In addition to Kuala Terengganu, there are also 6 other main administrative districts. Terengganu at the local Government level, the State has one local authority, namely the Municipal Council of Kuala Terengganu (MCKT). The average throwaway in Terengganu is around 0.85-1 kg of waste/person/day, which is higher than the national average (MOHLG, 2005).

This chapter presents the findings of a study on the attitude of households in Perak and Terengganu States on recycling of solid wastes. It seeks to find the reasons why the recycling campaign failed although all effort was taken by the Government, both at federal and State level, to encourage them to recycle. The chapter gives an overall view of the reasons for the failure.

Solid Waste Management and Recycling

What is solid waste? Since solid waste can be defined in many ways, it is appropriate to define what it is within the context of this study.

When we read news articles or hear people talking about solid waste, we might hear terms such as garbage, refuse, waste material or trash to describe what we throw away. Although the product may have value to someone (either in its present or in a converted state), if its producer doesn't ask for reimbursement for its removal, it is considered to be waste, and at the same stage, will enter a waste handling system, either private or public. Therefore, solid waste, within the context of this study, is non-gaseous and non-liquid waste that resulted from the daily activities of a community's residential, commercial, and industrial sectors.

It may take the form of combustibles, including paper, rags, wood, leaves, and weeds, or noncombustible, such as glass and metal materials.

Recycling, on the other hand, is a way of preserving the natural resources. Recycling helps reduce pollution, saves energy, and reduces the demands for virgin materials. Recycling diverts waste from overloaded landfills, provides materials that require less fuel for manufacture and helps make the Malaysian Ringgit (RM) more energy-independent (Agamuthu, 2001). Simply put, recycling means using things that have already been used to make new things. It also includes reusing things as they are, and giving things you no longer need for other people to use.

Status of Solid Waste Management in Malaysia

Solid Waste Management in Malaysia has become an increasingly important task of local Government or local authorities. Over the years, industrial and economic growth which brought about an increase in urban population and an increase in the standard of living have resulted in an increase in quantity and variation in the types of waste generated. Many types of solid wastes are generated which could be broadly categorized into four types, i.e. household wastes, commercial wastes, industrial wastes and city wastes. However, this study focuses only on household wastes. These are generally wastes generated by households in the preparation and consumption of food. Recyclables, which are commonly found in household waste, are paper, glass, plastic or metal containers.

In Malaysia, the management of solid waste is largely the responsibility of Municipal Councils (MCs), a unit within the municipal councils. More than 70 per cent of the MC's activity is related to collection, transportation and transfer of solid wastes from collection points to the landfills. Labourers employed by MCs previously did collection operation, which is highly labour-intensive but in recent years, most of these jobs are contracted out to private waste management companies. Overall, the annual handling cost for the whole of Malaysia is about Ringgit Malaysian 90 millions. This amounts to about 40 per cent to 70 per cent of the annual incomes from rates collected by the municipalities (Agamuthu, 2001).

Currently, two types of collection systems are employed. These are:

(i) Communal collection

In this system, the householder takes the waste material from the household to the collection point. The collectors will collect the waste from the communal storage. This system is commonly used in high-rise apartments and condominiums.

(ii) Curbside collection

In this system, waste materials are collected from the home. The residents leave their bins on the roadside in advance of collection time. After collection, the owners take empty bins back. Curbside collection is common in low-rise housing areas, which includes terrace, semi-detached and detached houses (Agamuthu, 2001).

The Recycling Campaign in Malaysia

Recycling is generally accepted as a Sustainable Municipal Waste Management (SWM) strategy. Several reasons are often advanced for participating and/or promoting recycling in both developed and developing countries. The general consensus among professionals and researchers is that recycling reduces the total amount of waste that is disposed of, and conserves natural resources (Muttamara, 1996; Noehammer and Byer, 1997).

As mentioned earlier, the Ministry of Housing and Local Government of Malaysia launched a nationwide recycling campaign in 1993. However, the campaign failed due to lack of response and participation from the people. A bigger and more aggressive campaign was initiated in 2000. Sixty-five drop-off or collection centres, located at schools, gas stations, shopping malls and other convenient public places were opened nationwide.

Recycling can be done in many ways. The method currently used in Malaysia can be divided into three types as shown in *fig*. 7.1:

In the first method, the householder separates recyclable materials from non-recyclable domestic wastes. The recyclable materials are then sold to recycling agents who made regular door-to-door visit. This method is most common for newspaper and paper products.

In the second method, householders are expected to separate and keep recyclable and non-recyclable materials in

Table 7.2
Recycling rate in Malaysia from 2001 until 2020

Year	*Total waste generated (tonnes/ year)*	*Recycling rate (per cent)*
2001	160,600	3.0
2002	164,615	4.0
2003	168,730	5.0
2004	172,949	6.0
2005	177,272	7.0
2006	181,704	8.0
2007	186,247	9.0
2008	190,903	10.0
2009	195,676	11.0
2010	200,567	12.0
2011	205,582	13.0
2012	210,721	14.0
2013	215,989	15.0
2014	221,389	16.0
2015	226,924	17.0
2016	232,597	18.0
2017	238,412	19.0
2018	244,372	20.0
2019	250,481	21.0
2020	256,743	22.0
	4,102,472	

Source: Chong, et al. (2005)

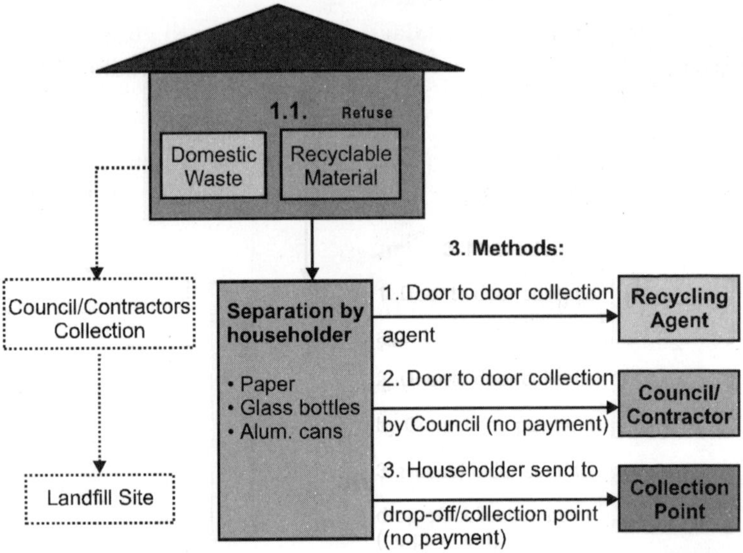

Source: Ministry of Housing & Local Government, Malaysia, 2005.

fig. 7.1 : Methods of Recyclingfs

separate plastic bags. Both materials which are placed in ordinary domestic waste-bins will be collected by workers employed by the council or appointed contractors. All recyclable materials will then be sent to recycling centre for storage and for further separation before it is sold to the recycling market.

The third method requires the householder to bring their recyclables to the drop-off or collection centres. Currently, there are more than 1400 collection centres available in the country. These are often located in shopping centres, resident associations, schools, etc. and are equipped with separate bins for paper, glass and plastics. This method is to cater for bigger amount and larger materials.

METHODOLOGY

This research was conducted in Terengganu and Perak States on recycling of solid wastes to explore the attitude of households. The study duration was from April to June 2006. Field data collection was done from April 2006 to June 2006, through participatory observation of attitude of household in the States mentioned above. In April 2006, we started to visit the households across the States. It was to gain information on Solid waste recycling campaign of the households in the two States. Specifically it was aimed to discover reasons why the nationwide recycling campaign that was organized by the local authority and the Government in both States failed to attract households to recycle. We gave a short survey on recycling solid waste programme and its campaign. The survey contained 14 questions distributed on sections which are focused on personal information, i.e. Awareness of the recycling activities/campaign? Types of materials recycled? Perception on the success of the recycling campaign and how can it be improved? And so on. The analysis is based on results of a questionnaire survey on 1000 households, 500 each from the States of Terengganu and Perak, Malaysia. The questionnaires were distributed within the period of three months beginning 1st of April 2006 to 30th of June 2006. To ensure good response, the strategy used was to distribute the questionnaire at selected socio-economic strata (lower, middle-class, and upper) areas on Terengganu and Perak States in order to see their attitudes towards the recycling of solid wastes, so that the results may be compared in order to verify whether the recycling campaign is a success or a failure. Four hundred and twenty five useable questionnaires (85 per cent) and three hundred forty seven also useable questionnaires (69.5 per cent) were received and analysed. Although the number of questionnaires received was small, it is sufficient to give some indication of the overall attitude of the households of Terengganu and Perak on recycling of solid wastes and is adequate to enable the findings to be generalized for the whole population of Terengganu and Perak. The descriptive analysis of the data collected is presented below.

FINDINGS

Awareness of Recycling Activities/Campaign

A majority (84.7 per cent) of the respondents in Perak said advertisements in the newspapers while television and radio ads ranked second followed by information in newsletters and the billboards. In contrast, in Terengganu the respondents (73.7 per cent) heard about recycling. As to their source of information, 73.7 per cent read about the campaign in the newspapers while 26.3 per cent heard about it over the television and radio.

Importance of Recycling

Asked on the importance of recycling, almost all (100 per cent) participants in Perak indicated that recycling is important. The same figure (100 per cent) was seen in Terengganu State. However, only about 71 per cent (247) of the respondents indicated that they participated in the recycling activities in Perak while 38.7 per cent (233) of the respondents indicated the same in Terengganu. The main reasons given, ranked according to the order of importance were: (i) Concern for the environment; (ii) Concern about availability of landfills; and (iii) Encouragement from their children. A small number indicated that they recycled for money.

Participation in Recycling

Amongst those who did not participate in the recycling activity 62 per cent in Perak and (61.3 per cent or 369 respondents in

Terengganu) indicated that the reasons are inconvenience and the lack of facilities (62 per cent) of the respondents in Perak and (49 per cent) in Terengganu. It is also interesting to note that a smaller percentage of the non-participating respondents (18 per cent in Perak) indicated that "they were unconcerned about recycling" or found it unimportant. Although the number of respondents within this group is small, particular attention should be taken to "persuade" them to change their attitude to recycling. A comparison with a similar study in Singapore (Foo, 1997) showed that only 9 per cent of the respondents practise regular recycling while another 11 per cent practise recycling "some of the time," whereas the rest only practise recycling once in a while (64 per cent). Some experts have noted that acceptance plays an important role when locating a SWM facility (Joos et al., 1999). It is interesting to note that about 31 per cent of the non-participating respondents indicated that they "weren't bothered" while 8 per cent considered recycling to be unimportant. Although the number of respondents within this group is small, particular attention should be taken to persuade them on the importance of recycling.

Facilities Provided

Respondents were also asked about the facilities provided for recycling. When asked whether they knew the location of the nearest collection point in their area, 61.7 per cent of Perak households and 62 per cent of Terengganu households indicated they knew the location. However, more than 52 per cent of households in Perak and 60 per cent of those in Terengganu State complained that the site could not be easily located. In terms of distance, only 31.8 per cent indicated that it was within one kilometre from their homes. In Perak 16 per cent stated that the site was located within the radius of 2-3 kilometres and 44 per cent indicated that it was within a 5 kilometres radius in Perak. While, 14.3 per cent in Terengganu stated that it was within 2-3 kilometres of the radius, 28.2 per cent cited that it was located within one kilometre of their homes, 6.8 per cent indicated that it was within a 4-5 kilometres radius and 50.7 per cent indicated that it was farther than a 5 kilometres radius. It was observed that, the farther the location of the collection point, the more discouraged were the householders to recycling. González-Torre and Adenso-Díaz (2005) commented that when citizens who are environmentally concerned have bins near to home, they appear to be willing to recycle more fractions than when they have to walk for a longer time to drop off the waste, due to the inconvenience of carrying the large volumes that this type of waste usually occupies. He concluded that distance and access to the bins is obviously an incentive to recycling. The benefit the facility may bring to local residents can influence attitudes (Lima, 1996). However, citizen's attitudes depend on knowledge about a facility (Rahardyan, 2004).

Types of Materials Recycled

Amongst those who recycled, the types of materials recycled in term of quantity were newspapers, aluminium cans, plastics, cardboards and glass. In response to the question "How often do you recycle," 46 per cent in Perak indicated they recycle waste weekly while about 24 per cent indicated they need to recycle more often, i.e. twice or three times a week. In contrast, in Terengganu 44 per cent indicated that they recycled more often, i.e. daily or twice a week while about 27 per cent did so daily. Finally, some participants mentioned that they recycled every 3 months.

Perceptions as to Success of the Recycling Campaign

The respondents were asked to give their opinion on the on-going recycling campaign hoisted by the relevant departments in the two countries. On the question whether the campaign had succeeded or failed, 90 per cent indicated that it failed to achieve its aims in Perak while 92 per cent stated that it also failed to do so in Terengganu as depicted in *fig*. 7.2. When queried about the reasons for the failure, there are many plausible reasons why recycling efforts have not been implemented with a great success in Malaysia. However, these reasons can be divided into three broad categories:

(i) Awareness of recycling and concern to environment should be inculcated from early ages. Unfortunately, there is no formal subject dedicated to achieve this purpose in the present education system at primary and secondary level.

(ii) Present campaign on recycling is currently done to general public. The dedicated target is very broad and the success rate is quite difficult to measure. It would be better if the campaign is targeted to a specific group of people such as school children, various income groups and the most producers of wastes.

(iii) There is no structured recycling mechanism being implemented to households at the moment. Recycling is done voluntarily with no incentives given. Some just do not bother to do it since there is no expected immediate return. On the part of Government, measurement of the success or failure of recycling is difficult without this comprehensive structure.

Blocks **1** and **2** indicate the responses of households in Perak and Terengganu. **Yes**: indicates the respondents who agree that the recycling campaign is a success. **No**: indicates the respondents who disagree that the recycling campaign is a success.

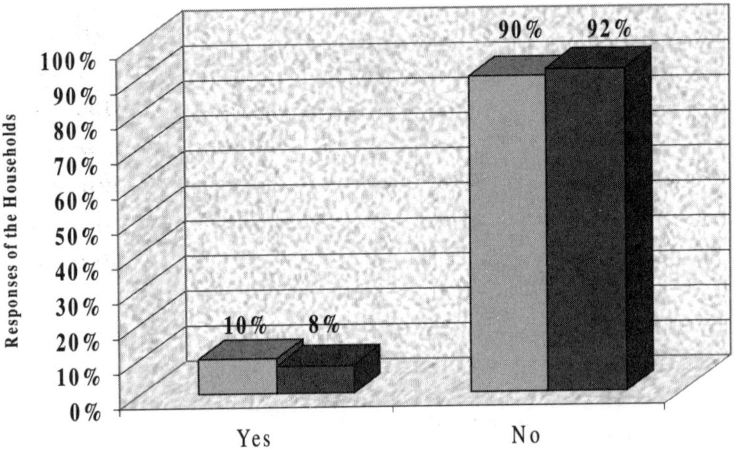

fig. 7.2: The Recycling Campaign situation in Perak and Terengganu

How can it be Improved?

The respondents were also asked of their views on how the situation could be improved. The majority of the respondents suggested that "more recycling facilities be provided." There should be "local collection centres," within easy reach of each community or housing area. Community or group recycling should be encouraged and more effort was needed to educate the people in the need and for the importance of recycling. Monetary incentives should also be considered, for example, upgrading the community facilities in an area as a reward, based on the quantity of recyclables collected. In this regard, it was observed that the high rate of newspaper recycling might be due to its marketability. When asked whether they will recycle in future, if all facilities were provided, 99 per cent of the respondents in both States said that they would willingly participate. This finding contrasts sharply with that of Grodzinska-Jurczak et al. (2003) in Jaslo City, Poland. In this study, he found that 41 per cent of 932 interviewed said they would recycle if all facilities are made available while the rest refused any participation (22 per cent) or did not respond (37 per cent).

Conclusion

Recycling has become a household word in Malaysia, based on the finding of this study; it is evident that the households in both States are of the opinion that recycling is a very important activity. However, result of the study gave a clear indication that the recycling campaign by the Ministry of Housing and Local Government in Malaysia failed. Even though the households agreed that recycling is important, not many of them did recycle. The quantity of recyclables collected in both States is indeed very small.

The main reason, as indicated by the study result, is due to misdirection in the campaign. Although much money was spent on advertisements, there is a clear misinformation. It is observed that advertisement campaigns are focused on informing households to sort their recyclables and place them in separate bins (Method 3). However, such bins can only be found at designated public places, which are usually at a distance from residential areas. It is therefore not surprising that most of the households find it too troublesome and cumbersome to bring their recyclables to the collection centres.

Furthermore, reasons such as "lack of facilities" or "distance of facilities too far from home" are also clear proof that most households are not aware that they can do their bit in recycling by simply putting the recyclables and non-recyclables in separate bags and placing them in the ordinary rubbish bins available at home which will then be collected by the council or appointed agents (Method 2). Therefore, the location of the recycling station is essential and the public attitudes or knowledge about source separation in general and recycling stations in particular are of interest for the functioning of the whole system (Petersen et al., 2004). In the final analysis, it is interesting to note that the actual reasons for the failure in terms of recycling, the lack of support and participation of households in Perak and Terengganu on recycling are not due to their negative attitude towards recycling but due to misinformation on the part of the authorities.

In order to increase the rate of recycling of solid waste and at the same time reduce the social problem related to Solid Waste Management the following suggestions were made to the Perak and Terengganu Peoples Committee as follows:

1. Improving the publics general knowledge and awareness concerning these issues is of prime importance to the minimization of waste, in general, and harmful effects of landfills on the environment, in particular.
2. Efforts are also needed to involve the public in the policy-formation, development plans, and implementation of waste management programmes. and landfill sitting decisions. Public support is essential for the success of such decisions.

However, according to Wolfe (1993), public information programming remains fundamental to the success of recycling programmes, but is often a last minute consideration by municipal decision-makers.

In summary, this study was successful in identifying some reasons of the household's attitude in Perak and Terengganu States towards the recycling situation in Malaysia.

Looking at the overall view of Malaysia, solid waste recycling has a lot to improve. Software and hardware tools should be introduced in the solid waste recycling. More legislations should be passed along with enforcements. Above all, there should be a target on what to achieve before any programme is implemented.

Abbrevations

MCI — Municipal Council of Ipoh

MCKT — Municipal Council of Kuala Terengganu

MCs — Municipal Councils

MSW — Municipal Solid Waste

MOHLG— Ministry of Housing and Local Government

RM — Ringgit Malaysian

SWM — Solid Waste Management

References

Agamuthu, P. (2001), *Solid Waste: Principle and Management with Malaysian Case Studies*, University of Malaya, Kuala Lumpur, Inc.

Chong, T.L. and Y. Matsufuji and H. Nasir (2005), Implementation of the Semi-aerobic Landfill System (Fukuoka Method) in Developing Countries: A Malaysia Cost Analysis, *Journal of Waste Management*, (25), pp. 702-11.

Evison, T. and A.D. Read (2001), Local authority recycling and waste awareness publicity/promotion. *Journal of Resources, Conversation and Recycling*, UK, (32), pp. 275-91.

González-Torre, B. and Adenso-Díaz, P.L. (2005), Influence of Distance on the Motivation and Frequency of Household Recycling, *Journal of Waste Management*, (25), pp. 15-23.

Grodzinska-Jurczak M., T. Marta and A.D. Read (2003), Increasing

Participation in Rational Municipal Waste Management — A Case Study Analysis in Jaslo City (Poland), *Journal of Resources, Conservation and Recycling*, (38), pp. 67-88.

Grodzinska-Jurczak M., P. Tomal, M. Tarabula-Fiertak, K. Nieszporek and A.D. Read (2006), Effects of an Educational Campaign on Public Environmental Attitudes and Behaviour in Poland, *Journal of Resources, Conservation and Recycling*, (46), pp. 82-97.

Joos W., V. Carabias, H. Winistoerfer and A. Stuecheli (1999), Social Aspects of Public Waste Management in Switzerland, *Journal of Waste Management*, (19), pp. 417-25.

Kathirvale, S., M.N. Muhd. Yunus, K. Sopian and A. Samsuddin (2003), Energy Potential from Municipal Solid Waste in Malaysia, *Journal of Renewable Energy*, Malaysia, (29), pp. 559-67.

Luyben, P.D. and J.S. Bailey (1979), Newspaper recycling: the effect of rewards and proximity of containers, *Journal of Environment and Behaviour*, (11), pp. 539-57.

Malaysian German Chamber of Commerce (MGCC) (2006), Market Watch Malaysia the Environmental Sector, via website http//: www.mgcc.com.my/12/2/2006.

McDonald S. and R. Ball (1998), Public participation in plastics recycling schemes, *Journal of Resources, Conservation and Recycling*, (22), pp. 23–41.

Mohd. Nasir, H. (2004), *What a Load of Rubbish*, Star Publication, 4th of May, Malaysia.

Noor, M.Z. (2005), *The Scenario of Solid Waste Management in Malaysia: A Case Study*, (Pre-Conference) Professional Training Programme on Solid Waste Management in SEA Cities, 4-5 July, Siem Reap, Cambodia.

Omran, A., A. Mahmood and H.A. Aziz (2005), "An Investigation into Public Participation on Recycling of Solid Waste in Malaysia: A Case Study of Kelantan State," Int. Conf. Proceedings on International Sustainability, 13-14th of October at Basel, Switzerland.

Rahardyan, B., T. Matsuto, Y. Kakuta and N. Tanaka (2004), Resident's Concerns and Attitudes towards Solid Waste Management Facilities, *Journal of Waste Management*, (24), pp. 437-51, Japan.

Read, A.D. (1998), Getting the message across: Recycling in Kensington and Chelsea, *Journal of Education and Information,* (17), pp. 299-314.

Read, A.D. (1999), A Weekly Doorstep Recycling Collection, I had no Idea We Could! Overcoming the Local Barriers to Participation. *Journal of Recourses, Conservation and Recycling,* (26), pp. 217-49.

Reams, M.A. and B.H. Ray (1993), The Effects of Three Promoting Methods on Recycling Participation Rates: A Field Study, *Journal of Environmental System,* (22), pp. 371-79.

Robinson, G.M. and A.D. Read (2005), Recycling Behaviour in a London Borough: Results from large-scale household surveys, *Journal of Resources, Conservation and Recycling,* (45), pp. 70-83.

Socio-Economic & Environmental Research Institute of Malaysia (2005), Via website http: //www.seri.com.my.

The Ministry of Housing and Local Government, Malaysia (MOHLG), (2005). Via website http//: www.kpkt.gov.my.

Thomas, C. (2001), Public Understanding and its Effect on Recycling Performance in Hampshire and Milton Keynes, *Journal of Recourses, Conservation and Recycling,* (32), pp. 259-74.

Wang, F.S., A.J. Richardson and F.A. Roddick (1997), Relationships Between Set-out Rate, Participation Rate and Set-Out Quantify in Recycling Programmes, *Journal of Resources, Conservation and Recycling,* (20), pp. 1-17.

Wolfe, P. (1993), Public Awareness Programmes, in *Lund,* editor, The McGraw-Hill Recycling Handbook: New York.

World Bank (1999), Urban Development Sector Unit, East Asia and Pacific Region, What a Waste: Solid Waste Management, May, via website http//: www.worldbank/html/fpd/publicant/whatawaste.pdf.

8

Knowledge Communication
The Essence of Sustainable Governance

Kendal Hodgman

Introduction

SUSTAINABILITY, known also as Sustainable Development and Ecologically Sustainable Development, is one of the greatest challenges now facing humanity. The world has been on notice on the seriousness of the sustainability challenges for a number of decades. It has been reported, with growing alarm, that such is the state of ecological decline that we are now in the midst of a species extinction event, the like of which has not been seen since the decline of the dinosaurs. The disturbing reality of the state of the world is outlined in the landmark Millennium Ecosystem Assessment 2005.[1] This collaborative global project depicts the enormity of human activity's devastating impact on earth's fragile eco-balance and heralds the anticipated impacts if serious human behavioural change is not implemented across the planet, quickly and systematically. Such is the level of current international concern that 2005 marked the beginning of the United Nations Decade for Education for Sustainable Development.

---

1. Millennium Ecosystem Assessment (2005), MA Synthesis Reports available at: <http://www.millenniumassessment.org//en/Products.Synthesis.aspx> viewed 14/5/2005.

Ultimately, sustainability requires that every nation, institution, group and individual move away from unsustainable practices, in order that earth's natural and human systems may survive. It is in this context that governments worldwide are grappling with the questions of how to create a coherent framework which meets the sustainability demands of integrating social, economic and environmental considerations in decision-making processes, whilst simultaneously encouraging best practice and learning.

A paradigmatic shift is required, one requiring new tools for communication, governance and sustainability. This article outlines the structural formation of such a tool, namely the Sustainability Analysis Framework (SAF)which has been successfully deployed in the largest State Government in Australia, New South Wales (NSW).

The Sustainability Analysis Framework, devised by the author, and detailed in her Report to the NSW Government, *Sustainability: A NSW Whole of Government Approach*[2] (hereinafter "The Report") has been implemented across 38 State agencies and demonstrates that a whole of government sustainability perspective is achievable.

At the heart of the article is the author's contention that one of the key problems which jeopardises our common future on earth is the lack of effective tools to communicate sustainability thinking and practice. In the course of the project, upon which this article is based, the author identified the need for a visually and conceptually accessible mechanism to accelerate the uptake of sustainability practice in a whole of organization context. In designing the SAF, which has

2. Hodgman, K. (2005), Sustainability: A New South Wales Whole of Government Approach. Premier's Department, Government of NSW, Sydney.

successfully bridged this knowledge communication gap, the author employed two of humanity's fundamental learning tools — the diagram and the story.

Stop for a Second to Think

> *Once a photograph of the earth, taken from the outside is available. . . . a new idea as powerful as any in history will be let loose.*
> — Frederick Hoyle, 1948

Think of the world today. Picture the blue globe of earth spinning through space. Imagine billions of human beings alive at this point of time. Consider how many individuals make up a billion. Now, place the concept of billions of people into something that is quantifiable in your own experience. It may be seeing, from an aerial perspective, a city you know contains millions of people, or maybe you have been part of a crowd of one hundred thousand people. Rest in that personal awareness of the biggest human throng you have ever experienced. Realize that that tangible multitude of people is but a tiny fraction of the number of human beings on earth right now. Expand your perspective back to imagine the billions of human beings who are all alive on the blue spinning globe. Picture them thinking and making and acting upon decisions every second. Comprehend how, in just one split second, so many billions of decisions are being made by so many people. Do you realize that most of those decisions are not benign and will result in an environmental impact? Now, imagine how quickly the world is changing each second, simply because of the enormity of the human population and the capacity for humans to act upon their decisions. Calculate how many decisions each of those individuals will make in a lifetime. Now, consider how many of those decisions are made with the knowledge and wisdom required for a sustainable future. Most are not!

The Nature of Change

The earth has, hitherto, never known such a dominant predator as the human being. Moreover, the planet has never before experienced such a population abundance of such a dominant species. It is, therefore, not surprising that the earth is changing more rapidly than ever before and that this rate of change will continue to quicken as human populations continue to swell, as indeed they are. There is nothing inherently alarming in this. This is the nature of change. However, if human beings wish to continue to survive, they should be alarmed at the rate at which the state of the world is changing. If humanity wishes to survive, a viable biosphere is essential. Thus far, earth provides the only viable biosphere known to humanity and earth's precious biosphere is now showing multiple and important signs of stress. This is not news. The world has been on notice for the past half a century that humanity cannot keep on exploiting and degrading natural systems at such a rate without serious repercussions. What has come as a surprise to many, though, is that nature's systems are changing ahead of "schedule" — as if there ever could have been one! Even now, when scientific consensus tells us that human activity is largely responsible for the drastic extinction of as many as forty species each day and that climate change is a reality, many of the decisions being made by humans bear the hallmarks of the proverbial ostrich, who, when under threat, rather then using its natural talent of speed to stand a chance of survival, puts its head in the sand, and blindly awaits its demise, as a sitting target.

Many people had been counting on the predicted nature feedback coming in 50 to 100 years. This, they hoped, would give scientists time to come up with technological solutions to the inevitable problems. Yet, it is now apparent that the feedback has started already and is speeding up exponentially. It is our generations that are bearing witness to the start of the calamitous legacy of man's contempt for nature — the foreseeable and tragic consequences of human folly and greed. It is our generations' responsibility to implement the changes in thinking and modes of operation that will be necessary for the survival of humanity and the other species for which this planet is home. It is widely acknowledged that these necessary changes are entailed in the principles and practices of sustainability.

Sustainability Thinking

Sustainability is generally defined as:

> *Development that meets the needs of present generations while not compromising the ability of future generations to also meet their needs.*[3]

The ringing warnings of the ecological implications of continuing with a business-as-usual-approach have been heard since the 1960's. Yet, the global discourse on the imperative to consider this concept began in earnest at the 1972 UN Conference on the Human Environment in Stockholm, during which the then Prime Minister of India, Indira Gandhi stated:

> The inherent conflict is not between conservation and development but between environment and the reckless exploitation of man and the earth in the name of efficiency.

The first formal global-scale determinations regarding definitions of the concept are contained in the 1980 World Conservation Strategy by the International Union for the Conservation of Nature and Natural Resources, wherein it is stated:

3. World Commission on Environment and Development (1987), *Our Common Future*, Australian Edition, p. 87.

> For development to be sustainable it must take account of social and ecological factors, as well as economic one; of the living and non-living resource base; and of the long-term as well as short-term advantages and disadvantages of alternative actions.

This needs to integrate the three aspects of social, environmental and economic considerations in decision-making and responsibility is the essence of sustainability thinking. Yet, all too often the world's decision-makers continue to claim that this form of thinking is beyond them and even utopian. In the halls of government, industry, justice and academia it is often claimed that sustainability thinking is amorphous and ill-defined, that it is more an aspiration than a direction. It is this attitude that needs to change. Such a change requires a paradigmatic shift, with new tools for communication, governance and sustainability.

This article outlines the structural formation of such a tool, the novel Sustainability Analysis Framework. It has been implemented across 38 agencies in the largest State Government in Australia. Moreover, it has demonstrated that a whole of government perspective is achievable in evaluating and communicating sustainability initiatives, issues, practice and models.

Australia's Sustainability Governance

The full gamut of the Australian governance structure in respect of sustainability is outside this article's scope. However, it is important to understand that the Commonwealth of Australia is a Federation of States. Each State Parliament has the constitutional authority to make laws on any subject of relevance to that State, meaning that, to a great extent, the States are, in many areas, stewards of their own destiny.

NSW is Australia's most populous State, with more than 6.6 million residents. Sydney, Australia's only global city is the NSW capital. Boasting the largest and most diverse economy in Australia, the NSW economy, alone, is larger than the national economies of Thailand, Malaysia, Singapore, the Philippines and New Zealand. With a Gross State Product of A$250 billion, NSW is undoubtedly the powerhouse of the Australian economy, which is the fifteenth largest in the world.[4]

The NSW Government has, for the past decade-and-a-half, committed itself, in its rhetoric and in a legislative and policy sense, to the principles of sustainability. Despite this, NSW, like Australia and the world generally, continues to slide backwards in its quest for sustainability.[5] Sustainability is an emerging area of administrative endeavour, with little global experience or wisdom to guide its process. It is to this end that the NSW Government commissioned the author to evaluate its extensive and diverse sustainability practice in "The Report." The level of the NSW Government's commitment to this process is evidenced by the fact that it was coordinated at the highest levels of the administration and engaged high-level input from a comprehensive portfolio of its agencies.

A Common Language and Form

A Sustainability Survey of NSW Government Agencies (hereinafter "The Survey") was undertaken, requesting

4. Government of New South Wales (2003), Sydney NSW Competitiveness Report 2003, Department of State and Regional Development, Sydney.

5. Government of New South Wales (2003), New South Wales State of Environment. Department of Environment and Conservation, Sydney.

selected agencies to submit all legislation, policies, strategies, projects and experience relevant to sustainability practice and thinking. The agencies' response was voluminous and unstructured. Thus, the author's first task was to evaluate the common sustainability issues facing the disparate arms of government.

From the data submitted to "The Survey," the following ten prevailing issues were identified:

(1) Conservation of Biological Diversity,

(2) Conservation of Resource,

(3) Partnerships and Synergies,

(4) Pollution Minimization,

(5) Research and Development,

(6) Social Equity and Education,

(7) Social Equity as a Regional/Spatial Driver,

(8) Sustainability Reporting,

(9) Sustainability Trade-offs, and

(10) Sustainable Quality of Life.

Once the commonalities were identified, the process of defining these sustainability issues was undertaken, in order that a common vocabulary was established for the purposes of the undertaking. The categorization and definition of the sustainability issues common across the government was an extensive process and is outside the scope of this article, but has been outlined in other publications by the author.*

* Queries regarding publication details should be directed to the author at K.Hodgman@murdoch.edu.au

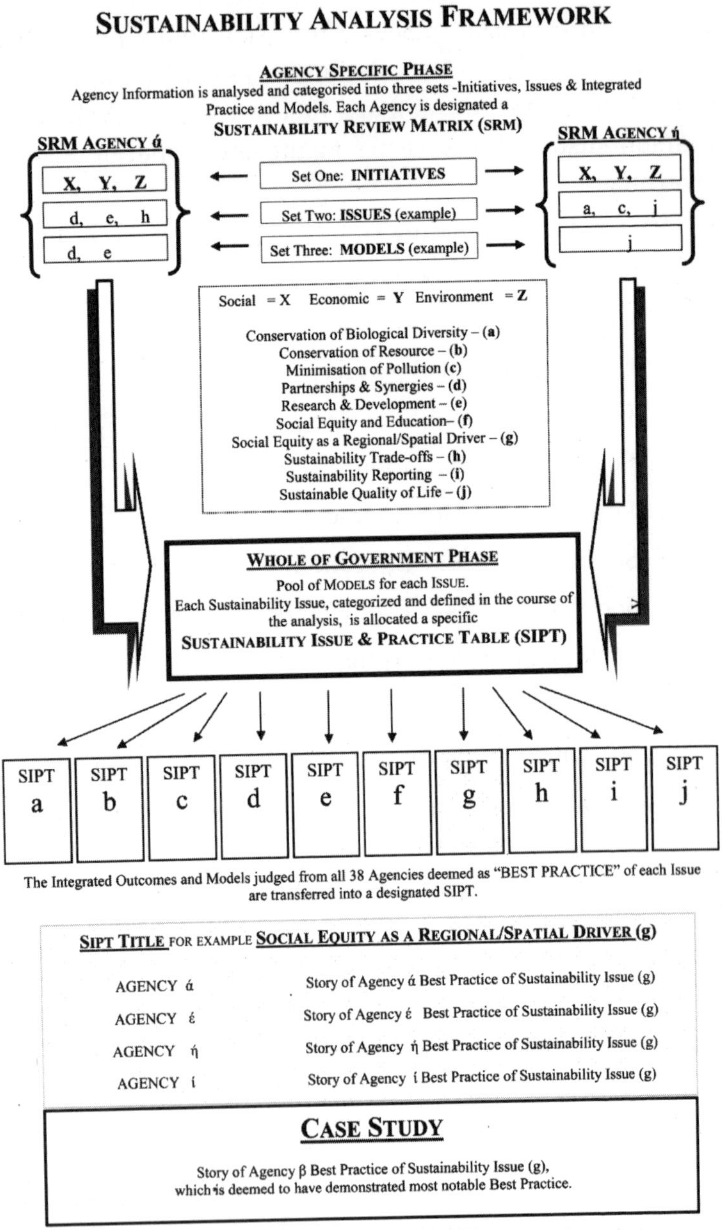

Figure 8.1. Sustainability Analysis Framework. © K. Hodgman (2006)

Following the categorization and definition phase, a visually accessible and structured mode of communication was devised, in order that the highlighted sustainability practice was able to be shared across the whole of government. The sharing of this practice was via short stories of specific project experience. These stories were positioned in uniform one page structures, namely the Sustainability Review Matrices and the Sustainability Issues and Practice Tables, the forms of which are detailed below.

See *fig.* 8.1 Sustainability Analysis Framework, which shows the flow of data and knowledge through the SRM and SIPT processes.

In its essence, the SAF draws upon two of humanity's fundamental learning tools — the diagram and the story.

The power of story is inestimable. It is a universal mode of human communication. It is through the sharing of stories across millennia that the cultures and technologies of humanity have grown. Civilizations have come and gone but their wisdom has remained in the annals of history. Yet, story is as modern as it is ancient. We still receive and give our news in the form of story and we conceptually communicate about the world, both imaginary and real, in story form. Thus, the central importance of deploying story, as a sustainability knowledge communication tool in the SAF was identified at the outset.

The framing of these sustainability stories within a visually accessible form was, however, a challenge. The challenge of visualization in complex problem-solving is not new, as this observation by physicist Richard Feynman, whilst working on the Manhattan Project in 1945 attests: "The single biggest problem we face is that of visualization." Thus, the importance of creating a framework which was visually accessible and simple, conceptually was deemed imperative for the SAF design.

Conceptually, the SAF is based upon communications and cognitive research, which concurs that, visually, readers are most likely to access and engage with single page documents, rather than lengthy reports.[6] Thus, the two mechanisms comprising the SAF, the Sustainability Review Matrix and the Sustainability Issue and Practice Table, are modelled to fit on either A4 or A3 single page formats, depending upon the nature and scope of the agency submissions.

Sustainability Analysis Framework

The SAF consists of two related parts, namely the Sustainability Review Matrix (SRM), which is the agency-specific assessment tool and the Sustainability Issues Practice Tables (SIPT), which are the whole of government communications tools.

The Sustainability Review Matrix (SRM) provides a world-first model for integrated analysis of sustainability initiatives, issues and practice. As a matrix in both the mathematical and literal senses, it treats each government agency/organization as an entity, comprising various sustainability components.

These components are outlined in three sets, namely Initiatives; Issues; and Integrated Outcomes and Models:

- Initiatives are categorized into the sustainability considerations of Social, Economic and Environment.
- Issues are categorized into the sustainability issues arising from the full data set analysis. How the agency addresses a prevailing challenge is then detailed.

6. Buzan, T. and B. Buzan (2003), *The Mind Map Book*. BBC Worldwide Ltd., London.

SYDNEY OLYMPIC PARK AUTHORITY (SOPA)

CREATION OF A SUSTAINABLE TOWNSHIP AT SYDNEY OLYMPIC PARK

INITIATIVES

SOCIAL		ECONOMIC		ENVIRONMENT
Range of existing management strategies to ensure an amenable, safe and accessible experience at SOP: Effective way-finding, signage, access g/lines & accessible designs; Strong access to public transport, extensive pedestrian/cycle networks; Visitor services; Interpretive tour products; Educational programs; Arts, cultural and heritage experiences	Developing first Social Plan for SOP: Proposed key outcome areas: Social Infrastructure - facilities, services etc Social diversity (incl. housing mix) Community engagement and participation Amenity safety and well being Regional leadership Social equity and accessibility	International recognition as a destination for best practice sustainability Plans for future expansion strongly positions SOP as a key location for sustainable industries. SOPA strategically partners with a diverse range of stake-holders including: research institutions, sustainable businesses, environmental organisations, educational institutions and government agencies	Economic strategy for SOP involves creation of business clusters: Science & technology, Health, recreation & well-being, Environment, Education, Sport, Culture, The Arts, Food & entertainment Each of these business clusters will enhance business investment and employment opportunities.	Sustainability is an integral corporate value for SOPA providing a solid platform for decision-making & management functions. SOPA recognises the challenges in creating a sustainable township at SOP. SOPA intends to build on existing environmental legacies, thereby ensuring it continues to "raise the bar' in its approach to social, economic and social sustainability. SOPA has a comprehensive Sustainability framework which includes: SOPA Act (2001); Environmental Guide-lines; Corporate Plan; Sustainability Policy & Strategy; Operational compliance procedures; Plan of Management: Parklands Master Plan & Vision 2025; WRAPP
- Recreational needs analysis undertaken to better understand differing demands for recreational space around the Homebush Bay region & more broadly Greater Western Sydney - MoU between the Authority and Dept. of Housing in relation to provision of affordable housing (3%) integrated as part of all residential developments - Close partnerships with surrounding LGA's, MoU with Parramatta and Auburn Councils - Assisting Auburn Council with its Social Plan - Ongoing engagement with residential, community and environmental ngo's		Establishing a "green hub" – or green economy at SOP covers a range of activities which reflect SOP's natural and built environment, the history of a site that has undergone intensive urban change – a brickworks, abattoirs, defence site and several rubbish dumps, the triumph of the "Green Games" in 2000 and SOPA's aspirations to create a sustainable township. SOP will have strong focus on R&D; research partnerships; demonstration of innovative environmental technologies. SOP is likely to have university sub-campus		Key Environmental Performance Areas: 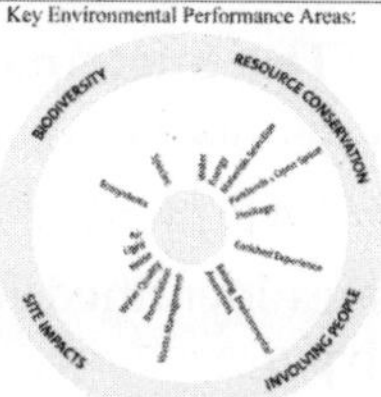

ISSUES

Social Equity as a Regional/ Spatial Driver	**SOP is ready to play an important role in Governments' desire to promote *healthy*, *liveable* communities** which address issues of human health & the relationship between health (both physical & mental) and our habitat. In this regard, SOPA is seeking to make SOP a national centre for well being – physical, social, emotional, intellectual & spiritual. SOPA is positioning SOP as the **Smart Community** - a community that enjoys an enhanced quality-of-life by the fact that SOP offers a ***smarter*** solution to modern urban living by: Facilitating a **healthy lifestyle** through interaction with SOP's world-class sporting & recreational facilities that offer unmatched opportunities for running, cycling, skating, tennis, swimming, golf and much more. SOP represents a 'green gym' in which human environment activities produce positive health outcomes; Providing opportunities for people to **learn** within a 'college town' setting in which a diversity of education providers offer secondary, higher education & vocational programs; Offering a built & natural environment founded on the principles of **environmental sustainability** & the importance of design to the human health condition; Providing **technology solutions** that can improve one's quality-of-life. This will be achieved through the enhanced utilisation of SOP's network of optical fibre infrastructure; & Providing a rich mix of cultural, artistic & entertainment offerings supporting **creativity & enjoyment**
Sustainable Quality of Life	SOPA's commitment to sustainability has been a guiding principle in the development of SOP. SOP's venues, facilities, infrastructure, parklands and environmental restoration & management initiatives have been recognised nationally & internationally for the approach to: environmental design, remediation and restoration, heritage conservation, ecological management, engineering, construction, project management, innovation, environmental education and environmental management. There is significant brand value attached to SOP's Sustainability credentials, deemed critical as SOP seeks to position itself to take a lead role in pursuing a sustainability agenda.
Resource Conservation	**Water Reclamation and Management Scheme** (WRAMS) at SOP saves 850 million litres of potable water each year. Mandatory connection of new dev'ts to WRAMS. Exploring options for extending WRAMS beyond SOP's geographic footprint; partnerships with research organisations, CRCs, Centres of Excellence. **Strong focus on the applied use of renewable energy** at SOP in urban core & parklands: solar, wind, tidal, co-generation. All new dev'ts encouraged to showcase renewable energy. SOPA purchases minimum 25% green power. All dev'ts must meet minimum 4.5 energy efficiency rating. **SOP was first precinct to mandate minimum 4 Greenstars** under Green Building Council (GBC), Australia environmental design tool for all new commercial building. SOPA is a GBC inaugural member. **Remediation**: SOPA responsible for ongoing management of 10 remediated land areas. Pioneered on-site treatment of scheduled chemical waste (using indirect thermal desorption & base catalysed destruction). SOPA is now exploring sustainable leachate strategy. Future dev't of urban core will retain the principle that as far possible waste is contained & managed on site – unique opportunity to demonstrate innovative engineering solutions & remediation technologies - research, R&D, "living lab". **Sustainable Materials**: Use of PVC minimised/ideally avoided, sustainable non-toxic natural materials prioritised in procurement processes and for new developments.

INTEGRATED OUTCOMES AND MODELS

Social Equity as a Regional/ Spatial Driver	The Vision is to create: "*an internationally recognised example of intelligent place-making - a dynamic and diverse township for living, working, learning and recreation - a place for all people set within a world class built and natural environment.*" Realising this combines strategies for Place Leadership, Place Management & Place Making. Approx 20 potential development sites throughout SOP - expected private sector investment over next decade in excess of $1 billion. Additional sites: educational facilities, entertainment, hotel & additional residential & commercial uses. SOP is evolving from an events precinct to a significant urban centre, which will offer a unique environment for living, working, learning & leisure pursuits. SOPA aims to promote a *smart community* in which residents, workers, students etc. share a unique value system including a commitment to sustainability & a belief in a holistic approach to all aspects of health including physical & environmental health. SOPA works closely with surrounding LGAs to interface & communicate SOP's social sustainability agenda of SOP.
Sustainable Quality of Life	Creating a **SOP sustainable township** will build on the significant environmental legacies of the site's initial urban renewal for the 2000 Sydney Olympic Games. The town will be an urban design exemplar - a multifaceted precinct, encompassing residential and commercial areas, education institutions, sports facilities, extensive parklands & still a major site for public events. **SOP's Green Economy** will focus on activities aligned with protecting/ improving sustainable outcomes now & into the future as SOP moves to being a dynamic township. Delivered strategically, the interface between the economic themes of environment, education, science & technology, health and well-being should succeed in attracting and retaining a diversity of businesses aligned with the sustainability sector. Delivering a SOP green economy will see the township established as a national destination for sustainable industries, businesses, research institutions, environmental organisations and government agencies which share SOPA's aspirations for innovation and creativity to realise a more sustainable future.

Figure 8.2. SUSTAINABILITY REVIEW MATRIX - SYDNEY OLYMPIC PARK AUTHORITY (SOPA), used largely to demonstrate Social Sustainability and the A4 page SRM layout. Excerpt from Hodgman, K. (2005), *Sustainability: A New South Wales Whole of Government Approach*, Premier's Department, Government of NSW.

- Integrated Outcomes and Models highlight innovation and notable practice in how the agency is dealing with a prevailing sustainability issue. This set of the SRM serves to demonstrate integration of social, economic and environmental considerations as well as when an activity has a net sustainability benefit.

See *fig.* 8.2, SRM Sydney Olympic Park Authority, one of 38 State Agencies from "The Report." It uses the A4 page SRM layout.

The Sustainability Issues and Practice Table (SIPT) is the whole of government mechanism. In the full execution of the SAF Methodology, each of the prevailing sustainability issues identified from the full data set analysis are allocated a SIPT.

Drawing from the SRM analysis,

- Best practice models and case studies of how agencies deal with the issue are selected for inclusion in the SIPT; and
- Selected case studies are utilized to showcase innovation and integration and agencies' experience of sustainable service delivery.

Rationale for Practice Model and Case Study Selection

While the NSW Government has underscored its commitment to sustainability with core directives, it has also allowed for a flexible and evolutionary approach to sustainability. This has enabled agencies to determine what sustainability means to them. This has resulted in the development of innovative practice models, which have been selected for inclusion in the SIPT on the basis of the following criteria:

- innovation;
- integration of the core sustainability principles;

- development of performance indicators;
- processes of reporting and evaluation; and
- general applicability.

Case studies selection was made on the basis of successful implementation, innovation and general applicability of the sustainability Practice Model.

To aid visualization of the SIPT method, this article draws from the report, *Sustainability: A New South Wales Whole of Government Approach,* a demonstrative SIPT model on the issue of Social Equity as a Regional or Spatial Driver. This SIPT, detailed in *fig.* 8.3, shows that the research done on the selected 38 NSW Government agencies can be brought together within the framework and that a whole of government sustainability perspective is achievable.

Findings

As the focus of this article is on the SAF's knowledge communication capacity, these findings shall be limited to this regard. The Sustainability Analysis Framework has proved itself flexible enough to be effectively deployed across all the selected 38 agencies of the NSW Government. Hitherto, there had been no established co-ordinated approach to communicating sustainability approaches across the Government. The SAF proved effective in providing and communicating a corporate history of sustainability initiatives, issues, practices, and models. Moreover, it provided a sustainability inventory of what is happening across a considerable sample of the NSW public sector and identified areas in need of development and support.

The educative capacity of the SAF was evidenced by the fact that all agencies were able to understand and effectively interact with the electronically transmitted SRMs in two phases

SOCIAL EQUITY AS A REGIONAL OR SPATIAL DRIVER

AGENCY	PRACTICE
Department of Infrastructure, Planning and Natural Resources	**The Metropolitan Strategy goal is to achieve a sustainable, competitive and liveable Sydney.** Over the next three years it will determine how the NSW Government intends to sustainably manage growth & change in Sydney and the Greater Metropolitan Region over the next 30 years. The Strategy will manage Sydney's ecological footprint by creating sustainable and liveable communities in greenfields areas, providing quality transport access and focusing development in existing urban centres & corridors which have capacity or require renewal. The Premier has announced funding totalling **$1.4 million for seven Western Sydney councils** (Penrith, Blacktown, Fairfield, Parramatta, Liverpool, Bankstown & Campbelltown) for town centre revitalisation plans & to identify growth opportunities. **Sustainability Commissioners, Peter Newman and Bernie Fraser,** have been appointed to: provide independent advice on Sydney's growth; establish a set of objectives by which to assess new housing & associated infrastructure; provide advice on major land release proposals to ensure they meet world's best practice in water & energy efficiency, accessibility & transport, air quality & conservation; and develop possible solutions to the population pressures on the NSW coast.
Department of Local Government	**To support councils in achieving sustainable outcomes in their communities, the Department has produced a number of policy documents**, including: ***Guidelines for State of the Environment Reporting*** - promoting ESD practices and a framework for identifying indicators; ***Management Planning Guidelines*** - promoting principles of ESD, social justice and integrated planning processes; ***Social and Community Planning and Reporting Guidelines and Manual*** – promoting the identification & use of social indicators & integrated planning processes. All available at < http://www.dlg.nsw.gov.au/ >. ***Cultural Planning Guidelines for Local Government*** – The Department and NSW Ministry for the Arts are the joint lead agencies for developing these guidelines, which have been endorsed by the Premier and the Minister for Local Government and are now being published.
State Library of NSW	**Public libraries are one of the few public services available to the entire community.** They are basic infrastructure & providers of environmental stability; they provide public meeting places & shared spaces that are welcoming, accepting and safe. In many rural, regional and remote communities the public library is one of the few community services & meeting places available to everyone. Public libraries are recognised community hubs offering insurance against the information & digital divides. Relevant initiatives: **NSW.net and Rural Link**, < www.nswnet.net>, network that links councils & public libraries throughout NSW to the internet. **Over 700 PCs** have been distributed for Internet access in public libraries. The Library's web presence & **Digital Library Strategy** ensure the preservation of unique heritage resources in the State Library's collection, & enable state-wide access through digitisation & online electronic service delivery; **Picture NSW**, a project to identify and provide access to public libraries' pictorial & local history collections; **State Library Total Asset Management** enables the protection & restoration of the heritage Mitchell Library; and **Public Library Development Grants** include target funds for building projects. (*People Places*, Library Council of NSW, 2000 < www.sl.nsw.gov.au/pls/publications/>)
Newcastle Port Corporation	**Working with others on new projects, NPC is utilising its port nexus role** to enhance the region's economy and increased social benefit. NPC continues to assist in the development of projects in and around the port precinct, which have the potential to generate significant volumes of new trade for the port. The optimum location of these developments & their supporting port facilities is critical to the longer-term development of the port. NPC has partnered in the Cruise Hunter project to enrich the Hunter region's capacity and reputation as an international or domestic destination of choice on cruise/navy port of call itineraries and for super yacht refits. Maximising the best use of port land is being furthered by a number of processes i.e. The Newcastle Port Environs Concept Study which is being developed by DIPNR, the proposed SEPP for the Port of Newcastle and a DCP process with Newcastle City Council; and a light industry Marine Precinct feasibility investigation of the Dyke Point and Carrington Area.
City West Housing Pty. Ltd.	**CWH's principal function is to develop and provide affordable rental housing to very low, low and moderate-income households in Pyrmont, Ultimo and Green Square.** The company houses people with a local connection (living or working in the area) so that those who otherwise might be forced out of the area (by gentrification and increasing prices of rental accommodation) can remain living close to family and their work. The company houses people over three income bands from low to moderate incomes, thereby, CWH maintains a range of socio economic groups across its portfolio and within each building. **CWH uses planning as an instrument to create social cohesion along with the technical implementation of energy and resource efficient living.**

CASE STUDY

AUSTRALIAN INLAND – ENERGY AND WATER UTILITY FAR WEST NSW

AI has made a commitment to its identified role as a regional development catalyst in the NSW Far West, which is a region with declining industry and population. AI's Strategic Plan highlights its need to engender community capacity, in order to align AI development with Community Development, hence, aiming to ultimately encourage regional development investment. **AI works to foster equity partnerships with Aboriginal, Welfare & Education providers.** AI, with Lifeline, has successfully obtained funding from the Department of Commerce for a financial counseling service for Far West people experiencing financial difficulties. AI has facilitated an environmental education partnership for Far West NSW, bringing together previously uncoordinated government initiatives and securing a 12 month position for a teacher to work with schools to establish Environmental Management Plans.This, along with landscape revitalisation & natural resource harnessing, is creating avenues for regional renewal as are industry partnerships to develop alternative energy programs for existing tourism ventures. **The Healing Gardens, Golf & Olives initiative** facilitates the reduction of a golf course from 18 to 9 holes; uses effluent water to feed land; converts 9 holes to an Aboriginal Healing Garden, research of native timbers, organic olive plantation; & responds to broader social fabric needs of South Broken Hill, where integration with the Aboriginal community is important.

Figure 8.3 (i) SUSTAINABILITY ISSUE PRACTICE TABLE - SOCIAL EQUITY AS A REGIONAL/SPATIAL DRIVER shows that the research done on the 38 Government agencies can be brought together within the SAF to demonstrate a whole of government Sustainability perspective. See next page for 8.3 (ii).

SOCIAL EQUITY AS A REGIONAL OR SPATIAL DRIVER

AGENCY	PRACTICE
Waterways Authority	**The Walsh Bay** precinct is one of Australia's major urban renewal undertakings. It displays reminders of Sydney's maritime heritage through the retention of historical items e.g. a wool bale elevator, the hydraulic lifting system, timbers recycled from Pier 6/7 and used as kerbs/public seating & in the drama theatre, & original bollards which can be seen from the public boardwalk. The site also reuses cobblestone paving in Ferry Lane & displays substantial remains of an 1820's cottage found whilst excavating for the theatre. Stone was reused for retaining walls at Pottinger St. & surplus material sold for recycling.
Roads and Traffic Authority	RTA has a key strategic sustainability objective of improving the State Road network. These major projects aim to promote economic growth, access to communities, road safety & use of public transport. **M5 East Freeway** is used as an example of injecting 30,000 new jobs & $500 million into Western Sydney over 5 years; travel times for commuters & business reduced by 50%; environmentally, traffic volumes & noise on local streets have decreased along with air quality improvements from reduced congestion (75,000 fewer vehicles a day on local streets). The key social benefits are improved safety; easier & quicker travel time & employment opportunities. **T-way Program** aims to raise public transport use & redress the social inequity of the job-housing imbalance of Western Sydney residents needing to travel to eastern Sydney for work. TBL considerations play an important part in option selections for major projects.
Landcom	**Moderate Income Housing Policy and Delivery Program** provides home ownership opportunities to moderate income households to which the median price of housing is unaffordable & would place such households in housing stress/ force them to rent. Landcom provides moderate income housing in all projects, where this is commercially sustainable. Landcom's target is 7.5% of annual yield. **Community Development Program – Welcome Program** aims to strengthen the new communities Landcom creates. A sense of belonging is vital for the creation of cohesive, sustainable communities. Through personal home visits, community events & networking, the Program lays the foundations of a culture of welcome & hospitality in Landcom estates. The Program has been in place in several Landcom estates since 1997. In 2003/04 alone, 668 new households were welcomed & 132 community functions & events were hosted, with more than 42,000 Landcom residents & other community members attending.
Department of Environment and Conservation	**Protecting Our Places** program est. 2002 funds Aboriginal communities and organisations to conduct environmental education projects & restore & rehabilitate land they own/is significant to them. In 2002, 15 funded projects totaled more than $400,000. In 2002 initiatives incl: Aboriginal environmental educators' workshop; working with 3 Aboriginal communities in western Sydney to improve stormwater run-off in the Georges, Hawkesbury–Nepean & Parramatta River catchments; Through NPWS **Aboriginal Place Program,** 5 new Aboriginal Places were declared 2002-03, & a total of 42 Aboriginal Places NSW-wide. Another 4 declarations are pending. **Aboriginal 'Living Places':** a 4-year study to record sites in NSW where Aboriginal people have settled since 1788. These places are a valuable part of NSW? heritage & will be placed on DEC Historic Heritage Information System & DEC Aboriginal Heritage Information System.
Community Relations Commission for a Multicultural NSW	**Community Relations Crisis Management Plan** has been developed *To maintain & manage cultural harmony within NSW in response to local or international events, which impact on relationships within the community & between people.* The CRCM Plan sets out protocols & procedures & is to be incorporated as a subsection of the NSW Displan. The CRCM was written in conjunction with NSW Police, DET, DoCS & the Anti-Discrimination Board. **Regional Advisory Councils** The 10 RACs (3 south, 3 west, 4 north NSW) create a vital network for rural & regional NSW. Each comprises community & government members to discuss & bring local matters of multicultural concern to the CRC attention. RACs work in partnership with local agencies & communities to foster improved communication between the community & government eg: access to interpreting services in remote & rural locations – Griffith Police Commander (RAC member) has confirmed video-conferencing facilities by any service on a cost recovery basis as one way to address on-site interpreter accessibility.

CASE STUDY

SYDNEY OLYMPIC PARK AUTHORITY - CREATION OF A SUSTAINABLE TOWNSHIP

The Vision is to create: *"an internationally recognised example of intelligent place-making - a dynamic and diverse township for living, working, learning and recreation - a place for all people set within a world class built and natural environment."* Realising this combines strategies for Place Leadership, Place Management & Place Making. Approx. 20 potential development sites throughout SOP - expected private sector investment over next decade is in excess of $1 billion. Additional sites: educational facilities, entertainment, hotel & additional residential & commercial uses. SOP is evolving from an events precinct to a significant urban centre, which will offer a unique environment for living, working, learning & leisure pursuits. SOPA aims to promote a *smart community* in which residents, workers, students etc. share a unique value system including a commitment to sustainability & a belief in a holistic approach to all aspects of health including physical & environmental health. SOPA works closely with surrounding LGAs to interface & communicate SOP's social sustainability agenda. The township will build on the significant environmental legacies of the site's initial urban renewal for the 2000 Sydney Olympic Games. It will be an urban design exemplar - a multifaceted precinct, encompassing residential and commercial areas, education institutions, sports facilities, extensive parklands & still a major site for public events. SOP's Green Economy will focus on activities aligned with protecting/ improving sustainable outcomes now & into the future as SOP moves to being a dynamic township. Delivered strategically, the interface between the economic themes of environment, education, science & technology, health & well-being should succeed in attracting & retaining a diversity of businesses aligned with the sustainability sector. Delivering a SOP green economy will see the township established as a national destination for sustainable industries, businesses, research institutions, environmental organisations & government agencies which share SOPA's aspirations for innovation & creativity to realise a more sustainable future.

Figure 8.3 (ii) SUSTAINABILITY ISSUE PRACTICE TABLE - SOCIAL EQUITY AS A REGIONAL/SPATIAL DRIVER. A3 Page Layout divided here into two A4 pages for formatting purposes. Excerpt from Hodgman, K, (2005), *Sustainability: A New South Wales Whole of Government Approach*, Premier's Department, Government of NSW.

of the process, firstly in the requests for additional information and secondly in the agency endorsement phase of the SRMs, in which information veracity was peer reviewed. Moreover, the enthusiasm for the project was evident at a number of seminars conducted by the author at Federal, State and Local Government levels. In the context of the NSW Government project, over 60 senior officers from across the Government attended a seminar, hosted by the Director-General of the Premier's Department, Dr Col Gellatly and championed by the NSW Sustainability Commissioner, Professor Peter Newman. Consequently, a number of agencies were emboldened to submit for analysis comprehensive and completed SRMs; others interacted with the electronically transmitted tools and updated their material; whilst others were enlightened as to the breadth and scope of sustainability and were able to identify projects which met the definitions. These indicative e-mails, which were received during either the SRM agency verification phase or following the seminar, also attest to the efficacy of the SAF as a knowledge communication tool:

> *I have tracked the changes made for ease of updating. . . . The changes are a result of further developments in this area since our original response to your request.*
>
> — Department of Local Government.

> *We can now better understand your intention of the report and have added information as appropriate.*
>
> — Sydney Harbour Foreshore Authority

> *A fair and accurate appraisal.*
>
> — Community Relations Commission for a Multicultural NSW

> *I really enjoyed your presentation on the framework . . . and I think that your report will make a significant contribution to understanding sustainability at a whole of govt. level.*
>
> — Sydney Olympic Park Authority

Conclusion

The Sustainability Analysis Framework acknowledges the enormous value of experience to organizations. It has demonstrated within a sample of only one government that much sustainability experience has already been gained and that this knowledge is ready and possible to be shared. Furthermore, this knowledge can be simply stored and thereafter utilized for the whole of organization's benefit and beyond.

The Sustainability Analysis Framework provides guidance by:

- Establishing a novel whole of government mechanism for evaluating and communicating sustainability initiatives, issues, practices and models;
- Identifying best practice and innovation, along with the wisdom gained from service delivery within sustainability thinking; and
- Educating public administrators, through their interaction with the simple whole of government mechanisms, of the imperative to integrate social, economic and environmental considerations in decision-making.

The simplicity of its form and method gives the SAF the flexibility to be deployed in various organizational contexts, to assist in the collection, maintenance, re-use, access and sharing of sustainability knowledge not only in particular instances but to aid in broader problem solving.

The successful deployment of the Sustainability Analysis Framework across the various agencies of such a significant bureaucracy as the Government of NSW shows that this generally applicable mechanism is effective in the collation of data, the sharing of information, the organization of knowledge and the communication of wisdom in a whole of government context.

There is no Time to Lose

Foreseeing consequences and strategic thinking are especially critical at times of crisis. It is through consideration and planning that disasters can be averted and successful outcomes achieved. There is already a wealth of sustainability knowledge waiting to be harnessed on local, regional, national and international scales. The Sustainability Analysis Framework provides a simple mechanism for the sharing of such vital sustainability information. It is the author's opinion that there is no longer time for continual "reinventing the wheel" exercises, when it comes to sustainability practice, as the earth is in the grip of harsh challenges posed by exponential growth.

Thus, in closing, let us consider the *Lesson of the Lily Pad*. This French children's riddle provides a powerful message to anyone considering the implications of exponential human population growth and resource consumption in the context of ecosystem fragility in earth's limited biosphere.

The *Lesson of the Lily Pad* asks you to consider a lily pad which starts growing in a pond. The lily pad will double in size each day. The lily pad will cover the pond in thirty days, exhausting the pond's capacity to sustain the lily's life. On what day will the lily pad cover half the pond? The answer is: on the second last day.

This *Lesson of the Lily Pad* demonstrates a number of important things, the most notable of which is that the consequences of exponential growth "sneak" upon us and can take us by surprise, often when it is too late. For instance, the lily pad as late as the 26th day covered only $1/16^{th}$ of the pond. Even more startling is how small the lily pad is for most of the month, as an example on the 20th day the pad covered only 1/980th of the pond. The fact that we are now seeing natural systems collapse on such a quickening and escalating scale echoes the riddle's lesson about the danger that exponential growth poses for a sustainable future on earth.

There is no longer any time to lose.

Abbreviations

SAF	—	Sustainability Analysis Framework
NSW	—	New South Wales
SRM	—	Sustainability Review Matrix
SIPT	—	Sustainability Issues Practice Tables

9

Linking Sustainable Development to Environmental Governance

Issues of Forest Villages in Chhattisgarh, India

R.N. Pati

CHHATTISGARH, a nascent State had been carved out of Madhya Pradesh on November 1, 2000. This State lies in eastern part of India between 17°46' N and 24° 05' N latitude and 80°15' E and 84° 20' E longitude. Forest covers 44 per cent of total geographic area of the State. Kurandi Forest, Kurchel valley, Kanger Reserve, Bailadilla Hills and Abhujmar constitute medicinal hot spots of the State.

The issue of environmental governance is correlated with sustainable livelihood in forest villages in and around Abhujmar and Bailadilla. Medicinal plant hot spots in Bastar are numerous and complex. These issues are deep-rooted in cultural, social and natural life support systems of communities living in this region.

The growing deforestation coupled with encroachment of steeper land and common productive resources in forest villages of Bastar region of Chhattisgarh have not only posed serious challenges to village ecosystem but also developed technological intervention for sustainable agriculture acquired through the process of globalization. Different studies conducted on Decan Bio Geographical zone of Central India have indicated that the population pressure on carrying capacity of land, traditional land tenure system and introduction of cash crops have led to wide use of steeper lands and intensified exploration of limited cultivable lowlands. The issues of household food security and poverty have forced a significant section of small holders of agricultural lands to acquire sloping lands for cultivation. The agricultural practices continuously carried on encroaching steeper and sloping lands with the use of local technical knowledge has rendered agriculture yield scaled down from the desired expectations of the community and sustaining an unsustainable agriculture.

The tribal women in these villages, being the producer and manager of agricultural produce and primary users of natural resources, have to face steep challenges from different quarters for up-keeping traditional mechanism of biodiversity conservation and sustaining equilibrium between social health and local environment. The forces of globalization spear-headed through popular democratic forces have undermined the natural, social and cultural life support system of these communities. The bio-wealth of these villages has been exploited commercially by the big players of globalization era violating the local traditional rules and hijacking the intellectual and cultural property rights of these forest communities and their innovators. The militant forces have obstructed the promotion of infrastructure network of geographically inaccessible villages and rendered these communities sustain their geographical isolation from the industrial world. The middlemen and agents of corporate pharmaceutical houses have found these areas their diamond mine for smuggling out rare herbs, mineral resources, elements of cultural heritage and rich indigenous knowledge for commercial gain without compensating the community as per provision of TRIPS and

Biological Diversity Act 2002, Government of India. A good number of international conventions and conferences such as Convention on Biological Diversity 1992, UN conference on Environment and Development, 1992, The Stockholm Conference, 1972, The World Commission on Environmental and Development, 1987, ILO conventions 169 in 1957, have been organized at global level to which India was a signatory. As a follow-up measure, Government of India have enacted appropriate legislative provisions and bills keeping women and biodiversities in the centre of the arena of sustainable development and promotion of sustainable life support system. There is a wide gap between macro-and meso-level planning in one hand and meso-and micro-level planning on the other. The resolutions and recommendations are taken at global, national and regional forums exploring vibrant think tanks, which never addressed the felt needs of the stakeholders taking them as the partners of the programme. They have been isolated from the forces of acquiring knowledge and technology required for enhancing their productive capacities to earn sustainable livelihood.

The Government of Chhattisgarh has framed people-friendly forest policy emphasizing on *in situ* and *ex situ* conservation, domestication, non-destructive harvest and propagation of medicinal plants involving indigenous herbalists, shamans and community-based organizations (CBOs). Gender mainstreaming approach has been well recognized in the State Government's vision for transferring the State into a herbal State as conceptualized in July 2001. After the change of Government, the priority has been shifted or sidetracked from the area of vision.

Peoples' Protected Area Programme (PPA) has been conceptualized not only to initiate participatory conservation of biodiversity resources but also to promote sustainable livelihood of communities involved. The Sacred Grove Conservation Movement (SGCM) initiated in the year 1992 has been incorporated in Government forest policy. It has given a new dimension to the bottoms-up approach in grass-roots level bio-diversity conservation and preservation initiatives backed up by State Biodiversity Strategy Action Plan 2002. The cultural barriers and taboos prevalent since time immemorial among Gond and Halba tribal communities have isolated women from participation in various rituals concerning conservation of sacred groves. It is observed that the tribal women among Gond and Halba communities extract numerous edible leaves, tubers and medicinal herbs from and around the sacred groves. The Women Self Help Groups (SHGs) popularly known as Vana Dhan Samiti have been empowered by Tribal Cooperative Marketing Development Federation of India Limited (TRIFED) to procure non-nationalized NTFP, non-timber forest produce, along with village forest protection committee, eco-development committee with award of 7 per cent commission. It is reported that during 2001 to 2003 well over 792 women SHGs along with other CBOs have contributed towards selling 40,000 tonnes of non-nationalized NTFP items — *tendu* leaves, *sal* seeds, *mahua* flowers and seeds, *amala*, *harra*, gum, lac, tamarind and *mahua* leaves — worth Indian Rs. 25 millions. It signifies the vibrant contribution of tribal women in strengthening the commercialization of NTFP apart from contributing to the sustenance of local health tradition.

The tribal women of Gond and Halba communities possess very rich knowledge on local health traditions and contribute towards family-level local health tradition (LHT) practices focusing mainly on obstetric care of pregnant women with administration of herbs and tubers collected from local biodiversity. The green leafy vegetables like *kanda bashi, logudi bashi* and tubers like *sagar kanda, dang kanda* are recommended to the pregnant and nursing women for revitalization of strength and vigour. Traditional food restrictions are imposed by senior women members of the family on consumption of tea, jaggery and groundnut during pregnancy. The women-folks in these tribal communities acquire traditional rules of dietary recommendations and dietary restrictions from their ancestors transferred and sustained through oral tradition. The nursing mothers after delivery are recommended various diet menu for restoring their reproductive health and vigour. Coconut, jaggery, *mong bashi* are prescribed to the nursing mother soon after delivery for eliminating the obstetric impurities from uterus. Two square meals containing adequate quantity of pulses (*arhar dal*), rice and drumstick leaves are recommended for nursing mothers. The dietary restrictions are imposed on consumption of green leafy vegetables, potato, brinjal and ladies finger by nursing mothers. The women play very significant roles in executing cultural restrictions on diet for pregnant women, nursing mother and children, which are interlinked with the community mechanism and local health tradition ensuring equilibrium between social health and eco-health.

The neonates are fed with *pan, roti,* i.e. the bread sandwiched with leaves of "mahua" containing nutritional ingredient for growth. *Dudh monga* a locally available herb is given to lactating mother for three days after delivery to enhance the secretion of breast milk. The juice of *koltha dal* is recommended to the lactating mothers for increased secretion of breast milk. The indigenous herbal tea prepared from *jaggery* and dry ginger is administered soon after the onset of labour pain as a booster dose for streamlining the labour pain and smooth delivery.

Research Design

This paper is an attempt to examine the role of tribal women being the custodians of localized environmental knowledge system in protecting social and cultural diversities and generating livelihoods over which the community has adequate controls. The tribal women play a vital role not only in sustainable agricultural production process but also in upholding the health tradition of the communities based on their understanding and knowledge of environment and growth and regeneration of various herbal species. They contribute a lot towards revitalization of life support system in these forest communities as interlinked with sustainable development and community-based environmental governance. The cultural values, social restrictions and taboos relating to home-based remedies and obstetric care, community-level harvest of rare herbal species constitute holistic community mechanism for biodiversity conservation which is deep-rooted in localized knowledge system. This paper examines issues of rapid deforestation caused by industrialization, overharvesting and exploitative trade of NTFPs and how these factors have eroded the habitat of medicinal herbs for the last five decades in these forest villages of Decan Bio Geographical Zone. This paper is based on three Focus Group Discussion (FGD) with 75 tribal farmers of Halba and Gond communities and FGDs with 40 herbalists, shamans and FGDs with 160 members of village Forest Communities in Dehari, Topal, Cilibahor, Lampuri, Mas-Barus and Pondgaon of Antagarh Block in the Kanker district of Chhattisgarh. These villages are located in forest zones in the south-western part of the Kanker district in the latitude 81°6"8' east and longitude 20°6"6', 212 kms from Raipur, State capital of Chhattisgarh, and 71 kms from district headquarters. The field work was conducted from July 2005 to January 2006 with administration of qualitative tools, participant observation, case study and PPA programmes. This piece of research study was conducted by two anthropologists and one ethnobotanist who made in-depth probing on role of women in conservation of biodiversity in terms of application of time-tested herb-based home remedies, application of low technology methods for processing of herbal remedies sustaining life support system for food security and facilitating community access to commonly used medicinal plants harvested in sacred groves of the villages. The local traditions manifested through observance of ceremonies and rituals are closely interrelated with social structure of the communities influencing indigenous mechanism for preservation and conservation of biodiversity. The community's ethics and values influencing environmental governance are embedded in women's contribution to household food security and participation in various rituals and ceremonies revolving around local health tradition, and preservation of sacred groves in these villages. This paper critically examines how tribal farmers in these forest villages add to existing body of knowledge and practices in agriculture and environmental conservation. These issues of environmental governance as related to agriculture and local health tradition are numerous and complex.

As many as 25,000 of wild plants have been identified in different forest regions of India out of which 7000 species are used as herbal medicine. In India, Unani, Siddha, Ayurveda and traditional healers in different tribal communities utilize herbal potencies of these herbs exploring indigenous knowledge system. The plant-based home remedies are widespread among tribal communities of Chhattisgarh, Madhya Pradesh, Orissa, Bihar, Andhra Pradesh and Rajasthan. In Chhattisgarh, several traditional treatment centres are run by healers in remote forest villages of

Dantewada, Bastar, Kanker, Korba and Sauguja. They render miraculous treatment for bonesetting, mentally retarded persons, snakebite and treatment of cancer, etc. The localized knowledge system on biodiversity in these forest villages have been sustained through oral traditions and informal network from one generation to another. The herbalist shamans, bone setters and tribal women are treated as the custodians of this localized knowledge system. The tribal women possess vast knowledge of medicinal herbs effectively administered as dietary supplement for debility in nursing mothers, expelling impurities from uterus of nursing mothers and herbal remedies for preventing tooth decay and conditioning hair etc. These tribal women can differentiate between the plants having medicinal potencies and the plants which do not have any. They use their finger and nose for identifying these herbal plants. There are several plants grown in the wild which look alike but do not have the same medicinal properties. Unfortunately, a good number of herbal species have not been covered under botanical classification through commercializing research initiatives. The tribal women as well as the shamans do not share the knowledge of many rare herbs to keep up the values and ethics of local health traditions. Secondly, they are haunted by professional insecurity and fear that others may commercially exploit their herbal habitat resulting in widespread bio-prospecting. The rare tubers like "Sagar Kanda" and "Dang Kanda" are recommended as food supplement for revitalization of strength and vigour in nursing mother. The herbal species locally known as "Dudh monga" have been over-harvested in village Dehari, Lampuri and Topal during the last couple of years in sacred groves of the village to combat malnutrition, debility, morbidity of nursing mothers and maternal mortalities widespread among Gond and Halba communities. The Key Informant Interview (KII) with herbalists and shamans of these villages reveal that the local herbs like "Chirchira' "Viskatia" "Arjuna" "Gondila" and "Bantulasi" containing medicinal potencies for revitalizing health and stimulating sexual vigour have been smuggled out in huge quantities by the agents of ayurvedic pharmaceutical companies who have not only hijacked the intellectual property rights (IPR) of the tribal herbalists but also exploited the traditional knowledge of these communities without compensating them as per Biodiversity Act 2002 and Biodiversity Rules, 2004. As per official record, 625 plant species from different forest regions of Chhattisgarh are traded through network of trading centres. The incidence of biopiracy has been growing day by day posing a serious threat to the equilibrium between social health and eco-health within these indigenous communities. Unfortunately the traders and big players have taken advantage of the gaps between macro-level policy formulation and micro-level implementation. The resolutions of Convention of Biological Diversity (CBD) focused on fair and equitable sharing of benefits derived from use of genetic resources and biodiversity has not been adhered to at local level administrative set-up. The Village Forest Committee (VFC) in many forest villages have failed to be properly empowered through capacity building initiatives launched by Forest Development Agency (FDA) through its network in Peoples Protected Area towards developing community-based mapping and management plan ensuring biopartnership campaign. The involvement of tribal women in Van Dhan Samiti in many villages has paved ways for regeneration of damaged plant habitats. The effect of globalization and militant infestation has sabotaged the efforts of local administration in gearing up innovative environmental governance initiatives.

The insignificant role of women in decision-making at local body level contributes to rural poverty and depletion of life support systems. The poorest of the poor are often ignored in the identification process due to political and social deprivations. The Women SHGs are found to be most potential facilitating agencies to initiate advocacy with Gram Sabha for identification and registration of potential poor families in the village following approved poverty identification yardstick. Van Dhan Samiti, women's forum for protecting natural resources, need to play a vital role not only in identifying potential poor families but also in recommending to the State Government for providing agricultural land to these landless families and access to utilization of common productive resources. The tribal women have been worst affected by syndromes of poverty and incapacities of modern agro-development initiatives to generate adequate livelihood for people. The poverty mainstreaming initiative with women involvement would yield best results. The appreciable action of Government of Madhya Pradesh in allocating agricultural land to at least 2.10 lakh tribal families out of special central assistance under tribal sub-plan during 2002-03 may be followed by Government of Chhattisgarh as a viable intervention of rural poverty reduction. The tribals constitute 33 per cent of the population of the State. But, they are availing 18 per cent of reservation in services which must be enhanced to 33 per cent on the basis of their population. This will facilitate alleviation of rural poverty. The rural poverty has been aggravated by poor rural infrastructure including village roads, culverts, water reservoirs, dispensaries, schools, Auxilliary Nurse cum Midwife (ANM) sub-centres, etc. in addition to geographical and social isolation. Integrated rural infrastructure development programme linked with income generation programme like community goatery, banana cultivation, sun flower farming, pisciculture, dairy farming, poultry farming, etc. will gear up intervention and experimentation on rural poverty reduction. The lessons of such best practices can be drawn from NGOs of Andhra Pradesh and Bangladesh.

The food security and ownership and access to forest resources among indigenous communities are major survival issues which are ignored to be prioritized and addressed through appropriate participatory interventions by Forest Development Agencies, Local Bodies and the Government. The local bodies and Panchayat Raj Institutions (PRI) are yet to be encouraged with appropriate sensitization and firm commitment towards shouldering the responsibilities of integrating ethno-healing with modern medical system bridging the gap between these therapeutic systems; facilitating practices of folkhealers, understanding and protecting their intellectual property rights; mapping the land and common productive resources of tribals, helping them to solve their land right issues, encouraging them to protect forest and biodiversity resources and generate income through exploitation of non-timber forest produce; and intensify farming of medicinal plants through well co-ordinated participatory interventions. Well co-ordinated intervention in these areas with involvement of women and their forum, Van Dhan Samities appropriately trained on conservation and development of NTFP species will boost up economic transformation in this nascent State.

The local bodies have been empowered by the State Government through enactment of Panchayat Upabandha Adhiniyam, 1996 to exercise ownership rights over NTFP. The members of the community are entitled to harvest, collect and sell minor forest produce. The legal provisions are very often misutilized which fail to fit within the framework of traditional community management mechanism of biodiversity. The farmers need to be supported with standard planting materials, market information, linkage with commercial manufacturing units promoted by corporate houses towards appropriate environmental governance within the framework of traditional management mechanism ensuring balance between eco-health and social health.

The biological resources in the indigenous territories of Chhattisgarh consists of various natural resources of agricultural, medicinal, ecological, veterinary and cosmological potencies which ensure equilibrium between local environment and social health of the tribal communities inhabiting the forest villages. The forest dwelling tribes interact with plant and animal diversity in a natural supportive way. The biological resources influence the customary practices, cultural resources and local knowledge systems not only among Gond and Halba communities but also among other indigenous communities. The above cultural practices, both customary and non-customary, prevalent among Gond and Halba tribes of Chhattisgarh are not only inherited territorially but also continue to evolve under influence of individual innovations and local environment. The deficiencies in careful customization of these cultural practices restrict opportunities for innovation and reproduction of these practices. The circulation and reproduction of natural and social environment and local system of production through vibrant role of tribal women are followed by these cultural practices which constitute potential substrates of local cultural resources.

There is a shift of development approach focused on exploration of marketing network from foreign market to domestic market after Independence. The Key Informant

Interview with community elders indicates that during colonial pre-Independence era very little effort was taken on enhancing food production and exploring the indigenous knowledge system. During colonial era very little room was allocated for research-based innovations. After Independence, indigenous knowledge of farmers has been explored intensively through research for developing sustainable agriculture technology. More focus has been given on enhancing food production and narrowing the gap between researchers involved in indigenous knowledge on one hand, and agricultural development practitioners on the other.

The tribal women of Gond and Halba communities in these forest villages have knowledge and understanding of 96 flowering plants, 87 medicinal herbs and 51 trees species grown around village forest and sacred groves of the village. Their participation in agriculture and collection of minor forest produce towards ensuring life support system not only contribute towards community-level management of natural resources but also towards promotion of livelihood for everyone in the community. A significant section of tribal women working as NTFP collectors live below poverty line. They lack adequate knowledge and information on market and support mechanism. They lack bargaining power to articulate their traditional rights to NTFP products. Besides, the forest policy of the State Government, 2001 also has very little room for recognizing their claims and rights to these products.

The tribal women have vast knowledge of the medicinal potencies of herbs which they grow in herbal habitats in the forest and sacred groves of the village for sustaining local health tradition and home remedies. The involvement of scientists is urged for commercializing research on chemical potencies of these herbs through laboratory tests.

Sl.no.	*Ailments*	*Plants with medicinal potencies administered for home remedies*	*Harvesting spots*
1.	Toothache	Sanwai, Mahua	Sacred groves, forest
2.	Cough	Harra, Ginger, Basil	Kitchen garden, Sacred groves
3.	Worm infection	Karra, Harra, Behra Kiwach	
4.	Acidity and indigestion	Harra, Dry Ginger	Kitchen garden
5.	Diarrhoea	Harra, Manga, Kodo, Paddy, Dry Ginger	Sacred groves, kitchen garden
6.	Dysentery	Tilsa, Arjun	Forest, sacred groves
7.	Menstrual Disorder	Koombhi, Arjun, Aonwla, Shisham Shilvling	Forest, sacred groves
8.	Vomiting	Kodo	Forest
9.	Normal fever and malaria	Bhoi-Lim, Ashwa-gandha,Black Pepper, Basil, Nagarmotha, Neem	Sacred groves and forest
10.	Itches or scabies	Karanj, Kusum, Kochla	Forest, sacred groves
11.	Boil	Gular (Doomar), Gudsukari, Thuo	Forest
12.	Dog-bite	Aak, Gudsukari, San	Forest
13.	Snakebite	Garud, Kochola, Garud	Forest
14.	Fracture or setting of broken bone	Amar Bel, Harisingar	Forest, sacred groves

Under local health tradition, the therapeutic norms are administered to extract medicinal potencies from fruits, leaf, stem, root, latex, bark, seed of different plant species which is kept confidential.

The cultural values associated with home remedy practices of tribal women in these villages ensure natural, social and cultural life support systems and prevent the communities losing their capacities in generating livelihood from common productive resources. There is an urgent need to promote a meaningful alliance between tribal women, herbalists, shamans bone setters on one hand and scientists, researchers, and agriculture development practitioners on the other. The enactment at national and regional level of legal provisions in conformity with international conventions would scale down biopiracy of genetic resources and promote benefit-sharing by the community from commercial exploitation of herbs and indigenous knowledge. The healthy interaction with the communities to acquire knowledge on rare herbs through licensing agreement will provide income to the community and create community-based business on harvesting of plants. There is enough scope for creating external demand of herbs which will gear up harvesting and regeneration of damaged plant habitat and create employment avenues for herbalists and women as NTFP collectors. The sector likes training on home remedies, creation of awareness on local health options, promotion of sustainable access to necessary raw materials, enhancing community confidence in traditional health practices and exploring strategies for sustainable management of biodiversity which would pave the ways for effective environmental governance by improving equitable access to benefits-sharing from commercial use of products of the biodiversities.

Abbrivations

ANM	—	Auxilliary Nurse cum Midwife
CBD	—	Convention of Biological Diversity
CBOs	—	Community-Based Organizations
FDA	—	Forest Development Agency
FGD	—	Focus Group Discussion
IPR	—	Intellectual Property Rights
KII	—	Key Informant Interview
LHT	—	Local Health Tradition
NTFP	—	Non-Timber Forest Produce
PPA	—	Peoples' Protected Area Programme
PRI	—	Panchayat Raj Institutions
SGCM	—	Sacred Grove Conservation Movement
SHGs	—	Self Help Groups
TRIFED	—	Tribal Cooperative Marketing Development Federation of India Limited
VFC	—	Village Forest Committee

References

Anon (1996), *The Useful Plants of India*, New Delhi: PID, CSIR, p. 918.

Gijtenbeek, J.M.M., M.J. Vanden Bent and C.J. Vecht (1999), *Cyclosporine Neurotoxicity*, J. Neurol, pp. 246, 339-46.

Gupta, Akshey K., S.K. Vats, and Brij Lal (1998), How cheap can a Medicinal Plant species be?, *Current Science*, pp. 74, 565-66.

Handa, S.S. (1992), Medicinal plants-based drug industry and emerging plant drugs, *Current Researches Medicine, Aromatic Plants*, 14, pp. 233-62.

Miaorong, P. and L. Jing (1996), Proceedings of the 40th Annual Conference on Chinese Medicine, Beijing University, pp. 28-30

Prajapati, N.D., S.S. Purohit, A.K. Sharma and Tarun Kumar (2003), *A Hand Book of Mediçinal Plants*, Jodhpur: Agrobios (India), p. 153.

Rajshekharan, P.E. (2002), Herbal Medicine, in World of Science, *Employment News*, 21-27 November, p. 3.

Roy, A.K. and H.K. Chaurasia (1989), Aflatoxin problems in some medicinal plants under storage, *International Journal of Crude Drug Research*, pp. 27, 156-60.

Shah, B.K. (1997), *Drugs, News Views*, pp. 4-7.

WHO (2000), General guidelines for methodologies on research and evaluation of traditional medicine, Geneva: World Health Organization.

10

Added Value in the Process Industry Through Integrated Environmental Engineering

Markus Thüer

Introduction

ENVIRONMENTAL protection measures can generate added value — although hardly anybody appears to believe it.

The concrete examples that follow show that pollution control requirements can lead to real savings if one is willing to study the existing processes and improve them where it makes sense. Sometimes this means leaving the trodden path and earnestly considering alternative approaches.

The most direct way to cut costs is to improve the actual manufacturing processes. Good concepts for this not only ensure that regulatory emission limits will be met, they improve product quality, increase production capacity, and reduce production costs.

Enhancing profits by improving production processes is increasingly recognized, but deriving cost benefits through waste treatment is seldom expected. Yet here too significant added value can be achieved through intelligent solutions, as many of the following examples show.

Conceptual Approach

How does one arrive at such economically and ecologically attractive solutions?

The amount of technical solutions for industrial pollution control is virtually unlimited (the immensity of the European Union's Integrated Pollution Prevention and Control (IPPC) documentation testifies to this). The application of these technical solutions depends on both the type of product and the manufacturing process. But these change constantly, so the optimal environmental protection techniques change accordingly.

What do not change are the fundamental principles of IPPC. These are mentioned in the IPPC documentation. In the case of the process industry the principles can be summarized as follows Table 10.1:

Process of Improvements

EXAMPLES OF IMPLEMENTED MEASURES

In the chemical industry the most promising way to increase eco-efficiency is fundamentally to increase yields, because all raw material that is not turned into product is waste. The equation is simple:

> Amount of waste = amount of raw materials times (100 per cent minus yield per cent)

If we manage to increase yield, we need less raw materials to make a product, which lowers operating costs. We produce less by-products, which reduces environmental impact and further improves profitability by lowering the cost of waste elimination. This principle also applies to auxiliary chemicals — although here the rule is not that simple.

Table 10.1
Basic concept for efficient environmental protection measures

Avoid and reduce	Environmental impact in general (waste in particular) that does not occur requires no elimination. Less waste means lower disposal cost. Conclusion: Optimize production processes.
Recover and recycle	Many types of waste such as by-products and unused raw materials can be recycled within production. This is rational and often relatively easy to do. In contrast, external recycling is attractive only as an exception, usually in the case of large and uniform production.
Treat	Treatment in so-called end-of-pipe systems is expensive (measured by unit cost), but usually unavoidable because emission regulations around the world prescribe concentration limits that can be met efficiently only with such special elimination systems.
Optimize effectiveness	Because emission limit values generally cannot be met by in-process techniques alone, the most efficient solution consists in a two-stage approach: (1) in-process and/or end-of-process measures to reduce volumes/loads combined with (2) end-of-pipe technology to reduce concentrations.

New Synthesis for an Intermediate in Pigment Production

This example from pigment production shows how in-process measures — direct process improvements — significantly reduced both environmental impact and costs.

DNS (dinitrostilbene-disulphonic acid) is an important intermediate in the production of optical brighteners. Originally DNS was being produced in a preliminary stage by oxidation with hypochlorite. The yield from this batch process was very low. Consequently the wastewater was heavily loaded with salts and organics difficult to degrade.

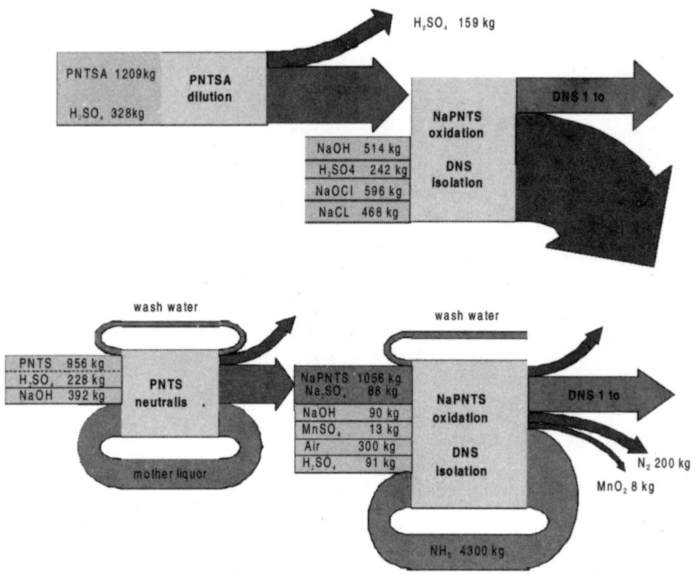

The thickness of the arrows corresponds to the volume flows:

- = product;
- = waste product;
- = educts (Techinical term) (raw materials, auxiliary products)

fig. 10.1: Mass flow diagrams of the old (upper figure) and new process

Characteristics of the Old Process:

Yield: (theoretical) 74 per cent

Environmental burden (per tonne of product)

- Salts:	1,500	kg
- Organics (most types difficult to degrade)	126	kg
- Wastewater volume	15	m^3

This unsatisfactory environmental picture plus the need to increase output spurred a complete revision of the process. Considerable development effort ultimately produced a completely new semi-batch process with air instead of chlorine as the oxidizing agent, significantly improving the balance.

fig. 10.1: shows that the new process greatly reduced waste amounts. The increase in yield also reduced raw material volumes.

Characteristics of the New Process

Increase in yield: 74% → 92%

Ecology:

- Water utilization (wastewater volume)	- 70%
- TOC (organic pollutants)	- 74%
- Coloration	- 62%
- NaCl	- 100%
- Na_2SO_4	- 46%

Economy:

Operating costs	- 25%

This case involved a completely new synthesis. Here the economic benefits can of course be fully realized only if a new production line is built. That was the case here.

Optimizing the Processing of Anti-Oxidants (Metilox)

This example shows the ecological and economic improvements, when the processing of melt, resulting from a chemical reaction, was changed from crystallization to a special form of distillation (rectification).

Ecology:

Water consumption	- 57 %
Steam consumption	- 47 %
Electrical power consumption	- 14 %
Liquid wastes	- 56 %
Wastewater - volume	- 92 %
Wastewater - pollutants -TOC	- 91 %
- BOD	- 80 %
- Acids	- 80 %

Economy:

Fixed costs	- 41 %
Variable costs	- 7 %
Absolute annual costs	- 9.1 mil. CHF

Optimizing the Process Parameters of a Light-Protection Agent

Here ecological and economic improvements were achieved solely by changing the process parameters — with no expensive changes to the equipment.

Again here the reason for reworking the (batch) process was wastewater loaded with salts and organics difficult to degrade.

The process was modified with the aim to continue using the multipurpose line with the fewest changes possible. Mainly the following process parameters were changed and optimized:

- Temperature of diazotization and coupling (cooling instead of heating).
- HCl instead of H_2SO_4 as a diazotization medium.

From these very simple changes resulted the following:

Improvements due to Change of Process:

Process data:

Increase in yield	86	→ 97 %
Theoretical waste amount	14	→ 3 %
Increase in production capacity	240	→ 800 t/a

Ecology:

Wastewater - volume	- 94 %
Organic pollutant load (TOC)	- 92 %
Waste - acids	- 69 %

Economy:

Production costs	- 21 %

End of Process Solutions that Boost Efficiency of end-of-Pipe Systems

The low concentration values for wastewater or exhaust gases prescribed by law in many countries are often so low that typical end of process methods such as stripping, extraction, condensation and distillation are no longer economically feasible. But when efficient end of process measures can significantly reduce the loads to be treated (for example by 70 to 90 per cent), existing end-of-pipe systems may suffice in spite of the tougher limits — or new end-of-pipe systems can be sized smaller.

Using an Existing Incinerator to Treat Exhaust at a Chemical Production Plant

To meet new clean-air laws a large production plant was required to cut Volatile Organic Carbon (VOC) emissions by

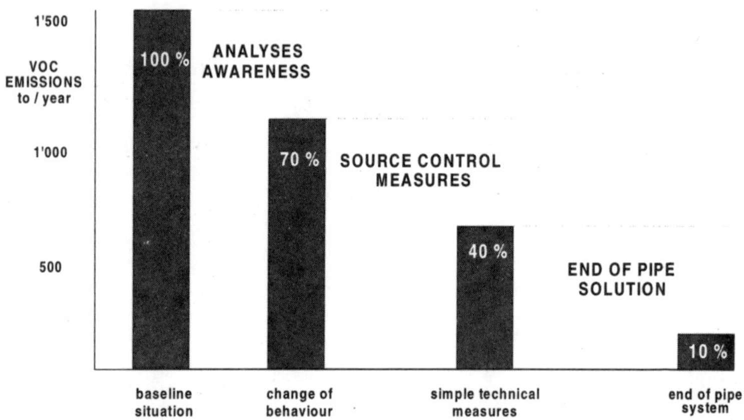

fig. 10.2: Integral exhaust-treatment concept for a large chemical plant

more than 90 per cent. As in other cases, it was possible to greatly reduce concentrations and exhaust gas volume by training the personnel and by employing relatively simple technical measures such as on-site scrubbers, aerosol separators, and the encapsulation of equipment. Still, end-of-pipe treatment was unavoidable. But because the organically loaded waste gas had already been reduced to a third of the original volume, instead of installing a new end-of-pipe system the solvent incinerator already in place at the plant could be used. Replacing fresh air the remaining contaminated waste air was used as a source of oxygen for combustion.

Alternative Approach Minimizes Capital Expense for end-of-pipe System

Positive experience with the wastewater treatment system at a production plant for agro-chemicals sparked the idea to build a similar system at a comparable but smaller plant.

Based on a comparison with the existing system, the budget of the plant master plan included the following investment:

(all numbers in CHF): 6 mil

- Alternatives were analyzed in a preliminary study. A system similar to that at the other plant was optimized: 5 mil
- Upgrading of the existing and somewhat inefficient system (though not recommended for various reasons): 4 mil
- In-plant handling was rejected; waste would be transported to an external facility for handling. Tank storage and rail loading station only: 1 mil
- In the detailed design phase the latter alternative was refined (simpler tank storage). This cut the cost by: 0.7 mil.

During the relatively long design and decision phase some changes in production arose, which allowed further optimization:

- Production improvements were realized which greatly reduced overall concentrations of organics.
- By separating waste streams a significant portion of the previous contaminants could be kept out of the water and could be eliminated as liquid organic waste.

- After cleaning up a landfill a system existing at the plant was no longer needed for treating groundwater. With wastewater loading greatly reduced, it was possible to expand this small existing system at low cost to handle the lightly loaded wastewater:

Final capital expense 0.3 million, instead of the initially budgeted 6 million.

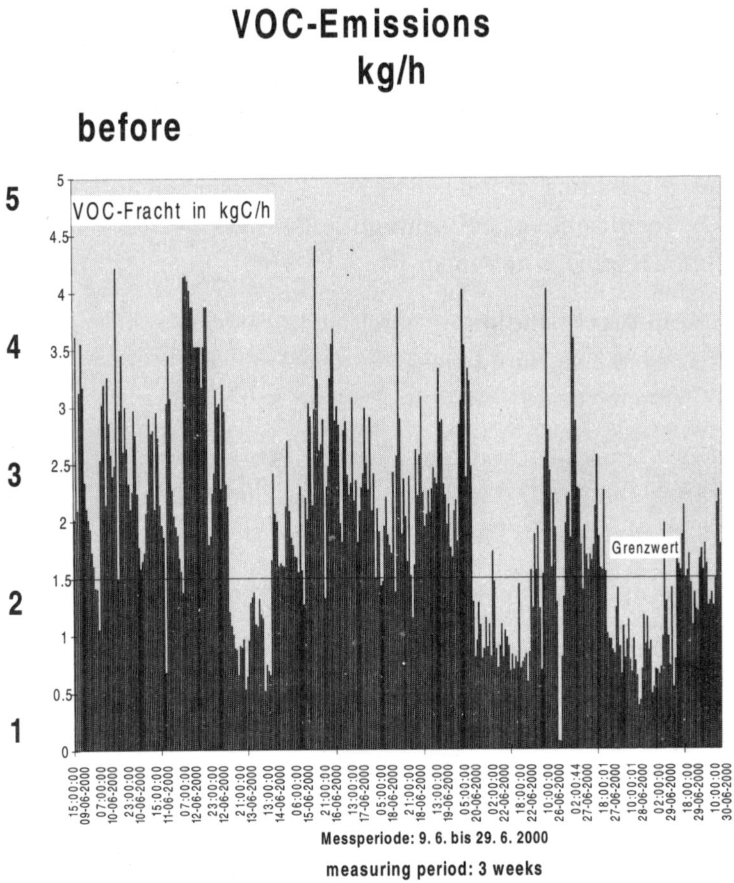

fig. 10.3A: VOC emissions at a chemical production plant before implementing simple in-process measures

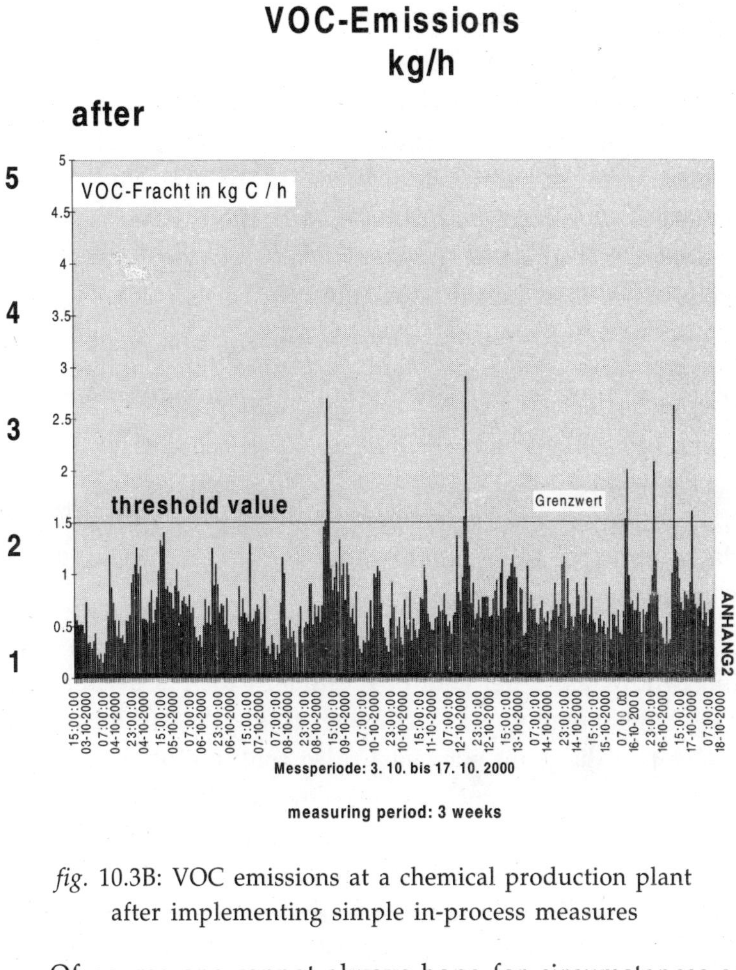

fig. 10.3B: VOC emissions at a chemical production plant after implementing simple in-process measures

Of course one cannot always hope for circumstances as favourable as these. Yet except for the groundwater treatment system that became available in this case, all the actions mentioned here are more or less applicable to other cases and can contribute to optimization moderately or greatly.

In fact, in certain cases one can do without an end-of-pipe system altogether, as the following example shows:

Simple Infrastructure Measures for Reducing VOC Emissions

Before taking up new production in an older factory, scrubbers were installed to collect acid gases. The existing coolers and condensers should have sufficed to handle the organic emissions. But once production started, the VOC emissions in the stack measured as shown in *fig.* 10.3A. Two alternatives were found to rectify the situation:

1. End-of-pipe system to separate the VOC's, or
2. In-process measures to prevent or greatly reduce the formation of pollutants.

Drawing upon our experience with similar cases, we first tried in-process measures alone. *fig.* 10.3B shows the effect of these measures three months after the initial measurements were made.

Instead of 70 per cent of the time, emission values exceed limits now just 2 per cent of the time, which is permissible. The improvement was achieved chiefly by training and motivating the plant personnel. Also contributing were minor technical measures such as correcting faulty connections to the exhaust duct to eliminate false air. Regularly closing openings (manholes, valves at vacuum hoses, etc.) greatly reduced the draw of ambient air into the system, which operates under negative pressure. This reduced the volume of air that can become contaminated by contact with solvents, and it raised concentrations in the exhaust gas, which improved the collection efficiency of the condensers.

The cost benefits or value added are as follows:

Standard solution		***In-process solution***	
End-of-pipe treatment		Simple on-site measures	
Activated carbon absorption unit	1,200,000	Technical modifications	100,000
Annual operating costs	150,000	Consulting	50,000
Total cost (2 years)	1,350,000	Total cost	150,000

Economical Alternatives for End-of-pipe Systems

JOINT SOLUTION FOR THE DISPOSAL OF NITRATE-LADEN WASTEWATER

A chemical plant produces wastewater that is heavily loaded with nitrates (NO_3), unavoidable due to stoichiometric reasons. Discharging the wastewater into the local wastewater treatment system was not possible, so the plant would have had to install a separate bioreactor for nitrate degradation. Because of the one-sided composition of the wastewater, the

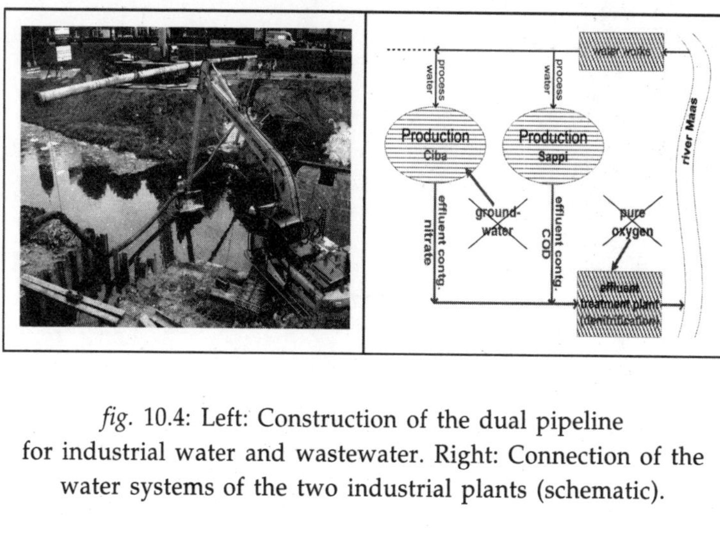

fig. 10.4: Left: Construction of the dual pipeline for industrial water and wastewater. Right: Connection of the water systems of the two industrial plants (schematic).

plant would have to add also large amounts of auxiliary chemicals, mainly Carbon.

Thus the search began for the local producer of wastewater with the highest carbon content. A paper factory was found whose overloaded biological treatment plant was being run on pure oxygen. That factory's one-sided carbonic wastewater required the continuous addition of nitrogen — the elements oxygen (O) and nitrogen (N) were lacking, precisely the two elements which the wastewater from the chemical plant offered in surplus.

The joint treatment of the two wastewaters in the existing system at the paper factory was made all the more attractive by a local pipeline that was to be built to carry river water to the industrial complex (to help conserve groundwater reserves). The wastewater line was built simultaneously with the freshwater pipeline, minimizing the cost of moving the wastewater.

The project received an award for good environmental practice — and saved substantial costs for both companies:

Company	*Chemical plant*	*Paper factory*
Approx. annual savings	0.5 million €	0.5 million €
Benefit	Costs avoided	Previous costs eliminated
Factors	Investment in bio-reactor Operating costs of bioreactor Cost of carbon source — Disposal of waste-water sludge	Cost of pure oxygen (O) Cost of nutrient (N)

Conclusion

The examples described here are concrete cases showing that environmental protection regulations — next to their original intent of protecting the environment — can very well lead to an outcome of economic value.

Attractive solutions like these hardly come from textbooks. They originate by creative thinking, experience, and an integrated approach. Such an approach does not stop with end-of-pipe systems. It scopes the entire problem, all the way to the beginning, production, and at the same time considers the safe final storage of the residues that inevitably result. (CO_2 is also a residue !)

Experience with comparable or similar situations is always an invaluable resource. It is the best guarantee that an environmental engineering project will fully deliver the expected performance.

Abbreviations

DNS — Dinitrostilbene-disulphonic Acid

IPPC — Integrated Pollution Prevention and Control

VOC — Volatile Organic Carbon

11

Types of Relationships between Firms, Communities and Government

And Their Obstacles

José G. Vargas-Hernández

Horizontal and Vertical Relationships of Firms, Communities and Governments

MACNEIL (1978, 865) defines the firm to be "in significant ways, nothing more than a very complex bundle of contractual relations." Klein et al. (1978, 326) also considers the firm as a particular set of interrelated contracts and suggests that these may be used to examine the economic rationale of different kinds of contractual relationships.

Collaboration between firms, social organizations and Governments is an important trend of the last three decades in order to engage in activities aimed to common goals and to have access resources otherwise not possible. There is an increasing recognition of relationships and linkages between firms, networks, business organizations, industrial associations, social and community organizations and Governments. There are institutionalized structures and formal-informal relationships of co-operation between firms, national States, communities, international organizations and non-governmental organizations. Public-Private Partnership

(PPP) is a kind of informal co-operation, which takes different forms.

State policy makers call on expertise, political support and manpower, for example, from associations, communities, firms, non-governmental organizations, etc. through a combination of conflict, competition and co-operation.

There are vertical and horizontal relationships with different nature of trade-offs between co-operation/harmony and competition/conflict. Close vertical ties characterized by rich information exchange and long-term commitments lead to greater co-operation and joint activities between the partners and higher levels of asset-specific investments, all of which translate into concrete performance benefits for the firms forming such ties (Helper, 1991; Heide and Miner, 1992).

Through the formation of horizontal alliances firms seek to strategically co-operate having resulted in the emergence of new organizational structures in order to manage the relationships of co-operation. The set boundaries of the firms are blurring. A firm can be involved simultaneously in different types of horizontal and vertical relationships to other firms based on the value chain, but involving economic and non-economic exchanges.

Podolny and Page (1998, 59) define a network form of organization as "any collection of actors (N=2) that pursue repeated, enduring exchange relations with one another and, at the same time, lack a legitimate organizational authority to arbitrate and resolve disputes that may arise during the exchange. . . . This definition . . . includes a wide array of joint ventures, strategic alliances . . . franchises . . . relational contracts, and outsourcing agreements."

Network's Associations and the Effects of Institutions on Beliefs and Decision-Making

A network is a distinct, highly differentiated, heterogeneous organizational form (Powell, 1990). A network binds relations between complementary resource owners, tied together by personal relationships in order to accomplish a variety of purposes and tasks, allowing them to use each other's core competencies. Networks bind the independent social and technical entities of two or more organizations by relationships of trust, common culture, interdependence, and complementarity. A network remains more open to admit new participants. Networks evolve into multiple webs of technical, financial and social interactions (Kogut and Zander, 1992; Gulati, 1995).

Co-operation networks as an element of agile organizations (Goldman et al., 1994) increased with the emergence of flexible specialization depending on cultural requirements (Amato Neto, 2003) of the market infrastructure, financial conditions, characteristics of the partners, and so on. Cultural infrastructure is related to co-operation among partners. Goranson (1995) lists the requirements in terms of legal infrastructure such as economic agreements, physical infrastructure such as communication technologies and the cultural barriers represented in the lack of trust which facilitates co-ordination and co-operation forms among inter-firm networks.

Tie modality is the set of institutionalized rules and norms that govern appropriate behaviour in the network spelled out in formal contracts or simple understandings that evolve within the dyad and the network (Laumann, Galaskiewicz and Marsden, 1978). The modality of ties created by firms maintains the relationship characteristics of the network, such as the degree of co-operativeness or opportunistic with implications in the strategic behaviour and performance. The relationships in most strategic networks are mixed-motives of partners neither strictly competitive nor co-operative (Gulati, Khanna and Nohria, 1994). Networks determine the

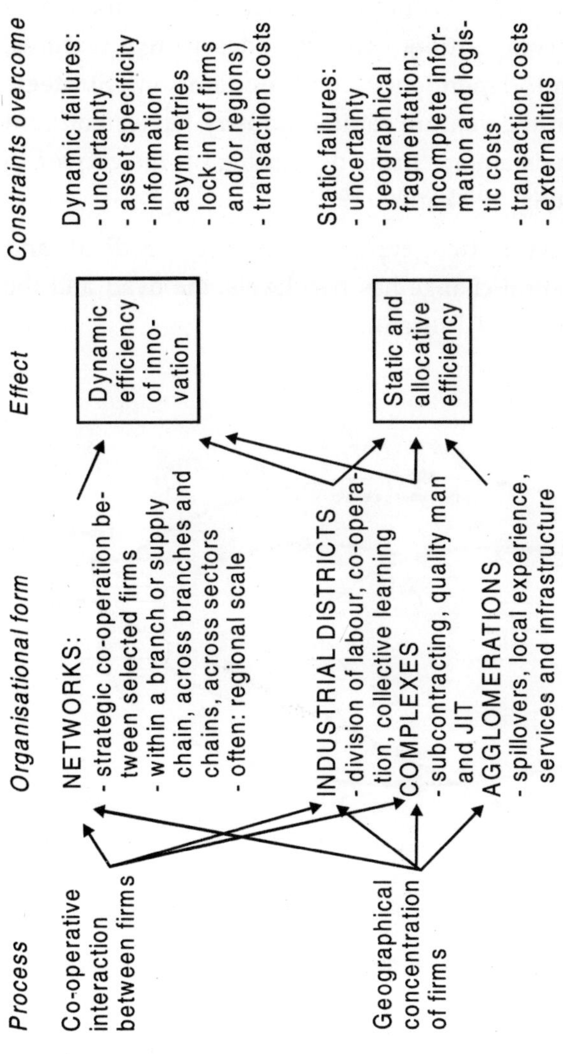

Source: Visser, E.J. & R. Boschma (2004).

fig. 11.1. Organizational forms of co-operative interaction between firms and geographical concentration of firms.

choices available to partners and network structure determines private and common incentives to compete or co-operate.

Chalmers, Martin and Piester (1997) define associative networks as the "non-hierarchical structures formed through decisions by multiple actors who come together to shape public policy." Chandler (1977) emphasized the co-ordination in hierarchical structures. Within any given network, there may or may not be competition, conflict, a descriptive features, domination and dependency, or co-operation. Strategic networks within the venture capital industry have significant profit differentials among firms depending on the cliques to which they belong. (Piskorski, 1999).

Networks have two types of changes, radical and incremental. Radical change has two levels, the dyad and the network (Knoben and Rutten).

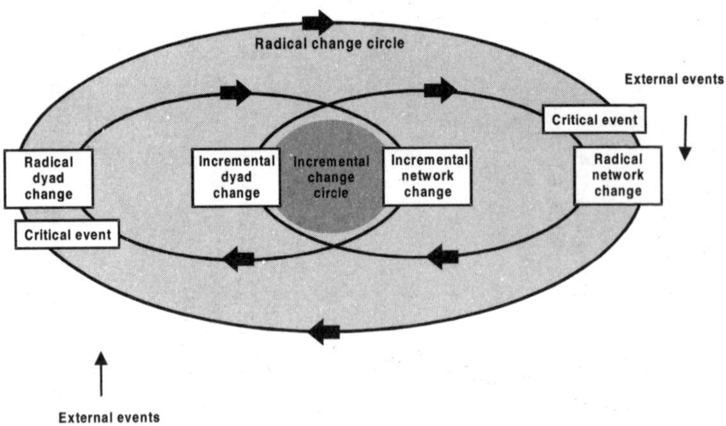

Source: based on Halinen et al., 1999.

fig. 11.2. A framework of change in networks and dyads

Four types of horizontal relationships are based on trade-offs between co-operation and competition (Easton and Araujo, 1992; Easton et al., 1993). In a no-clear pattern, the content of the relationships can change from competition to co-operation, or co-existence, steered by the other relationships in the environment.

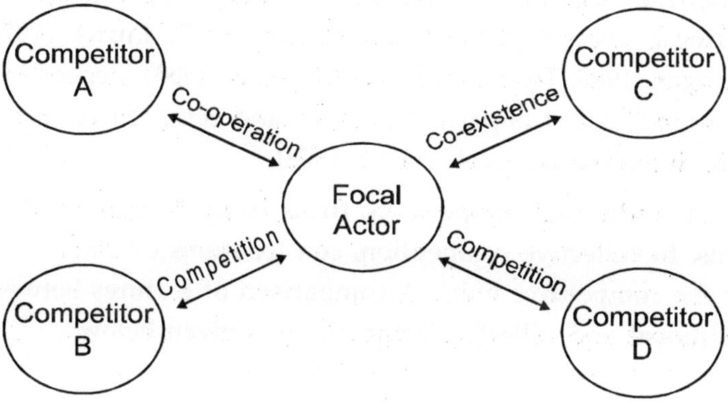

fig. 11.3. Horizontal relationships between competitors

A. Relationships of Competition

The notion of competition derives from the structural equivalence of firms, or the extent to which they share the same resources or customers. Power and dependence are related to the actor's position and strength. Dependence is more equally distributed but related to the actor's strength and position in the business network. Conflicts arise frequently due mainly to invisible norms as part of the climate. The goals are object-oriented. Proximity of competitors that have common goals is based on psychological and functional factors. Competitive relationships have not been analyzed between vertical actors.

Competition allocates resources by unilateral actions, and creates internal and external pressures. Competition is a process of selecting the best practices to innovate as source of profits.

In neo-classical economic theory, competitive relationships take place between different structures. Criticism from industrial organization theory introduces the concepts of strategic groups (Caves and Porter, 1977; Porter, 1979; Harrigan, 1985; Thomas and Venkatraman, 1988), dependency between firms at imperfect markets, and competitive rivalry at an intermediate level (Hunt, 1972).

In traditional competition, firms compete against other firms. In collective competition, constellations of allied firms are the competitive units. A comparison of features between traditional and collective competition is given below:

	Traditional competition	*Collective competition*
Competitive units	Firms	Constellations
Industry structure	Oligopoly of firms	Oligopoly of Constellations
Source of differentiation	Firm-based advantage	Group-based advantage
Valuble resources	Controlled by the firm	Assembled by constellation
Governance of resources	Corporate structures	Constellation structure
Source of Profit	Rent in the value chain	Rent in the constellation

Source: Gomes-Casseres, 2003.

fig. 11.4. Features of traditional competition and of collective competition

The notion of "hyper competition" is similar to high velocity environments between individual firms, which is shifting towards one more dynamic model of "hyper-co-operation" (D'Aveni, 1994). Firms competing in hyper competitive environments exhibit behaviour that differs significantly from behaviour in more static environments (Thomas, 1996). The identified drivers for a shift towards hyper competition are consumer demand, the knowledge base of firms and associated workers, declining entry barriers, and the increasing frequency of alliances among firms.

To assess the structure of competition in the global currency, trading industry has been used in interactions between banking firms in a global electronic network (Zaheer and Zaheer, 1999).

B. Collusive Relationships

Collusive relationship takes place when two competitors join forces to damage a third one. Collusive behaviour dominates the study of co-operative behaviour. Adam Smith (1776) wrote, "people of the same trade seldom meet together, even for merriment and diversion, but the conversation ends in a conspiracy against the public, or in some contrivance to raise prices."

Obstacles for Co-operation and Co-ordination

The ability to provide co-ordination, for hierarchical controls especially in situations involving high interdependence and uncertainty in inter-organizational relations is a challenge (Barnard, 1938; Thompson, 1967; and Chandler, 1977).

The ability of organizational hierarchies to mitigate the uncertainty resulting from co-ordination and control of complex and interdependent tasks is aided by creating co-operation and co-ordination among organizational members (Barnard, 1938).

Anticipated interdependence resulting from the logistics of co-ordinating tasks can create considerable uncertainty at the outset, "since there is both conflict and co-operation and formal authority structure is lacking." (Litwak and Hylton, 1962, 399).

Chandler (1977), emphasized the significance of co-ordination in hierarchical structures. Transaction cost economists have begun to examine issues such as "temporal specificity," or the importance of timing in receipt of goods or services, that are related to co-ordination costs (Masten, Meehan, and Snyder, 1991).

Genefke (2001), draws the path from the goal of the collaboration over the difficulties inherent in non-closed partnerships to the collaborative fate, which can evolve into a tight-knit co-operation or drift into some un-manageable entity.

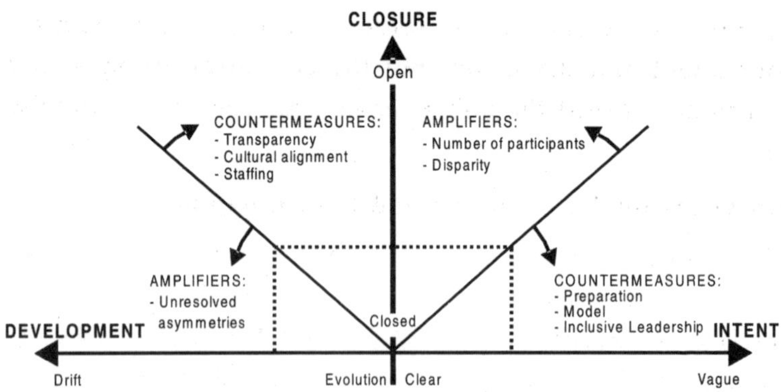

Source: Genefke (2001).

fig. 11.5. The 2001-Model of Factors Influencing Collaborative Success

Any assessment of formal co-operation is based on benefits, costs and risks. Global and local governance establish limits and problems to solve the areas of potential co-operation. Some obstacles to co-operation in clusters are:

Table 11.1
Obstacles to co-operation in clusters

Obstacles to co-operation between firms	*Obstacles to co-operation between firms and supporting institutions*	*Obstacles to co-operation between private and public sector*
Prisoner's dilemma in an unco-operative environment	Difficult relationship between SMEs and associations, in particular chambers	Local governance issues (political rivalry, collective conservatism, and role of chambers)
Costs and risks of co-operation	Common problems of co-operation between firms and supporting institutions	Global governance issues (externally owned firms, foreign buyers)

Source: Amato Neto (2003).

According to Amato Neto (2003), the social and cultural barriers for creating co-operation networks among SME's in Latin America, among others are:

1. Lack of real commitment and confidence among the partners.
2. Lack of resources in terms of information technology (IT).
3. SME's are not used to co-operating with each other.
4. The precarious organizational structure and the specific organizational culture.
5. SME's are in general just concentrated in performing everyday operations and there is no vision for the long run.

To establish a co-operative relationship between firms requires some elements. León (1998), presents different aspects to consider in a trustworthy situation:

- The importance of the pre-existent social relations networks.
- The importance of the mutual respect.
- The learning of the relationship.
- The importance of the reputation of each partner.
- The risks involved in cases of opportunistic behaviour, mainly in terms of the necessity of shouting out some partner from the network.
- The learning of the social "savoir-faire," among others.

A successful collaboration involves a shared mental picture of the dependencies between the participating organizations' work, goal and need systems. A messy picture gives misunderstandings and conflict (Genefke, 2001).

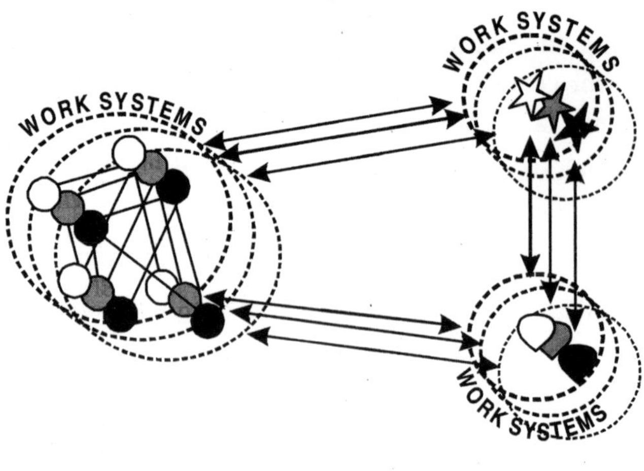

Source: Genefke (2001)

fig. 11.6: A human system view of collaboration

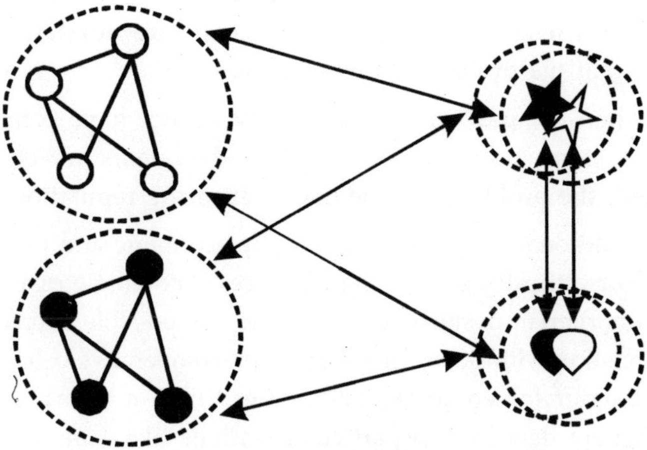

Source: Genefke (2001)

fig. 11.7. Problem of trust in collaboration

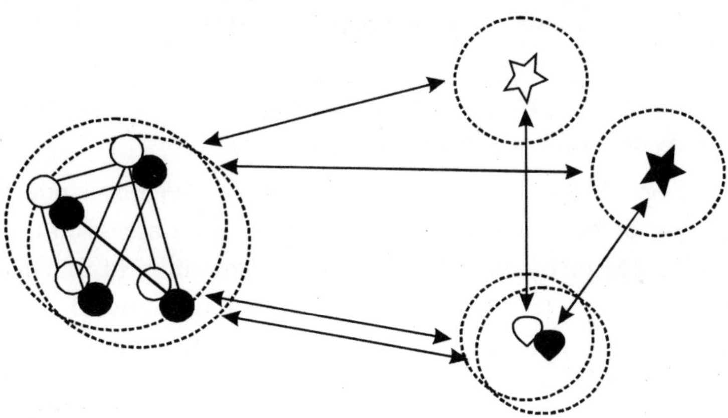

Source: Genefke (2001)

fig. 11.8. The ensuring reputation's problem

A partner who perceives that the two partners' goals and needs are related, but the work-systems' are unrelated can mean that the problem is one of trust.

When the partners perceive they do not have common goal-systems but the work- and need-systems are closely related, the problem may be one of ensuring reputation.

Traditional sets of beliefs held by economic and political elites or attitudes suggesting distance, clientelistic relations, or authoritarian postures, etc. blockade any possible interaction and relation with other actors. This non-co-operative behaviour is a barrier for complex social co-ordination to make and implement decisions in particular settings like communities, firms, Government agencies, etc. Social co-ordination and governance requires more collaborative and co-operative attitudes between the different private and public stakeholders involved, more specifically when public goods are scarce and common-pool resources need to be managed.

To promote co-operation in associative network between popular sectors (workers) and elites (managers), it is necessary to develop cognitive skills. Such network is an arena where outcomes will not be determined by political resources associated by property, class, social status or access to the means of coercion (Chalmers et al., 1997).

Regardless of whether collaboration is driven by strategic motive or by learning considerations to gain access to new knowledge or by embeddedness in a community of practice, connectivity to an inter-organizational network and competence at managing collaborations have become key drivers of a new logic of organizing.

This view of organizations and networks as vehicles for producing, synthesizing and distributing ideas recognizes that the success of firms is increasingly linked to the depth of their ties to organizations in diverse fields. Learning in these circumstances is a complex, multi-level process, involving learning from and with partners under conditions of uncertainty, learning about partner's behaviour and developing routines and norms that can mitigate the risks of opportunism, and learning how to distribute newly-acquired knowledge across different projects and functions Powell (1998).

References

Amato Neto, J. (2003), Cultural requirements for creating small and medium size companies co-operation networks, http://www.prd.usp.br/redecoop/SME'SCultur.pdf.

Barnard, Chester I. (1938), *The Functions of the Executive*, Cambridge, MA: Harvard University Press.

Caves, R. E. and M.E. Porter (1977), "From Entry Barriers to Mobility Barriers: Conjectural Decisions and Contrived Deterrence to New Competition," *The Quarterly Journal of Economics* 91(2), pp. 241-62.

Chalmers, Douglas A., B. Martin Scott and Kerianne Piester (1997), "Associative Networks: New structures of representation for the popular sectors," pp. 544-82 in Douglas A. Chalmers et al. (eds.), *The New Politics of Inequality in Latin America: Rethinking Participation and Representation*, Oxford: Oxford University Press.

Chandler, Alfred D., Jr. (1977), *The Visible Hand: The Managerial Revolution in American Business*, Cambridge, MA: Harvard University Press.

D'Aveni (1994), "*Hypercompetition: Managing the Dynamics of Strategic Manoeuvring*," Free Press.

Easton, Geoff and Luis Araujo (1992), Non-economic exchange in industrial networks in *Industrial Networks: A New View of Reality*, B. Axelsson, and G. Easton (eds.), London: Routledge.

Easton, G., R. Burrell, R. Rothschild, and C. Shearman (1993), *Managers and Competition*, Oxford: Blackwell Business.

Genefke, Jens (2001), *Conjectural Collaboration Theory.*

Goldman, S., R. Nagel and K. Preiss (1994), Agile Competitors —

Concorrência e Organizações Virtuais (ed.), Érica, São Paulo.

Gomes-Casseres, Benjamín (2003), Competitive advantage in alliance constellations, *Strategic Organization*, vol. 1(3), pp. 327-35

Goranson, T. (1995), "Agile Virtual Enterprise — Best Agile Reference Base," http://abse.amef.lehigh.edu/Ex_Proj/MAVE/Mave.html.

Gulati, R. (1995), Does familiarity breed trust, The implications of repeated ties for contractual choice in alliances, *Academy of Management Journal*, 38, pp. 85-112.

Gulati, Ranjay, Tarun Khanna and Nitin Nohria (1994), "Unilateral commitments and the importance of process in alliances," *Sloan Management Review*, 35 (3), pp. 61-69.

Halinen, A., A. Salmi and V. Havila (1999), "From dyadic change to changing business networks: An analytical framework," *Journal of Management Studies* 36(6), pp. 779-94.

Harrigan, K.R. (1985), *Strategies for Joint Ventures*, Lexignton, MA.: Lexigton Books.

Heide, J.B. and A.S. Miner (1992), "The shadow of the future: Effects of anticipated and frequency of contract on buyer-seller co-operation," *Academy of Management Journal*, 35 (2), pp. 265-91.

Helper, Susan (1991), "Strategy and irreversibility in supplier relations: The case of the U.S. automobile industry," *Business History Review*, 65, pp. 781-824.

Hunt, M.S. (1972), Competition in the major home appliance industry, Doctoral dissertation, Harvard University.

Klein, B., R.G. Crawford and A.A.E. Alchian, Vertical Integration, Appropriable Rents, and the Competitive Contracting Process, *Journal of Law and Economics*, XXI(2), October, 1978, pp. 297-326.

Kogut, B. and U. Zander (1992), Knowledge of the firm, combinative capabilities, and the replication of technology. *Organization Science*, 3, pp. 383-97.

Laumann, Edward O., J. Galaskiewicz and P. Marsden (1978), "Community Structure as Interorganizational Linkages," *Annual Review of Sociology*, 4, pp. 455-84.

León, M.E. (1993), Uma anàlise de redes de cooperação das pequenas e médias empresas do setor das telecomunicações, São Paulo, 1993.

Dissertação (Mestrado) – Escola Politécnica, Universidade de São Paulo.

Litwak, Eugene and Lydia F. Hylton (1962), "Interorganizational analysis: A hypothesis on co-ordinating agencies," *Administrative Science Quarterly*, 6, pp. 395-420.

Macneil, I.R. (1978), Contracts: Adjustments of long-term economics relations under classical, neo-classical and relational contract law, North-western University Law.

Piskorski, Misiek (1999), "Allocation to Open and Closed Portfolios," Harvard Business School Working Paper.

Podolny, J.M. and K.L. Page (1998), Network forms of organization, *Annual Review of Sociology*, 24, pp. 57-76.

Porter, M.E. (1979), "The Structure within industries and companies performance," *The Review of Economics and Statistics*, 6, 1, pp. 214-27.

Powell, W. (1998), Learning from Collaboration: Knowledge and Networks in the Biotechnology and Pharmaceutical Industries, *California Management Review*, 40, 3, pp. 223-40.

Powell, Walter, W. (1990), "Neither market nor hierarchy: Network forms of organization," In B. M. Staw and L. L. Cummings (eds.), *Research in Organizational Behaviour*, 12, pp. 295-336, Greenwich, CT: JAI Press.

Smith, Adam (1776), An inquiry into the nature and causes of the wealth of nations, Londres.

Thomas, L.G., III (1996), Dynamic resourcefulness and the hypercompetitive shift, *Organization Science*, 7, pp. 221-42.

Thomas. H., N. Venkatraman (1988), Research on strategic groups: Progress Thomas, L.G., III (1996) and Visser, E.J. and R. Boschma (2002) Learning in districts: novelty and lock-in in a regional context. Revised version of a paper presented at the Euram conference on Innovative Research in Management, May 9-11, 2002, Stockholm. http://econ.geog.uu.nl/visser/tabfig.pdf.

Zaheer, Akbar and Srilata Zaheer (1999), "The Structure of Global Competition: A Network Approach," *Strategic Management Journal*.

12

Co-operation and Conflict Between Firms and Communities

The Cerro de San Pedro Case

José G. Vargas-Hernández

THE aim of this write-up is to analyze relationships of co-operation and conflict between a mining company and the involved communities, New Social Movements and the three levels of Government. The presence of the mining company Minerva San Xavier (MSX) in Cerro de San Pedro has caused a severe social conflict among the inhabitants of San Pedro, Soledad y San Luis and has called the attention of all who are concerned by historic heritage, cultural and environmental issues. At the centre of the controversy is the cheap and efficient technology. Federal and State laws were violated. It is quite evident of the lack of sensitivity of foreign mining companies toward the consequences of their activities upon the communities and environment. This case also shows the lack of negotiation between firms, communities, new social movements and Governments.

Geographical Localization

Cerro de San Pedro is a semi-abandoned historic mining town located in the centre of Mexico, the State of San Luis Potosi. Cerro de San Pedro is a small village 10 miles east of the city of San Luis Potosi, the capital of the State of San Luis Potosi.

Cerro de San Pedro is located in the mountains above the valley of San Luis Potosi and is part of the watershed area for the valley and its major cities. The valley is the source of 73 per cent of the water for the area.

It is a ghost town containing the ruins of shops, churches, estates and a hospital. Today there are only about 100 people living in the Cerro. The Real hamlet covers the hills on both sides of the canyon; large and small houses flank the narrow streets (Cordero de Enciso, 1997). The remains of the 400 year old town are still there, along with an active church and municipal office. Cerro de San Pedro sits in the high desert in the heart of Mexico, the kind of place with lots of road runners and big cacti. 400 years of mining did not alter the original appearance of Real, which is irregular and whose centre is the parish of San Pedro. The artistic and urban development that started in the seventeenth century is represented in Cerro de San Pedro. There are two structures particularly important from the historical heritage perspective. The Church of San Nicolas dates from seventeenth century and San Pedro Apostle which dates from the eighteenth century.

Tarascan Indians settled around the church and they adopted San Nicolás as their patron saint; the avenue in front of the church was used as an exchange and socializing place (Cordero de Enciso, 1997). Two churches were built in Cerro de San Pedro attended by the secular clergy helped by the Franciscan monks, and later by the Augustines who were able to speak Tarascan. The two churches built in the first half of the seventeenth century are identical, though the San Pedro church was later modified. The church of San Pedro is a rare example of a seventeenth century church; and its colouring is in aesthetic harmony with the hill behind it. The San Nicolás de Tolentino church is built on one side of the canyon and has become an urban area. The San Nicolás church kept its primitive appearance of only one nave and barrel vault.

There are several diverse historical monuments protected by the National Institute of Anthropology and History (Instituto Nacional de Antropología e Historia — INAH). The section of town known as "La Colonia de los Gringos" contains what once were company offices and living quarters of the American Smelting and Refining Co.

Legal Background

Since the prehispanic times in México, mining has played an important role in the economic and political history. From 1986 to 1990, the World Bank granted credits to support the structural adjustment economic policies. The credit 3359 supported structural adjustment of the mining sector categorized as B to eliminate environmental requirements and public hearings (Border Ecology Project, 1994). Under a neo-liberal economic policy, amendments to constitutional Article 27, a new Agrarian Law, a Mining Law (1993) and a Foreign Investment Law during the nineties, allow the ejidatarios, originally limited owners of land rights, to change the ownership. Investors now could associate with and ejidatarios, exploit land resources without buying it. The North American Free Trade Agreement (NAFTA) offer advantages and opportunities for investors.

The Mining Law (1993) and the Regulation to the Mining Law (1999) opened to foreign capital areas that were reserved for national investors and defined new rules for the development of national and foreign investments in exploration and exploitation of minerals as activities of public utility. The granting process of mining concessions does not require public hearings and most of the times the affected communities are the last ones to know about the project. There are some references about considering this and other "competitive advantages that offer Mexico compared to their partners in NAFTA" (Bardake, 1993). A mining concession cannot be cancelled for polluting the environment and only can be fined.

Historical Antecedents

The Guachichiles inhabited the area of Cerro de San Pedro hills before the Spanish came. The first original urban plan of Cerro de San Pedro dates from 1412. A couple of missionaries visited the area in the 1570s, and silver was found in the Cerro de San Pedro hills. Cerro de San Pedro used to be one of the biggest mining towns of the colonial New Spain five hundred years ago. Spanish conquistadores carved up the earth as they plundered the town's riches, sending most of the treasure back to Europe. In March 1592, Don Miguel Caldera, a mestizo and Commander of the Spanish army sent a group of miners to reconnoitre the land in the hills of the valley of San Luis Mexquitic and register the mines of the gold and called it Real de San Potosí.

Some 60 discoveries were registered with metals rich in lead. The richest minerals lay near the surface. After 40 years of struggle with the Guachichiles during the last decade of the sixteenth century, the conquistadores convinced the Indians on planting crops and to have a sedentary life. Real de Minas de Cerro de San Pedro was founded in 1583 after several mines in the vicinity began operations, although it was established in 1592. Before that the capital of San Luis Potosi, discovered in the sixteenth century, due to its wealth was baptized by the Spanish as the Potosi. Martín Pérez was one of the discoverers of the mines of el Cerro de San Pedro (SLP), on March 4, 1592 (P.F.V.: Col. Doc., vol. I, p. 254, cited by Del Hoyo, 1979).

Cerro de San Pedro dates back to the sixteenth century and was the original location of the State capital of San Luis Potosi. But at the San Pedro Hill there wasn't enough water to support the town and for washing the metals, so they ended up moving, and the Spaniards founded the village San Luis Potosi in the valley. The San Luis Potosi city's Coat-of-Arms had the Cerro de San Pedro on a blue and gold background with two silver and two gold cross bands, over which is lying Saint Lous King of France, testimony to its mining origins. The mountain is the symbol of their heritage.

Some Spanish families mestizos, mulattos and Indians founded Real de Cerro de San Pedro further up in the sierra which had their own governors and unions. Tlaxcalans, Tarascans ad Otomies were brought in to work in the mines and the cattle ranches. The mining district Cerro de San Pedro has supported various periods of significant mining activity and has seen many production mining campaigns since its discovery over the past 500 years. There are no records of production during the period (1575 to 1660) of mining activity in the Cerro de San Pedro. The mines produced wealth in the first thirty years and some 62 million pesos were paid in rights alone during its first 60 years of existence; that is, some 10 million pesos per year (Cordero de Enciso, 1997).

In 1613, the mayor, Pedro de Salazar had the famous Socavón del Rey built; a horizontal tunnel that gave access to deeper veins which produced around thirty tonnes of silver mixed with gold in a year. After 15 years of mining, the amount of precious metals reduced although there was a "gold affair" that stirred greed among a group of men, who colluded in an enormous fraud and the owners of the Briones mine lost their property, and finally in 1628 the houses in San Luis Potosí's main square were vacated. The last rich mine, the San Cristóbal was closed down in 1656 although there were some bonanzas on El Cerro.

In 1690, the Mayor, Alonso Muñóz Castilblanque, opened the San Cristóbal mountain pass with the help of a loan made to him by the Viceroy, the Count of Galvez, and production increased to one fifth of what it was in 1620. In 1740 one hundred furnaces and sixty mineral crushers still existed in the region.

In the eighteenth century, the area had a reputation for maltreatment of indigenous people and anger. The poverty of the inhabitants of the hill and its surroundings increased and became worst in 1767. The donations of silver given towards the reparation of the church were lost. The expulsion of the Jesuits resulted in an uprising in 1767. Cerro de San Pedro in 1767 was the focal point of a popular insurrection against the excess of Borbonic reforms. The serranos had demands and opposed the removal of the Jesuits but had to surrender. Viceroy Marquis de Croix sent Don José Galvez with 400 soldiers to punish the rebels and their families cruelly, but the serranos managed to have their taxes reduced and the church was repaired and improved.

By the mid eighteenth century, after two hundred years of mining industry, it was underdeveloped and had low productivity due to a lack of capital, technological insufficiency, the limited capacity of the specialized workers, and a shortage of supplies and labour, among other things (Villalba, 2002). A few years later, Don Joseph de Castilla y Loaeza, a knight of Santiago founded the Compañía Patriótica that invested 20,000 pesos and used old-fashioned techniques. In 1773, San Luis Potosí had around twenty mining communities in deplorable state of unproductiveness. By 1774, Cerro de San Pedro had to continue to struggle to restore exploitation of the local mines (Lopez Miramontes y Urrutia, 1980).

In 1816 a horizontal tunnel was built in the Pópulo hill and the Socavón Aventurero de la Victoria, the tunnel of adventure and victory, restarted 60 years later. Compañía Metalúrgica Mexicana owned the railway that extended towards Río Verde to transport the minerals from San Pedro to San Luis Potosi. A major period of mining activity began in 1870 and continued through the early 1950's. In 1930, the American Smelting Company (ASARCO) worked the horizontal tunnel and the work continued until 1948 when the miners' strike broke out and the mine closed down.

By the late 1940s, the gold, lead, iron, manganese and mercury deposits finally began to give out. By the early 1950's it is estimated that approximately 2.5 million ounces of gold and 40 million ounces of silver had been produced from the Cerro San Pedro district. In 1993, the region of Cerro de San Pedro was declared ecologically protected area. Local firms continue to extract limited quantities of minerals from the mines. Visitors can enter La Descubridora, the town's first mine. Guide service is available.

The Conflict

According to the company MSX, the 100 per cent-owned Cerro San Pedro gold and silver heap leach project is located in the historic Cerro San Pedro mining district in the State of San Luis Potosi, Mexico. The presence of MSX in Cerro de San Pedro has caused a severe social conflict among the inhabitants of San Pedro, Soledad y San Luis and has called the attention of all who are concerned by historic heritage, cultural and environmental issues.

MSX argued that its operations would have some benefits: 40 millions of pesos in taxes will be paid to the federation in eight years and would buy materials and provisions from local suppliers which would be the minimum because most of these suppliers would be foreign. The company never referred the mining operations as an ecocide, contamination of watersheds, pollution of air and destruction of the historical heritage. The inhabitants of these communities supported by environmental groups and NGOs argue that the project will pollute sources of fresh water besides perturbing the environment and the ecology of the region.

At the centre of the controversy is the cheap and efficient technology. It is alarming to learn of the use of cyanide and its impact on watersheds, the environment and human health. Lixiviation consists in piling up mineral mixed with cyanide over a platform in such a way that gold will be residual. Cyanide is used for the extraction of metals since 1887 as a chemical reactive to solve gold in water (Logsdon et al., 2003). about 20 per cent of global production is used in a process of lixiviation to get gold. Almost 99 per cent of gold is separated from a rock and it is profitable to spend one tonne of cyanide to extract 6 kilos of gold (Ronco, 2002)

Studies done by Minera San Xavier to evaluate pollution risk to the watershed of the valley of San Luis and to quantify the use of millions of cubic metres of water and its evaporation are insufficient and with a tendency. The hydrological card of INEGI the subterranean waters of San Luis Potosí and Cerro de San Pedro are the same in the geo-hydrological zone. The daily use of 16 tonnes of cyanide and 32,000 tonnes of rock material that would require one million cubic metres of water per year would have residuals of cyanide, heavy metals, toxic material and mercury stem which can contaminate the watershed favoured by inclination of land and put population at risk.

According to the Environmental Impact Manifestation presented by MSX, there should be erosion by deforestation, alteration of drainage patterns, cancellation of productive activities, pollution caused by deposits of toxic residuals and severe, irreversible and permanent damages. The Manifestation of the Environmental Impact of the company considers that "the impact is significant and adverse for the extraction of water" (page 16). Ninety per cent of water consumption comes from the valley of San Luis which can be contaminated by the cyanide used in the lixiviation process (Martínez Ramos, 2004).

In the last 25 years, the major causes of cyanide spill-over have been: 76 per cent due to imperfections in the lixiviation yard, 18 per cent due to pipes and 6 per cent due to transportation accidents. (State Environmental Resource Centre, 2004). Mining companies have caused ecological catastrophes that have provoked reactions of civil society groups and governments around the world. Governments of many countries have prohibited open pit mining exploitation using cyanide. (Governor's office, 2003; Friends of the Earth y Oxfam America, with support from Mineral Policy Centre, 2003).

The company had bought up buildings in the village to be used for offices. The open-pit silver and gold mine planned for the area would have a devastating effect and is being challenged in court by environmentalists. Environmentalists have a long battle against the company Minera San Xavier, a subsidiary of Canada's Metallica Resources, that plans to build an open-pit silver and gold mine that would decapitate the mountain that looms behind the town of Cerro de San Pedro. In a post-production model developed by the company, the area looks like a lunar landscape. The ore-processing plant, where the toxins would be used, sits just 20 minutes from San Luis Potosí, the capital of the State and home of about one million people.

Excavation for the mine will take place in an area of 67.7 hectares, digging a crater 1,150 ft. deep and a half-mile wide to gain access to the 90,500 oz. of gold and 2.1 million oz. of silver the mountain could yield each year for the next decade. The mountain will be demolished and in its place will be large deep pits filled with the residue of the mining process. Soil cover will be lost in an area of approximately 500 hectares.

The pit is only about 600 metres from the town square and the tunnels from the old town go under the church and the square. If the mine project goes forward, a 1,150-ft., half-mile crater would be blasted at the top of the mountain that, sits behind the town of Cerro de San Pedro, Mexico. The proposed mine would destroy the historic remains of the old town and destroy the environment because of the cyanide leaching and potentially poison the water of San Luis Potosi. Greenpeace says cyanide poses a high risk in the mining plans by a Canadian firm in the Mexican district of Cerro de San Pedro. The firm Cambior has been involved in two most disastrous cyanide spills in mining history. Millions of litres of water were contaminated.

The project would entail moving part of the town and its historic buildings, but the people don't want to move. To avoid damage to the buildings, the company plans to move the municipal buildings and the centuries old church another 600 metres away. The company would destroy the environment for a yield that would last only 6-8 years. MSX only vaguely gave an outline on the environmental-impact report of how it would restore the mountaintop, clean up the massive piles of bulldozed waste, protect rare plants and wildlife like the biznaga cactus and the desert tortoise, and safeguard the town's sixteenth-century structures. Actual profit from the exploitation would be low in comparison to the amount of destruction and permanent ecological damage that would result.

Most troubling was the company's unclear plan for the management and disposal of the toxins, including cyanide, that are used in gold mining. The daily use of 13 tonnes of explosives composed of nitrate "Anful" will produce great quantities of dust which can cause irreversible ills. 640 millions of m^3 of cyanide materials would be residuals covering a surface of 178 hectares which will not allow agricultural or cattle activities for generations. The potential poisoning of the watershed lands alone would have dramatic consequences for the inhabitants of San Luis Potosi. (Campbell, 2004). However, MSX argues that it has clarified its plans and is implementing the 100 changes suggested by a group of Mexican academics who studied the environmental-impact report.

In spite of the fact that permits have been cancelled, the company has huge trucks, big tanks and workers on site, and the land has been cleared for future use in an environmentally protected area, so the clearing is obviously illegal. A test drill resulted in the street collapsing because of the tunnels under the street, and the company had "repaired the damage" by dumping a load of gravel. If the project goes forward, MSX would add about 170 jobs to its existing staff of 34 to work on the mine, but the new jobs will require education and training that people from Cerro de San Pedro often lack. Some qualified residents would receive temporary housing a few miles from town. Other villagers could choose to stay here and receive a monthly payment based on the typical wage here, from MSX that could be used to strengthen their houses to protect them from the blasts.

The company violated federal and State laws. Among federal laws:

- Presidential Decree of June 2, 1961 which forbids extraction of water in the valley of San Luis Potosi.
- Article 35 of Federal Law of fire arms and explosives. Store and consumption of explosives is only 50 metres from town instead of at least one kilometre.
- The Agrarian Law establishes the obligation of the agrarian authority to staff and protect the ejidtarios. The Company leased ejidal lands from fake ejidatarios.

State Laws violated are:

- Article 7 of the Environmental Law of San Luis Potosi which does not give power to the governor to authorize licences of land use. The Governor exceeded his authority to grant authorization of land use in May 2000.
- Article 15 of the State Constitution of San Luis establishes the right of citizens to enjoy a healthy environment and to prevent and combat environmental pollution.

Final Remarks and Conclusions

Mining activities are perceived as the main factor of marginal regions and depressed zones. Mining concessions granted by Mexican government are centralized, brief and against public hearings, in such a way that affected groups and communities cannot react immediately and mobilize against potential risks and dangers or negotiate rights and interests.

The Canadian firm Metallica Resource Incorporated was at the point to destroy part of the environmental, cultural and historic heritage of the country, although there were three judicial resolutions to halt operations granted by different authorities upon request of the ejidatarios who, have rights to own the land and had been dispossessed. It was assumed that operations of the firm were in complicity with the Federal, State and local governments. The environmental and health risks would have side-effects on more than one million people living in the localities of Cerro de San Pedro, la Soledad and San Luis Potosi. Norms were violated by the transnational when it started operations without obtaining legal permit of construction and operations and authorization to manage and to store explosives.

Exploitation of gold through open pit mining and use of cyanide will lead to destruction of natural environments and irreversible geomorphologic alterations, distortions of watersheds, reduction on the quality of available water, transport accidents of dangerous substances and spill-over during the exploitation, irreversible destruction of natural scenery and generation of deposits of highly risky pollutant materials which have social, cultural and environmental impacts at short, medium and long terms (Montenegro, 2004).

The negotiation agenda and international mobilization around the debate over the concept of sustainable development and defence of the environment is a paradigm presented as a model of co-operation and consensus where the needs of all are incorporated and the greater have a compromise to support the weaker. Intervention of the State and international community is imperative to benefit the public interest and the common good and to control forces of the State and to achieve more equity among populations together with the implementation of more sustainable production and consumer patterns.

It is quite evident of the lack of sensitivity of foreign mining companies toward the consequences of their activities upon the communities and environment. To a certain extent, we disagree with Sánchez-Mejorada (2000) who argues that facts will not convince the fringe environmental activists, and the best defence is to address all environmental concerns and to have an aggressive community relations programme that will put the facts before the general population that will be affected by the project. Keeping a low profile will rarely work when being assaulted by activists on all fronts. But, an aggressive community relations programme will escalate the conflict.

This case also shows the lack of negotiation between firms, communities, new social movements and governments. Information about externalities and future costs of company activities is crucial but more crucial is formulation and implementation of more sensitive policies to avoid damage of the environment, biodiversity and health of population. Governmental institutions must be aware that their decisions may affect the community quality of life of actual and future generations only for a small increment in economic growth and large increase in private benefits of a small group of investors.

Abbrevations

INAH	—	Instituto Nacional de Antropología e Historia
NAFTA	—	North American Free Trade Agreement
ASARCO	—	American Smelting Company
MSX	—	Minera San Xavier

13

Educational Systems Under Reform
A Comparative Perspective

Adela Coman

Introduction

Recent dramatic changes in Eastern and Central Europe raise new scholarly interest about this region. Higher education is a topic for study for a variety of reasons, out of which two are particularly significant.

First, as the ideological adherence to one prevailing ideology, in this case Marxism-Leninism and its national derivations, has been abolished in the process of democratic revolutionary transformations, which in Romania had a dramatic character due to the specific nature of the communist regime, the role and functioning of the society's institutions have to be redefined. Reform of higher education was expressed since the very beginning of the call for revolutionary transformations.

Secondly, the university and other higher education institutions play a significant role in search of the new identity of the changing society. They are *per se* related to the past, since one of their main functions is to serve as repositories of knowledge, ideas and cultural traditions of the country and its people. Their own position *vis-à-vis* society is often related to their institutional heritage. Therefore, any realistic educational strategy has to, or at least should, take into account the historical past of the educational system and its academic traditions. At the same time, their foundation, mission and governance was always strongly related not only to the educational, but also to the political, social and economic doctrine of the country and its evolution. Therefore, *a better understanding of higher education can often be one of the keys* to more general conclusions about the directions of the national or regional development, as the universities are frequently called to serve as agents of social and economic transformations or are subject to policy changes indicating major changes within society. As Romania is now undertaking such major changes, the study of its higher education is particularly relevant.

The evolution of the Romanian higher education, especially between 1948 and mid-1960's has been subject to significant distortions in Romanian academic publications. Studies on higher education in Eastern and Central Europe have not reflected the diversity and specific traditions of Romanian higher education. A closer look at the period 1948-62 may help us all understand the democratic Revolution of 1989 and why students and some academics played an important role, confirming that higher education can be, in certain conditions, a hot-bed of political changes. But higher education can also be, as will be shown in this paper, used by those in power for other purposes than society's educational, professional, cultural and scholarly development.

Tibet is another example of the idea that when used as a political right, education can be an instrument of domination and in the end, it may sometimes contribute not to the development of the region/country, but to the disappearance/ destruction of a civilization.

During the four decades of Chinese occupation of Tibet, for educational and professional reasons the younger generation has been tempted to learn Chinese rather than Tibetan, and as a result is assimilating Chinese values. Among Tibetans in exile, the youth are tempted to pay more attention to the English language than their own, because they find that English is more marketable. Fortunately, at present, there are still a large number of patriotic first-generation exiles who have sacrificed their personal interests to work for the preservation of Tibetan culture and language. But, for how long will they be successful? Is the harm done irreparable or not?

In the end of this paper I present some personal reflections on possible directions of a new post-communist strategy in Romanian higher education, based on the previous developments of my comparative perspective and present-day discussions.

The Romanian Higher Education — A Short History

The general conditions under which Romanian higher education system functioned in the initial years after the Second World War, needs to be seen in the context of the insecurity dominating the first postwar period in Romania. The country was, practically, under the *Soviet military occupation*. But, despite the financial burden of the postwar reconstruction and severely limited resources, there were some positive developments in Romanian higher education.

For example, in the University of Jassy, the number of students increased from 2,390 in the academic year 1944-45, to 3,306 in 1947-48, and the tuition fees was made almost symbolic. The number of students in all higher educational institutions reached around 54,000 in 1946-47, which was more than twice their number in 1937-38. In 1946-47, one in five students received free lodging and maintenance. In 1945, in order to democratize access to higher education, the differences between the vocationally oriented, commercial and industrial *lycees*, and the theoretical *lycees* where humanities and science subjects were taught at a more theoretical and advanced level, sometimes assured by university teachers, were reduced by the introduction of the same curriculum and the transformation of those *lycees* into the so-called "unified gymnasium." After the third grade, students, according to their academic aptitude and choice, could continue their education in the same school or in a specialized *lycee.* Graduates of both types of *lycee* received a "baccalaureate certificate" which gave them the right to seek admission to higher education.

The major reason for the greatly delayed developments of the Romanian academic institutions was that the general political and ideological conditions under which Romanian higher education had to function changed dramatically when, against public desire, but *with the support of the Soviet Union, the political power passed into the hands of the communists.* The Soviet military administration gave such control to the "progressive forces" of the National Democratic Front and, in doing so, were allowed to form a new Government, as the earlier elections were falsified. The new Government was headed by Petru Groza, a non-communist, one of the leaders of a small peasants' party, who was very sympathetic to communists. The actions of the new Government soon revealed the intentions to establish the foundations for a "people's democratic" system in Romania. One of the consequences would be the introduction of the new conceptual framework of a so-called *"people's model" of higher education.*

After King Michael's abdication in 1948, imposed by the communist-led forces and the Soviet military administration, the country was renamed the Romanian People's Republic. A new Constitution adopted in 1948 gave complete power to the Communist Party. Its actions, such as the total elimination of any political opposition, the forced disinvestment of privately owned businesses, the land reform followed by forced collectivization and central planning and expansion of heavy industry, revealed that its real intention was the establishment of a political, economic and social system based on the communist ideology. Deriving from this doctrine, measures concerning the objectives, tasks and structure of higher education were soon to be drastically enforced.

The reorganization of Romanian higher education according to the "people's model" of higher education was introduced by a decree of the Presidium of the Great National Assembly which was adopted in August, 1948, entitled the *Law of the Educational Reform* (1). The model was based on the principle that *education is state-provided, laic, based on a realistic and scientific basis, and on the ideological principles of Marxism-Leninism* (Sipos, 1955). Three main "orientations" were to guide the development of higher education: *Change of the ideological context in teaching and research, increase of access to higher education of the "working class children" and education of students in the "spirit of patriotism and socialist internationalism"* (Pascu, 1971). In reality, it provided a uniform, highly-centralized system, intended to maintain a strong link between higher education and the needs of the national economy. It emphasized political supervision of the students, teachers and research workers to assure their adherence to communist ideology and the decisions of the Romanian Workers' Party. In many respects, decisions were based on the Soviet model, such as decisions related to the role and mission of the universities and the specialization of higher education institutions, the central accreditation commission on academic diplomas, the "aspirantura" system of postgraduate studies, the "faculties for the working class," the reorganization of the academy of sciences, etc.

The basic tasks for higher education were said to be the training of intermediate and higher specialists needed to administrate the people's democracy and to build socialism, the training of teachers needed in the development of a "new and democratic people's model" of education, the training of research workers and artists. Thus, the new law combined higher education development with presumed manpower needs, and with a conviction that Marxism-Leninism must guide the progress in higher education and science. In the words of Gheorghe Gheorghiu-Dej (1901-65), who was at that time First Secretary of the Romanian Workers' Party and the Chairman of the State Council, the new policy represented a complete rejection of the old "liberal-bourgeois" idea of education and replaced it with a "new type of education," corresponding to the principles of the people's democracy, so that it would become the "principal source of cadres for the construction of socialism" (Gheorghiu-Dej, 1952). The replacement of the pre-war intelligentsia and the opening of higher education to the "sons and daughters of workers and farmers" was also one of the main objectives of the "Cultural Revolution" which the Romanian Communist Party carried out between 1948 and 1952.

This was to be done, partly by introducing *criteria of class background* and *political screening* to the admission to higher education and to academic appointments. The Romanian Cultural Revolution was meant to contribute to the formation of a new socialist intelligentsia (Imangulova, L.M., 1958). It was expected that the new socialist elite, through professional and ideological training, would develop a capacity for materialistic and dialectical thinking. In other words, it meant that the "elite" would be more eager to accept the policy of the communist party. The relationship between the intelligentsia and the socialist State would also express the unity of professional endeavour with obedience to the party's teaching in professional and social activities, as well as in private life.

This stance might sound quite empty nowadays. But, it should not be forgotten that such political dogmas, often supported by the interpretation of "scientific materialism" repeatedly encouraged brutal measures such as *forced dropping of studies* and *aggressive ideological indoctrination* of students and staff. Moreover, it brought personal tragedies for those students and academics who were affected by such repressive measures because of their social origin, views or convictions. In most cases, the repressive measures introduced by the communists were met only with minor opposition. However, dissent was particularly difficult since the regime had eliminated all non-communist, even if symbolic, political organizations. Besides, unlike some other countries in the region, its religious institutions, among which was *the dominant Orthodox Church, had too easily given up any form of opposition* to the ideology of the communist State. In this climate, any "politically unreliable" academics, particularly members of the law and humanities faculties, were forced to retire or were dismissed from their positions.

The new people's regime eliminated any religious participation of the religious denominations as well as secular private bodies in the "people's higher education." The elimination of the theological faculties/specializations from the universities was one of the consequences of the new policy. These faculties were amalgamated into the Academic Institute of Theology in Bucharest, which was placed under the administration of the Office of Cults and which was not regarded as part of the higher education system. Theology then practically disappeared from Romanian higher education, both as a field of study and as a subject for research. This "organizational" change in Romanian universities coincided with the founding of "Stefan Gheorghiu" Higher Party School since the late 1960's officially known as the Academy for Training and Development of the Leading Cadres. It was ascending to an academic institution and an integral part of the higher education system. In a short time, it became an elitist training centre of the party and State officials, journalists and managers. Since the beginning of 1970's, it was also in charge of updating courses for teachers of social and political sciences, who have been since required to take them every three years.

The law of 1948 introduced the vision of higher education which was supposedly "placed on democratic, popular, realistic and scientific basis" and led to profound *changes in the role of the university and the modification of the structure of the higher education system* and its institutions. Based on the Soviet policy of the 1930's, the universities were assigned the task of developing an *education focused on theory* while more professional specialized higher education was provided in separate higher education institutions. University researchers, along with those in the research institutes of the Academy of the Romanian People's Republic (which replaced the Romanian Academy), were to concentrate on more theoretical, non-utilitarian types of programmes. This was similar to the tasks assigned to the reorganized academies of sciences. This reorientation of the university's mission and emphasis on specialization led also to the modification of the faculty structure in the Romanian universities. It was done through the transfer of the faculties of medicine, pharmacy and veterinary medicine into separate academic establishments known as "institutes." Some of them, with sufficiently large teaching and research staff and student bodies were later called "academies." Moreover, as a part of this process, new, specific discipline-oriented faculties were created by the breaking down of multi-section "sciences" and "humanities" faculties.

Another "organizational" change introduced in the context of the "people's model" of higher education was the so-called *"faculty for the working class,"* which was also copied from the Soviet academic system (Zavorykin, A.A., 1970). For example, between 1953 and 1955, such a faculty functioned along the University in Jassy. It provided full-time and evening courses for a group of model workers called "labour heroes" in such fields of study as Romanian history, mathematics, physics, chemistry, natural sciences, geography, technical design and sports. Its graduates took the State examination which became equivalent to the traditional first university-level degree-licenta. Unfortunately, it is difficult to evaluate the effectiveness of these educational innovations, but it shows again how *academic institutions were used by the new regime in its desire to reward efficiency drives or certain types of behaviour among workers.*

The reform of higher education of 1948 changed also the *governance of higher education institutions.* The faculties, still headed by deans, were now divided into larger units called "departments," but some of them were allowed to keep the traditional name of "chairs." A more significant change for their institutional governance was the reduction of the role of the academic Senate to narrowly defined academic problems. A collectivist approach to governance led to the creation of a new entity — the Academic Board — which was composed of the rector, the vice-rectors, deans of faculties, chairmen of departments, the administrative director, the representative of the organization cell at the particular institution of the

Romanian Workers' Party, representatives of local industrial enterprises and representatives of the student association. This board which was a combination of traditional academic Senate and of a board of trustees was, in fact, an organ of the "nomenklatura." Central political supervision and ideological conformity replaced any traces of collective academic freedom and academic autonomy.

Students in the Early Years of "People's Model"of Higher Education

A distinctive feature of the "people's model" of higher education was its closer integration with the real and alleged needs of the economy, the central and local public administration, as well as the "requirements" of socialist education, culture and arts. As a result of the "integration," the number of students in all institutions of higher education had substantially increased – from 48,676 students in the academic year 1948-49, to 77,663 students in the academic year 1955-56, and to 81,206 students in 1956-57, the highest level attained in the 1950's. Students in the "socialist" universities, reorganized according to the reform of 1948, represented some 30 per cent of the total student population in the academic year 1948-49. Even if, in the following years, their number was growing due to a great extent of part-time studies, the percentage of students in the universities in total student enrolment was mainly declining. In the academic year 1955-56, it was as low as 18,150 students, approximately 23.4 per cent of the total student population. It can hardly be said that the doors of higher education had been "widely opened" as it was often claimed by the communist regime (*Romanian Statistical Yearbook, 1948–1958*).

In the following years, a reversal of the declining trend was achieved but, again, mainly by increasing the number of students in part-time studies. They included "evening" courses and "correspondence" courses. Part-time studies were seen as a form of enhancing opportunity for university studies for those who were from the working class and were academically disadvantaged in the past.

In 1957, the Communist Party and the Government set a long-term objective that at least 40 per cent of all students should come from a working class background and about 30-35 per cent should belong to families of farmers (Gheorghiu-Dej, 1952). It was the last time when such political policy goals were set in relation to Romanian higher education.

These trends might reflect the policy dilemma of the communist regimes when adopting the "people's model" of higher education. On the one hand, the universal need to observe a certain quality of training provided in the system of higher education by complying to a more rigorous observance of the academic and graduation requirements, independent of the form of study. On the other hand, the ideologically motivated commitment to "open the door" and admit more students from the lower classes to replace the old intellectual stratum and train the new "people's intelligentsia." These were to be achieved by the introduction of *part-time studies* and the *elimination* of the selection by *"ability to pay,"* as a prerequisite to benefit from university-level education.

One of the main characteristics of the "people's model" of higher education was that there were *no fees.* It was free as what was frequently used in international propaganda.

Contrary to the general policy adopted in other Eastern European socialist countries, in Romania educational fees were not abolished until the beginning of the academic year 1961-62 (Lapidus, Gail W., 1976). The fees, established by the Ministry of Education and the Ministry of Finance, were modest but not insignificant. The annual fee represented 60 per cent of the monthly average salary which was of approximately 850 lei per month in the mid 1950's. In addition, there were relatively small fees for enrolment, examination and graduate certification.

Altogether, the first decade of Romania's experience with the "people's model" of higher education was marked by profound transformations whose main result was the destruction of the pre-communist structure of higher education, its system of governance and its institutional administration. Academic freedoms and autonomy, whose bottom line is the freedom to research, teach and publish without being subject to victimization because of the nature or content of what is researched, were considered as being incompatible with the new role assigned by the political authorities to higher educational establishments and research organizations. The content of studies and research were subject to scrutiny from the perspective of its economic and ideological "usefulness."

Education for What?

Tibet has had four distinctly different sets of rights served by successive educational systems: one derived from *religious influences*, one intended *to open the country to a larger world*, one designed *to serve ideology* and one dedicated *to restoration and renovation of the traditional culture.*

The educational system in Tibet is examined here at three levels: the first deals with the educational system that was prevalent in traditional Tibet before the occupation of Tibet in 1959. The second part looks at the politics of the Chinese in the development of modern education in traditional Tibet. The third part focuses on the use of the Tibetan education system as a propaganda tool during the Chinese invasion of

Tibet which began in 1950 and later, as a tool to indoctrinate Tibetans into Communism. It also addresses the issue of the curricula and the use of Chinese as a medium of instruction, from the secondary to the university level.

Religious Influences

The secular educational system in Tibet was traditional rather than modern, and emphasis was more on Tibetan literature and handwriting and on the study of ecclesiastical and temporal treatises (Mackerras, 1995, Dorjee, 1977). There were two types of schools: Government financed and private. The Government-run schools admitted only children of aristocrats and Government officials. The general public had no access to them, except by becoming monk-officials.

In the eighth century, the concept of private schools seems to have spread. It was common practice for a teacher, usually a monk or a male retired Government official, to use his own home as a school. Due to the lack of records, it is unclear as to how many of these schools existed in Tibet. In private schools, admission was open to children of both rich and poor families and the admission prerogative remained solely with the teacher, who also acted as a school administrator. School fees were unknown, and education was mostly free. Students gave gifts, and rich students donated cash to teachers during the Tibetan New Year. The practice of not charging fees reveals an old-age belief that *to impart wisdom is good for the community*, with students giving gifts as a sign of gratitude. With this practice, rich families did enjoy extra opportunity because they had the choice to lure better teachers if the teacher in the village or town was not to their satisfaction. Obviously, children from poor families, because of financial constraints, could only make use of the school in their village or otherwise remain without education if they were denied admission or if there was a lack of local schools.

The Chinese invasion and occupation of Tibet in the early 1950s led to the virtual destruction of most of the 2,242 monasteries and nunneries (Avedon, 1986, Barnett, 1989), which were the main source of education in traditional Tibet. Tens of thousand of monks suffered and died at the hands of the Chinese during that time, and continue to do so (Asia Watch, 1990). Contrary to conventional belief, the destruction of most of the monasteries took place long before the Cultural Revolution. Even today, under the recently introduced "strike hard campaign," hundreds of Buddhist monks have been expelled and many were tortured in prison for political as well as religious reasons.

Education for Ideology: Occupied Tibet

With the advent of communism in Tibet, from 1950 onwards, *the Chinese opened schools to spread the communist ideology and power base.* In the initial period, the communists made an astute movement by recruiting from the upper strata and aristocratic families (Norbu, 1997). The main thrust of Chinese policy was to give special attention to the prominent members of the Tibetan Government, "so as to use the influence and prestige they commanded among their own people to facilitate the successful performance of the mass work" (Walt van Praag, Michael C., 1987). *The Communist Chinese Party paid silver coins as a reward to anyone joining the party,* and everyone had a price. For example, most of the 82 students in the Sakya Primary School, children of aristocrats and officials, were paid 30 silver coins per month to join the school and study communism (Norbu, 1997). There was initial euphoria, generated with the imposition of communism, because people thought that an egalitarian society would replace the hierarchical society of traditional Tibet.

In practice, the Chinese did not make substantial changes in the socio-political structure of Tibet. Instead, the communists and some Tibetans were making strategic moves to recruit powerful families to control villages with their support, rather than empowering the poor families. Even the aristocrats, who were supposed to be the vanguard of the "Peaceful Liberation," gave no chance to the commoners (Norbu, 1997). Ordinary people rose against the Chinese occupation of Tibet. The largest expression of their dissatisfaction was shown in the famous revolt of March, 1959. Another group unhappy with the spread of communism was the monasteries. Their suspicion was based on the belief that communists were enemies of religion and would destroy their culture and tradition. This is, in fact, what the Chinese and their Tibetan supporters did, and this reinforced the suspicions of ordinary Tibetans which continue today.

During the Cultural Revolution, any sense of minority consciousness was suppressed; in Tibet, "books of blind faith" was the label applied to works on Tibetan language, grammar and culture. In effect, everything about Tibetan society was condemned as backward. In this milieu, use of the Tibetan language in schools took a nosedive. For example, when there were 70,000 Tibetans and fewer than 40 Chinese in one particular area, the Chinese language was still used in the schools (Sangay, 1991). Tibetans grew up unable to write independently in either Chinese or Tibetan.

The era of Deng Xiaoping brought some changes in the outlook of the Chinese Government toward the Tibetan people. Deng's pragmatism was reflected in his *education policy,* which was keyed on *supporting China's economic development.* He declared that, other than independence, anything could be discussed to find a solution to the Tibetan issue.

Literacy and Modern Schools

The Chinese Government claims to have made "tremendous efforts to promote the culture and education of the minority nationalities," (State Council, 1992), adding that farmers and herdsmen enjoy free boarding and education. Indeed, *education in Tibet is free under the Chinese Government as it was in traditional Tibet* where school fees were also unknown. Free schools do give ordinary Tibetans better access to primary education as compared to the limited availability of schools in traditional Tibet. So, the number of students going to school has increased markedly; there are 93 secondary schools with 33,915 students and 3,500 primary schools. This is definitely a great leap forward from only three Government schools in traditional Tibet.

But, this number of schools seems to show a different picture when analyzed closely. An independent Chinese source shows that in 1986 out of 2,451 schools, only 451 were financed by the Government, the rest being community-run schools (Li, 1986). When 451 Government-financed schools are compared with the destruction of almost 2,242 religious institutions, the main source of traditional learning, the Chinese Government has established only a quarter of the number of institutions it destroyed. This is not to justify the monasteries. Rather, the interpretation should be limited to infrastructure accessibility to education in traditional Tibet which is significant because the Chinese Government claims to have "liberated" and replaced the old system of Tibet with a modern one (State Council, 1992).

In fact, there is a *huge disparity of budget allocations for China and Tibet*. China spends 19 per cent of its total Government spending for education, compared to about half in Tibet. Moreover, the figures for Tibet include expenditures for separate schools and facilities for the large number of Chinese students studying there, the large sum spent on 13,000 Tibetan students sent to schools in inland China, and the salaries and facilities for the incoming Chinese teachers and other educational staff.

An interesting development is the pattern of *school distribution*, which tracks the Chinese population expansion. According to Bass (1990), the better Government-funded schools are located in urban areas where the Chinese are the majority. The primary as well as secondary schools are unevenly distributed throughout Tibet. There are 14 secondary schools in urban areas, half of which had senior departments. At the country level, there are 61 schools, of which 11 per cent had senior departments. In rural areas, there were two junior secondary schools, but no senior ones. It is clear that *a major beneficiary of secondary education in Tibet is the Chinese population.*

Chinese as the Medium of Instruction

The National Minority Law's provision that the language of the majority be used as a medium of instruction (art. 37) is commonly ignored. Even if Tibetans constitute the absolute majority in a particular class or school, Chinese is used as the medium of instruction. The exception used to be the Tibetan primary schools, where all the courses are taught in Tibetan, but recently these have begun to teach in the Chinese language. According to a senior official in Tibet, this is because many parents feel that the sole use of Tibetan may not help their children's future. As a result, the regional Government has reversed its 1987 decision, and both the Tibetan and Chinese language are being taught (*China Daily*, 1997). Tibetan is regarded as "unscientific and not sufficient" to translate all the courses. Of course, by this reasoning, English rather than Chinese would be indicated. Tibetan schools in India do, in fact, use English as well as Tibetan and Hindi, not only for students at the primary level, but also at higher levels.

The use of Chinese as the medium of instruction in Tibetan schools has a *negative impact on Tibetan students*, especially because Chinese is the language of the examinations (Tsering, 1997). Students with native fluency in Chinese have a clear advantage over Tibetans. No matter how hard Tibetans work, it is difficult for them to surpass Chinese students in their own language. According to Li (1986), almost 90 per cent of Tibetan primary school students fail to be admitted to middle school. The national examination is repeated for high school and for college admission. The *drop-out rate* of Tibetans continues at every level of examination (Tsering, 1997). For example, according to a Chinese Government source, the enrolment was 63,488 students in the first year of primary school with a sharp fall to 12,594 by the final year of primary school (*Tibet Statistical Yearbook*, 1995). This drop of almost 80 per cent of students shows the seriousness of the situation.

Thus, like lower stream classes 8-12 throughout China, *Tibetan classes became part of a system, justified by the strategy of gaining maximum returns*, that assigns them poorer facilities and less qualified teachers. Tibetan students who embark on a secondary school career must not only contend with learning in a second language, but also with inferior teaching. The majority of Tibetan students, unless they have connections, will fail in the lower stream classes. The failure rate and limited opportunities of Tibetan students discourage them from pursuing higher education. They are made to feel that there are no bright prospects so long as the examinations conducted to test their abilities are in the Chinese language. This becomes a vicious cycle for Tibetans, from which there is no escape, unless the Tibetan language is used in selection examinations as legally required under the Law of Regional Minority.

Therefore, intentionally or not, *the structure of the school system works in a systematic manner to discriminate against Tibetans,* and those who persist are left with few options but to be assimilated into the Chinese culture.

Assimilation and Use of "Guanxi" or Connection

Another systematic way to assimilate Tibetans has been by *sending students to China* (Bass, 1990). Every year, the top-ranking students from primary schools are selected to go to either special Tibetan classes attached to local secondary schools, or 18 other "Tibetan Secondary Schools" in China (Kormondy, 1995). There is no doubt that facilities in the schools in China are better and students get a better education there. However, Tibetans do not necessarily enjoy all the facilities available to Chinese students.

The policy of retaining Tibetan students in China even in the case of sickness and depriving them of the chance for education in Tibet weakens the Chinese Government's claim of good intentions in sending students to China.

There are two other ramifications of sending Tibetan students to China. First, since 1984, a significant proportion of the educational funding allocated to Tibet has been spent for students sent to study in central China. Instead, much of the money could have been used to train teachers or improve the already existing facilities of Tibetan schools in Tibet. Secondly, the students, being very young, return home substantially assimilated into Chinese culture and find it difficult to reintegrate into Tibetan culture. A remedy was proposed by the Panchen Lama, who suggested that older students, who are in a better position to understand Tibetan language and culture, be sent to China (Panchen Lama, 1991). The Chinese Government, instead of responding positively to the Tibetans, increased the number of Tibetan students sent to China from 4,000 in 1986, to 13,000 in 1994 (*Beijing Review*, 1995). When 13,000 of the total 33,915 secondary students go to China, then automatically the standard of education as well as educational expenditure within Tibet is seriously affected. In this situation, Tibetan schools in Tibet are not likely to improve. Tibet will continue to remain backward, and the education system will not show significant improvement. With no alternative, some parents without "Guanxi" or connection take risks and send their children to be educated in schools in the Tibetan exile community.

The low standard of education and drain of resources are exacerbated by *the illegal use of connections to get Han children admitted in Tibetan schools* (Bass, 1990). The low pass mark for the secondary school graduation examination and the university entrance examination in Tibet has led to a situation where less able children from central China enrol, unofficially, in the final year of Tibetan secondary schools in order to pass the graduation examination. Since they are likely to get a higher mark for the school graduation exam in Tibet than they would at their own school in China, where standards are generally higher, they improve their chances of getting a place at university or a good job in urban areas. However, this influx of below-average secondary school students not only lowers the academic levels of secondary education; it is a drain of resources which are already unable to meet the needs of children in Tibet (Tibet Information Network, 1993a).

The use of "Guanxi" continues in the four modern universities in Tibet: Tibet University, the Institute of Nationalities, the Agriculture and Animal Husbandry College and the Tibetan Medical College. It should be noted that the establishment by the Chinese of these colleges in Tibet is a welcome sign of progress. Moreover, the departure from the traditional concept of monastic universities is definitely a contribution that the Chinese have made in Tibet. But, these universities seem to serve the interest of the Chinese better than the Tibetans, with a disproportionate representation of the Chinese in the student body.

The use of "Guanxi" and systematic discrimination is made clear by *the division of courses*. In Tibet University, science courses were allocated 60 per cent of seats, although only 40 per cent of the total applicants opted for the science courses, while arts or humanities get just the opposite, namely, 40 per cent per cent of seats for 60 per cent of total applicants (Tibet Information Network, 1994). More seats are allocated for science and commerce because Chinese students prefer to take those courses, while arts or humanities are predominantly left for Tibetans. However, in technical, financial, business and science areas, all vital to the Tibetan economy, as much as 50 per cent of the places were taken by Han Chinese. At Tibet University, although 60 per cent of total places are allocated for science courses, out of 135 seats only one Tibetan qualified in the general competition, while 45 could be admitted only after their marks were adjusted, because they scored the least among the selected students. It can be said that although the adjustment does help Tibetans to get into higher education, it does not seem to make much long-term difference, because even these Tibetans are not likely to fare well in class, as they have to continue to sit for examinations in the Chinese language. Consequently, Chinese students will be at the top of the class and will be in an advantageous position for further studies in inland universities. Thus, in 1979 the whole of Tibet sent 600 students to institutions of higher learning in inland China. But of that 600, only 60 (10 per cent) were ethnic Tibetans (Tsering, 1986). Ironically, *these seats were especially created to encourage students from remote areas like Tibet to get a better education by sending them to China; yet 90 per cent of seats are in fact taken by Chinese.*

Conclusion

The people's model of higher education which claimed the possibility to combine educational and professional activity, knowledge enhancing and loyalty to Marxism-Leninism ideology failed. As it embarks on the search of a new model of higher education which will be more appropriate to the new needs and expectations of post-communism, Romania will have to cope first with its institutional, educational and psychological heritage and the consequences of the communist governance of academic life which allowed non-academic "uses" of the university and other higher learning institutions. It can be assumed, based on the declarations of the new leaders of the country and of the academic institutions that further efforts will be made for the total de-ideologization of studies and research, the rediscovery of Romanian positive experiences in teaching and research and the revival of academic autonomy as well as the return to its European roots.

As it can be seen from this study, the destruction of the academic system in Romania has been substantial; it resulted in years of intellectual isolationism, the substantial deformation of staff policy and of the functioning of academic institutions. The experience of Romanian higher education makes it an extremely significant case for studying *mechanisms and consequences of unaccountable political interventionism in higher education*. The replacement of academic autonomy which, in principle, characterized the relations between the State and the academy in Romanian higher education until 1948, with a system of close political, ideological and administrative control had overall negative consequences for academic life and society at large. But, we can also observe that past developments can be favourable or unfavourable to those wishing to introduce substantial reforms in higher education. Moreover, long-term outcomes are not always those which had been expected. The "people's model" of higher education and the communist policy in this field are convincing examples of the negative consequences of such undemocratic policies.

Tibet is another example of region whose educational system went through major changes within the same period.

While, in Romania, the communism was meant to lead to an equalitarian society in which concepts such as "individual," "property," and "values" disappear, one may say that in Tibet, the Chinese communist invasion aimed at indoctrination of the Tibetan population by means of assimilation. In both cases, the tool used for achieving purposes was the *educational system.*

In case of Romania, the repeated aggressions in the structure of higher education institutions, by way of the so-called "reforms," contributed to the beheading of the Romanian intellectual elite. Deprived of its elite, the Romanian people was easy to manipulate and terrorize along the almost 50 years of communism.

In case of Tibet, the indoctrination by assimilating the indigenous population and young Tibetans in particular, had as a main consequence the destruction of the Tibetan civilization — mentalities, traditions and culture. There were some attempts to preserve the national culture, efforts supported by the Tibetan Government in exile (India), but the chances of survival are little, as long as the Tibetan youth, educated in China, does no longer feel the "pulse" of the community.

There are quite a few years since Romania and Tibet are well engaged on their way to modernization; Romania, as a candidate country for the integration into the European Union and Tibet, as a "de facto" constituent of China.

The Romanian higher education faces again profound changes in its attempt to adopt European standards. Traditionally, a Romanian graduate could get his graduation diploma at the end of 4 years of study, with few exceptions. Today, according to the European Union standards, the first cycle of higher learning is supposed to be of only 3 years.

In this context, the question is to what extent would these graduates be prepared to face challenges, risks and uncertainties on the labour market? How many of them will be able to access a field of specialization — a master's degree — and become, in the end, high class specialists/intellectuals?

Recent studies show another interesting fact: almost 80 per cent Romanian higher education graduates have basic knowledge of English! In this perspective, Romania's integration into the European Union may be a success. But, what would be the price?

To what extent working abroad, the use of foreign languages and the brain drain will help this people save its originality and national identity?

It is clear that for Romania, the way to modernity is similar with the integration into the European Union. If we define it as an assimilation process of the Romanian people into the great European nation, the risks are enormous.

Instead, if we design integration as a process of selection of what is favourable, valuable and consonant with the traditions, identity and indigenous knowledge of the Romanian civilization, we still have a chance: not letting uniformity become the boring equivalent of civilization.

References

Avedon, John F., *In Exile from the Land of Snows*, New York: Knopf, 1986.

Barnett, Robert, *The Role of Nuns in Tibetan Protest*, London: Tibet Information Network, 1989.

Bass, Catriona, *Inside the Treasure House — A Time in Tibet*, London: Gollancz, 1990.

Beijing Review, Tibetan Special, August 1995.

China Daily, 19 April, 1997.

Dorjee, Tashi, "Education in Tibet," tr. By K. Thondup, *Tibet Journal*, 31, 1977.

Gheorghiu-Dej, Gheorghe *Articole şi cuvîntări*, Bucharest: E.P.L.P., 1952.

Imangulova, L.M., "Partidul Muncitoresc Romîn-Organizatorul revoluţiei culturale din Republica Populară Romînă," *Revista de Pedagogie*, no. 6, June, 1958.

Kormody, Edward, "Observation on Minority Education, Cultural Preservation and Economic Development in China," *Compare*, Volume 25, 1995.

Lapidus, Gail W., "Socialism and modernity: education, industrialization and social change in the USSR, in P. Cocks, R. Daniels," and N. Heer, (eds.), *The Dynamics of Soviet Politics*," Cambridge: Harvard University Press, 1976.

Li Mangteh, Ta Hongchun and Tsung Wunchu, "Intensifying the Education Drive in Tibet to Overcome Nationalities' Inequality," *Tibet Weekly*, Issue 2, 1986.

Mackerras, Colin, *China's Forty Millions*, New York: St. Martin's Press, 1995.

Merciless Repression, New York: Asia Watch, 1990.

Norbu, Dawa, *Tibet: The Road Ahead*, New York: Harper Collins, 1997.

Panchen Lama, *Panchen Lama Speaks*, Dharamsala, India: Department of Information and International Relations, 1991.

Pascu, Stefan, L'Universite de Cluj au fil de l'histoire, in "*L'Universite Babes-Bolyai de Cluj*," ed. Stefan Pascu, Întreprinderea Poligrafică Cluj, 1971.

Sangay, F., "It is Our Historical Duty to Study and Use Tibetan Language." *Tibet Educational Review*, Issue 1, 1990, published by China's Institute of Tibetology.

Sipos, Nicolae Grija Partidului Muncitoresc Român pentru dezvoltarea învățământului de cultură generală în Republica Populară Română, *Revista de Pedagogie*, no. 4, 1955.

Tibet Information Network 1993a. Lhasa City CPPCC, Bulletin no. 2 "Problems that People Have Serious Complaints About." London: Tibet Information Network, 15 July 1993.

Tibet Information Network, 1994, TIN Updated 19 April, 1994, London: Tibet Information Network.

Tibet, Its Ownership and Human Rights Situation, Beijing: Information Office of the State Council of the People's Republic of China, 1992.

Tibet Statistical Yearbook, 1995.

Tsering, Tashi, *Petition in Dhonkun Drubpa Mishikpa, Brief History of Tibet: A Glance at the Period of Blood and Tears*, Dharamsala: Tibetan Government-in-Exile, 1986.

Tsering, Tashi, Melvyn Goldstein and William Siebenschuh, *The Struggle for Modern Tibet, An Autobiography of Tashi Tsering*, Armonk, NY: M.G. Sharpe, 1997.

Walt van Praag, Michael C., *The Status of Tibet*, Boulder: Westview Press, 1987.

Zavorykin, A.A., *Cultural Policy in the Union of Soviet Socialist Republics*, UNESCO, Paris, 1970.

———, Perspectivele dezvoltării învățământului superior în patria noastră, *Revista de Pedagogie*, no. 7, July 1957.

———, Legea pentru reforma învățământului din, 03 August, 1948, *Monitorul Official*, no. 177, August 1948.

Part III

Poverty Alleviation and Sustainable Development

14. Treadle Pumps : Improvements and their Contribution towards Poverty Alleviation
    — *C. Pereira, J. Malça, M.C. Gaspar* and *F. Antunes*

15. Managing Complexities in Sustainable Development
    — *Wolfgang Amann* and *Shiban Khan*

16. Viable Alternatives for Sustainability : Economic Reforms in Forest Villages of Chhattisgarh
    — *R.N. Pati*

17. Sustainable Development : Concept, Scope and Ecological Perspectives
    — *Prafulla Kumar Kara*

14

Treadle Pumps

Improvements and their Contribution towards Poverty Alleviation

C. Pereira, J. Malça M.C. Gaspar and *F.Antumes*

Introduction and Background

POVERTY and hunger still persist in many parts of the world. Today, 1.1 billion people worldwide are very poor, earning less than one dollar a day and suffering from food insecurity (FAO, 2004; Polak, 2006). In particular, more than 800 million people lack adequate access to food, out of which 31 per cent are in East and South-East Asia. Similar *figure* of 31 per cent is in South Asia while Sub-Saharan Africa has 25 per cent (Pretty et al., 2003; Uphoff, 2002; Pinstrup-Anderson et al., 1999). The majority of them live in rural areas of developing countries with limited livelihood opportunities other than agriculture (Molden and Fraiture, 2004; Polak, 2004; FAO, 2004; IRN, 2006). Besides energy deficiency, micronutrient deficiencies frequently occur in association with protein-energy malnutrition. Every year, six million children under the age of five, die of malnutrition and related preventable diseases. Millions more have physical and cognitive development problems and susceptibility to infectious diseases, negatively impacting future generations (Avila and Gasperini, 2005; MDGR, 2005).

At the beginning of the new millennium, more than 180 governments signed the Millennium Declaration, a shared commitment to the world's poor people setting a comprehensive set of goals — the Millennium Development Goals (MDGs) — for human development in its various dimensions (MDGR, 2005). These goals address many of the problems affecting poor people and provide tangible benchmarks for measuring progress in a 25-year period (1990–2015) in several areas. For instance reducing the number of poor and hungry people by 50 per cent and cutting under-five child mortality by two-thirds by the year 2015. However, many countries are off track for most of the MDGs. Focusing solely on the first MDG, the percentage of people living in extreme poverty in South Asia and in Sub-Saharan Africa only decreased by 16 per cent and 2 per cent, respectively between 1990 and 1999 (Sachs et al., 2005). This shows that over half the number of people were living on less than US $ 1 a day. In this context, a revolution is required to achieve the millennium poverty and hunger targets (Polak, 2006). Since most poor people live in rural areas and derive their primary livelihood from agriculture, achieving the MDGs will require a set of measures to address their basic needs, particularly by increasing their income from farming (Toulmin and Gueye, 2005; Polak, 2006). This assumes even higher relevance since the percentage of $1-a-day people living in rural areas in developing countries will not fall below 50 per cent until 2035 despite rapid urbanization (Ravallion and Chen, 1997). Thus, developing and supporting more effective strategies that focus on agriculture and rural development — with particular emphasis on small farmers — could be a powerful engine for (i) economic growth, increasing both employment and wage rates; (ii) progress in education and health; and (iii) poverty reduction and eradication. Moreover, promoting gender equality and empowering women is also an essential aspect in countries where agriculture is still labour-intensive, because in these circumstances women are responsible for more than 60 per cent of the food produced (FAO, 2004; Molden and Fraiture, 2004).

Summing up, to achieve the MDGs and attaining the overarching goal of sustainable and widespread poverty reduction, specific strategies and plans of action sharpening their focus on rural development are urgently needed in developing countries.

Irrigation and Food Security

Basic needs are defined as the minimum standard of living which a society should set for the poorest groups of people. For certain communities, basic needs are simply confined to food and water (Brinkerhoff et al., 1997). An adequate and appropriate food supply — for example induced by modern agricultural methods — is a necessary condition for eliminating hunger. However, increased food supply does not automatically mean increased food security for all (Pretty et al., 2003). If the households are continuously below the poverty line, they lack the ability to access enough food, maintain a healthy life, thus leading to conditions of undernourishment. To overcome this situation, low-cost and easy-to-use technologies and practices to increase food production are crucial in rural areas, where the overwhelming majority of poor and hungry people live (Pretty et al., 2003). Moreover, the problem of food security is exacerbated by the rapid growth of population and hence the demand for food (FAO, 1997). In sub-Saharan Africa, for example, the population is projected to double by the year 2025, with respect to the 1995 levels (UN, 1997). Therefore, a great effort must be made to assist the developing nations in improving their prospects for food security.

Pretty et al. (2003) point out three options for agricultural development if food supply is to be increased, namely (i) expanding the area of agriculture, by bringing new lands into production; (ii) increasing per hectare production in agricultural exporting countries (mostly industrialized); and (iii) enhancing total farm productivity in developing countries. The first option may result in negative impacts on biodiversity, while the second option remains beyond the financial possibilities of those who most need the food, i.e. the poorest. Developing agricultural water use is pivotal for increased land productivity and also for increased labour productivity in developing countries (Van Koppen, 2003). Irrigation is the supply of water to agricultural crops by artificial means, designed to permit farming in arid regions and to offset drought in semi-arid regions (Hillel, 1997). Agriculture is seriously affected by the lack of access to sufficient water or the appropriate means to use it. Many of the most marginalized people record the lowest level of access to "safe water" with the highest percentage of income poverty, suffering from regular and extreme food deficit associated with the severity and variability of weather (DFID, 2001; UN, 2003; Hope, 2006). Even in areas where total seasonal rainfall is adequate on average, it may be poorly distributed during the year and variable from year to year. In these cases, irrigation can help to ensure stable agricultural production (Hillel, 1997). For poor farming families, finding sufficient water for irrigation and the provision of affordable and acceptable irrigation technologies are the principal ways to raise and stabilize food production, and consequently one of the major challenges to improving food security, agricultural commercialization and successful poverty alleviation in developing countries (Hamdy et al., 2003;

Heltberg and Tarp, 2002; Chancellor et al., 1999; Chancellor and O'Neill, 1999).

Hussain and Hanjra (2004) conducted a thorough study to clarify the linkages between irrigation and poverty. They addressed the role of irrigation development and management in poverty alleviation, its magnitude and key determinants. The extensive review suggested that the linkages between irrigation and poverty are undeniable. In general, irrigation is productivity enhancing, growth promoting, and poverty reducing. Moreover, irrigation helps to alleviate poverty in its worst forms, namely chronic poverty. According to Hope (2006), people lacking access to water are often the poorest, hungriest, and most vulnerable in the world. This author investigated the impact of water availability in the households of two communities with poor water access in a semi-arid zone. He identified improved water accessibility as the most important intervention for social welfare gains, particularly benefiting female water collectors. Through irrigation, farmers can achieve significant increases in food production, whether as yield improvements, increases in cropping intensity or diversity of produce (Pretty et al., 2003). By prolonging the effective crop-growing period, farmers are able to harvest a second or third crop in the dry season and plant new crop varieties, which reduces vulnerability to seasonality and increases the nutritional value of crops (Hillel, 1997; Daka, 2001). Additional benefits, such as the generation of jobs and higher incomes, leading to local marketing initiatives and thus to better living conditions, can also be achieved in rural areas (Hussain and Hanjra, 2004). Bhattarai et al. (2002) estimate a multiplier of about 3 for irrigation in India. This figure means that for every $1 generated by irrigated crop production that directly benefits farmers, another $2 benefits the local economy as an induced effect. This is particularly important because a large share of these benefits accrue via indirect channels and in the long term (Hussain and Hanjra, 2004). Polak (2004) also states that affordable small-plot irrigation technology for the production of high-value marketable crops can add around US $ 500 to the annual incomes of people currently living on less than $1 per day.

According to Van Koppen (2003), public and private authorities and technology manufacturers should create the supporting environment that facilitates the massive uptake of cost-effective small-scale technologies for water lifting and application of surface and groundwater, and for better exploitation of wetlands and other water bodies. Several programmes have been implemented in many developing countries of Asia and Africa, with the central aim of livelihood creation for the poor, based on groundwater development. Compared to large surface water systems, whose design is driven by topography and hydraulics, small-scale groundwater development is often much more amenable to poverty targeting. Nowadays, there are various opportunities available for institutional and technological innovations that can put groundwater irrigation at the service of the poor (Molden et al., 2001; Postel et al., 2001).

The lack of alternative water sources has resulted in partially diluted and sometimes untreated wastewater being used for local irrigation in agriculture by the poor (Raschid-Sally et al., 2005). Due to year round availability that allows for multiple cultivation cycles, different cropping patterns emerge with this practice. Several benefits have been demonstrated for wastewater use, namely to sustain land productivity, lift farmers out of poverty and ensure food security for the poorer households. On the other hand, a number of problems, particularly concerning health risks to farmers and consumers, cannot be ignored and require immediate solutions (Perry, 1997; Raschid-Sally et al., 2005). However, the measures for safely managing the use of wastewater in irrigation require concerted efforts by multiple stakeholders — farmers, consumers, municipal, environmental and health authorities, etc. — and, thus, are difficult to come into play (Raschid-Sally et al., 2005).

Data available on the irrigation potential of sub-Saharan Africa, a particularly vulnerable region to climatic instability and frequent draughts, indicates that a projected area of 10 to 35 million hectares could be irrigated — *circa* 2 to 7 times the area under irrigation — and, thus, contribute significantly to the food security of the African continent (FAO, 1997). Currently, less than 4 per cent of the total renewable water resources in Africa are drawn each year for agriculture, domestic water supply and industry and only about 25 per cent of the irrigation potential is being utilized (Bedoumra, 2006). How to find sufficient water for irrigation is one of the major challenges facing farmers because technologies to use the water are basic or non-existent. Sub-Saharan Africa illustrates this reality well with the so-called "economic water scarcity": The water resources are available, but the economic means and incentives to harness water resources are lacking (Molden et al., 2001; Van Koppen, 2003). To increase the potential of irrigable land it is necessary to make use of the appropriate technology, (Brabben and Pearce, 1999). When adopting new technology, social and cultural issues can play an important role, but they vary from country to country (Kay and Brabben, 2000). So, it is important that the end-users of irrigation are capable of making profits and improving livelihoods by choosing the systems that best suit their needs (Chancellor et al., 1999; Chancellor and O'Neill,

1999; Chigerwe et al., 2004). Several irrigation systems are available in market, ranging from sophisticated technologies — e.g. automated canal and piped water delivery systems; laser land levelling for surface irrigation applications; set and automated sprinkle irrigation — to more conventional equipment such as drip and sprinkler systems. However, they often require motorized pumps for water lifting (electric, gasoline or diesel powered pumps). These devices are very efficient, increasing production by irrigating larger areas, giving greater yields and reducing irrigation labour time. Additionally, they allow raising water from the ground which is a potential source of irrigation. Nevertheless, these technologies are unaffordable and uneconomical for three quarters of the farmers in developing countries, who cultivate less than one or two hectares of land (Perry and Dotson, 1996; Postel et al. 2001; Amarasinghe et al., 2005). These farmers simply cannot afford to buy motorized devices, as most of them are imported, often at prohibitively high prices. In fact, an important design requirement of these modern technologies has been the optimization of efficiency rather than affordability. However, when customers are the small farmers of developing countries affordability is one of the first requirements in the design process, so a revolution at design level is needed (Polak, 2004).

The productivity of micro-farmers is now determining the growing problem of food security in the world. Irrigation can use human power instead of a modern technology. In most African countries, irrigation is mainly performed using the traditional rope and bucket system. Although this method may have the advantage of requiring little capital investment for the typical farmer, it is a low-efficiency and labour-intensive water raising technique, creating highly unfavourable production conditions. Thus, alternative technologies that exhibit specific characteristics such as: affordability, low investment cost, rapid return on investment, suitability for different field sizes (i.e. divisibility and expandability), simple and cheap maintenance, portability (lightweight), ease of operation and higher water efficiency could be the keys to solving that weakness. All improvements in developing and disseminating alternative low cost irrigation solutions are needed to achieve the goals of alleviating poverty, ensuring household food security and enhancing profitability (Postel et al., 2001; Polak, 2004).

The Treadle Pump

Among the most exciting innovations in manual irrigation technologies one very effective solution is the treadle pump: a simple low-cost water raising device that has helped

fig. 14.1: Woman irrigating with a treadle pump in Bangladesh. (Photo courtesy: International Development Enterprizes, www.ide-international.org)

millions of the world's poorest communities from developing countries to improve food security and family incomes (Daka, 2001; Molden et al., 2001; Postel et al., 2001; Polak, 2004). The combination of treadle pumps for water lifting, low-cost drip and sprinkler irrigation systems for efficient water application and minimization of evaporation losses, and plastic water tanks to store water collected during the rainy season are the key elements for irrigation success (Postel et al., 2001).

The treadle pump employs the user's body weight and leg muscles to lift water from surface water sources (for example rivers, watercourses, swamps) and shallow water tables, over a reasonable depth below the ground surface (*fig.* 14.1). Changing the driving power from arms and hands to feet and legs has been one of the most important innovations brought by the treadle pump, being much less tiring than other manual pumps that use the upper body and arm muscles (Perry, 1997). Compared to other manual lifting devices, the treadle pump is an effective low-cost alternative solution, since it combines higher water discharge rates with ease of operation (Chigerwe et al., 2004). Field and laboratory tests have shown that these human powered water lifting devices provide affordable means of irrigating small plots of land, like small and marginal farms (Thomas, 1993; Kay and Brabben, 2000; Srinivas and Jalajakshi, 2004). Depending on the geometry of the pump, there can be two operators who may be men, women or children (DTU, 1991). If more than one operator is working on the pump, the irrigated area can be greatly increased (Kay and Brabben, 2000). Its considerably lower cost when compared to motorized systems and also the operating simplicity are two key aspects that show the potential of the treadle pump. In summary, the beneficial impacts ensuing from the adoption of the treadle pump include: (i) benefits to farming practices — larger agricultural area under irrigation, additional and new crops grown each season, irrigation required less often, reduced working time and less tiring irrigation work when compared with bucket irrigation, direct access to groundwater, etc.; (ii) improved family nutrition — full irrigation resulting in improved crop quality and yield, variety of crops grown, increased number of growing cycles as crops are able to grow faster with full irrigation; and (iii) benefits at the economic level — significantly increased agricultural production (attributed not only to increased crop yields, but also to increased irrigated area), farmers are more willing to take risks such as trying new crop varieties or fertilizers (due to increased water availability), extra family income due to marketing of vegetables and employment opportunities for the whole supply chain of manufacturers, retailers and selling agents of treadle pumps (Malça et al., 2005). Polak (n.d.) states that treadle pumps help farmers earn an average of US $ 100 more per pump per year, or even more according to Shah et al. (2000). As a result, the treadle pump can be considered as "the harbinger of a new agricultural revolution greening millions of postage stamp sized plots in the world's poorest and hungriest areas" (Polak et al., n.d.). Putting irrigation at the service of the poor, the treadle pump is a way to hunger and poverty eradication and incomes generation (Kay and Brabben, 2000; Postel et al., 2001). This type of water lifting device has achieved considerable success in many countries, e.g. Bangladesh, India, Zambia, Kenya and Tanzania.

Operating Principles

A treadle pump comprises twin cylinders fitted with pistons that rise and fall when an operator, standing on the treadles connected to the pistons shifts his body weight side to side in a walking motion (*fig.* 14.2). In this manner, a suction

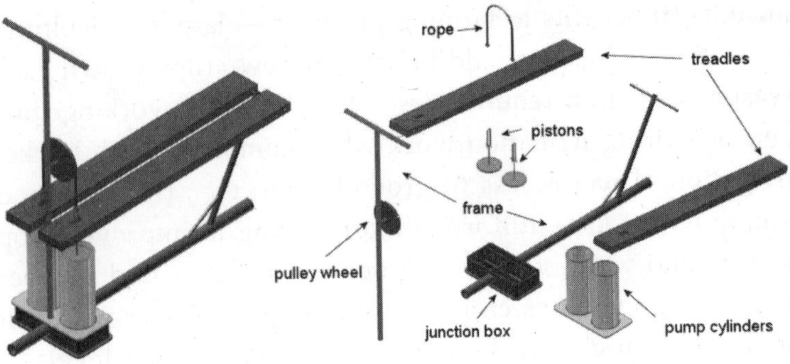

fig. 14.2. Treadle pump: Perspective and exploded view (Malça et al., 2005).

pressure is created inside the cylinders and water is forced to enter the pump cylinders through the inlet pipe connected to the junction box. A non-return valve is fitted to the end of this pipe, allowing water to enter the pipe and preventing it from flowing back to the water source.

Depending on the way water is discharged, treadle pumps can be classified into two main types: (i) suction pumps and (ii) pressure pumps. The suction pump discharges water on the upward stroke through a spout attached to the lips of the cylinders. The spout can be fitted with a round pipe, from which water can easily flow by gravity through a hose pipe into an irrigation channel or tank. This is possible because the metallic frame of the pump elevates its head to approximately one metre height. Since the ability of a suction pump is merely lifting water from a lower level to the height of the pump, it has to be at the highest level.

The pressure pump operates exactly on the same suction principle as the suction pump, but the delivery end has been modified so that water can be fed — under pressure — into a pipe rather than an open channel. During the downward movement of the pistons, the leather or rubber cups fit watertight in the cylinders and water is pressurized through the junction box to the outlet pipe connected to it. Thus, the pump will both lift water from a source and lift it further to a greater height than the pump. In fact, pressure pumps can deliver water at elevations of up to seven metres above pump level, which represents an increase of versatility compared to suction pumps. This advantage overcomes certain limitations presented by the first type of pumps namely for (i) irrigating crops in steep or undulating soils; (ii) pumping water through hoses over long distances; and (iii) delivering water to header tanks to satisfy domestic demands or drive drippers and sprinklers of irrigation systems (Kay and Brabben, 2000; Daka, 2001; Malça et al., 2005).

Treadle Pump Performance

The main objective of a treadle pump is to elevate water from shallow aquifers or surface water bodies using a human-actuated pumping device. The elevation height and the operator's force are two parameters that act on the linear pumping system of the pump. Besides depending on the binomial operator-pumping device, the treadle pump's efficiency is also associated with its base operating mechanism. The overall performance of a treadle pump is therefore closely related to the triad operator-pump-mechanism, as illustrated in *fig.* 14.3.

The Role of the Human Operator

The pressure with which water is discharged depends on the operator's energy. The operators can be men, women or children; hence the operator's related parameters can vary significantly, namely weight, height and physical shape. Flexibility is, therefore, an important parameter since the equipment may be used by different members of a family or

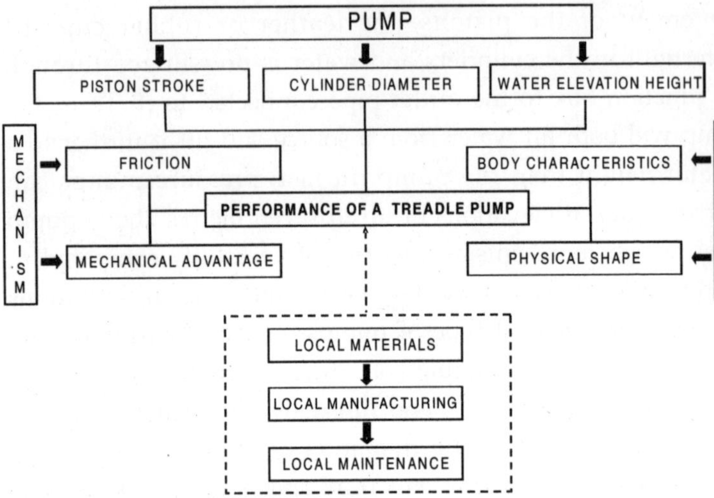

fig. 14.3. Conceptual issues related to the pump's performance.

community. These individuals are able to produce different forces. The gait and posture of the treadle pump's user, and particularly the feet position, play a significant role on the performance of these human-powered water lifting devices. In addition, the user's weight and physical shape are also essential, as the treadle pump's efficiency depends mainly on its operator's performance. However, the influence of the user on the treadle pump's design and constructive solutions has not been completely analyzed so far.

Force, Power and Fatigue

In the treadle pump the leg's movement is similar to the combination of step climbing and walking, so it is easily acquired and repeated sequentially in a mechanized way. The climbing period corresponds to the work of the muscle. The weight moves upward a distance equal to the stairs height or treadle stroke. For long pumping periods, the force transmitted by the user to the treadle must not exceed 50 per cent of his weight. For short pumping periods this limit can be increased up to 70 per cent. Since the treadle pump can be used by different types of operators (males, females and children) it should be designed for resistance forces between 15 and 50 kgf (DTU, 1991; Fraenkel, 1997). However, the fatigue of human body is quickly reached when an isolate number of muscles is used or when the body is forced to work in an uncomfortable anatomic position.

The operator can select the foot position in relation to the pivot point (see *fig.* 4), which modifies the cadence and the force on foot. Lower cadence corresponds to a higher force and lower stroke, which is adequate for heavier persons. On the other hand higher cadence, higher stroke and lower force are adequate to young people. Recommendations can be found in the literature for cadences lower than 60 cycles/min and foot strokes between 100 and 350 mm, with the upper value corresponding to a conventional bicycle pedalling stroke (Thomas, 1993; Kay and Brabben, 2000). Table 14.1 presents the power capabilities of human beings. For longer periods a healthy adult, well fed and having an age within 20-40 years, is able to produce an average power of 75W (Kay and Brabben, 2000). However, considering the poverty related sub-nutrition aspects, 30 to 40W is a more realistic power range.

Table 14.1
Power capabilities of human beings (Fraenkel, 1997)

Human power by duration of effort [W]						
Age (years)	*5 min*	*10 min*	*15 min*	*30 min*	*60 min*	*180 min*
20	220	210	200	180	160	90
35	210	200	180	160	135	75
60	180	160	150	130	110	60

The water elevation height, which is a main input to the pumping system, defines the increase of potential energy according to:

$$\Delta E_p = \rho.V.g.h = 9810\ .h.V \quad \ldots (1)$$

being ρ the specific mass of water ($\approx$1000 kg/m^3), V the volume of water, g the acceleration of gravity and h the elevation height. Therefore, the water pump rate [m^3/s] is:

$$P = \frac{9810\ .h\ .}{\eta} \frac{dV}{dt} \quad \ldots (2)$$

being η the efficiency and P the human power available. For $dV/dt = 2.77 \times 10^{-4}$ m^3/s, which corresponds to 1 m^3/h, h = 4m and a mechanical efficiency of 90 per cent, the human power needed is 12.1W, which is an acceptable value, considering the power capabilities presented in Table 14.1.

Muscular fatigue is the decay in the capacity to generate muscular tension and occurs due to a sub-critical extended activity, or due to a high intensity and low duration activity. Long working periods are achieved with an aerobic regime effort that avoids premature exhaustion. In this sub-critical exercise fatigue is a consequence of reduction in glycogen stocked in the muscles, even if oxygen is available. Regular cadence pumping with relatively small strokes is aimed as an efficiency input to the pump mechanism. During prolonged exercise water ingestion and feeding are also fundamental. The fatigue of the human body is quickly reached when an isolate number of muscles is used or when the body is forced to work in an uncomfortable anatomic position, as discussed next.

Ergonomics

Ergonomics is the science that promotes adaptation of human and material resources for the best performance. This requires a deep knowledge of the human body in terms of anthropometry and comfort. The main aspects of the interaction between ergonomics and anthropometry are the sizes of human body segments, muscular forces, posture, and movements, since they are intimately related with comfort, safety and functionality. Data on human body sizes vary from person to person and from country to country. They also vary from youth to oldness and with historical time. Height of people has increased since antiquity and particularly during the twentieth century as a result of improvements in food and life conditions. Modern societies have recognized the importance of anthropometry, and technical data is already available. However, in developing countries this is not a central issue, and data is scarce.

The gait and posture of the treadle pump's user, and especially the feet position, plays a significant role on the performance of these human-powered water lifting devices. In addition, the user's weight and physical shapes are also essential, as the treadle pump's efficiency depends mainly on the operator's performance. Hence, the user's anthropometric influence must be carefully analysed. Unfortunately, few words can be found in the literature concerning this key aspect of the treadle pump. Thomas (1993) presented a definition of ergonomic efficiency as the relation between the (real) energy effectively transmitted by the operator to the treadles and the energy transmitted in ideal operation conditions. However, the parameters involved in this relation are difficult to quantify. Srinivas and Jalajakshi (2004) evaluated the operationality and ergonomic behaviour of these devices inquiring of several users. The results showed that the majority of the pump operators did not feel physical tiredness in excess; nevertheless, the operating times were short. In fact, ergonomics is one dimension of the investigation where improvements are promising and needed (Kay and Brabben, 2000). The analysis of the treadle pump's ergonomic aspects is expected to help deriving new effective design directives. Geometry and size of the different pump components should be designed and selected to guarantee the operator comfort and thus optimize the human power during large operating times.

Fig. 14.5 represents the extreme angular positions of feet. The equipment should be designed in order to guarantee that the mean position of operation matches a neutral angle of $\theta = 0^0$ — horizontal position — since in this position the foot force is

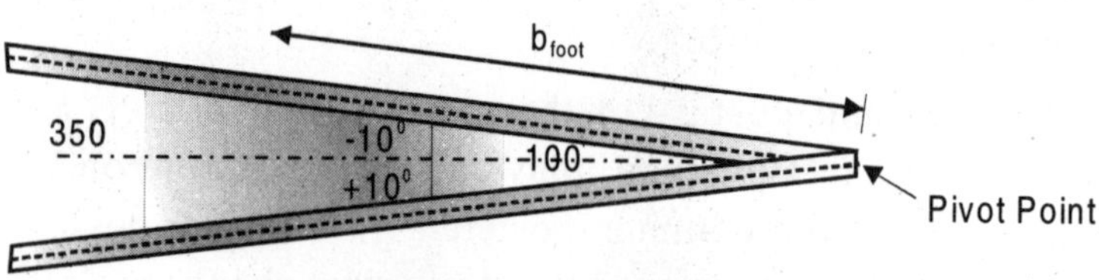

fig. 14.4: Feet extreme positions related to the pivot point of treadles.

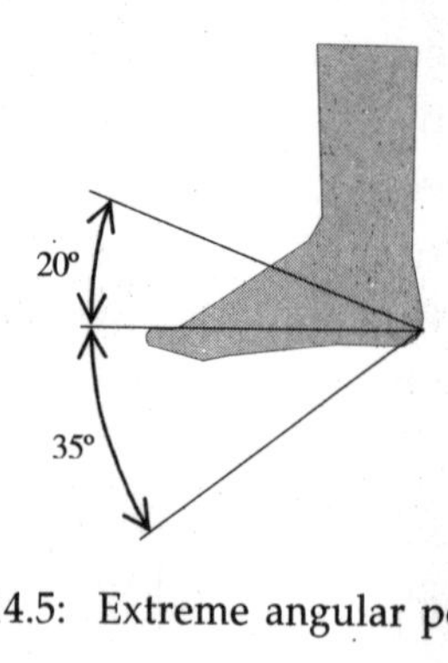

fig. 14.5: Extreme angular positions of feet.

maximum because the force acts vertically (Panero and Zelnik, 2002). However, a comfortable pumping posture requires feet angular positions between -10^0 and $+10^0$. These values depend on the cylinder's position along the lever and on the cylinder's stroke (Silva et al., 1997). Considering that the foot stroke should vary from 100 to 350 mm and θ between -10^0 and $+10^0$, as illustrated in *fig.* 14.4, and then the distance from foot to the pivot point — b_{foot} — can vary between 280 and 1000 mm.

The angular position of the legs depends on feet distance and represents another important ergonomic parameter. In fact, treadles must be large enough to be suitable for different operator's height and allow selection of the best position. Additionally, relatively large treadles allow flexibility for the angular position of feet. On the other hand, enlargement of feet supports increases weight, with a negative impact in terms of pump's portability, which is another key design parameter.

The Mechanism

Different mechanisms can be designed to elevate water. The selection of the most appropriate is based on different design constraints. The number of bodies and joints must be minimized to reduce complexity, friction forces, and wear. Bearings are adequate for joints in mechanisms with frequent stops and inversion movements; however, their availability in developing countries is quite limited. Nonetheless, lubrication is fundamental to reduce energy dissipation and to increase efficiency. A parametric modelling approach was developed by the authors on the design of the base mechanism of human actuated linear pumps. Conceptual issues related to the pump's working sequence were established and the main geometric constraints identified (Gaspar et al., 2006).

Linear pumps have pistons with linear movements to force water upwards or downwards inside the cylinders. Several one-degree-of-freedom mechanisms can be developed to transform the operator's foot stroke into a linear movement

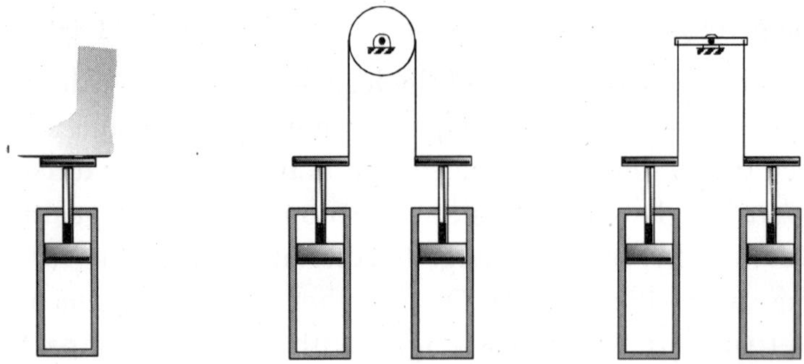

(a) (b) (c)

fig. 14.6: (a) Direct actuation of foot; (b) and (c) Solutions to alternate movements (pulley wheel and string *vs.* lever and string).

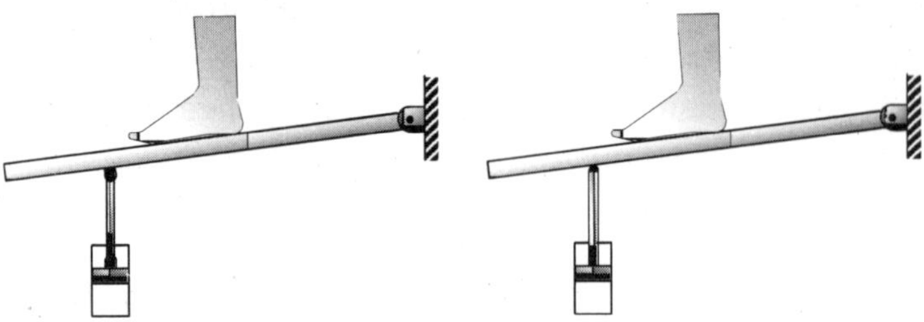

(a) (b)

fig. 14.7: Treadle pump with: (a) rotational joints, and (b) translational joint.

of the pump's piston to elevate water. The simplest transformation of the linear movement of foot into the linear movement of piston is direct actuation (*fig.* 14.6a). This is a simple and compact solution, however, without flexibility. The load required at the foot depends on the resistance force imposed by the pump. Two pumps side by side give opportunity to alternate movements. The stroke range was considered from 100 to 350 mm. Return can be achieved with a linear spring. On the other hand both cylinders can be connected and returned by foot force directly (*figs.* 14.6b and 14.6c).

Another solution is the use of treadles, as illustrated in *fig.* 14.7. This is an extremely flexible solution from a mechanical point of view, but portability of the resulting device is limited by the dimensions of the treadle. The cadence, stroke and force are changed when the position along the treadle changes. Therefore, different users can pump water with comfort, and even the same user can vary its position during pumping. The resulting flexibility is a major benefit, as the same type of device can be efficiently used by a wide range of people. *Fig.* 14.7b shows a variant of

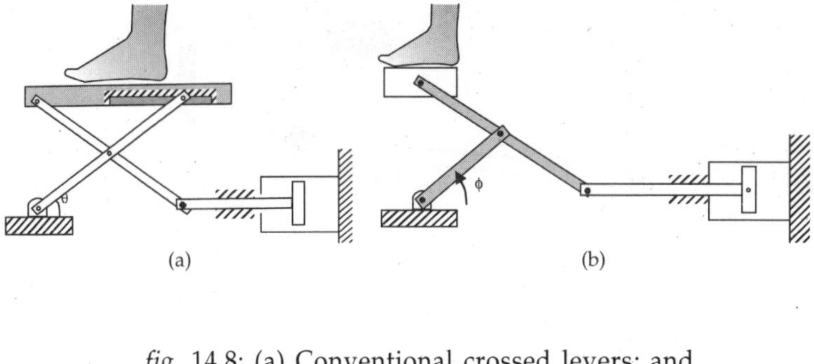

fig. 14.8: (a) Conventional crossed levers; and
(b) Simplified alternative solution.

the arrangement of *fig.* 14.7a, with a translational joint used instead of two rotational joints on the pump's cylinder piston.

The solution illustrated in *fig.* 14.8a is based on elevation devices, since it gives a parallel movement of the loads being elevated. The mechanism is composed of four moving bodies, four rotational joints, one sliding joint and one mixed joint (sliding plus rotation). The elevated number of joints can give poor efficiency. *fig.* 14.8b presents an alternative solution with four moving bodies, four rotational joints and one sliding joint, therefore reducing the number of joints.

The relations between velocities and between forces are:

$$v_{piston} = v_{foot}.tg(\phi) \quad (3)$$

$$F_{foot} = F_{piston}.tg(\phi) \quad (4)$$

Tangent of ϕ is higher than one for $\phi>45^o$, and $F_{foot}>F_{piston}$.

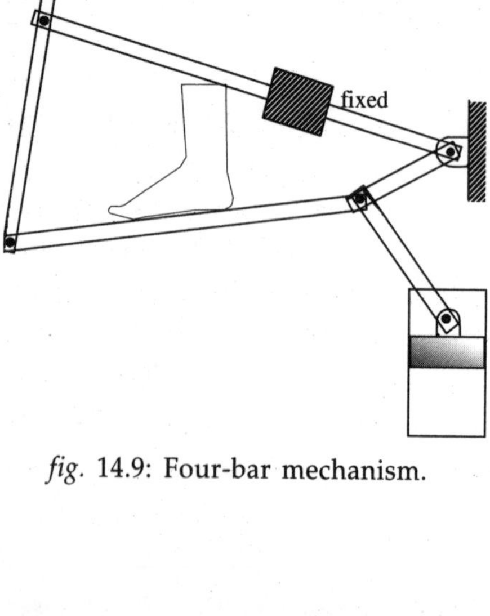

fig. 14.9: Four-bar mechanism.

Alternative solutions for the human-actuated pump's mechanism can be defined by transforming the linear movement of feet into rotation, and this into linear movement of the pump's piston. The intermediate rotation can be obtained using a four bar mechanism as illustrated in *fig.* 14.9.

Different parameters can be considered when comparing the proposed solutions. Relevant parameters include the number of bodies and joints, which quantify the complexity of the solution. Another important parameter is flexibility, considering that the device must be used by different members of a family or community, including men, women and children.

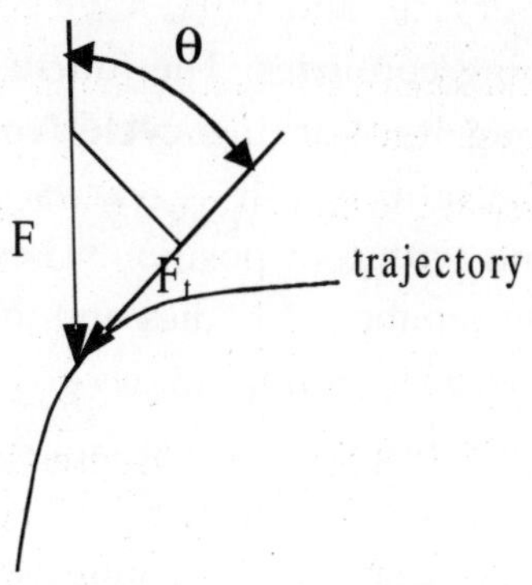

fig. 14.10: Efficiency of human force.

The variability of ratio (foot force/pump force) can be used to quantify this concept. Finally, the efficiency of human force defined as the angular deviation of human force relatively to the trajectory's tangent (*fig.* 14.10) is also a pertinent parameter:

$$\cos(\theta) \quad = \quad F : F_t \qquad (5)$$

For the maximum efficiency of human force, θ must be 0°.

Table 14.2, compares the four solutions. Note that the number of bodies and joints were defined for the complete mechanism (i.e. for both feet). Solutions of *figs*. 14.8 and 14.9, have more bodies and joints, which is disadvantageous. On the other hand, the direct actuation of force presents a major disadvantage in terms of flexibility, since the force at the foot is always equal to the piston's resistance (neglecting friction). The treadle pump enables a significant variation of foot force for the same piston resistance. The user only has to change its position along the treadle. The efficiency of the user's force is also quite high, considering that the extreme angular positions of the treadle are $\pm 10^{\circ}$. Solutions of *fig*. 14.8 have apparently the greatest flexibility in terms of applied load. However, the large number of bodies and joints of this solution turns it into a very complex device, and thus, not very appealing to be used in developing countries. The four-bar mechanism has dead points along its working cycle ($\cos\theta = 0$) which is inconvenient. The ratio F_{foot}/F_{piston} varies significantly along the load cycle and with foot position. Therefore, considering the relatively low number of bodies and joints, and the great flexibility, the treadle pump (a lever-based solution) is probably the best solution.

Table 14.2

Comparative analysis of the proposed solutions

Fig.	Bodies	Joints	F_{foot}/F_{piston} *	$\cos(\theta)$
14.6	3	3 (2T+1R)	1	1
14.7a	7	9 (2T+7R)	0.5-3	0.98-1
14.7b	5	7 (4T+3R)	0.5-3	0.98-1
14.8	9	11 (2T+9R)	0-∞ ($tg\phi$)	1
14.9	9	11 (2T+9R)	-	0-1

T – translational joint
R – rotational joint
M – mixed joint (T+R)
* neglecting friction.

Other Aspects

Furthermore, parameters such as portability, reliability, and ease of manufacturing and repair cannot be neglected in the design of treadle pumps. Portability is especially important in some applications — e.g. irrigation — as well as for security reasons, when the pump cannot be left in the field overnight. Reliability has been guaranteed, because several parts of treadle pumps, mainly the junction box (which connects the inlet and discharge pipes to the pump cylinders), the cylinders, the pistons, the metal rods (which connect the pistons to the treadles) and the non-return valves are commonly built in metallic materials. However, this design option implies increasing costs of manufacturing and maintenance. In fact, the cost (less than 100€) of these human-powered pumps is many times prohibitive for the developing world of small-scale farmers. Many pumps in use today in developing countries were donated under Government programmes or NGO initiatives, and are thus community property. Furthermore, failure tends to occur sooner because maintenance is poor and conditions are sometimes more hostile in developing countries. Therefore, treadle pump's repair and maintenance requirements constitute also great constraints to its widespread use in these countries. In fact, poor farmers typically are unable to maintain the machines, which eventually break down and are abandoned. However, it has been observed that individually owned pumps are much better maintained than those owned by the whole community (Kay and Brabben, 2000). If spare parts are not available, or if the local skills are insufficient to cope with routine maintenance and repair tasks, pump maintenance is unlikely to be sustainable in the long term. Resources may be available in a nearby town but this means that transport is needed and time

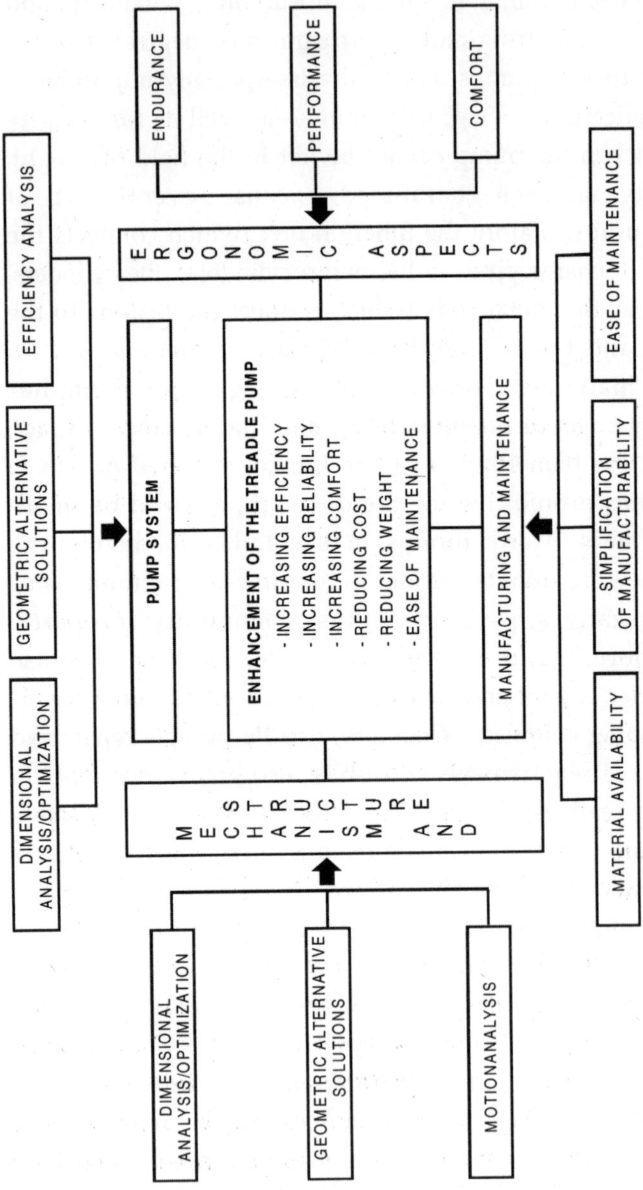

fig. 14.11: Treadle pump enhancement: Key aspects of the methodology.

is spent to get to them. These two commodities are usually in short supply in most rural communities. One of the solutions to overcome these problems and to allow an extensive availability of pumps among farmers is to produce them in local workshops from locally-available materials. This would boost employment in rural areas, with artisans manufacturing pumps, carpenters producing treadles and additional people helping on the farm to handle the additional agricultural production. In addition, wealth increase among native population and reduced national import costs would be attained, while solving the maintenance and assistance problems. Although some solutions have already been tried in using local materials as an alternative to metal-based treadle pumps, the weakness shown does not allow its intensive use and failure tends to occur precociously. Therefore, development still continues, with tests looking at long-term performance and maintenance needs of treadle pumps, in particular pressure pumps (Srinivas and Jalajakshi, 2004).

The possibility for the developing countries of locally manufacturing the treadle pumps using local materials as an alternative to metal-based pumps has two additional motivations for native populations. The lower cost of locally manufactured pumps would result in an increased availability amongst those who would effectively benefit from them. On the other hand, the start/effort on achieving the skills and interest of manufacturing would be the first step on industrialization of those populations (Gaspar et al., 2005).

Moving Towards an Integrated Approach

The principles of human powered pumping systems depend mainly on the binomial operator-pumping device and must be fully understood to provide practical, constructive solutions with improved performance. Many features must be studied and enhanced; therefore, a multi-disciplinary methodology focusing on dimensional and structural requirements, manufacturing and maintenance aspects, cost reduction as well as ergonomic aspects is expected to obtain significant results in the treadle pump enhancement (Malça et al., 2005). This methodology is summarized in *fig.* 14.11.

The use of treadle pumps for long periods requires physical strength, thus comfort is an important issue. The geometry and size of the different pump components should be designed and selected to guarantee the operator comfort. In order to perform the optimization of this type of devices and deriving new effective design directives for long operating times, the first step is to study ergonomic aspects like endurance, comfort and efficiency. A human centred approach has been developed (Pereira et al., 2006) searching for improved comfort and thus optimized user's performance, because the amount of water pumped on this type of pumps depends significantly on the user, his physical shape and how his energy is converted into pumping power. The analysis of the treadle pump's ergonomic aspects is expected to help derive new effective design directives. The gait and posture of the treadle pump's user, and especially the feet position, plays a significant role on the performance of these devices. In addition, the user's weight and physical shapes are also essential. Hence, the user's anthropometric influence must be carefully analyzed.

The pump-operator binomial study must be completed with a dynamic analysis in order to obtain the working forces to which a treadle pump is submitted. A dynamic modelling should be carried out considering different types of human operators. *fig.* 14.12 shows some frames of the simplified

fig. 14.12: Treadle pump working sequence modelled in multibody software.

dynamic modelling of the treadle pump and its operator performed using multibody software. The full modelling of the working sequence allows calculation of the maximum stresses on the treadle, in order to subsequently carry out its optimal dimensioning. Different geometric solutions must be considered to obtain the most efficient results when considering the target user populations.

As mentioned before, aspects like cost reduction, and manufacturing and maintenance simplicity must be considered in order to permit the massive availability of this type of water lifting devices to very poor populations. Therefore, a parametric study must be carried out based on the above referred design directives to consider the applicability of alternative locally available materials. An efficient parametrization permits analysing different materials in the manufacturing of the treadle pumps in order to obtain tailored solutions for different geographical regions. Strategically, parameters and dimensions must be defined and an adequate numerical model of the enhanced solutions has to be obtained.

These works must be accompanied by field and laboratory tests towards an integrated optimized solution taking into account alternative designs and materials.

References

Avila, M. and L. Gasperini (2005), MDGs and Sustainable Rural Development in Sub-Saharan Africa: Challenges and Implications for Education for Rural People, Ministerial Seminar on Education for Rural People in Africa: Policy Lessons, Options and Priorities, Addis Ababa.

Bedoumra, K. (2006), African Development Bank water sector initiatives: Experience and lessons, Workshop on Financing and Cost Recovery in the African Water Sector, Tunis, 13-15 June.

Bhattarai, M., R. Sakthivadivel and I. Hussain (2002), Irrigation impacts on income inequality and poverty alleviation: Policy issues and options for improved management of irrigation systems, Working Paper, International Water Management Institute (IWMI), Colombo.

Brinkerhoff, M., K. Fredell and J. Frideres (1997), Basic minimum needs, quality of life and selected correlates: Explorations in villages in northern India, Social Indicators Research 42, pp. 245-81.

Chancellor, F. and D. O'Neill (1999), Gender-Sensitive Irrigation Design, Gender considerations relating to treadle pump adoption: Experiences from Zambia, Report OD 143 (Part 3), HR Wallingford Ltd., Wallingford, December.

Chancellor, F., N. Hasnip and D. O'Neill (1999), Gender-Sensitive Irrigation Design, Guidance for smallholder irrigation development, Report OD 143 (Part 1), HR Wallingford Ltd., Wallingford, December.

Chigerwe, J., N. Manjengwa, P. van der Zaag, W. Zhakata and J. Rockström, (2004), Low head drip irrigation kits and treadle pumps for smallholder farmers in Zimbabwe: a technical evaluation based on laboratory tests, Physics and Chemistry of the Earth, 29, pp. 1049-59.

Daka, A. (2001), Development of a Technological Package for Sustainable Use of Dambos by Small-Scale Farmers, Doctoral Thesis, University of Pretoria, South Africa.

DFID (2001), Addressing the water crisis: Healthier and more productive lives for poor people, Strategies for achieving the international development targets, Department for International Development. London.

DTU — Development Technology Unit (1991), The Treadle Pump, Working Paper no. 34, Department of Engineering, University of Warwick, Coventry, UK.

FAO (2004), The State of Food Insecurity in the World 2004, Food and Agriculture Organization of the United Nations, Rome.

FAO (1997), Irrigation potential in Africa: A basin approach, FAO Land and Water Bulletin 4, Rome.

Fraenkel, P. (1997), Water pumping devices, IT Publications, London.

Frausto, K. (2000), Developing irrigation options for small farmers: Harnessing the potential of the poor, Contributing paper to the World Commission on Dams.

Gaspar, M.C., F. Antunes, J. Malça and C. Pereira (2006), Parameterization and Parametric Design of a Human Powered Water Lifting Device, International Water Conference (IWC, 2006), Porto, Portugal, 12-14 June.

Gaspar, M.C., J. Malça, C. Pereira and F. Ventura (2005), Engineering Supported Solutions for Sustainable Development in Arid and Semi-Arid Regions, International Sustainability Conference, 2005 (ISC 2005), Basel, Switzerland, 13-14 October.

Hamdy, A., R. Ragab and E.S. Mugnozza (2003), Coping with water scarcity: Water saving and increasing water productivity, Irrigation and Drainage 52, pp. 3-20.

Heltberg, R. and F. Tarp, (2002), Agricultural supply response and poverty in Mozambique, Food Policy 27, pp. 103-24.

Hillel, D. (1997), Small-scale irrigation for arid zones — Principles and Options, FAO Development Series 2, Rome.

Hope, RA., (2006), Evaluating Water Policy Scenarios against the Priorities of the Rural Poor, World Development 34 (1), pp. 167-79.

Hussain, I. and M. Hanjra (2004), Irrigation and poverty alleviation: Review of the empirical evidence, Irrigation and Drainage 53, pp. 1-15.

International Rivers Network (2006), Spreading the Water Wealth: Making Water Infrastructure Work for the Poor, IRN Dams, Rivers and People Report, Berkeley, CA.

Kay, M. and T. Brabben (2000), Treadle pumps for irrigation in Africa, Synthesis report, Food and Agriculture Organization of the United Nations (FAO), Rome.

Malça, J., C. Pereira, M.C. Gaspar and F. Ventura (2005), Low cost water pumping systems for developing countries, International Conference on Water, Land and Food Security, Bari, Italy, 6-11 September.

MDGR (2005), The Millennium Development Goals Report, United Nations, New York.

Molden, D. and C. Fraiture (2004), Investing in Water for Food, Ecosystems and Livelihoods, Comprehensive Assessment of Water Management in Agriculture — Blue Paper, Stockholm.

Molden, D., U. Amarasinghe and I. Hussain (2001), Water for Rural Development. IWMI, Colombo.

Panero, J. and M. Zelnik (2002), Dimensionamento humano para espaços interiores (ed.), Gustavo Gili, S.A., Barcelona.

Pereira, C., J. Malça, M.C. Gaspar and F. Ventura (2006), Human Motion Analysis in Treadle Pump Devices. In: T. Clemmensen, P. Campos, R. Orngreen, A. Mark Petersen, W. Wong (eds.), Human Work Interaction Design: Designing for Human Work, The First IFIP TC 13.6 WG Conference: Designing for Human Work, IFIP International Federation for Information Processing, volume 221 (Boston: Springer), pp. 155-65.

Perry, E. (1997), Low-cost irrigation technologies for food security in sub-Saharan Africa. In: Proceedings of the Workshop "Irrigation Technology Transfer in Support of Food Security," Harare, Zimbabwe, 14-17 April.

Pinstrup-Anderson, P., R. Pandya-Lorch and M. Rosegrant (1999), World Food Prospects: Critical Issues for the Early 21st Century. International Food Policy Research Institute (IFPRI), Washington, DC, October.

Polak, P. (2004), Water and the Other Three Revolutions Needed to End Rural Poverty, Water Science and Technology, 51 (8), pp. 133-43.

Polak, P., (no date), Dismantling the barriers to the green revolution for small farmers, International Development Enterprises (IDE), Lakewood, Colorado.

Polak, P., B. Nanes and J. Sample (no date), Opening Access to Affordable Micro-Plot Irrigation for Small Farmers, IDE report, Lakewood, Colorado.

Polak, P., and R. Yoder (2006), Creating wealth from groundwater for dollar-a-day farmers: Where the silent revolution and the four revolutions to end rural poverty meet, Hydrogeology Journal 14, pp. 424-32.

Postel, S., P. Polak, F. Gonzales and J. Keller (2001), Drip Irrigation for Small Farmers, A New Initiative to Alleviate Hunger and Poverty, International Water Resources Association, Water International 26 (1), pp. 3-13.

Pretty, J.N., J. Morison and R.E. Hine (2003), Reducing food poverty by increasing agricultural sustainability in developing countries. Agriculture, Ecosystems and Environment 95, pp. 217-34.

Raschid-Sally, L., R. Carr and S. Buechler (2005), Managing wastewater agriculture to improve livelihoods and environmental quality in poor countries, Irrigation and Drainage 54, pp. S11-S22.

Ravallion, M. and S. Chen (1997), What can new survey data tell us about recent changes in distribution and poverty? World Bank Economic Rev. 11(2), pp. 357-82.

Sachs, JD. (ed.), and UN Millennium Project (2005), Investing in development: A practical plan to achieve the Millennium Development Goals, Earthscan, New York (cited in Polak and Yoder, 2006).

Shah, T., M. Alam, D. Kumar, R.K. Nagar and M. Singh (2000), Pedalling out of poverty: Social impact of a manual irrigation technology in South Asia, Research Report 45, IWMI, Colombo.

Silva, M., J. Ambrósio and M. Pereira (1997), Biomechanical Model with Joint Resistance for Impact Simulation, Multibody System Dynamics, vol. 1, pp. 65-84.

Srinivas, S., and C. Jalajakshi (2004), Alternatives to Micro-Irrigation: Evaluation of the Treadle Pump, *Economic and Political Weekly*, September 18, pp. 4271-75.

Thomas, T.H., (1993), The Performance Testing of Treadle Pumps, Working Paper no. 39, DTU, Department of Engineering, University of Warwick, Coventry, UK.

Toulmin, C., and B. Gueye (2005), Is there a future for family farming in West Africa?, IDS bulletin — Institute of Development Studies 36 (2), pp. 23-29.

UN (2003), Water for People, Water for Life — UN World Water Development Report, Paris: UNESCO.

UN, Population Division (1997), World Population Prospects, 1950–2050. The 1996 Edition.

Uphoff, N. (ed. 2002), Agroecological Innovations: Increasing Food Production with Participatory Development. Earthscan, London.

Van Koppen, B. (2003), Water reform in Sub-Saharan Africa: What is the difference?, Physics and Chemistry of the Earth 28, pp. 1047-53.

15

Managing Complexities in Sustainable Development

Wolfgang Amann* and *Shiban Khan

Introduction

SUSTAINABILITY is currently a crucial issue on governments, managers, executives and non-profit organizations' radar screens. Simultaneously, the theorizing process has started in academia. However, almost twenty years ago, the World Council on Economy and Development's Brundtland Commission had already defined sustainable development as "development that meets the needs of the present without compromising the ability of future generations to meet their own needs" (WCED 1987, p. 8).

One may justifiably ask what has been achieved in twenty years, or for that matter, why progress has been slower than it should have been. After all, signs of unsustainability continue to crop up: poverty, hunger, pollution and climate change. For many, the wave of attention directed towards sustainability first led to a peak of inflated expectations, followed by a "trough of disillusionment" due to the disappointing outcomes. We are now experiencing a promising move towards a plateau where solutions really work, as illustrated in *fig.* 15.1.

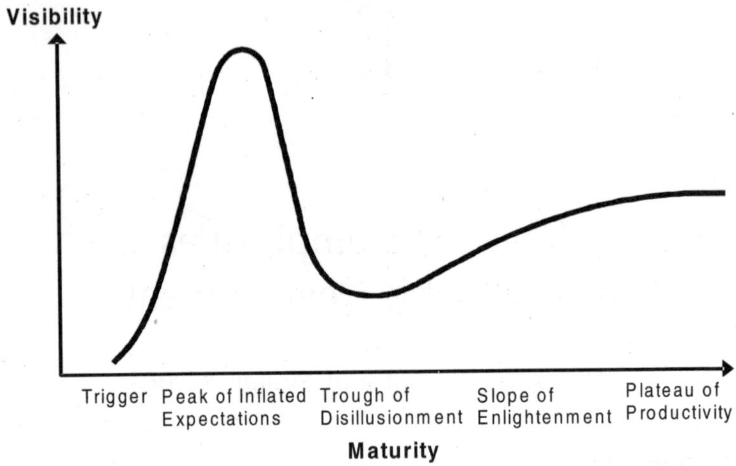

fig. 15.1: Development of sustainability over the time

The ongoing signs of unsustainability may be attributed to a number of factors. These are: (1) From an economics perspective: imperfect markets, or the unfeasibility of holding companies accountable for all negative externalities; (2) From an education perspective: a generation of project managers, executives and policy makers for whom the topic of sustainability is rather new and has not been part of their education; (3) From a concept maturity perspective: the need for more time to develop and test innovative strategies, concepts, measurement tools, e.g. for the business case, and for ways to master their implementation as each concept first emerges as an idea followed by the development of tools and implementation ideas; and, finally, (4) From a stakeholder perspective and tension field analysis: less pressure is exerted than needed for fast progress.

In this chapter, we argue that there may be an additional factor that could influence progress in the field's pace: the complexity hidden in the phenomenon, i.e. sustainability itself lags behind its expectations, as its inherent complexities could easily be overwhelming. The first step in mastering its complexities naturally calls for a comprehension of the complexity drivers. In the following, we present a framework for understanding the complexity inherent in sustainability. This conceptual chapter is structured in such a way that empirical evidence is woven into it to illustrate the framework, replacing the more traditional, but in this case less helpful, division of the conceptual foundation and empirical evidence into different sections.

Sustainability Defined

Sustainability — what does it mean? Drawing upon the Brundtland Commission's legendary definition of sustainable development, corporate sustainability (CS) is best understood as "a strategy for corporate sustainability that meets the needs of a firm's stakeholders without compromising its ability to also meet the needs of future stakeholders" (Dyllick and Hockerts, 2002, p. 131). The conceptual development of CS owes much of its roots to sustainable development's core idea. As Wilson (2003) outlines, CS results from a synthesis between the theories of sustainable development (SD), corporate social responsibility (CSR), stakeholder theory, and corporate accountability as portrayed in *fig.* 15.2.

A truly sustainable firm seeks to achieve the integration of the economic, ecological, and social aspects of its activities, the ground-breaking concept known as the "triple bottom line." Aiming for a true integration of the economic, ecological, and social aspects of a firm's activities, the triple bottom line (TBL) has in recent years become the most prominent model for CS and has gained popularity as the preferred model for firms to follow in order to be responsible for their societal and environmental impacts.

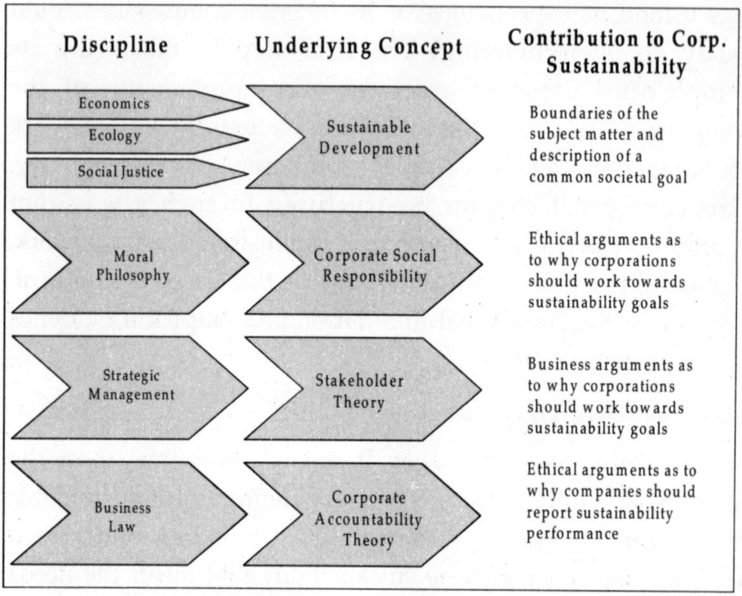

fig. 15.2: Pillars of corporate sustainability

However, there is lively controversy among scholars who are in the process of selecting terminology in respect of corporate sustainability. The rich perceptive and definitional diversity regarding SD's core concept has contributed to the variety of ways of depicting CS in relation to SD and other related concepts (e.g. CSR) in the field. Van Marrewijk (2003), for example, regards CS and CSR as synonymous, and advocates a context-specific content for a definition that is adjusted to the individual organization's awareness and goals. In earlier studies, CSR was also construed as corporate social performance (Wood, 1991; Carroll, 1999), while a popular contemporary equivalent of CS is corporate environmentalism (Hoffman, 1997, Banerjee et al. 2003). On the other hand, Rubenstein (2003) considers the TBL to be the same as CS. Schaltegger et al. (2002) regard "corporate sustainable development's" central challenges to be the integration of the economic, ecological and social aspects. Moreover, all the topics discussed within this context are often placed under the corporate citizenship umbrella (cf. Birch and Moon, 2004).

The business case for corporate sustainability in which an ecologically sustainable organization also achieves a healthy financial bottom line emerged as the dominant paradigm in CS research. The most important question in the context of CS research is whether being environmentally responsible actually results in profits, or, as scholars often phrase it: "Does it pay to be green?" Basing sustainability decisions on economics as their driver ensures an easier dialogue with organizations — internal and external stakeholders. Such initiatives would be maintained even in tougher times, while mere philanthropic projects may be abandoned. But whether there is a positive, neutral or negative bottom-line impact is clearly one of the most controversial topics in contemporary management research. Thus, the debate on the ambiguous relationship between a firm's financial performance and its social/ environmental responsibilities will surely be prolonged for some time to come.

In most cases, the business case for sustainability is determined by a firm's efficient use of natural capital, a concept known as eco-efficiency. It refers to the relation between a firm's economic value added and its aggregated ecological impact. Eco-efficiency is also heavily patronized by the World Business Council for Sustainable Development (WBCSD). However, eco-efficiency as the sole basis of an indicator of achieved sustainability is rather limited, as it concentrates on the issue from a cost-efficiency viewpoint. As evident from the preceding sections, the triple bottom line is realized in firms when their social and environmental achievements are considered by measuring their financial accomplishment. Therefore, the concept of eco-effectiveness is gaining ground as an alternative to eco-efficiency, highlighting the former's financial orientation. Eco-effectiveness largely relies on a technical viewpoint of effectiveness and has been defined as a "strategy for designing human industry that is safe, profitable, and regenerative, producing economic, ecological, and social value."

Applying a Complexity Framework to Sustainability

In the following, four drivers render the discussion on and solutions for sustainability more complex, as shown in *fig.* 15.3. Diversity is the first key driver of complexity. Internationalizing organizations are complexity incarnate, because they face a complex set of challenges characterized by two types of diversity. First, there is internal diversity, which executives must either manage or respond to due to the higher diversity in the HR pool, the greater variety in management systems, and/or the business models required for the different types of business units, etc. Second, there is external diversity, which materializes in the form of varying customer needs, different cultural values, or heterogeneous political, economic and legal environments. India, for example, faces huge diversity, also in a comparison of urban and rural India.

In addition to these general growing challenges, the sustainability debate also entails a growing level of diversity, as major business goals become more comprehensive. But even before the emergence of the sustainability discussion, corporate business cycles have always resembled sine curves of high and low performances. Maintaining successful businesses is a true art only mastered by a few. Only one in seven companies, for example, achieves its set and publicly announces growth and profit goals. About 70 per cent of mergers and acquisitions fail, 80 per cent of strategic innovation projects fail, 80 per cent of the companies do not survive industry consolidations and around 90 per cent of family businesses do not survive long enough to have a third

fig. 15.3: Generic complexity drivers

generation to continue the legacy. Being able to ensure a solid financial performance – based on a single bottom-line logic – is thus the exception.

Sustainability adds to the level of challenge, first because it increases the overall level of complexity with which companies have to cope. Besides the financial ends mentioned above, companies should also pursue ecological and social contributions, although they are already struggling with just the financial performance dimension. As if this triangle of goals or triple bottom line were not complex enough, Dyllick and Hockerts (2002) broke these goals down into six criteria that truly sustainable companies have to meet. This results in a rather diverse and complex goal system, as shown in *fig.* 15.4:

In practice, there is a plethora of actual motives for sustainability, as shown in *fig.* 15.5. However, sustainability is not a panacea. Less clarity and a lack of prioritization can only lead to deception, or an overwhelming complexity.

Diversity emerges in other fields as well, a crucial one being "transmission belts" that cause either direct or indirect external pressures (e.g. from NGOs, legislators, customers,

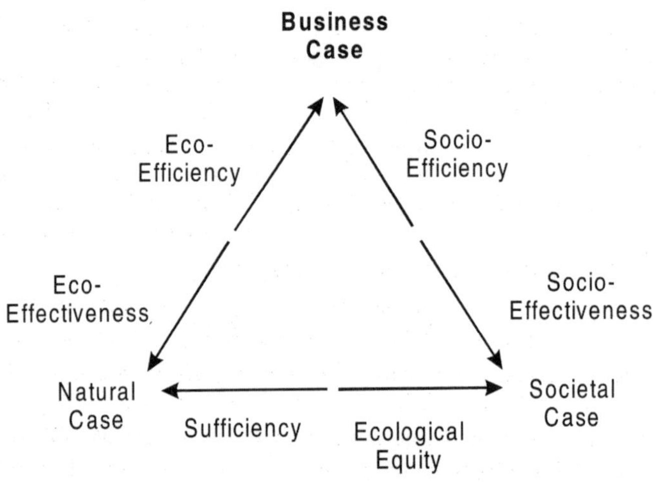

Source: Dyllick and Hockerts 2002, p. 138

fig. 15.4: Diversity of ends and criteria

capital markets, etc.). Each "transmission belt" requires a tailored stakeholder management approach as well (cf. Steger, 2003). The financial investment community demands a different treatment than governments. Diversity is enhanced by the fact that sustainability challenges and the importance of sustainability in general differ from industry to industry.

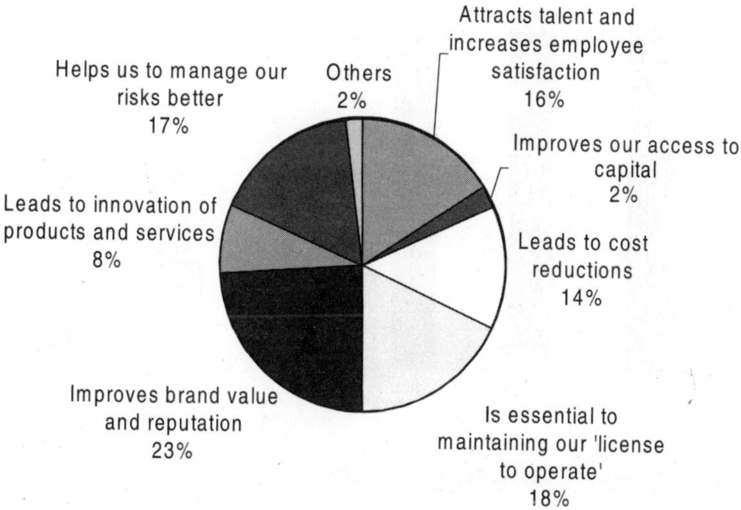

N = 123 sustainability officers. Source: IMD-CSM Research.

fig. 15.5: Diversity among drivers

Even within industries, a variety of topics matter, calling for a difficult prioritization, as revealed in *fig.* 15.6. There is also diversity in a comparison of developed and developing countries.

The interdependence of (sometimes highly diverse) factors is the second driver of increasing complexity. Companies must — to an unprecedented degree — manage the effect of increasingly international interdependence within businesses. Cross-company value webs have replaced traditional value chains. Corporate boundaries have practically vanished. Reputation, financial flows, value chain flows, and top management and corporate governance issues have reached advanced levels of interdependence. Managers even have to take non-local events' repercussions into account. The less clear-cut the boundaries of a company become, the more it is exposed to impacts on

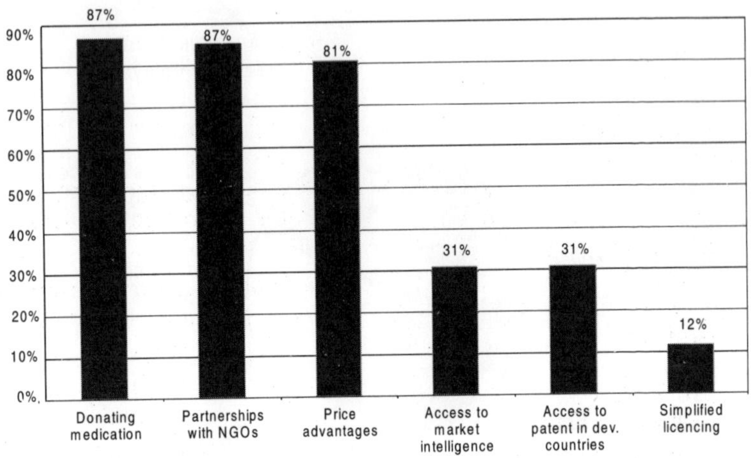

Source: SAM (2004), p. 3

fig. 15.6: Importance of sustainability issues in the pharmaceutical industry

the value creation process through mistakes, frictions, reverse trends, or even shocks. Risks appear as quickly as opportunities are either captured or missed. The sustainability discussion increases interdependence by adding an additional dimension. There are interrelations between green investments and reputation, safety and workforce motivation, brand and "green" policies, sustainability achievements and actual costs or competitive advantages, to name but a few examples.

Ambiguity emerges as the third driver of complexity. Too much information with less and less clarity on how to interpret and apply insights characterizes the business world. A diversity of accounting standards renders financial *fig.*s ambiguous. Studies, scenarios, survey results, and reports become less reliable due to an ever-increasing uncertainty, with true ambiguity being at its highest level. Cause-effect relationships become difficult to determine, e.g. to discover what the clear value drivers are. Are they image or price-related services, privileged relationships, speed, or knowledge? Cause-effect relationships have indeed become blurred.

Ambiguity is a major issue with regard to sustainability, as precisely these cause-effect relations may lack certainty. Even within companies, our research indicates a plethora of motives for embarking on more sustainable practices. Measurement problems associated with long-term effects, or with qualitative aspects challenge sustainability officers.

The fourth and final element in our framework of complexity deals with fast flux. As if these three complexity drivers weren't enough, managers have to face yet another — the fast flux. Even if sustainability officers and managers *fig.* out (temporary) solutions regarding interdependence, diversity and ambiguity for their specific company, industry, and personal situation, the situation could change the next day. Today's solutions (and especially those of the past) may be outdated tomorrow. Changes occur in many directions at once, and at increasing rapidity. While corporate sustainability programmes are well received at a certain point of time, competition may soon render acknowledged efforts outdated and insufficient. DaimlerChrysler serves as a real world, real learning example of fast flux:

1. CEO heads Global Business Coalition on HIV/AIDS.
2. Supports the UN Global Compact, a Kofi Annan initiative requiring multinationals to fulfil minimum standards (against child labour, pro-environmental technologies, human rights, etc.)
3. Formulated own Social Responsibility Guidelines quite early.

4. Supports the World Business Council for Sustainable Development (an association of approximately 170 companies from more than 35 countries and 20 industrial sectors that seeks to secure the sustainability of economic development).
5. Has fuel cells en route to the customer.
6. First car manufacturer to offer cars with a diesel particle filter that works without additives and fully meets the EURO 4 emission regulations, including the limits set for nitrogen oxide.
7. The CHOREN project is exploring the production of gasoline from biomass.
8. In India, the production of bio-diesel fuel from the Jatropha plant is being investigated.
9. Researchers in Windsor, Canada, are finding new ways to make cars more eco-friendly by making them more recyclable or developing efficient painting processes.
10. DaimlerChrysler is a leader in the use of natural fibres. POEMA is a project in which automobile parts are made of natural, renewable raw materials like coconut fibre or natural rubber. At the same time, jobs are being created for the people who harvest these plantations. Other projects with a positive knock-on effect include, for example, the Abaca project. If applied properly, Abaca fibre shows striking similarities to steel.

In spite of all these efforts, this package of initiatives (of which only a selected few are mentioned here) soon met its limits. Other companies have closed the gaps and even overtaken DaimlerChrysler since then. The company is no longer represented on the Dow Jones Sustainability Indexes, nor is it any longer a best practice company. In spite of leading efforts and substantial investments in the industry, it is no longer a benchmark company — has practically overnight become this.

Conclusion

In this chapter, we argue for the management of the often-underestimated level of complexity in sustainability. The presented framework provides a tool for the better comprehension of the phenomenon and its complexity drivers. Key drivers enhance complexity in successfully implemented sustainability strategies and practices. Is the management of sustainability doomed or are there solutions? From our point of view, accepting the reality about complexities and gaining a profound understanding of how to handle them are crucial first steps. Developing the capability to cope with them represents the subsequent necessity. Coping with the inherent complexities will allow all involved stakeholders ranging from governments to businesses and non-profit companies to reach the mentioned next phase in sustainable development — delivering the desired results.

Abbrevations

WCED — World Commission on Environment and Development
CS — Corporate Sustainability
SD — Sustainable Development
CSR — Corporate Social Responsibility
TBL — Triple Bottom Line
WBCSD — World Business Council for Sustainable Development

References

Banerjee, S., E. Iyer and R. Kashyap (2003), "Corporate Environmentalism: Antecedents and Influence of Industry Type," *Journal of Marketing*, vol. 67, issue 2, p. 206.

Brich, D. and J. Moon (2004), "Introduction" *Journal of Corporate Citizenship*, vol. no. 13, pp. 18-23.

Carroll, A. (1999), "Corporate Social Responsibility: Evolution of a Definitional Construct," *Business and Society,* vol. 38, issue. 3, pp. 268-95.

Dyllick, T. and K. Hockerts (2002), "Beyond the Business Case for Corporate Sustainability," *Business Strategy and the Environment,* vol. 11, no. 2, pp. 130-41.

Hoffman, A. (2001), *From Heresy to Dogma: An Institutional History of Corporate Environmentalism*, San Francisco, CA: New Lexington Press.

Rubenstein, R. (2003), "A Keynote: Triple Bottom Line Investing," *International Journal of Business Performance Management*, vol. 5, issue 2-3, pp. 109-13.

SAM (2004), Changing pharma, *SAM Insight* 2/2004.

Schaltegger, S. and A. Sturm (1998), *Eco-efficiency by Eco-controlling,* VDF, Zurich.

Schaltegger, S., C. Herzig, O. Kleiber and J. Müller (2002), *Sustainability Management in Business Enterprises,* BMU, Bonn.

Steger, U. (2003), Corporate diplomacy, Chichester, Wiley.

van Marrewijk, M. (2003), "Concepts and Definitions of CSR and Corporate Sustainability: Between Agency and Communion," *Journal of Business Ethics,* vol. 44, issue 2/3, pp. 95-105.

Waddock, S. and S. Graves (1997), "The Corporate Social Performance — Financial Performance Link," *Strategic Management Journal,* vol. 18, issue 4, pp. 303-20.

WCED (1987), *Our Common Future,* World Commission on Environment and Development, Brussels.

Wilson, M. (2003), "Corporate Sustainability: What is it and Where Does it Come From?," *Ivey Business Journal,* vol. Mar/Apr 2003, pp. 1-5.

Wood, D. (1991), "Corporate social performance revisited," *Academy of Management Review,* vol. 16, no. 4, pp. 691-718.

16

Viable Alternatives for Sustainability
Economic Reforms in Forest Villages of Chhattisgarh

R.N. Pati

Introduction

REDUCTION of poverty has become global priority these days. A good number of international conventions have been organized and different national governments have been sensitized on this global development goal. World Summit on Sustainable Development (WSSD) 2002 at Johannesburg provided a platform to all participants and international leaders to rethink on Millennium Development Goals (MDGs) and address the issues of poverty. The poverty reduction strategies adopted in many developing as well as less developed countries have failed to achieve the desired goals. Because, the social programmes of these countries fail to address the felt needs of the poor appropriately. The voice of the poor has been ignored in the policies developed for them. Their voice and participation was overlooked in different phases of programme at designing as well as implementation level.

Globalization, an international incarnation of capitalism and neo-colonialism, has affected the agriculture of rural India adversely. The globalization has converted all developing countries like India into markets for dumping the products of advanced countries like USA, Japan and UK. The agriculturists have failed to compete with the multinational forces and sell their local products. They are reduced to the poorest from the poorer. Under Millennium declaration, as many as 191 countries including India have taken a vow to eliminate poverty by 2015. This declaration emphasized more on human centric and equitable globalization model, which will benefit the rural poor. Globalization may be treated as potential tool for economic development as well as reduction in rural poverty under neo-liberal reforms. The economic reforms under neo-colonialism and globalizing process have adversely affected the tribal peasants and tribal communities of India in various ways. The adverse economic effect of globalization has far-reaching effects on indigenous economy and political structure in numerous forest villages of Chhattisgarh, one of the tribal dominated States in India. Well over 70 per cent of indigenous people of the world live in Asia and the Pacific. India accommodates 8 per cent tribal population who constitute 40 per cent of displaced groups affected by mining, industrialization and trade liberalization.

The issues of poverty and sustainable development among indigenous communities of Bastar region focuses on their self-reliance, control over productive resources and self-assertion of their ownership over natural resources and indigenous knowledge system. Indigenous knowledge is locally managed and owned. Self-reliance is a local approach to development as perceived by the forest tribes of Bastar region, Chhattisgarh. The policy-makers, development actors and implementers of development agenda go to great lengths to help empower women, poor and unprivileged communities. The true empowerment cannot come from outside. Sustainable

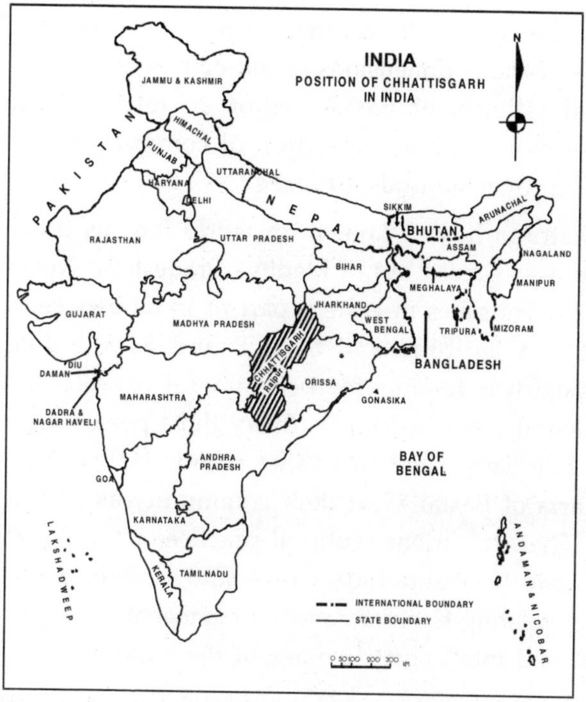
INDIA
POSITION OF CHHATTISGARH IN INDIA
N
JAMMU & KASHMIR
HIMACHAL
PUNJAB
HARYANA
DELHI
UTTARANCHAL
PAKISTAN
NEPAL
SIKKIM
BHUTAN
ARUNACHAL
ASSAM
NAGALAND
MANIPUR
MEGHALAYA
TRIPURA
MIZORAM
RAJASTHAN
UTTAR PRADESH
BIHAR
JHARKHAND
WEST BENGAL
BANGLADESH
GUJARAT
MADHYA PRADESH
CHHATTISGARH
Raipur
ORISSA
GONASIKA
DIU
DAMAN
DADRA & NAGAR HAVELI
MAHARASHTRA
ANDHRA PRADESH
BAY OF BENGAL
GOA
KARNATAKA
LAKSHADWEEP
KERALA
TAMILNADU
ANDAMAN & NICOBAR
INTERNATIONAL BOUNDARY
STATE BOUNDARY

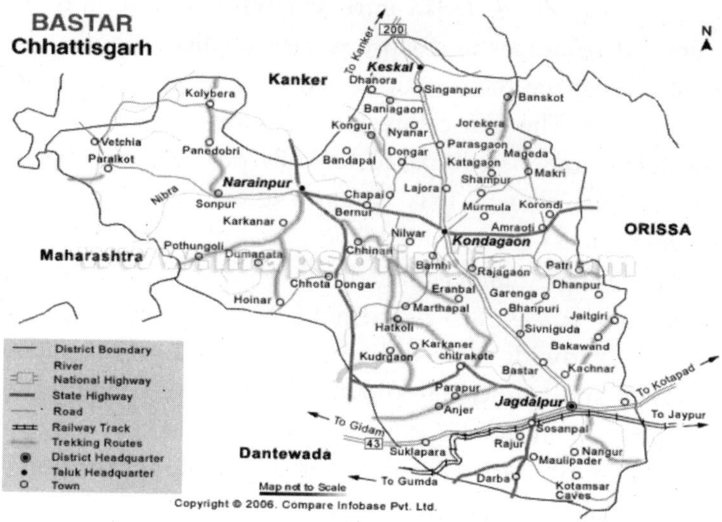
BASTAR
Chhattisgarh
N
200
To Kanker
Keskal
Kanker
Dhanora
Singanpur
Banskot
Kolybera
Banlagaon
Kongur
Nyanar
Jorekera
Vetchia
Paralkot
Panedobri
Bandapal
Dongar
Parasgaon
Mageda
Katagaon
Makri
Shampur
Narainpur
Nibra
Sonpur
Chapai
Lajora
Murmula
Korondi
Bernur
Karkanar
Amraoti
Nilwar
Kondagaon
ORISSA
Maharashtra
Pothungoli
Dumanata
Chhinari
Bamhi
Rajagaon
Patri
Chhota Dongar
Eranbal
Garenga
Dhanpur
Hoinar
Marthapal
Bhanpuri
Jaitgiri
Hatkoli
Sivniguda
Karkaner
Bakawand
Kudrgaon
chitrakote
Bastar
Kachnar
Parapur
To Kotapad
Anjer
Jagdalpur
To Gidam
Sosanpal
To Jaypur
43
Rajur
Suklapara
Dantewada
Maulipader
Nangur
To Gumda
Darba
Kotamsar Caves
Map not to Scale
District Boundary
River
National Highway
State Highway
Road
Railway Track
Trekking Routes
District Headquarter
Taluk Headquarter
Town
Copyright © 2006. Compare Infobase Pvt. Ltd.

empowerment is self-empowerment. The present chapter examines various dimensions of self-empowerment of women in tribal villages of Bastar region in terms of economic empowerment and self-assertion of community rights and ownership over natural resources.

Chhattisgarh, well known for world famous tribal region of India, was carved out of Madhya Pradesh on November 1, 2000. This State lies in eastern part of India between 17°46'N and 24°06'N latitude and 80°15'E and 84°51'E longitude. Chhattisgarh is famous for rich mineral resources, cultural heritage and medicinal herbs. Every third person of the State is a tribal. The tribal folks like Gond, Halba, Muria and Abujmaria of Bastar view their community as an integrated whole. Their traditional cultural practice, art and craft, local health tradition and indigenous knowledge and cultural practices relating to environmental management constitute the cultural and intellectual heritage of the State.

The Bastar region of the State covers Decan Biogeographical Zone (DBZ) enriched with unique and rich biological resources and various rare medicinal herbs. The forest area of the region can be classified as open forest and dense forest. The dense forests constitute 67.10 per cent of total forest area as compared to 32.89 per cent of coverage under open forest. This forest region covering Decan Biogeographical Zone upholds medicinal plant hotspot of the State covering Abujmar, Bailadila Hills and Kanger Reserve wherefrom at least 625 medicinal plants species have been traded worldwide. The indigenous art and crafts, sacred materials and traditional knowledge of tribal communities have been commercially exploited without the knowledge or permission of the indigenous people and appropriately compensating them. Many museums have been established to derive commercial benefits from art and crafts of these tribes of Bastar. A series of trade fairs exhibitions, and tribal dance programmes have been regularly organized both at state and national community level commercializing art, craft and heritage of the tribes of Bastar. Under the influence of globalization, liberalization and privatizations, the tangible and intangible aspects of cultural heritage of tribal communities of Bastar have been commercialized without compensating these indigenous people. The vital components of the cultural heritage have been isolated from traditional territory through over-exploitation of biological resources, illegal felling of trees and brutal exploitation of mineral resources. The tribal herbalists have estimated that well over 75 per cent of rare herbs have been wiped out from the biodiversity by clandestine operation of the traders.

The concept of sustainable development among these forest tribes of Bastar region revolves around livelihood issues and protection of basic rights and equity for everyone in these tribal communities. The life support systems in these tribal communities have been challenged as the government has failed to provide alternative livelihood for these communities. The forces of globalization and industrialization under the banner of so-called "development" have undermined the cultural, social and natural life support systems of these forest tribes. These tribal communities have lost their capacities to produce from common productive resources. They feel the cultural treasures, traditions, customs and lifestyle have been eroded under the process of development more rapidly after formation of the new state. The germ plasm of good number of medicinal species has been plundered. The medicinal species like *Ruvolfia serpentina* have disappeared from many parts of Bastar forests. The species like *Acacia concinna, Emblica glandulifera, Swertia Chirayta* and *Emblica Officinalis* have high market value both inside and outside the country.

The present write-up aims at exploring the following research questions in context of issues of sustainable development in forest villages of Bastar region, Chhattisgarh.

(a) How the tribal communities assert their rights to determination in protecting their customary rights over natural resources, life support system and equity.

(b) How economic empowerment of tribal women supported through Van Dhan (Forest Wealth) Self Help Groups (SHGs) network promotes community access to and control over natural resources by safeguarding their cultural and biological integrity.

(c) How international, national and state level legislations have been actualized through grass-roots level interventions in reduction of poverty and promotion of sustainable development in micro scale.

These research questions have been probed through development of appropriate research tools and undertaking of empirical investigation.

Research Design

The present chapter is based on anthropological appraisal of ethical and social issues of sustainable development among Dravidian forest tribes in nine forest villages of Bastar district under Decan Bio-geographical Zone in Eastern India. It further explains how economic globalization has affected the political and economic systems of these forest communities and isolated them from local biodiversity. A team of two social anthropologists and one ethno-botanist had conducted four months' field work in Chota Dongar, khadakagaon, Dhoudei, Dhanura, Gourdanda, Brehabeda, Palki, Bijili and Keralakha forest villages of Narayanpur Block in Bastar district during August to October 2003 and June to July 2005. As many as 46-

community leaders, 18 tribal herbalists (*baiga*), 12 Shamans (*gayata*) were covered under in-depth Key Informant Interview (KII). The study has drawn valuable insights from success stories of community-based initiatives focused on women empowerment, experimentation on community biodiversity registry, documentation of the indigenous knowledge on bio-wealth facilitated by a consortium of 50 women SHGs (Van Dhan Samities) under guidance of the NGO, *Dandakaranya Sarankhyan Evam Sodha Saṅstha*, Narayanpur. The in-depth anthropological case studies have been conducted on bottom-up experimentation by this consortium towards documentation of Peoples Biodiversity Registry (PBR) and related indigenous knowledge. The study has drawn insights from case study of 85 seasonal outmigrant families of these villages. Focus Group Discussion (FGD) has been conducted with members of women SHGs, lineage elders and herbalists separately. The study has drawn inputs from analyzing of oral histories and participant observation on rituals associated with collection and use of biological resources.

The semi-structured precoded schedule, interview guides for FGD and case study were administered during the fieldwork. The study adopted both qualitative and quantitative research tools including in-depth personal interview, case study, Focus Group Discussion and Participant observation. Appropriate cross checking and validation of data have been exercised through adoption of on-the-spot, sample check up and verification.

Secondary information on morbidity and mortality statistics have been collected from Primary Health Centres (PHC) and related sub-Health Centres of these villages. The secondary information on statistical data pertaining to illegal felling of trees and legal cases lodged against culprits have been collected from Forest Department and the local police station. The insights drawn for this study are based on demonstrative experimentation of one NGO translating the resolutions of international debate, Convention of Biological Diversity (CBD) and provisions of Biological Diversity Act, Government of India, into grass-root reality through women empowerment, self-assertion of community rights and ownership over natural resources.

The present study has critically assessed the deeper and cultural factors inter-related with the economic transformation of tribal communities at micro-level and curbing down of poverty in Bastar regions of Chhattisgarh. The tribes in Bastar need to be shifted away from their parental habitat towards alternative life support system focusing on land, pastoral enterprise and exploitation of mineral and natural resources as basic source of livelihood. The issues of alienation of traditional habitat and parental land aggravate frustration and force a significant section of tribal communities into adopting alternative life support systems.

Impact of Economic Globalization on Biodiversity Conservation and Sustainable Development

The sustainable development and economic transformation in the nascent State of Chhattisgarh, where one-third of population are tribal, lie in promotion of pastoral enterprise, exploitation of rich cultural heritage through spiritual, health and eco-tourism interventions, promotion of tribal arts and crafts, intensification of medicinal plant farming, protection of biodiversities and appropriate exploitation of mineral and natural resources through indigenous entrepreneurship and resource management initiatives. The globalization has affected the life of tribals of Chhattisgarh in various forms. The cultural diversities of the tribes have been eroded within a very short period. The tribals have been deprived of leading their indigenous lifestyle, up-keeping their traditional customs, values and cultural heritage. They have been exposed to various forms of exploitation by traders, forest officers, exporters, forest contractors, politicians and Maoist activists. The promotion of infrastructure and rural development interventions including feeder roads, culverts, bridges, water management and water conservation programmes in forest villages of Bastar regions has been obstructed and threatened by intermediary militant forces.

Trade liberalization and linkage with international market have promoted export of tribal art and crafts of Bastar region. Internet and promotion of website on rich tribal cultural heritage of Bastar region have attracted attention of foreign markets during the last couple of years. But the benefits have been monopolized by non-tribal exporters. The tribal artisans have not been benefited but excluded from the process of participation in global economy. The forces of globalization and trade liberalization have led to increased use of biological resources and related traditional knowledge of tribals in the forest regions of Chhattisgarh. India is one among the group of 17 mega biodiversity countries of the world. India has been pushing for an amendment to TRIPS (the International Trade Related Intellectual Property Rights agreement) to curb down the growing biopiracy in these tribal territories of Chhattisgarh. It has emphasized on the incorporation of the principles of consent and benefit sharing in TRIPS as per the resolutions of UN Convention on Biological Diversity (CBD). The users are not only required to disclose the source of biological resources that have been used in their innovations but also obtain the prior informed consent (PIC) of the community who are the customary guardians of biological resources as well as related traditional knowledge system.

These proposed amendments of TRIPS cannot be appropriately applicable without enabling the stakeholders to develop Peoples Biodiversity Registry by creating Intellectual Property Rights (IPR) region. These aspects are very closely related with the economic reforms and initiatives for sustainable development in these tribal territories.

The Government of India has enacted Biological Diversity Act in 2002, which seeks protection and regulation of the country's natural resources and traditional knowledge. This initiative has been stimulated by resolutions of International Convention on Biological Diversity to which India was one of the signatories. This Act has prescribed three-tier system of regulation ranging from national level to grass-roots level. National Biodiversity Authority (NBA) has been created at apex level to coordinate the activities of State level Biodiversity Board (SBB) and local level Biodiversity Management Committee (BMC). The Government of India has drafted the rules of Biodiversity Act (BA) in 2004, which entrusted the National Biodiversity Authority to take appropriate steps for creating database and documentation system for biological resources through biological registers and electronic data bank. The Ministry of Environment and Forest, Government of India convened a series of workshops for preparing detailed manuals for People's Biodiversity Registry. It has been visualized that each Gram Panchayat of the country would be encouraged to promote Biodiversity Information System (BIS) and Peoples Biodiversity Registry (PBR). This would serve as a storehouse of all biodiversity-related information and be used as a tool towards gaining access to forest produce. People will be sensitized to know the biodiversity around them and curtail its use and plan ecological conservation accordingly. At the initial stage, Centre for Ecological Sciences (CES), Bangalore has been entrusted by Government of India to prepare manuals for PBR to be launched at least in 300 Gram Panchayats of the country, which would promote Intellectual Property Right region and ensure conservation of bio-wealth.

The Government of India has taken praiseworthy stand at international circle and denied IPRs on life forms at the World Trade Organization (WTO) level. But, the flaws in domestic legislative provisions have not been prioritized and rectified so far. It has allowed IPRs on plant varieties. No policy has been enacted to empower the stakeholders in preventing biopiracy in terms of obtaining prior informed consent directly from the communities. Biodiversity Rules, 2004 enacted by Government of India have entrusted power to National Biodiversity Authority to grant permission to foreigners seeking access to biological resources and traditional knowledge without taking prior informed consent from local Biodiversity Management Committee. The representation of community at State and National Level Biodiversity Boards has been ignored. The role of local Biodiversity Management Committee has been confined to documentation of traditional knowledge and developing people's biodiversity registry only. Besides, the provisions for equitable benefits-sharing by stakeholders from commercial use of biowealth and indigenous knowledge have not been well-defined in the Biodiversity Rules. The district administration has been authorized to receive the benefit on behalf of the community. The principles of consent and benefit-sharing need to be revised and restructured incorporating room for empowerment of stakeholders as well as local Biodiversity Management Committee in terms of granting prior informed consent to users and availing benefits-sharing directly without involvement of any bureaucratic hurdles.

A good number of international conventions have been organized since the last two decades to which India was a potential signatory. Rio Earth Summit, 1994, Convention of Biological Diversity (CBD), ILO Convention, and UN Draft Declaration on Rights of Indigenous People are the important international debates which have aired concerns for Human Rights and development issues of indigenous people. There exists a wide range of vacuum between these international debates and grass-root realities. The resolutions take years together to be transformed into action at the grass roots. The stakeholders have been deprived, denied and are isolated.

After formation of the new state in 2001, the Government of Chhattisgarh enacted people-friendly forest policy empowering the community access to control over natural resources. The provisions have been made to protect customary rights to tribals over forest management apart from meeting their requirements for fuel wood, fodder, minor forest produce, etc. The important component of Chhattisgarh Forest Policy of 2000 covers feasible mechanism for *in situ/ex situ* conservation, domestication, propagation and non-destructive harvest of medicinal plants, with the active support from local people including traditional healers and *vaidya*s. The State Government has encouraged the tribal communities for active participation in natural resource management by endowing the ownership rights of minor forest produce on Panchayati Raj Institutions through provisions of the Act, Panchayati Upabandh Adhiniyam, 1996. As many as 6687 community-level committees have been formed under the Joint Forest Management (JFM) programme. This has yet to initiate efforts in the conservation, sustainable and utilization of medicinal plant resources and restore the degradation of forests in the State. The Government of Chhattisgarh has envisaged schemes on People's Protected Area (PPA) to translate the policy into meaningful action in terms of network of PPA, for sustainable livelihood including health cover. The Forest Department has annually adopted one thousand hectares of forest area rich in medicinal plants for *in situ* conservation. Besides, the Forest Department of Government of Chhattisgarh has launched a wide range of programmes directed towards conservation of biodiversity as well as providing sustainable flow of natural products and services to local forest communities. These schemes are: Training for conservation and development of non timber forest produce; Promotion of medicinal plant nurseries; and Marketing of medicinal herbs and plants. The Government here has also prepared State Biodiversity Strategy Action Plan (SBSAP, 2002) under the National Biodiversity Strategy Action Plan (NBSAP).

The sacred groves covering patches of natural vegetation dedicated by the tribals to their ancestral spirits or deities, play an important role in the socio-religious life of these tribal communities. These groves provide benefits to local communities in terms of grazing of animals, harvesting of certain rare herbal species, collection of firewoods and celebration of different festivals. These groves serve as living nurseries of ancestral and community identity. The commercial forest policies coupled with encroachment by local community, modernization and market forces, and religious conversions have isolated tribal communities exercising their customary rights over these natural vegetations.

The Sacred Grove Conservation Movement (SGCM), initiated in the year 1992, has been incorporated in the Government Forest Policy of Chhattisgarh. It has given a new dimension to the bottoms-up approach in grass-root level biodiversity conservation and preservation initiatives backed up by State Biodiversity Strategy Action Plan, 2001.

The Government of Chhattisgarh has made experimentation on innovative scheme, "Van Dhan" (Forest

Wealth) empowering women Self-Help Groups (SHGs) to market non-nationalized, non-timber forest produce. The authorized-women SHGs are entitled by the government to procure non-nationalized Non-Timber Forest Produce (NTFP) from local market along with village Forest Protection Committee, Eco-development Committee with award of seven per cent commission. It is reported that during 2001 to 2003, well over 792 women SHGs along with other Community Based Organistaions (CBOs) have contributed towards selling over 40,000 tonnes of non-nationalized NTFP, items like *tendu* leaves, sala seeds, *mahua* flowers and seeds, *amla, harada*, gum, tamarind and *mahua* leaves worth of Indian Rs. 25 millions. It signifies the vibrant contribution of tribal women in strengthening the commercialization of NTFP items apart from contributing to the sustenance of local health tradition. The women Self Help Groups have been encouraged to initiate various micro enterprise activities with assistance from government and loan from commercial banks.

The plight of tribals in Bastar region of Chhattisgarh continues to be miserable despite the pumping of huge resources through various programmes under the tribal sub-plan. The Governments both at Centre and State levels have not ensured tribals' inclusion in economic growth process. The benefits of economic growth have neither evenly spread nor occurred evenly. The success stories of Indian economic growth in terms of low rate of inflation and huge foreign exchange during 2002-03 have not helped in raising the quality of life of the poorest of the poor and tribals in forest regions of Chhatisgarh. The economic growth has not been equitable. Due to lack of employment opportunities coupled with natural calamities threatening the agriculture sector in forest villages of Bastar, large number of men, women and youth are reported migrating from villages to town and cities as seasonal migrants and living in unenviable conditions. The seasonal emigration from these forest villages have not only added expansion of urban slums with growth of urban poor in Delhi, Mumbai, Kolkata, Surat, Ahmedabad and Chennai but also intensified the episodes of feminization of poverty. Frequent droughts and irregular monsoons have forced more than 40 per cent of these farmers to leave villages with families to these metropolitan cities in search of employment in industry and construction sectors. Poor infrastructure development and marketing network have retarded the economic growth in tribal villages in Bastar regions of Chhattisgarh.

Sustainable Development: A Different Concept Among Forest Communities

The sustainable development has been conceptualized among community elites of these villages in terms of addressing the basic survival issues, promoting access to flora and fauna, creation of ownership on biological resources and protection of indigenous knowledge as well as intellectual and cultural property rights. These components of development are very closely interwoven with livelihood opportunities and substructure of economic and political systems. In industrial society, GDP has been considered as an indicator for measuring development. The concept of sustainable development differs among forest communities of Decan Bio-geographical Zone. The concept of sustainable development is deep-rooted within cultural values, environmental ethics and socio-economic and political structures of these communities directed towards protection of their human rights.

The efforts of network of 50 women Self Help Groups (SHGs) in mobilizing weekly savings at the rate of Indian Rs. 20 per head from 527 members have accumulated adequate fund for investment in micro-enterprise activities at community level over a period of last eight years. The arrangement of appropriate linkage with commercial banks has enabled these Van Dhan Samities raising of loans towards effectively carrying out various micro-enterprise activities like promoting pisciculture in community ponds, running of paddy, pulses and millet processing units, broom stick binding, operating Grama Panchayat level Public Distribution System (PDS) dealing with consumer items, promoting petty enterprises like production of *agarbatti,* mosquito coils, detergent powder, etc. This experimentation has enhanced women's entrepreneurial ability for appropriate exploration of physical and human resources as well as boosting up gender mainstreaming initiatives. The grass-root women forums are instrumental for integration of community assets within political, social and economic structures of their communities, which have been reflected in manifestation of their social, economic and political empowerment.

The tribals of this State lack ability to develop and apply entrepreneurial and business skill required for economic exploitation of physical and human resources available within indigenous territories of the State. Lack of appropriate local enthusiasm to explore available opportunities towards integration of community assets within regional, political, social, and economic structures has restricted local development initiatives in transforming local enterprise initiatives and grass-root co-operation involving local networks and community partnership into a desired economic development scenario.

The issues of food security, group ownership and access to forest resources among indigenous communities are major survival issues, which are ignored to be prioritized and addressed through appropriate participatory interventions by

NGOs, CBOs, Panchayati Raj Institutions (PRIs), community and Government. The NGOs are yet to be encouraged with appropriate sensitization and firm commitment towards shouldering the responsibilities of integrating ethno-healing practices with modern medical systems. Besides, the NGOs have to work in tandem to bridge the gap between these therapeutic systems, to facilitate the practices of folk healers and understand and protect the tribals' Intellectual Property Rights. They have to work in mapping the bio-resources and habitats of the herbs, the common produce of the tribals, and help them to solve their land rights issues. Tribals must be encouraged to protect forest and biodiversity resources. They must learn to generate income through exploitation of non-timber forest produce and intensive farming of medicinal plants through well co-ordinated participatory interventions. All these have to be explained to these tribals by the NGOs. Well co-ordinated intervention in these areas will surely boost up economic transformations in this nascent State.

The elites of some villages in Narayanpur Block of Bastar expressed their frustration over losing their cultural diversity and inability to maintain secrecy of their customary rules. The conversion initiative by some missionary groups in remote forest villages has isolated them from their religious faith and rendered them refugees on their own heartland. The local markets in these tribal regions have been flooded with chemical fertilizers, harmful products and drugs dumped by multinational companies. The agents of concept-sale and net work marketing of foreign products have trapped a significant number of unemployed youth. The empowerment of local bodies has been diluted by bureaucratic hurdles and has diverted the access of big players to common productive resources in these indigenous territories. The hijacking of

Intellectual Property Rights of tribal herbalists and shamans, premature exploitation and smuggling of rare medicinal herbs and commercial use of indigenous knowledge without appropriately compensating the custodians of knowledge system have not only destroyed the local health tradition but also destroyed the base of time-tested traditional knowledge on medicinal potencies in various species of animals, plants and minerals. The premature tapping of herbal habitat is treated unethical by tribal herbalists. These issues threaten the process of sustainable development as perceived by elites of the forest communities of this region.

Globalization and Transfer of Technology

The globalization has introduced a new technology in tribal heartland of Bastar, famous for tribal handicrafts, folk dances and hidden natural beauty. The tribal artisans of Kumbharapara village are found interacting with foreign buyers for their unique products of art and craft in brass, bronze and bell metal through the tireless efforts of one NGO. This linkage has, no doubt, excelled the export of tribal art and crafts on one hand, and boomed tourism on the other. The introduction of IT in the globalization era has empowered tribal artists to keep a computer at home and interact with international customers through Internet. This boom of tourism and visit of foreign tourists to this forest region of Bastar have not only posed huge threats to sensitive eco-system but also paved ways for violating cultural property rights. The biodiversity hotspots of Bastar region (e.g. Bailadilla Hills and Abhujmar) have been altered by infrastructural development programme and other human activities.

In the globalization era, a series of development initiatives have been launched in these tribal regions through industrialization and trade liberalization. Due to the absence of written contract between users (industrialists, pharmaceutical companies, traders) and custodians of bio-wealth (tribal communities) and lack of *sui generis* legislation, these tribal communities have not only been isolated from natural resources but also been deprived of sharing equitable benefits from commercial use of indigenous knowledge system. Their human rights including rights to land and rights to self-governance have been violated. Various forms of cultural expressions along with traditional songs, dance and oral traditions have been commercialized by business houses and multinational companies in this era of trade liberalization. The knowledge of tribal shamans on rare medicinal herbs has been commercialized by pharmaceutical companies.

Grass-Root Initiatives and Community Empowerment

The cultural practices of the Dravidian tribes, Gond, Halba, Maria, Abuja Muria and other tribal communities of this region, who are mostly agro-silviculturist groups, constitute substrates of cultural resources influencing not only reproduction but also circulation of social and natural environment. These tribal communities have adopted indigenous mechanism of conservation of bio-wealth through various cultural practices prevalent from time immemorial. They draw livelihood, elements of agriculture, veterinary, medicine and cosmopological utility from forest. Their cultural practices sustain a strong interaction with biodiversity and ensure equilibrium between local ecology and social health. They are the custodians of the rich tribal heritage, which is inherited from one generation to another and presented through oral tradition and cultural expression. The cultural practices and indigenous knowledge system among these forest tribes of Decan Bio-geographical Zone in eastern India have been evolved by individual innovations of herbalists, shamans and bonesetters.

Self-realization and participatory assessment by tribal women on overexploitation of biological resources around their community have united them and infused a drive towards repairing and restoring the damaged bio-resources. "We have destroyed our own forest," was the guilty feeling which knocked the hearts of as many as 527 tribal women working in at least 50 Van Dhan Samities across 30 villages to promote a common platform for initiating ecological restoration, intervention and documentation of bio-wealth. They have realized that the big players of the globalization era have posed devastating challenges for their survival. The challenges are appropriation of indigenous knowledge developed through ages and dispossession of land and common productive resources within the tribal territory. They have also realized that, in the absence of appropriate documentation of indigenous knowledge system, it has been treated as a commodity by multinational companies for acquiring patent without honouring it as a cultural heritage of the tribal communities. The tribal innovators (shamans, herbalists and bonesetters) have been handicapped to challenge the patent claim and community-based rights to secure equitable benefit from commercialization of this knowledge by external agencies. The tribal herbalists have realized that not less than three-fourths of rare herbs have been eliminated from the biodiversity by smuggling of medicinal herbs and exploitation of forest contractors over the last decade.

The assessment of ecological loss as perceived by the tribal women through the opinion poll conducted over 527 women during the survey indicates that regular firewood collection contributes a major cause of vegetation degradation followed by illegal felling of trees, exploitation by forest contractors, smuggling of medicinal herbs and increased grazing of animals. The ecological damages have led to changes in monsoon reflected through reduction of rainy and winter seasons and outbreak of frequent droughts over last two decades. Different species of birds, animals and plants have been eliminated from the biodiversity. The duration of summer has become longer.

Poor health and nutritional status contributes significantly towards poor political, economic and social empowerment among tribal women. The complex nutritional and reproductive health issues aggravate their situation of poverty. Study of 315 pregnant women indicates that malaria and anaemia are major health risks among pregnant women. Sexual tract infections (STIs) and reproductive tract infections (RTIs) prevail among a small section of pregnant women in these communities. Inappropriate lifestyle is attributed to occurrence of some respiratory diseases whereas consumption of contaminated pond water, upholding traditional dietary preference and inappropriate menstrual hygiene contribute significantly to poor health and degraded nutritional status among tribal women in these villages.

The frequent drought and natural calamities owing to irregular monsoon and climate changes have broken down the agriculture sector. The seasonal emigration of female labour force with their families has multiplied the episodes of feminization of poverty which is deep-rooted in patriarchal social structure. The low status of women, increase of female-headed households and absence of appropriate platform to air and articulate common concerns focusing on gender discrimination have rendered the women from poorer to poorest in these communities.

The efforts of these grass-root women SHGs towards restoration of damaged ecosystem covered organizing a series of workshops with facilitators in main villages, orientation on PRA (Participatory Rural Appraisal) and mapping exercise, organizing exhibitions, fairs, and mobile biodiversities festivals across the villages. These interventions have resulted in tremendous public sensitization on biodiversity restoration. The facilitators organised village-level workshops for conducting PRA and mapping exercise. As many as 30 village resource maps covering inventory on habitat of plants, local names of plants, birds, animals and insects have been prepared under guidance of the NGOs and environmentalists. Three copies of biodiversity registers have been prepared with endorsement of all the villagers. These signatories of communities took mass oath to conserve, protect and document the bio-wealth of the villages on the occasion of national Republic day witnessed by government authorities.

The community-based nurseries have been promoted in all the adopted villages raising the saplings of native species and fast growing varieties of fuel wood species. The members of the participating SHGs contributed free labour inputs towards replanting the damaged village forest with saplings raised in the village nurseries. Besides, the women farmers of these Van Dhan Samities have raised 27,000 saplings of local variety of bio-diesel plant, "Ratan Jot" in at least 20 village nurseries with financial support from IFFCO, a corporate house promoting partnership with farmers for renewing the vegetation. A large chunk of farmers are encouraged to explore utility of this plant variety as fencing plant of the crop fields. The wide scale utilization of this plant in fencing the crop fields has expanded the community bio-wealth resource base.

The intervention initiated by members of women SHGs towards restoration of damaged biodiversity has infused a sense of community ownership on bio-wealth among half of the villagers and curbed drastically illegal felling of trees within a short period of five years beyond expectation of the district administration. The cultural integrity and harmonious co-operation among women SHGs boosted up their self-confidence, self-assertion and claim over bio-resources for which they raised a war against forest contractors and initiated legal action against a good number of traders involved in clandestine exploitation of forest and smuggling of herbs from these tribal territories.

Conclusion

The food security and control over common productive resources among forest dwellers are major survival issues. The commercial forest policy, encroachment of forest land, and exploitation of mines have challenged the customary rights of tribals to natural resource management. The population pressure in these forest communities has led not only to shrinkage of productive resources but also to reduction of livelihood supporting role of natural resources. The globalization forces have isolated tribal communities from forest and from exercising indigenous management norms over natural resources. The new industrial policy of the Government has paved ways for corporate houses exercising control over land and productive resources in forest regions of the State. The efforts of forest community in restoring their rights over biological resources and resisting mining adventures have been failed. The efforts of women SHGs have restored a spirit of harmony and socio-cultural identity in preventing degradation of natural resources. The traditional value of distribution of resources has been incorporated in group-based control of natural resources as observed from the intervention of women Groups. Their efforts have created self-assertion and enhanced community influence in terms of management of natural resources, facilitating growth of nurseries of medicinal plants and preservation of valuable species. The challenges of denial and erosion of separate cultural identity imposed by market economy and adverse globalization forces have been appropriately managed. The efforts of these women groups have minimized the destruction of traditional resource base and promoted new vegetations around temples and schools at par with Sacred Groves exploring sustainable partnership with community, government and local people. The experiment of these women SHGs enhances participation and empowerment of community to adopt alternative life support system with enhanced capacities for utilizing common productive resources. The cumulative effects of all these components would go a long way in ensuring sustainable practices of natural resources management and reduction of household poverty.

The vibrant intervention of women SHGs in cleaning the water resources, educating rural mass on prevention of malaria and water-borne diseases through the roles of plays, exhibitions, drawing competition among students, and health fairs have led to reduction of malaria and water-borne diseases to a considerable extent. The Ante Natal Care (ANC) and Post Natal Care (PNC) screenings have been enhanced with motivation of women which created a far reaching positive impact on child survival.

The vibrant interventions of women SHGs have brought about economic reforms among poorest families, which have been reflected in reduction in seasonal out-migration in these villages. The household indebtedness has been reduced with economic empowerment of women and adoption of alternate livelihood options facilitated through micro-enterprise initiatives. The political empowerment of women has been reflected through return of a couple of elected women candidates as office bearers of Panchayati Raj Institution, 2005. The documentation of community knowledge in the form of community biodiversity registry, initiated by women SHGs network in partnership with NGOs and community, has empowered the women in particular, and community in general, claiming ownership and rights over biodiversity and infused the forces for challenging the patent claim on knowledge of medicinal herbs. Such innovation experimentation has facilitated integration of community assets within political, social and economic structures of the community and ensuring protection, preservation and documentation of local knowledge system. Community achievement at micro-scale corroborates the concept of sustainable development defined as: "Indigenous people have the right to their traditional medicine and health practices, including the right to the protection of vital medicine plants, animals and minerals" (Article 24, UN Draft Declaration on the Rights of Indigenous People).

Abbrevations

ANC	—	Ante Natal Care
BA	—	Biodiversity Act
BIS	—	Biodiversity Information System
BMC	—	Biodiversity Management Committee
CBD	—	Convention of Biological Diversity
CBOs	—	Community Based Organistaion
CES	—	Centre for Ecological Sciences
DBZ	—	Deccan Bio-geographical Zone
FGD	—	Focus Group Discussion

IPR	—	Intellectual Property Rights
JFM	—	Joint Forest Management
KII	—	Key Informant Interview
NBA	—	National Biodiversity Authority
NBSAP	—	National Biodiversity Strategy Action Plan
NTFP	—	Non Timber Forest Produce
PBR	—	Peoples Biodiversity Registry
PDS	—	Public Distribution System
PHC	—	Primary Health Centres
PIC	—	Prior Informed Consent
PNC	—	Post Natal Care
PPA	—	People's Protected Area
PRA	—	Participatory Rural Appraisal
PRIs	—	Panchayati Raj Institutions
RTIs	—	Reproductive Tract Infections
SBB	—	State-level Biodiversity Board
SBSAP	—	State Biodiversity Strategy Action Plan
SGCM	—	Sacred Grove Conservation Movement
SHGs	—	Self-Help Groups
STIs	—	Sexual Tract Infections
TRIPS	—	The International Trade Related Intellectual Property Rights
WSSD	—	World Summit on Sustainable Development
WTO	—	World Trade Organization

References

Agrawal, A. (2002), Indigenous Knowledge and Policies of Classification, UNESCO, pp. 289-97.

Alcoff, L.M. (2000), Power knowledge in the colonial unconscious: A dialogue between Dussel and Foucaut. In E. Medieta and L.M. Alcoff (eds.), *Thinking from the Underside of History*, Lanham, MD: Rowman and Littlefield, pp. 249-68.

Aseby, E.J. (1996), Indigenous knowledge and intellectual property: towards equitable compensation, In *Biodiversity, Biotechnology and Sustainable Development in Health and Agriculture Emerging Connections,* Washington, D.C.: Pan American Health Organization, Pan American Sanitary Bureau, pp. 191-210.

Galison, P. (2001), Material culture, theoretical culture and delocalization, In J.W. Scoot and D. Keates (eds.), *Schools of Thoughts : Twenty-Five Years of Interpretive Social Science,* Princeton University Press, pp. 179-93.

Gallopin, G.C., S. Funtowicz, M. O'Connor and J. Revetz (2001), Science for the twenty-first century: From social contract to the scientific core, *International Social Science Journal,* 53 (2), pp. 219-29.

Guyer, J. and S.M.E. Belinga (1995), Wealth in people as wealth in knowledge: Accumulation and composition in Equatorial Africa, *The Journal of African History* 36(1), pp. 91-120.

Hall, K.T. and S.A. Laird (2004), Bioprospecting arrangement and benefit sharing with local communities, In J.M. Finger and P. Schuler (eds.), *Poor Peoples Knowledge: Promoting Intellectual Property in Developing Countries,* Washington, D.C., The World Bank/Oxford University Press. pp. 133-58.

Kuramoto, J. and F. Sagasti (2002), Integrating local and global knowledge, technology and production system: Challenges for technical co-operation. In Fukuda- S. Parr, C. Lopes and K. Malik (eds.), *Capacity for Development: New Solutions to Old Problems,* London: Earthscan, pp. 203-28.

Legassick, M. (1980), The frontier tradition in South African historiography, In S. Marks and A. Atmore (eds.), *Economy and Society in Pre-industrial South Africa,* London: Longman. pp. 44-79.

Nakashima, D. (2000), Traditional knowledge: Resisting and adopting to globalization. Paper prepared for the UNCTAD Expert Meeting on systems and National experiences for protecting Traditional knowledge, innovations and practices, Geneva, 30th October to 1st November 2000, Geneva: UNESCO, pp. 1-8.

Odora-Hoppers, C. (2002), Indigenous knowledge and integration of knowledge systems: Towards a conceptual and methodological Framework, In C.O. Hoppers (ed.), *Indigenous Knowledge and the Integration of Knowledge Systems: Towards Philosophy of Articulation,* Claremont, South Africa: New Africa Books, pp. 2-22.

Pati, R.N. (2004), Impact of Globalization on primitive tribes of India: An anthropological appraisal, unpublished research paper, pp. 4-12.

——— (2005), Cultural Dimensions of poverty among primitive tribe Kamar in Chhattisgarh: A critical Appraisal, unpublished research paper, pp. 1-15.

Ranger, T. (1983/1992), The Invention of Tradition in colonial Africa, In E. Hobsbawn and T. Ranger (eds.), *The Invention of Tradition,* Cantoed, Cambridge: Cambridge University Press, pp. 211-62.

Reeves, J. (1998), Report of the Review of the Aboriginal Land Rights (Northern Territory), Act 1976 — Building on Land Rights for the Next Generation, Canberra: Aboriginal and Torres Strait Islander Commission, pp. 3-9.

Singh, P. (1996), "The Role of Entrepreneurship in Economic Development," in *P.S. Lokanathon 72nd Birthday Commemorative Volume, Economic Development: Issues and Policies*, Bombay: Vora and Co., pp. 2-5.

Shukla, H.L. (1988), *Tribal Heritage of Madhya Pradesh,* Delhi: B.R. Publishing Corporation, pp. 6-10.

Svarstad, H. (2000), Reciprocity biopiracy, heroes, villains and victims, In H. Scarstad and S.S. Dhillon (eds.), *Responding to Bio-processing: From Biodiversity in South to Medicine in the North,* Oslo: Spartacus Forlog As, pp. 19-35.

Taylor, J. (1997), *The Opportunity Costs of Future Indigenous Labour Force Status,* CAEPR Discussion Paper no. 128, Canberra : Canter for Aboriginal Economic Policy Research, Australian National University, 1984, pp. 6-8.

Tiwari, D.N. (1984), Primitive Tribes of Madhya Pradesh, Strategy for Development, GOI, MOHF, Tribal Development Division, New Delhi, pp. 10-15.

Yunupingu, B. (1991), A Plan for Ganma Research, in *Aboriginal Pedagogy: Aboriginal Teachers Speak Out,* Geelong: Deakin University Press, pp. 2-9.

Watson-Verran, H. and D. Turnbull (1995), Science and other indigenous knowledge systems. In S. Jasanoff, G.E. Markle, J.C. Petersen and T. Pinch (eds.), *Handbook of Science and Technology Studies,* Thousand Oaks: Sage, pp. 115-39.

17

Sustainable Development
Concept, Scope and Ecological Perspectives

Prafulla Kumar Kara

Introduction

WITH the onset of the era of newly independent states the concept of development all over the world has become an increasing concern for the social scientists, planners, bureaucrats and political elites. The term *Sustainability* and its corollary *Sustainable Development* though not entirely new and hitherto unknown was introduced by Brundtland Commission (1987) in its seminal report called **Our Common Future** and popularized by World Bank and United Nations Environment Programme. Since that time there has been much discussion on the concept and various ideas inextricably connected with it.

Sustainable development is development that meets the needs of the present generation without compromising the ability of future generations to meet their own needs. This definition contains within it two concepts:

(a) the concept of "needs" especially the essential needs of the world's poor to which overriding priority should be given, and

(b) the idea of limitations imposed by the state of

technology and social organization on the environmental ability to meet present and future needs.

Sustainable Development cannot be a static concept and hence cannot be defined once for all. It is a dynamic process and will be applied by different countries in tune with their own cultural, political and economic perspectives. To the extent that "sustainable" implies continuity and "development" implies change there is even perhaps a contradiction in the term, though we shall see the words can be interpreted more creatively than that. Now emphasis is being given on economic growth and technological aspects. The general feeling is that development processes can continue provided the technological innovations are rapid and appropriate enough to reduce environmental side effects. So unless there is a broad agreement on goods, directions and means the concept of sustainable development will prove sterile and the business of development will continue as usual with more tensions among the nations, states, regions and localities within the nation and state. So it is important to know what constitutes sustainable development or how sustainable development differs from development.

Sustainable Development has to be a long-term process, and one may say a continuing process. In general,

(a) It cannot be achieved in the short run,

(b) Its approach is balanced and integrative,

(c) It has common goals but different routes,

(d) It accepts nature not only as a resource for development but also as the earthly womb for survival and development of human kind,

(e) It is participatory in nature, and

(f) It is based on equity and justice. Equity and justice are important for sustainable development. It is four-dimensional :

- Equity among nations — rich nations, poor nations, developed nations, developing nations,
- Equity within countries — between regions, social classes, genders, sectors of activities,
- Equity between generations, and
- Equity between economics and ecology and science and spirituality.

Goals of Sustainable Development

Sustainable development has a fixed set of goals. These are:

(a) Basic needs of all human beings, i.e. food, clothing, shelter, education, health, security and self-esteem must be met adequately. Level of these needs will be determined by natural and technological resources available and the global socio-economic context.

(b) Development process should be so articulated that ecological balance and environmental purity is least disturbed.

(c) All nations and people must join hands to support each other and work with each other to create a world in which the above two goals are optimized.

Sustainable Development : Underlying Principles / Premises

Some of the principles / premises underlying the concept of sustainable development are:

1. It is an alternative design for development which by definition should be environmentally benign and eco-friendly.

2. That the present generation should meet its needs without compromising the ability of future generations to meet their own needs, i.e. to ensure that the productive assets available to future generations are not unfairly diminished.
3. That those who enjoy the fruits of economic development today must not make future generations worse off by excessively degrading the earth's exhaustible resources and polluting the earth's ecology and environment.
4. That there is a symbiotic relationship between consumerist human race and producer natural systems.
5. That environment and development are not mutually exclusive — healthy environment is essential to sustainable development and healthy economy.
6. That economic development which erodes natural capital is often not successful.
7. That environmental mistakes of the past need not be repeated, as past patterns of degradation are not inevitable.
8. That development is not growth only, it should stand for broader goals of social transformation.
9. That sustainable development in the long run has to do with ecology, resources and people along with their service agencies, institutions and other aspects of their social organizations.
10. That sustainable development has two major aspects — internally sustainable development and externally sustainable development — without both no sustainable development would exist.

11. That sustainable development is accountable to the poor and hence it should ensure that the poor have adequate access to sustainable and secure livelihoods.

Considering all the above aspects, sustainable development at the conceptual level can be assumed to maximize three goals: *biophysical, economic and social.* Sustainable development advocates a development process that is biophysically permissible, economically viable and socially acceptable. In other words it is a process of development that should operate within a framework bounded by the biophysical, economic and social co-ordinates. To operate within these three co-ordinates, it is necessary to recognize that there are certain limits within which the development process has to function. These limits can be broadly identified as *biophysical and ethico-social limits* (Daly, 1989).

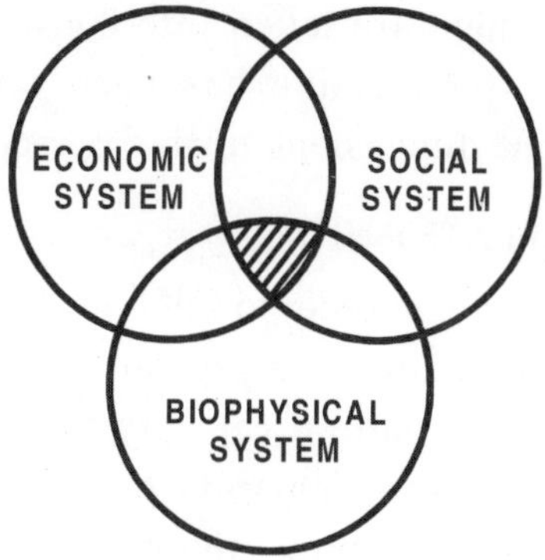

Sustainable development aims to maximize the goals across three system (Modified after Barbier, 1987). The biophysical limit which actually controls resource availability, resource use and economic viability is due to: (a) Finitude; (b) Entropy; (c) Complex Ecological Interdependence (CEI); and (d) Resilience or self-ameliorating capacity. Apart from these four, photosynthetic limit is another factor to impose restrictions.

The ethico-social limit is equally important in the matter of achieving sustainability. This dimension is supposed to provide philosophical backdrop of a society including the legal, executional and policy-making authorities.

Sustainable Development : The Ecological Perspectives

The concept of sustainable development emerged as an important theme in 1987. The Brundtland Commission on Environment and Development in its report **Our Common Future** called for application of sustainability as a criterion for all development initiatives. Sustainable development can be looked at from a variety of perspectives such as ecological, economic, social, political and cultural. None of these perspectives can stand alone. Sustainable development is possible if all of them are taken into consideration. In this article ecological perspective has been taken for deeper analysis. Important dimensions of this perspective are:

MAN-NATURE RELATIONSHIP

Man is a part of nature. In order to fulfil his desires man exploits the environmental factors to a greater extent, by which the environment loses its natural capacity for self-stabilization. To meet the increasing demands of time human beings deliberately exploit the natural environment to improve their quality of life. Unknowingly, different environmental activities such as construction of roads, dams, airports, buildings, power plants and industries have some negative repercussions on the environment in which man lives. Thus, the developmental activities are unsustainable for global ecosystem. But we can't stop these activities. For the development of the nation these activities are essential. Industrial growth is directly related to nation's economy. Construction of major and minor irrigation projects and development of new power plants must not be frozen. Hence at the present context, when man has reached the twenty-first century, nobody would want for technological stagnation. On the other hand, excessive exploitation of the environment through these technological implications lead to disaster. So what is needed is *environmental sustainability,* i.e. environmental management and sustainable development.

"Environmental Sustainability" implies to regulate the demands of man in such a manner that the ability of the same environment to sustain his development will remain un-repaired. Environmental sustainability aims at ensuring the protection, conservation and better management of earth's natural resources. The idea is not to debar people from using these resources. It rather aims at such a pattern of use, that resources, particularly those which are so vital for human survival, are neither exhausted nor polluted nor destroyed. This would require a change in our attitude towards nature as also towards what we call economic development.

ECOSYSTEM INTEGRATED

Ecosystem is the sum total of all life in a given area plus life's interaction with the non-living portions of the area. It is the largest functional unit in ecology because it includes both living (biotic) and non-living (abiotic) environments. All natural ecosystems are characterized by four qualities namely — *complexity, stability, diversity and resilience*. If any of these qualities are weakened or jeopardized the system collapses.

Ecosystem is integrated, i.e. its constituent elements are interdependent. Destruction of any of the constituents will harm the whole system. The ecosystem integrity can be maintained if we know *its carrying capacity, its assimilative capacity* and *its renewability*. Carrying capacity is the ability of an ecosystem to feed a certain population of humans and/or animals. Assimilative capacity is also directly linked to carrying capacity. All systems including the ecosystem have a metabolic process to remove the waste. Certain amount of waste discharged in soil, air or water will be purified in the natural course. Problem arises if the amount of waste is beyond the natural capacity to clean or of a kind that cannot be handled by the ecosystem. Waste therefore has to be treated before it is released or its quantity and quality have to be controlled.

Recharging capacity of the ecosystem is its third characteristic. All renewable resources need time to recoup. The impression that the renewable resources can be misused or mismanaged without any adverse effects is totally wrong. What is needed urgently as a policy measure is to see that renewable resources are not diverted to other uses. Secondly, the waste emission must be restricted to conform to the assimilative capacity of the ecosystem.

BIODIVERSITY

The third dimension of ecological perspective is biodiversity which can be seen from three perspectives — *genetic diversity, species diversity* and *ecosystem diversity*. Genetic diversity refers to the chromosomal information carried by genes of individual plants and animals. If we destroy any plant or animal species we would lose that gene for ever.

Species diversity is the second perspective. Many plants and animals live in association with each other and the destruction of any of them may lead to the destruction of associated life also. This is because each plant and animal species is interdependent and contains gene pool of great importance. In order to preserve the biodiversity, natural ecosystem as well as whatever is left of the modified ecosystem must be protected. Further man-made ecosystems should now be so planned that in the next 50 years or so we have more such areas where nature has its own sway.

MAN-LAND RATIO

The fourth aspect of ecological perspective that needs attention is population. "The quality of human life is inseparable from the quality of the environment. It is increasingly clear that both are inseparable from the question of human numbers and concentration," says UNFPA (1990). The carrying and assimilative capacities of the ecosystem depend on man-land ratio (land-nature). If the human population increases without proportionate increase in natural resources, the carrying capacity of the ecosystem, i.e. the quantity and quality of natural resources, gets reduced. This problem is further accentuated, if the population increase takes place in those regions and nations where most of the people still depend upon agriculture and other primary activities. As part of their survival strategy they cut trees and kill animals.

Movement of rural population to urban areas is another dimension having direct implications for environment and sustainability. The slums of Indian metropolises tell us more of what population concentration does to environment than anything else.

ENVIRONMENTAL PLANNING

The last dimension of ecological perspective brings us to environment planning. Its aim is fourfold :

(a) Environmental Protection;

(b) Rehabilitation and restoration of degraded ecosystems;

(c) Augmentation of the carrying capacity of both natural and human-managed ecosystems; and

(d) Creation, expansion and development of new ecosystem-s, both minor and major.

Conclusion

Sustainable development is not possible if it remains the responsibility of the government and private companies alone. It is the business of the people in general. It is an admitted fact that many environmental problems cannot be solved without the active participation of local people and people-centred grass-roots environmentally-active non-governmental organizations. Their involvement in environmental protection programmes is essential for discharging a variety of vital functions. The participatory approach offers three main advantages:

(a) It gives planners a better understanding of local values, knowledge and experience;

(b) It wins community backing for project objectives and community help in local implementation; and

(c) It can resolve conflicts which arise when large infrastructural investments in dams, irrigation facilities, roads, etc. are made.

Sustainable development is essentially a process of empowering and enhancing the organizational capacity of local institutions, with only little technical and financial support from external agents/agencies, if at all required.

References

Barbier, E.B., "The Concept of Sustainable Development & Environmental Conservation", *Environment Impact Assessment Review*, 1987.

Daly, H.E., "Sustainable Development: From Concept & Theory Towards Operational Principles", *Population & Development Review*, Washington D.C. 1989

Maler, Karl Gozan, "Environment, Poverty & Economic Growth" article presented in Annual World Conference on Developmental

Economics, 1977.

Mishra, R.P., *Understanding Development: Development Issues of our Time*, New Delhi: Concept Publishing Company, 1985.

Ramchandran, K.S., *Developmental Perspectives*, New Delhi: Centre for Earth Science Studies and Concept Publishing Company, 1989.

Sharma and Chattopadhaya, *Sustainable Development-Issues and Case Studies*, New Delhi: Concept Publishing Company, 1998.

Srivastav, S.P., "Sustainable Development-Issues and Considerations", *Geographical Review of India*, 1990.

World Commission on Environment & Development (W.C.E.D.), *Our Common Future*, Oxford University Press, 1987.

Part IV

Sustainable Agriculture

18

Globalization of the Potato
An Ancient Andean Indigenous Crop

Elayne Zorn* and *Leslie Sue Lieberman

Introduction

THE potato (*Solanum tuberosum*) is the world's fourth largest food crop (Messer, 2000; CIP, 2002). Potatoes were first domesticated more than 7,000 years ago in southern Peru's Andean high plateau from a single, wild progenitor, *Solanum brevicaule* (Weber, 2005). Raw, boiled, roasted, or freeze-dried, it has had central roles in indigenous Andean culture and cuisine (Woolfe, 1987). Introduced to Europe by Spanish invaders in the mid-1500s, it has circled the globe and is grown and consumed in about 150 countries (Salaman, 1949; Messer, 2000).

Production and Consumption

Potatoes can be grown from sea level to approximately 14,000 feet in elevation. Only bitter varieties can be grown at the highest altitudes. Potato production in 2005 was 321 million metric tonnes (Table 18.1). Surprisingly, countries and regions with the greatest production (China, the Russian Federation, India, the U.S.) are geographically dispersed with vastly different climates. Together, they accounted for half of worldwide potato production in the last decade (FAOSTAT,

Table 18.1
World Potato production of some selected countries from 2003–2005 (in metric tonnes)

Country	2003	2004	2005
China	68,139,264	70,048,000	73,026,500
Russian Federation	36,746,512	35,914,240	36,400,000
India	25,000,000	25,000,000	25,000,000
United States	20,766,100	20,680,770	19,111,030
Peru	3,151,355	2,229,090	3,200,000
World	315,478,323	327,624,417	321,060,852

Source: Food and Agricultural Organization of the United Nations, 2006 <http://faostat.fao.org/faostate/servlet> (4/27/06).

2006). In India, where potato is the most important food crop after rice and wheat, production is primarily industrial (Grain, 2000). Potato consumption in 2003 was estimated to be 206.5 million metric tonnes, which supplies 32.9 kg per person per year at approximately 61 kcal per person per day (Table 18.2) (ibid.). Unexpectedly, countries with the highest production do not have the highest per capita consumption. Andean consumption is estimated the highest: 150-200 kg per person per year (ibid.). In the U.S., annual consumption is about 60 kg per person and potato consumption in China and India is about 14 kg (ibid.).

Classification

The potato (*Solanum tuberosum*) belongs to the diverse Family Solanaceae. An extensive Andean classification and naming system also exists (Arnold and Yapita, 1996). This Family includes tomatoes, chili peppers, tobacco and many nightshade species, such as belladonna and jimsonweed, often used as

Table 18.2
World Potato consumption of some selected countries in 2003 (in metric tonnes)

Country	*Weight (mt)*	*Supply Cap /Yr (kg)*	*Cal/Cap /Day (number)*	*Prot/Cap /Day (gr)*	*Fat/Cap /Day (gr)*
China	46,168,314	35.2	68.4	1.6	0.1
United States	18,730,892	63.7	100.8	2.7	0.2
Bolivia	491,121	55.8	102.3	3.7	0.4
World	206,520,423	32.9	60.9	1.4	0.1

cal = calories; cap = per capita; gr = grams; mt = metric tonnes; prot = protein; yr = year

Source: Food and Agricultural Organization of the United Nations, 2006 <http://faostat.fao.org/faostate/servlet> (4/27/06).

medicinal plants (Hawkes, 1990). The International Potato Centre (CIP) and other groups have described the evolution and genetic diversity of the Andean potato *Solanum tuberosum* spp. *andigena*. They have identified nearly 1,500 wild types and 5,000 cultivars worldwide (Hawkes, 1990; CIP 2001, 2002). The bitter varieties with high levels of potentially toxic protein-sugar compounds, the glycoalkaloids, are grown in the Andean altiplano or high plateau (3,900–4,200 metres) where they are subjected to nearly nightly frost. Cultivars grown in other regions of the world have lower glycoalkaloid levels (Johns, 1986; Messer, 2000).

Nutrient Values

Potatoes are the most important Andean food crop, complemented by corn and quinoa. Although nutrient values vary with variety, climate, soil conditions, and processing, potatoes are a good source of calories, carbohydrates, dietary fibre, potassium, phosphorus, magnesium, iron, thiamin, niacin, pyridoxine, folic acid, and particularly vitamin C (Table 18.3 (Woolfe, 1987; Messer, 2000). The Peruvian yellow variety has 35 g of ascorbic acid per 100 g of fresh weight and by comparison an orange has about 55 g. The starch is easily digested. Potato protein content is comparable by dry-weight to cereals. The protein is high in lysine and low in sulphur-containing amino acids. Potatoes contain pigments that act as antioxidants, including the yellow carotenoids and the red and purple anthocyanins (Woolfe, 1987; Messer, 2000).

TABLE 18.3

Nutrient content changes with traditional processing (100 g)

Nutrient	*Raw Potato*	*Chuño blanco*	*Chuño negro*
Calories	75-80 kcal	300-350 kcal	300-350 kcal
Water (moisture)	83-78% by lot	14-18%	14-18%
Protein	2.0 g	2.0 g	4.0 g
Carbohydrate	18.5 g	78.0 g	78.0 g
Calcium	9.0 mg	90.00 mg	45.00 mg
Phosphorous	50.00 mg	54.00 mg	200.00 mg
Niacin	1.50 mg	0.40 mg	3.40 mg
Vitamin C	20.00 mg	1.00 mg	1.50-2.00 mg
Iron	0.80-1.50 mg	3.30 mg	1.00 mg

Sources: Various, cited in Woolfe, 1987, *The Potato in the Human Diet*, Cambridge: University of Cambridge Press, pp. 148-49; Tablas Peruanas de Composición de Alimentos, cited in INCOPA 2003.

Traditional Processing Technologies

Potatoes are very watery; dry matter comprises only about 20 per cent of average weight (Werge, 1979; Woolfe, 1987) although native Andean varieties "have more dry matter than commercial potatoes" (W. Amorós, cited in Portillo, 2004: 3). Various processing techniques were discovered by indigenous populations in the Andes (CIP website) and continue to be used to reduce water content and toxicity, and to increase nutrient concentration and duration of preservation. Indigenous Andeans were the first to discover "freeze drying." This technology takes advantage of the unique Andean tropical mountain environment in the dry season, with heat and intense sunlight during the day and extreme cold at night.

Although glycoalkaloids and other potato constituents such as the lectins and proteinase inhibitors protect the plants, conferring resistance to cold stress, insects, other vertebrates, and fungi, they are toxic to humans (CIP, 2002). Similar to other dietary tubers such as bitter cassava or manioc that require processing to reduce concentrations of cyanogenic glycosides, some varieties of potatoes require processing to reduce concentrations of the glycoalkaloids (Johns, 1986). High levels of glycoalkaloids (20-30 mg/100 g) inhibit the neurotransmitter cholinesterase and injure the lining of the gastrointestinal tract, leading to nausea, vomiting, diarrhoea, headaches, dizziness and possibly death (Johns, 1986; Woolfe, 1987). Because heating does not destroy glycoalkaloids, other drying, freezing, and leaching techniques are used to reduce glycoalkaloid content (Johns, 1986). Andean potatoes are *always* peeled (Arnold, 1996), eliminating most glycoalkaloid content (Woolfe, 1987). Reducing toxicity is important because processed potatoes are often the foods consumed in high quantity when little else is available.

On the Peruvian coast, drying is used to prepare *papa seca* (dehydrated potato), which is produced by first cooking, then peeling and drying the cooked potatoes in the sun (CIP 2002). *Tocosh* is prepared in several Andean countries by fermenting potatoes for several weeks or months, then drying them in the sun (Cruz, n.d.; Patiño, 1992). In the Andean highlands, freeze-drying is used to produce *chuño* (*ch'uñu*). Two varieties are made: *chuño negro* (black) and *chuño blanco* (white). Chuño negro (or simply, *chuño)* almost always is made from bitter and/or small, irregular, poor quality potatoes; it has an average concentration of 16 mg of glycoalkaloids/100 g of potato (Woolfe, 1987). Chuño blanco is made from large, regular potatoes, and averages only 4 mg of glycoalkaloids/100 g (INCOPA, 2003).

Chuño negro is produced by placing the potatoes on a bed of straw, freezing them for one or more nights, then drying them in the sun (Mamani, 1978; REDEPAPA website). Before drying they are gently stepped on to squeeze out water. After drying thoroughly, which can take two weeks, the potatoes are rubbed to remove the peel and stored away from sunlight. Two chuño blanco varieties are made, with regional variation in production and terminology (Mamani, 1978; Patiño, 1992; Arnold and Yapita, 1996, Guido, Esprella, Aguilera and Devaux, 2002; INCOPA, 2003). After freezing, potatoes are soaked in a running stream for about two weeks to make *tunta* or in stagnant water to make *moraya*.

Creating chuño significantly alters the potatoes' nutritional content, by decreasing moisture content from an average of 80 per cent to 16 per cent (Woolfe, 1987; INCOPA, 2003). Compared to 100 g of raw potato, 100 g of chuño has a fourfold increase in energy (Table 18.3) and a fourfold increase in carbohydrate. Freeze-drying markedly increases calcium, but reduces ascorbic acid (vitamin C). Chuño negro compared to chuño blanco shows a twofold increase in protein, a fourfold increase in phosphorous, and a ninefold increase in niacin (Table 18.3). Chuño is easily transported because of its light weight. It can be stored for many years: three years is average but there are many ethnographic reports of storage for 10 years or more. Long periods of subsistence on chuño as the primary food source are legendary.

Traditional Knowledge and Cultural Associations

Traditional Andean knowledge about the potato has considerable time depth. Extremely complex civilizations developed in the south-central Andes more than a thousand years ago with a subsistence base of tuber agriculture and camelid herding (Moseley, 2001); potatoes were the major high altitude crop. This agro-pastoral system permitted the growth of dense populations and major civilizations, including the Inca empire. This system is disappearing due to factors that include floods and droughts, modernization, and rural to urban migration.

However, an elaborate indigenous vocabulary still exists for cultivating potatoes, drawing on inherent properties including colour and reproduction (Apaza, 1996). Indigenous knowledge in relation to the potato is increasingly recognized globally for its potential to restore ancient Andean farming systems to help solve local food scarcity (Arnold and Yapita 1996; Roach, 2001; CIP, 2001, 2002; Guido, Esprella, Aguilera, and Devaux, 2002; Thiele and Devaux, 2002; Portal Agrario, n.d.; Cruz, n.d.; Tapia, n.d.). Knowledge about potatoes is used globally in the developing world in applications such as the technology of storing potatoes away from light to improve nutrient retention and sprouting (CIP website). The study of traditional knowledge also provides significant insight into Andean thought and logic. This knowledge is encoded in language and concepts shared across multiple semantic domains, which function through metaphor and analogy, and also describe values and ways of thinking in ethics and philosophy (Arnold and Yapita, 1996).

Gender permeates Andean knowledge. Women are responsible for seed selection and storage, management of ecology, and potato biodiversity (ibid.; FAO, n.d.; Tapia and De la Torre, 1998), and thus must be central to scientific efforts to improve food and seed security (FAO, n.d.). In the Andean sexual division of labour, men open the earth and women plant seeds, so both genders are essential. Potato seed is related to female fertility, but potato flowers symbolize the human head and the masculine power of war (Arnold and Yapita, 1996).

Stories about the potato's origin vary by region and ethnic group. Potatoes are described as animate beings with social lives; their growth is understood by analogy with humans and animals. For example, potatoes are carefully sorted after harvest by variety, size, and future use, but two or more varieties are sown together in each field. In one Bolivian region, potatoes are said to "compete" to see which variety will produce more when planted in Mother Earth: "I will win," No, I will win," each variety proclaims (Jiménez and Yapita with Arnold, 1996).

The Andean system of potato classification is based on colour, gender, shape, use, frost resistance, and other characteristics (Arnold and Yapita, 1996). Numerous regional and ethnic group variations exist, with greatest variation in the highlands (the site of domestication). In Aymara (an indigenous language), popular varieties include *Janq'u Imilla* (White Girl) and *Saq'ampaya* (Long Male Potato). In Quechua (Inca), popular varieties include *Yana Imilla* (Black Girl) and *Kusi Sonq'o* (Happy Heart) (CIP 2001). Although not sexually reproducing, potatoes are ascribed a gender (Apaza, 1996; Arnold and Yapita, eds. 1996; Jiménez and Yapita, with Arnold, 1996): red potatoes are female and white are male. Potatoes have nuclear family kinship relations: a husband and wife, and their babies (Jiménez and Yapita, with Arnold, 1996).

Applications of potato metaphors and analogies to other domains link crops and music, and agriculture and textiles. In Bolivia, the *pinkillu* flute is played between the festival of San Sebastian and Carnival in the rainy season when potatoes flower above ground (Stobart, 1996). The flutes have openings like potato "eyes" and are considered "alive." In contrast, the panpipe, which has no openings, is played in the dry season at harvest; it is "dead" like chuño and cannot grow (ibid.). Cloth (the most important expressive medium in the Andes for 5,000 years; Zorn, 2004) provides a structuring principle for understanding other aspects of life. In this system of analogies (Arnold and Yapita, 1996) between cloth and crops, textile designs symbolize potatoes as the first crop planted in the Andean crop rotation system. Furrows of potato fields are compared to lines in weavings (Arnold and Yapita, with Apaza, 1996). Images "growing" in the textile as it is woven are like potato flowers growing in fields and tubers growing underground.

Culturally, potatoes in general and chuño in particular have extremely strong ethnic/racial associations with native Andeans, who still have low social status (Zorn, 2004). This has led to a pejorative perspective on *chuño*, which is commonly described as "tasteless," "dirty," and of low nutritional value. Recently, these negative perceptions may be changing as a result of the 2005 election of Bolivia's first indigenous President, who has served native foods at state functions.

Conclusion

Potatoes are a food crop fundamental to the daily lives of Andeans. As a plant they provide the basis for organizing lives around agricultural cycles, designs for textiles, and metaphors for human kinship and social relationships. The potato has become a component of cuisines worldwide. It offers increasing nutritional value to tropical regions of the developing world. However, preference for diverse varieties and traditional ways of processing and cooking, including freeze-drying, boiling, and roasting, are diminishing in favour of a fewer varieties often prepared by frying. This globalizing trend is exemplified in the consumption of french fries (chips), which are the number one vegetable consumed in the US — primarily as a fast-food item (Spurlock, 2005). The International Potato Centre and affiliate research centres, including India's Central Potato Research Institute (CPRI), are committed to preserving the potato's genetic diversity and to assisting other groups in utilizing food processing technologies to develop new varieties of foods from potatoes (CIP n.d.a, n.d.b). The twenty-first century has seen the Andean potato de-localized from its Andean roots and globalized by farmers and fast-food franchises.

References

Apaza, C. (1996), La Aparición de la papa, In *Madre Melliza y sus crias*, D. Arnold and J. Yapita (eds.), La Paz, Bolivia: HISBOL/ILCA, pp. 27-138.

Arnold, D. (1996), Somos lo que comemos, In *Madre Melliza y sus crias*, D. Arnold and J. Yapita (eds.), La Paz, Bolivia: HISBOL/ILCA, pp. 195-222.

Arnold, D. and J. Yapita with C. Apaza (1996), Mama Trama y sus crías: Analogías de la producción de la papa en los textiles de Chukiñapi, Bolivia, In *Madre Melliza y sus crias*, D. Arnold and J. Yapita, (eds.), La Paz, Bolivia: HISBOL/ILCA, pp. 373-411.

Arnold, D. and J. Yapita (eds. 1996), *Madre Melliza y sus crias*: *Ispall Mama Wawampi/Antología de la papa*, La Paz, Bolivia: HISBOL/ILCA.

CIP (Centro Internacional de la Papa, International Potato Centre), (2001), *World Potato Atlas*: Bolivia, <http://www.cipotato.org/wpa/samerica/Bolivia.htm> (5/24/04).

———, (2002), *CIP Potato Facts,* <http://www.cipotato.org/market/potatofacts/growprod.htm> (5/24/04).

———, (n.d.a) *Hojuelas de papas de colores: Conservando la biodiversidad ancestral con nuevos habitos de consumo,* <http://www.cipotato.org/potatoes/Postharvest/Flyer_hojuelas_colores.pdf> (5/19/04).

———, (n.d.b) Reducción de la Pobreza en los Altos Andes a través de la Producción, Transformacióny Comercialización de Productos Agropecuarios, <http://inrm.cip.cgiar.org/home/sp3spa02.htm> (11/23/05).

Cruz, G. (n.d.) Traditional peasant's [sic] *in situ* conservation of native potatoes (*Solanum spp*) in Ragracancha, highlands of Huanuco, Peru, In Situ Project, PNUD-AAP-CCTA-IDMA. <http://www.unu.edu/env/plec/cbd/Montreal/abstracts/Cruz.pdf> (7/6/04).

FAO, (Food and Agriculture Organization) (n.d.) Mujeres conservacionistas. <http://www.fao.org/DOCREP/x0227s/x0227s07.htm> (5/17/04).

FAOSTAT (2006), Food and Agricultural Organization of the United Nations, FAOSTAT Database, <http://Faostat.fao.org/faostat/servlet> (4/27/06).

GRAIN (2000), Potato: A Fragile Gift from the Andes, Seedling: The Quarterly Newsletter of Genetic Resources Action International. <http://www.grain.org/seedling/?id=23> (8/7/06).

Guido, A., R. Esprella, J. Aguilera and A. Devaux (2002), Análisis Prospectivo de la Cadena Agroalimentaria del Chuño y la Tunta en el Altiplano Central de Bolivia, <http://www.cipotato.org/papandina/Documentos/UltimoInforme % SYAL.pdf> (5/21/03).

Hawkes, J. (1990), *The Potato: Evolution, Biodiversity and Genetic Resources,* Washington, D.C.: Smithsonian Institution Press.

INCOPA (Inovación Tecnológica y Competitiva de la Papa), (2003), Rescatando un sabor ancestral: El chuño blanco. INCOPA Hoja Divulgativa 1 (November), <http://www.cipotato.org/potato/Postharvest/642-tunta.pdf> (5/14/04).

Jiménez, D. and J. Yapita with D. Arnold (1996), La metafisica de la papa, In *Madre Melliza y sus crias,* D. Arnold and J. Yapita (eds.), pp. 139-

93, La Paz, Bolivia: HISBOL/ILCA.

Johns, T. (1986), *Taste Evaluation of Potato Glycoalkaloids by the Aymara: A Case Study in Human Chemical Ecology*, Human Ecology 14, pp. 437-52.

Mamani, M. (1978), El chuño: Preparación, uso, almacenamiento, In *Tecnología Andina*, R. Ravines (ed.), Lima: Instituto de Estudios Peruanos, pp. 227-39.

Messer, E. (2000), Potatoes (White), In *The Cambridge World History of Food*, Volume one. K. Kiple and K. Ornelas (eds.), Cambridge: Cambridge University Press, pp. 187-201.

Moseley, M. (2001), *The Incas and Their Ancestors: The Archaeology of Peru*, London: Thames and Hudson.

Patiño, V. (1992), Tecnología Poscosecha Aplicada a Agricultura y Horticultura, Chapter XII, In *Historia de la Cultura Material en la América Equinoccial* (Tomo V), Biblioteca Virtual: Banco de la República (Colombia), <http://www.banrep.gov.co/blaavirtual/letra-h/historia5/cap12.htm> (7/7/04).

Portal Agrario (n.d.) Papa: Industralización, Perú: Ministerio de Agricultura. <http://www.portalagrario.gob.pe/papa_ind.shtml> (5/20/03).

Portillo, Z. (2004), Community Potato Banks Preserve Ancestral Treasures, CIP Press Release, <http://www.cipotato.org/news/pressreleases/2004/aymara_eng.htm> (7/9/04).

Roach, J. (2001), Saving the Potato in Its Andean Birthplace. National Geographic News, <http://news.nationalgeographic.com/news/2002/06/0610_potato.html> (7/14/03).

Salaman, R. (1949), *The History and Social Influence of the Potato*, Cambridge: Cambridge University Press.

Spurlock, M. (2005), *Don't Eat This Book: Fast Food and the Supersizing of America*, New York: G.P. Putnam's Sons.

Stobart, H. (1996), Los Wayñus que salen de las huertas: música y papas en una comunidad campesina del Norte de Potosí, In *Madre Melliza y sus crias*, D. Arnold and J. Yapita (eds.), La Paz, Bolivia: HISBOL/ILCA, pp. 413-30.

Tapia, M. (n.d.), The Role of Under-Utilized Plant Species with Regard to Increased Food Security and Improved Health of Poor People, in Mountain Regions, Project IIAP-PNUD, Peru, <http://

www.underutilized-species.org/events/w_shop_leipzig_documents/ plenary_presentations/m_t/m_t.pdf> (7/7/04).

Tapia, M. and A. De la To rre (1998), *Women Farmers and Andean Seeds*, FAO/IPGRI. <http://www.ipgri.cgiar.org/publications/ pubfile.asp?ID_PUB=308> (7/8/04).

Thiele, G. and A. Devaux (2002), Adding Value to Local Knowledge and Biodiversity of Andean Potato Farmers: The Papa Andina Project, *Info Agrar News* no. 12, pp. 2-3.

Weber, K. (2005), Finding rewrites the evolutionary history of the origin of potatoes, EurekAlert, AAAS. <http://www.eurekalert.org/ by subject/archaeology.php> (11/23/05).

Werge, R. (1979), Potato Processing in the Central Highlands of Peru, *Ecology of Food and Nutrition*, 7: 229-34.

Woolfe, J. with S. Poats (1987), *The Potato in the Human Diet*, published in collaboration with International Potato Centre, New York: Cambridge University Press.

Zorn, E. (2004), *Weaving a Future: Tourism, Cloth, and Culture on an Andean Island*, Iowa City: University of Iowa Press.

WWW Sites

CIP (Centro Internacional de la Papa, International Potato Centre) <http:/ /www.cipotato.org>

Global Potato News <http://www.potatonews.com>

REDEPAPA (Red Electrónica de la Papa, Electronic Network about Potatoes) <http://www.redepapa.org/index.html>

19

Incorporating Indigenous Knowledge Challenges and Opportunities

Perspectives from Maya Kacquikel Guatemala

Benjamin Levy

Introduction

"INDIGENOUS peoples in Guatemala are the poorest of the poor" according to the World Bank (O'Kane, 1999). Approximately 50 per cent of Guatemala's population is indigenous. Indigenous peoples have passed down their knowledge through the generations. This knowledge is beginning to be recognized by the development community as a valuable resource. Development programmes and projects have thus far lacked community participation towards sustainable development. Guatemala, and its high proportion of indigenous peoples, provides the ideal research location to gain insight into the perspectives of indigenous peoples on the appropriate methodology and use of their Indigenous Knowledge (IK) in development. Through in-depth interviews, participants provided recommendations that could improve development within an indigenous context. Voices from the indigenous community will aid in a more equitable and culturally appropriate alternative model for the incorporation of IK in development.

Country Background

Guatemala is a multilingual, multicultural State with a high density of indigenous people who are distinguished by 22 dialects, dress, self-identification and other characteristics (Fischer, 2004). Since the time of early colonization by the Spanish, indigenous peoples of Guatemala have been marginalized and taken advantage of their knowledge, labour and resources. The Mayans are the largest of the four main indigenous groups in Guatemala. They have a subsistence-based culture and have received the most international publicity during the 36-year war. They are the most well known of the main groups in Guatemala.

Agriculture has always been the predominant foundation and core of the Mayan cultures of Guatemala. Corn (*maiz* = maize), for example, is not just a crop to the Mayans, but also a symbol of their history and culture. The four colours of corn represent the four main skin tones of human beings and the four main cardinal directions. It is believed that corn has its origins in Guatemala (Lec-Ajcot, 2005). Hence, it is no wonder the Mayans are sometimes referred to as *Hombres de Maiz*/ Men of Corn (Asturias, 1996).

The traditional form of agriculture practised by the Mayans is called *milpa* agriculture. *Milpa* is a well-defined, three-crop system developed over millennia, consisting of corn (*maiz*), beans (*frijoles*), squash (*calabza*), and sometimes livestock. This form does not require large tracks of land due to its high efficiency. Yet, through various strategies by the colonialists and various regimes over the years, the Mayans have lost the majority of their lands. (O'Kane, 1999) Often communal, these lands were mistaken as fallow, and therefore were re-distributed to the government, churches and powerful individuals and businesses. *Ladinos*, those of Spanish origin, have often received a raised status within Guatemalan society due to their economic positions and received greater access to social services as a result (education, health, etc.) (Choy and Borrell, 1997).

Since the 36-year war/genocide ended in the mid-1990s, there have been numerous agreements made by the Guatemalan Government, the United Nations, and many other organizations (UN, 1995). These agreements have created a formal recognition of the indigenous peoples of Guatemala, offered legal rights to them and have led to discussions about what their place is within mainstream society (Govt. of Guatemala, 1995). In addition, there has been much greater decentralization of the government into municipal units and a greater presence of NGOs, both local and international, within the country.

Conceptual Framework

This research follows the Critical Humanist Paradigm, originally presented by Burrell and Morgan in 1979, which acknowledges that there are certain "social processes [which] deprive individuals and organizations of important satisfactions." These social processes can include systematic ethnic cleansing, colonization, slavery, torture, child labour, inequitable education, lack of access to health care, education, food, water and other human rights. These sources of contradictions or oppressions can be restrained or overt in their execution. There are no universal truths and the perspectives within this paradigm are highly dependent upon the context of the community and the individual. Individuals have the ability to transform their social structures to bring about social change (Rossman and Rallis, 2003).

The ethnographic research tradition seems to be the most appropriate to deal with the context of this topic and the research. Cultural context is a critical aspect of this topic, and an ethnographic study allows a researcher to gain an ethnic perspective of the communities and culture while building relationships and trust in order to conduct a qualitative study (Rossman and Rallis, 2003).

The research included a foundation in Critical Modernist Theory, which posits that rather than discount development? there is a need to analyse other perspectives (Peet and Hartwick, 1999). The central ideas of this theory lie in a broad-based and participatory approach to a decentralized democracy, development and progress, while aiming for positive political change (Arce, 2003). Through this theory we must critique the context in which these people live: a patriarchal, class-based system placed within a capitalist structure.

Research Problem

In Guatemala, history has displayed a disregard for indigenous perspectives for the development of the country and society. The absence of strong organization within indigenous communities; a fragmentation between classes, communities and generations; and a lack of necessary resources for survival have all contributed to the neglect of the integration of indigenous peoples into the development discussion in Guatemala. The disregard of indigenous perspectives has resulted in the continuation of unsustainable development within indigenous communities and their surrounding environments.

As a result of this lack of participation in development and the new trend for developmental organizations to incorporate indigenous knowledge (IK) into their strategies, this research aims to gather perspectives of one indigenous group, the Maya-Kacquikel, regarding the incorporation of

IK in development, the current state of development within their context, their historical context, what challenges and opportunities they envision with this incorporation, and their vision for the future.

METHODOLOGY

Research Design

This research was designed to be a field report and using the research I was able to present the opinions and perspectives from the research participants, as well as the literature, on the research topic. Participation was open, except for the following criteria: participants should be indigenous, from the local region, involved with agriculture and development in some aspect during their lives and must be an advanced speaker of Spanish. When choosing participants, there was a motivation to create a demographic variance in the participants. All participation was voluntary and participants signed consent forms prior to commencement agreeing that they understood the research and its objectives. Participants included both men and women from age 19 to 45. Some were directly involved with farming as their primary source of income and some were involved indirectly with local NGOs.

Data Collection

This study consisted of two phases of data collection. The first phase was a review of relevant literature, discussions with key players in the field, proposal writing and gaining access to the communities. Upon completion of the first phase, I developed a three-part interview guide. The first dealt with general demographic and cultural information; the second collected information on the definitions, methods and conservation of IK; and the third consisted of topics concerning current trends in development, the incorporation of IK in development, intellectual property rights and the participants suggestions for the future of this topic.

Data Analysis

Since the entirety of this study was qualitative, content analysis was applied to examine the data and present conclusions. First, all of the interviews were transcribed and then translated from Spanish to English. After a preliminary review of the data a series of descriptive codes were created to assist with interpreting and discovering patterns within the data. An interpretative analysis and conclusions were finally drawn from the coded data.

Findings/Data Collected

The findings were categorized into five main categories: Indigenous Identity, Indigenous Knowledge (IK), Agricultural Practices, Sustainable Development (SD) and the Incorporation of IK in SD the following is a brief summarization of the major findings from the data collected.

Indigenous Identity: The cultural indicators that participants utilize for indigenous self-identification include: united extended family unit, language, clothing (*traje*), subsistence agriculture, cooking methods and typical foods, music and dance, environmental stewardship, and strong community ties. However, the indigenous participants consider the social inequalities and injustices experienced by members of their cultural group (lack of access to education, land, health, etc. and poverty in general) as indicators of their identity, as well.

According to participants, the Guatemalan Government does not understand the indigenous peoples because of their low economic positions, and therefore actively discriminates against indigenous peoples. The Government needs to "connect with communities," according to one participant, in order to understand the indigenous peoples and begin to create a just and equal Guatemalan society for all its citizens. Participants often speak about a split society of the indigenous and the *Ladinos* (people of Spanish origin.) They feel there is a direct economic link in this division. As a result of inequitable access to social services, indigenous peoples are pushed into positions of migrating out of their communities in order to provide for their family's basic needs. It is nearly impossible for indigenous peoples in modern Guatemalan society to own land as they once did. While speaking with the research participants, there is also a sense of normalization present in their responses when asked about the discrimination they have experienced in their lives.

Indigenous Knowledge (*IK*): The general consensus among participants conclude that IK is the root of Mayan ancestry and culture and it must be recovered and maintained. Major distinctions from Western knowledge systems are noted through the use of languages and dialects, use of clothing, agricultural and subsistence work, family ancestry, respect for nature and transmission through an oral and practical manner. They also speak about a sense of obligation to share knowledge with someone they encounter who does not possess the knowledge. However, participants also speak about a variety of factors placing these knowledge systems in danger, including the modernization of traditional society, Western education systems, a shift to cash crop agriculture and the fragmentation of the Mayan society, especially between generations.

Agricultural Practices: "Agriculture is something sacred, something that is valuable, without it, we can't survive," one participant articulated. Nevertheless, indigenous agricultural systems in Guatemala have changed. Some of the traditional practices that are less common or no longer followed include: crop diversification, traditional *milpa* agricultural system, organic production, use of organic fertilizers, sustainable field layout, use of live and dead barriers, native crop/seed production, native seed saving, and conservation of soil. As a result of the reduction in available and accessible land, it is becoming more and more challenging for local farmers to sustain their communities. As this shift in traditional agricultural system occurs, "the seeds of humans are also being lost. Each time we become more modern, we lose something of the indigenous," declared one of the interviewees.

One of the major themes the research participants discuss deals with the generational divide. As the sustaining of one's family becomes increasingly difficult within the current context, younger generations are viewing agriculture as a challenging and unproductive career choice. Therefore, they are gradually attempting to become further educated and migrate towards urban centres. However, "you can't eat paper in an office, who is going to produce the food?" proclaims one of the participants.

Sustainable Development (*SD*): When the discussion focusing on sustainable development commenced, it became quickly obvious that there are dissimilar perspectives and definitions of this concept. The Mayan indigenous of Guatemala define SD as an integrated, multi-sectoral approach that begins with local people, is defined by local people, and is done in a collective and sustainable manner. Participants feel that the Guatemalan Government has a different conceptualization of SD, one that is based primarily on economic development and the establishment of infrastructure but disregards sustainability.

Additionally, the discussion progressed towards the topic of the lack of dialogue and participation regarding development in Guatemala. The indigenous participants feel as though they possess beneficial insights about development within Guatemala, but they are neglected as a result of ignorance and disrespect on the part of the Guatemalan Government and large international organizations. Local NGOs have played an important role in the development of the local indigenous communities and their surrounding environments, according to the participants. There was a general consensus among the local peoples that they have been routinely consulted for their knowledge concerning specific development projects implemented by local NGOs.

Incorporation of IK in SD: The main theme of the research focused on the current trend to incorporate IK systems into SD projects and policies driving international development organizations. Based on discussions with local Kacquikel-Maya peoples in Guatemala, I quickly discovered that many view this trend as having enormous benefits for the conservation of IK and yet there are many challenges when it comes to the implementation of these initiatives.

Participants express their thoughts about incorporation as a unifying factor towards the defragmentation between the many cultural groups in Guatemalan society and of Mayan society. With greater awareness, non-indigenous peoples may begin to place value on the experiences and knowledge of the indigenous peoples, and, at the same time, indigenous peoples can begin to develop further pride and strengthen their cultural identity by the sharing of indigenous knowledge systems. This initiative will allow indigenous peoples to build their capacity from through access to resources, technologies and training workshops. As a result, greater leadership would be expected within communities, creating, once again, a sense of community among indigenous peoples and a reduction in the divide between generations.

Since written documentation is not a traditional practice among the indigenous people of Guatemala, this strategy could create some obstacles during the implementation of this initiative. With low literacy rates and untrained indigenous peoples, one question the research participants asked was: whom will this knowledge system be presented and who will benefit from it? Thus, the issue of access to appropriate education is brought into the discussion as a potential obstacle to the access of this documented knowledge by the very people who provided it.

Conclusions, Recommendations and Implications

CONCLUSIONS

In the past, indigenous peoples have been hesitant to document their knowledge systems for fear of commodification by Western organizations or individuals. In addition the colonial history of indigenous peoples in Guatemala, there currently exists a concern for the expropriation of intellectual property. Agreements need to be created when conducting research within indigenous communities.

There are a limited number of Mayans who still practise and transmit particular cultural practices. While this number rapidly declines, it is becoming essential to shift the focus of IK conservation onto the younger generations. In order for change to occur it is necessary to encourage greater pride among indigenous peoples and a better understanding of these indigenous peoples by non-indigenous members of Guatemalan society.

Incorporation of IK into development projects is an important support to development and could increase conservation and survival of IK and increase awareness of indigenous peoples as well. Today, there are barriers that exist in Guatemalan society that have inhibited the use and exchange of IK, as it had existed historically in the Mayan culture. These challenges are discussed in more detail below.

Challenges

When organizations attempt to incorporate IK into their policies and projects one important challenge is to gain an understanding of local and regional context. Often, large organizations choose to create policies that can be implemented globally without context-specific consideration. Greater human and financial resources should be made available for the appropriate execution of programmes when integrating IK into all projects and programmes.

If there is a greater understanding and awareness of Mayan indigenous peoples and their position within Guatemalan society, then it may be possible to create more unity among all the cultures present. Greater awareness and understanding may help to combat discrimination and provide indigenous peoples greater access to social services, thereby elevating them from their current position within the power structure in the country.

Furthermore, there is a de-valuation of (something) by many large organizations of indigenous knowledge as trivial when compared to modern, Western knowledge systems that are generally accepted in the Western world as the norm. Historically, Western knowledge has been the foundation for development projects. Collaboration with local indigenous peoples has been limited or altogether non-existent. In the last ten to twenty years there has been a shift concerning the recognition of these knowledge systems. In this transition period, it is essential to be cautious not to negatively affect indigenous culture and to strive to create a system that is effective and provides positive benefits for those communities.

Many barriers need to be considered, namely the generational divide and low literacy levels among indigenous peoples. The Mayan youth of today have grown up witnessing the struggle experienced by their parents and grandparents, and most have now made a conscious decision to change those patterns. They are attempting to become more educated and/or migrating towards urban centres to work in jobs that create greater stability in their lives. Aligned with this shift, younger generations have found it possible to provide for their families financially, but at the expense of their traditional culture. It is true that culture is dynamic, but current changes in the knowledge of Mayan culture are inescapable due to present social conditions. For example, it is common throughout all cultures that farmers experiment and adopt new practices and technologies to maximize their production; however, current external forces (GMO technology, Green Revolution technologies, pesticides, international trade agreements, and US subsidies), are forcing indigenous farmers to quickly adapt with little choice.

One significant challenge discussed by the indigenous research participants was the methodology relating to the incorporation of IK in SD. There are concerns regarding who would be the ones to document IK systems. Would they be indigenous or non-indigenous? Currently, the development model excludes local peoples from fully participating in projects. However, it is necessary to analyze this approach to determine new strategies to increase indigenous and community participation. It is important to remember the many restrictions this could present. With statistically lower levels of education and literacy, it would be imperative to provide training and work with the Guatemalan Government to create change in the current social structures in order to permit easier access for indigenous peoples. This will be an enormous but crucial element to the discussion concerning the incorporation of IK in SD. Without social change in Guatemala, the incorporation of IK in SD will be neither sustainable nor successful.

Finally, while creating policies to integrate IK into SD projects, it is important to include sections that manage their intellectual property rights. Without these directives, the integration of IK into the mainstream will become another form of colonization to the indigenous peoples and their knowledge. As such great care needs to be considered to ensure the protection and conservation of these important knowledge systems.

Opportunities

Although significant challenges are present with the integration of IK into development projects, we can also see opportunities. Greater collaboration with indigenous peoples will increase the sustainability of projects as a result of greater investment from local communities. Also, the use of local knowledge and resources will allow local peoples to continue with project objectives after organizations choose to depart from their communities.

One of the by-products of the implementation of indigenous forums during the documentation phase of IK integration will be a greater sense of unity and pride among indigenous peoples. These forums and training workshops will also help to build greater capacity among indigenous individuals and organizations to function independently and collaboratively with international organizations, thus providing greater project sustainability for the future.

Collaborating with indigenous peoples on development projects and the integration/documentation of their knowledge will create a greater global awareness of these people and the walls of discrimination should crumble as a result.

RECOMMENDATIONS

1. With modernization, there has been a dilution of cultural identity within Guatemala through social constructions. Programmes for the empowerment of indigenous leaders should be a priority for building cultural pride and sustainability amongst the indigenous communities.
2. Creation of initiatives to support sustainable systems of agriculture which focus on the promotion of native crops in an internal market and a phasing out of unreliable external cash crop market.
3. An agrarian reform that looks at the historical ownership of lands and redistributes based on these lines. This reform will create greater access for indigenous communities to continue their agricultural way of life and safeguard the associated knowledge systems through continued practice and transmission of knowledge between generations.
4. Through training activities and the encouragement of indigenous leaders to enter into more political positions, many of the issues that are rampant in Guatemalan society can begin to be addressed.
5. The establishment of indigenous awareness programmes to build greater appreciation and understanding of indigenous peoples to the greater population of Guatemala. Through these programmes,

perhaps discrimination can be left to isolated events.

6. Lack of access to education and other social services is a crucial issue to be addressed at an international level, if integration of indigenous peoples is to be truly successful. Until these issues are brought to the forefront and a strategy to deal with them is created, integration will not function within Guatemala.
7. The addition of a section within the national development plan of Guatemala that specifies special considerations and conditions for working with indigenous peoples.
8. The establishment of a Government entity that deals with indigenous issues as a liaison between the indigenous peoples of Guatemala and the Government is essential for bringing attention to the current situation.
9. The integration of IK into SD is a prime opportunity for the training and utilization of indigenous researchers and development workers for the provision of local knowledge and more effective collaborations with communities.
10. A literacy campaign, similar to the ones in Nicaragua and Cuba (Ozideas, 2000), is urgent to increase literacy levels in Guatemala of which the higher percentages of low literacy lay within the indigenous sector of the population.
11. Valuable links should be encouraged for the assimilation of both Western and indigenous knowledge systems and technologies within the current development model.

12. Efforts should be made for a revival of indigenous practices and knowledge that has been applied less or has been completely lost. The incorporation of IK systems into predominantly indigenous school curricula could be an important pedagogical approach to the conservation of IK systems.

IMPLICATIONS

Based upon the research findings, conclusions and recommendations, many implications can be made of which a few are mentioned below. First, it is important and essential that the attitudes and perspectives of indigenous peoples be brought into the discussion of IK utilization in development within Guatemala and elsewhere. Second, the documentation of IK can be an important tool towards the conservation and preservation of these knowledge systems. Thirdly, there is a need for greater enforcement of intellectual property rights to ensure ownership which remains with indigenous peoples. Finally, the Guatemalan Government should make concerted efforts to establish awareness programmes of indigenous peoples, policies ensuring just and equitable access to social services for all citizens, and a progression of the current model of development and agriculture for greater sustainability and stability.

Abbreviations

IK — Indigenous Knowledge

SD — Sustainable Development

References

Arce, Alberto (2003), Re-approaching social development: A field of action between social life and policy processes, *Journal of International Development*, vol. 15, Issue 7.

Asturias, Miguel Ángel (1996), *Hombres de Maíz*, Editorial Losada: Madrid, Spain.

Choy, Alberto Esquito and Victor Galvez Borrell (1997), *The Mayan Movement Today: Issues of Indigenous Culture and Development in Guatemala*, FLACSO: Guatemala.

Fischer, E.F. (2004), "*Guatemala and the Maya,*" Vanderbilt University, Webpage: www.vanderbilt.edu/AnS/Anthro/Anth210/guatemala_and_the_maya.html. Accessed: 09 Sept. 2004.

Government of Guatemala (1995), *Acuerdo Sobre Indentitad y Derechos de Los Pueblos Indígenas*, México: UNDP, SAQB'E, and CHOLSAMAJ.

Lec-Ajcot, Ronaldo (2005), Personal communication, Instituto Mesoamericano de Permacultura, Pachitulul, San Lucas Tolimán, Guatemala.

Levy, Ben (2006), "The Incorporation of Indigenous Knowledge in Sustainable Development: Perspectives from the Maya-Kacquikel of Lake Atitlan, Guatemala," Thesis Paper, School for International Training, Brattleboro, Vermont, USA.

O'Kane, Trish (1999), *Guatemala : In Focus*, New York: Interlink Books.

Ozideas (2000), "*Spelling and Literacy in Cuba and Nicaragua,*" Website: http://home.vicnet.net.au/~ozideas/ whispanref.htm. Accessed: 24 April 2006.

Peet, Richard and Hartwick, Elaine (1999), *Theories of Development,* New York: The Guilford Press.

Rossman, G. B. and F. Sharon Rallis (2003), *Learning in the Field: An Introduction to Qualitative Research*, London, England: Sage Publications.

United Nations (1995), *Accord on Identity and Rights of Indigenous Peoples,* Mexico, D.F., 31 March, 1995.

20

Life, Culture and Care of Polynesians

Serving Food is a Big Ritual

Salei'a Afele-Fa'amuli

Introduction

INHERENT in the Polynesian food culture is "super" size servings of food as a display of love, gratitude, and joy. To date, to a large extent, Polynesians in the United States and other developed countries remain true to their cultural norm of respect, hospitality, thanksgiving and gratitude by greeting and serving large or whole portions of food to family guests, visitors and elders or adults in the family. Food plays a significant role in Polynesian cultural events, from village chief council meetings to birthdays, weddings, funerals, to family and church group gatherings and celebrations. [1, 2, 8, 12]

While some ancient ways of life and culture disappeared since the arrival of European and American influence in Polynesia during the nineteenth century, [11, 12] the traditional foods cooked on hot stones in a ground pit or oven is still popular today. Unfortunately, due to heavy labor in cooking traditional foods, the daily meals of traditional food may be served once a week or less.

The traditional meals would include complex carbohydrates such as taro, breadfruit, green banana, sweet potato and yams; protein sources include fish and/or other seafood choices including lobster, crab, and seaweed; greens include okra and sweet potato, hibiscus manihot leaves, and taro leaves garnished with coconut milk. Spring water, home-made hot cocoa or hot tea made from lemon or other herbal leaves accompany all meals. Unfortunately, Western foods, which are primarily refined and high in sugar and fat, may be easier to prepare and cook on stoves, but are served in large pieces in the same cultural perception and spirit of hospitality and respect for family guests and elders. The routine of large portions of food is a regular practice each and everyday.[2, 5, 7, 8, 12]

It is not uncommon to find whole cooked chickens, fish, pig, taro, yam, and large cuts of lamb flaps, beef, or other fattening meats such as corned beef on the family dining table or on individual placemats. This manner of service is a demonstration of cultural pride, respect, kindness, hospitality, appreciation for company, and a form of welcome for new or ongoing familial courtship and friendship. Especially for guests or visitors, it is expected to return respect for respect by consuming a good size meal in addition to a "care package" of food to take home particularly for guests who are not spending the night. The same hospitable treatment is extended to guests lodging at a hotel to assure they never go hungry.[12] An understanding of this important cultural value in "super" sizing food portions is very important for nutrition and health professionals to consider in their clinical or outreach educational programs. The population of Polynesian minorities in the United States and other Western societies is increasing.[11, 13, 14] Without consideration of this reality in order to counter escalating rates of obesity among Polynesian minorities will be ineffective programming and poor investment.

Polynesian History

Polynesia lies within the somewhat triangular frame between Hawaii to the north, Fiji to the west, New Zealand to the south-west, and Easter Island to the south-east. Of a common ancestry, the Polynesians migrated from South-East Asia around 5000–2000 BC. They are believed to have migrated from south-eastern China eastward to New Guinea, the Philippines, Indonesia, Indo-China and the Malay Peninsula and ultimately into the Pacific islands or Polynesia.[11, 12, 13, 14]

To the amazement of European explorers, the Polynesians depended on their traditional skill and knowledge of the ocean, wind, and stars for voyaging and navigation to new fishing grounds, thus discovering new islands that became home. European explorers found the islanders to look alike, speak alike, and had similar cultural practices. Their tools of stone, bone, and coral to build their canoes and fishing tools were very similar. Their stocks of domesticated plants such as taro, yam, breadfruit and other plants and animals such as pigs and chickens were of similar species.[11, 12, 13]

To date, the Polynesian languages which are spoken readily and fluently in almost all the Pacific islands, have many common words with common reference and application. Polynesian entertainment, dance and music in their respective island tongue is well known and popular world-wide today. Polynesian performances are seen from coast to coast all throughout North and South America, Canada, Japan, and other parts of the world.[11, 12, 14]

Population

According to the 2000 US Census Bureau, the population of Native Hawaiians and other Pacific Islanders (including Guam and Micronesia) in the United States was 874,414 or 0.3 per cent of the total U.S. population. In the 2002 U.S. Census, 12.5

million or 4.4 per cent of the total population was Asian and Pacific Islanders (about 7 per cent). At least 50 per cent of the Asian/Pacific Islander population lives in the west; 19 per cent lives in the south; 12 per cent lives in the mid-west; and, 19 per cent lives in the north-east. Overall, the Asian/Pacific Islander population is young: 26 per cent is under 18 and 7 per cent is 65 and above. About 95 per cent of Asian/Pacific Islanders live in metropolitan areas. There is growing awareness among Polynesians that there are now more of them migrating and living in the United States including Hawaii and other developed non-U.S. countries than back in the islands.[11, 13, 14]

Polynesian Body Frame

NFL football players and servicemen of Polynesian descent are known for being big, tall and heavy weight which I'm often asked why. Most Polynesian women, compared to their age-adjusted peers in other countries, are tall, have large frames, and heavy weights. An ongoing research is fielding this wonder on the large build of Polynesians, particularly Samoans, exploring and comparing traditional to modern diets, eating habits, daily physical activity, and overall lifestyle changes. The study further explores attributes to obesity which is rampant among Samoans in Samoa, American Samoa, Hawaii, and west coast U.S.[4] Obesity is also observed in the diverse population of Polynesians in New Zealand including the native New Zealanders or Maori, and among Polynesians living in Australia.

Health Status

Similar to health status of inhabitants of other developed countries and continents, the overall health of Polynesians has changed drastically come modernization, change, and introduction of imported foods and fast foods. For instance, recent research claims Samoans in American Samoa are among the most obese in the world.[8, 9] Further, Samoans in Hawaii and west coast United States are primarily overweight and obese. Generally, all of the Polynesian islands including Hawaii, Tonga, Tahiti, Fiji, non-U.S. Samoa, American Samoa, and New Zealand have growing obesity problems and other related non-communicable diseases such as cancer, cardiovascular disease, hypertension, diabetes, renal disease and gout. Obesity is further enhanced by the change in lifestyle from intensive physical labor to minimal physical activity and sedentary desk jobs.[3, 5, 6, 11]

The overall diet in the Pacific islands has gone from wholesome to refined: daily complex carbohydrates to simple and refined carbohydrates of unenriched bread and rice; fish to daily fatty meats such as lamp flaps, pig's feet, pork, turkey tails, beef and corned beef. Soda pops are readily available and preferred over spring water.[1, 2, 3, 12]

Polynesian Food Culture to Date

Island hospitality remains and is assured by having lots of food for self service. Unfortunately, the popular food choices rarely, if at all, include vegetables or greens and fruits.[1, 6, 10, 11, 12]

Throughout my visits to the United States, Hawaii, New Zealand and Tonga, super-sizing of island and non-island foods is observed in Polynesian households. The islanders are not hesitant to serve large portions of Western food in place of island food to guests and visitors. Whether a Polynesian lives in Seattle, Washington D.C., Dallas, or New York City, "fast food" would take the place of island wholesome food in large servings to demonstrate gratitude and respect.

Recommended Nutrition and Health Education Approach

The Polynesians, referred to in the census as Native Hawaiian and Other Pacific Islanders or mingled with Asians in the Asian and Pacific Islander data,[13, 14] are increasingly aware that unhealthy choices of food contribute to obesity and other related non-communicable diseases such as chronic diseases of the heart, liver, blood and bones. They also are aware that food over-consumption and physical inactivity are unhealthy.[1, 2] However, awareness is only the beginning of the roadmap to meaningful change.

The purpose of this write-up is to bring to the attention of nutrition and health professionals working with Polynesians or Pacific Islanders some understanding of the Polynesians' deeply embedded cultural value in super-sizing food servings. From less complex socio-economic systems of physical labor and wholesome food to industrial and electronic technology and refined foods, delivery of an effective and culturally appropriate nutrition education to Polynesians now residing in Western culture is plausible.

To a large extent, health/nutrition professionals with respect, knowledge and consciousness of things Polynesian including recognizing island food culture and traditional foods prior to establishing an educator-learner relationship are welcomed with open arms. A suggested model is recognizing, reminding and perpetuating consumption of wholesome food choices of fruits, vegetables, fish and lean meats, and drinking lots of water. These were traditional foods of their ancestors who had no known record of obesity and chronic heart diseases. Studies and reports today verify that the diet of Polynesians in the islands and abroad is both very low in fruits and vegetables.

Cost and availability may be realistic hindrances to accessing traditional fruits such as mango, papaya, passion fruit, young coconut, and guava; likewise vegetables that are deep green such as taro, hibiscus manihot, and sweet potato leaves; pumpkin and breadfruit. However, once empowerment and trust are in place in the educator-learner relationship, the island fruits and vegetables, abundant all-year round in the islands could be successfully substituted with local fruits and vegetables of similar taste, colour, nutritional value, in their recommended serving sizes for different ages.

Compared to cooking today using lots of frying oil, soy sauce, monosodium glutamate and salt, meat was grilled on hot stones ridding most of the fat, and sea water was used in place of salt for flavoring. Food was wrapped in mango, banana, breadfruit and taro leaves which added natural flavour and nutrition. Papaya leaves were used to tenderize octopus before cooking. With the exception of salt, these practices are ongoing for special occasions in the islands, but not in the United States.

To further encourage participation in health and nutrition education lessons, Polynesians prefer to learn in small groups of neighbours, family and friends.[1, 2, 12] Church groups are preferred and have been successful sites for learning and applying new knowledge in other studies. Polynesian family is hardly nuclear. Neighbours, related or unrelated are embraced by Polynesians like family and would enjoy learning together with them.[1]

The concept of recipe cooking is not new to Polynesians abroad. However, lesson presentation without hands-on learning is unlikely to transfer to home cooking. Further, handouts and other printed materials including recipes may not be successful teaching tools. There is preference for hands-on learning like their ancestral upbringing in a very oral culture. Despite relocating to Western culture, parents continue to perpetuate their oral culture through story telling, dance, music, and display of island craft. High regard for elders and adults in the home is central and the best of the best are theirs. Given these ongoing cultural practices away from island home, respect for respect is imperative and undoubtedly will find success in health and nutrition engagement upon entering Polynesian households.[1, 11, 12]

Notes

1. Afele-Faamuli, Saleia, Learning Preferences of Adult Non-formal Learners in American Samoa: Implications for Extension and Continuing Education in American Samoa, 1992, unpublished doctoral dissertation.
2. Afele-Faamuli, Saleia, A Pilot Study in Nutrition and Exercise for Cancer Prevention: Implications for an Island-wide Cancer Intervention for All Adults in American Samoa. Funded by the National Cancer Institute, National Institutes of Health, U.S. Department of Health and Human Services, 2000, unpublished.
3. American Samoa Department of Health, 1999.
4. DePrince, Kristin M., S.T. McGarvey, L. Bausserma, C.E. Aston, M.I. Kamboh, Genetics of Plasma Lp(a) Levels in American Samoa, Department of Medicine, the Miriam Hospital, Brown Medicine, Providence, RI 02906.
5. Galanis, D.J., S.T. McGarvey, C. Quested, B. Sio, S. Afele-Faamuli, Dietary Intake Among Modernizing Samoans: Implications for Risk Cardiovascular Disease, *Journal of American Diet Assoc.*, Feb 2000, vol. 99, no. 2.
6. Gershater, E, S.T. McGarvey, *Fourteen Year Changes in Adiposity and Blood Pressure in American Samoa Adults*, 1995, Wiley-Liss Inc.
7. McGarvey, S.T., Thifty Genotype Concepts and Health in Modernizing Samoans. 1995, *Asia Pac Jn of Clin Nutr.*

8. ———, Obesity in Samoans and a Perspective on its Etiology Polynesians. *AmJ Clin Nutri* 1991 53: 1586S-94S.

9. Mishra, S. et al., Identifying the Cancer Control Needs of American Samoans. *Asian Am and Pac Islander Jn of Health*, 1998, vol. 6, no. 2.

10. Murphy, J.K. and S.T. McGarvey, Pressor Reactivity in American Samoan Children: Comparisons with Mainland American Children, *Ethnicity and Disease*, 1994, V4.

11. Google web search for Polynesian culture, history, food and health: www.google.com.

12. Shaffer, Robert J., *American Samoa: 100 Years Under the United States Flag*.

13. US Department of the Interior, Office of Insular Affairs, 1999.

14. US Department of Commerce, Economics and Statistics Administration, U.S. Census Bureau, 2002.

21

Indigenous Knowledge Practices in Sustainable Agricultural Production
In Villages of Benue State, Nigeria

G.A. Abu, E.P. Ejembi **and** ***O.G. Okpachu***

Introduction

THE need to change from a high, costly and imported input agricultural production to a more sustainable one dependent on indigenous knowledge became imperative in Nigeria. The economic crisis of the mid 1980's formed the basis for the transition. The Nigerian State could no longer sustain the food, agro-chemicals, fertilizers, machineries and other costly inputs that were usually imported since political independence. Farmers have to fall back on indigenous knowledge inherited as the only option. The indigenous knowledge was intended to complement Western scientific knowledge. However, there are challenges limiting the generation and utilization of the indigenous knowledge system. Such challenges include colonialism, wars, conflicts and natural disasters. All these events dislocated and altered the indigenous base of the rural communities. HIV/AIDS is the latest challenge ravaging the rural communities with high death toll on the custodians of treasury of indigenous knowledge. This further depleted the reservoir of indigenous knowledge. It, therefore, became apt to carry out an inventory and document indigenous knowledge system-cum-practice in the face of these challenges. Using Focus Group Discussion (FGD) and observer participant methodology in three villages in Benue State, north central Nigeria, this article focuses on documenting proven indigenous practices in crop and animal production. The results showed important indigenous knowledge in crop protection, farming systems and animal disease control. The mode of transmission of indigenous knowledge from one generation to another is via oral tradition of folk tales, story telling, ceremonies, arts and culture. This knowledge, if systematized and extended will guarantee sustainable agricultural production. The chapter recommends that similar studies be conducted in different geo-political zones of Nigeria, given that the indigenous knowledge is influenced by history, culture, ethnicity, location and belief system.

Indigenous Knowledge and Agriculture

The issues of food self-sufficiency, provision of industrial raw materials to feed the agro-allied industrial, income generation and job creation in the rural areas have been the major issues of debate lately amongst well meaning Nigerians. In spite of the vast agricultural potentials of Nigeria, the issue of good security is still a problem and this is because these potentials till date are not harnessed properly. Inquiries are, therefore, on to find out why development efforts have not been able to provide solutions to these problems. One element which we hope can facilitate efforts to deal with these problems, especially in agriculture, is the awareness, understanding the use of indigenous knowledge and the structure of the existing institutions via which changes must be transmitted if success is to be registered.

The agricultural sector of the Nigerian economy is of critical importance because of its close linkage to the overall development effort through food production and provision, job creation in the rural areas, income generation and raw material provision for agro-allied industries. The influence of the sector is, therefore not in doubt. However, the sector tends to be scored very low because, it neither provides sufficient food for the entire populace nor reduces the associated problems of rural poverty. The scenario depicted from the foregoing stems from a blend of social and economic crisis, part of which is the reason for embarking on this empirical research work with the aim of generating a data base of indigenous knowledge practices and to see how it complements Western scientific practice.

COLONIAL STYLED ECONOMY

Nel (2005) contended that indigenous knowledge systems inquiring has forced itself the agenda of serious reflection in both the academic and practitioner context. In the Nigerian case, it was orchestrated by the fact that indigenous knowledge has hitherto been misunderstood and suppressed as well as ignored by "outsiders" in spite of its incredible wealth of potentials. This was so because of the colonial antecedents. After independence in 1960, Nigeria inherited a colonialist-styled economy. Because of the *comprador* elites that emerged at independence, little or nothing was done to change the colonial economic system. Agricultural commodities were regulated by a board introduced by the colonialists, production of agricultural commodities was geared towards the industrial needs of the west and the farming system was sole cropping as against the indigenous mixed cropping system before the coming of the colonial masters. By mid 1980s, Nigeria experienced economic crisis that was not only symbolized by declining aggregate growth rates, but also the occurrence of macro-economic disequilibria. Agriculture no longer could feed the Nigerian population. Modern inputs were recommended to local farmers such as hybrid seeds, fertilizers, agro-chemicals and machineries. It was hoped that these inputs would increase productivity in the agricultural sector. The Nigerian State could not guarantee the timely supplies of these modern inputs that were imported most of the time. Even when provided, the relatively high cost associated is unaffordable to the local farmers. Against this backdrop, indigenous knowledge practice became an option. Very often, when indigenous knowledge is mentioned, it is erroneously assumed to be "straight jacket" that you can go to any rural setting and collect. Colonialism was a violent encounter, the colonial educators created a carbon copy of Europe in Africa, thus yielding evil fruits by distorting and discouraging the heirs of what is now called indigenous knowledge from paying serious attention to their knowledge heritage. In addition to colonialism, wars, conflict, natural disasters all toiled with indigenous knowledge by dislocating them.

HIV/AIDS and Indigenous Knowledge

HIV/AIDS is another pandemic that is straining the reservoir of indigenous knowledge system and constitutes a new challenge. HIV/AIDS is most prevalent in the rural areas. It is taking a toll on the old and aged of the farm population. Given that indigenous knowledge is passed from generation to generation, a vacuum is being created by the incessant death of old people who are the custodians of the treasury of indigenous knowledge, thus depressing the reservoirs of indigenous knowledge. It is thus apt to systematically document and create a database of indigenous system against the foregoing challenges. Specific research questions addressed in the study include: What local knowledge exists in the study area pertaining to agricultural production? How is such knowledge transmitted from generation to generation? How is indigenous knowledge utilized in sustainable agricultural practices?

Methodology

STUDY AREA

The study area is Otukpo local government area which was created in 1976 by the General Murtala Mohammed's administration. The local government area is one of the twenty-three local government areas that constitute Benue State. It is made up of predominantly the Idoma speaking ethnic group occupying a land area of 82,298 km^2 and has Otukpo as its headquarters. Its latitude is 7.45-8.15^{0}E and longitude 7.0-7.45^{0}N. According to the census result of 1991, the population *figure.* of the study area was estimated to be 181,000. Out of this *figure.* 100,000 were males whereas the remaining 81,000 were females. The area is marked by guinea savannah grassland and experiences two seasons; dry season which starts from November-March with temperature ranging between 21-33^{0}c and wet season which starts from April-October with an average annual rainfall of 800-1500 mm. The climate and vegetation experienced tends to be conducive for agricultural practices, and this has led to most of the inhabitants taking to farming as their major occupation (Ministry of Information, 1986). Farmers cultivate food crops like yams, maize, cassava, millet, sorghum, rice and groundnut. A few numbers of the farmers diversify their farming activities by keeping livestock on a small scale. Examples of the livestock include; goat, sheep, cattle, pigs, poultry and rabbits. There exist credit institutions like community of Banks, Nigerian Agricultural Co-operative and Rural Development Bank (NACRDB), co-operative associations and lending agencies as well as Non-Government Organizations (NGOs) that help boost farmer's agricultural productivity.

DATA COLLECTION AND SAMPLING TECHNIQUES

The study relied greatly on primary data obtained with the help of Focus Group Discussions and Oral Interviews (OIs) to evoke responses from respondents.

Using the Benue State Agricultural and Rural Development Authority (BNARDA) system of zoning, the study area comprises four districts, namely: Adoka, Akpa, Otukpo and Ugboju. The study focuses on Otukpo districts and specifically, Edikwu, Upu and Obaganya villages. To evoke responses from respondents FGDs and OIs were employed. Focus group is typically composed of 7-10 participants who are unfamiliar with each other. These participants are selected because they have certain characteristics in common that relates to the topic of the Focus Group Discussion. A total of 90 respondents were selected from the three villages represented by sample size respondents of 30 farmers. The 30 respondents from each of the villages are further divided into three focus groups comprising 10 members each (10 adult males, 10 adult females and 10 youths (5 males and 5 females), respectively bringing it to a total of 15 male youths and 15 female youths for the villages). It is worth noting that in rural communities, rural members are familiar with each other and this quality does not invalidate the use of Focus Group Discussions.

Results and Discussion

INDIGENOUS KNOWLEDGE PRACTICES IN THE STUDY AREA

The responses evoked from the respondents in Edikwu, Upu and Obaganya villages with respect to indigenous knowledge system tends to have a lot of similarities as such, the results listed below cover the villages in question. Most of the responses were evoked from the adult males and adult females group. The youth groups of both males and females were also able to provide one or two vital informations. For each of the crops grown by the farmers, the **problems** associated in their productions are stated clearly below:

Cassava

The leaves and the stems as well are eaten up by pest (insects) like grasshopper and crickets.

Yam

Post-harvest losses occur in tubers harvested due to poor storage and termites attack. Seed yams that are planted are eaten up by termites. Also termites and cricket eat up the vine and leaves.

Maize

Post-harvest losses occur in cobs due to poor storage and weevil infestation. The seeds that are extracted from cobs and bagged are also attacked by weevil. Grasshopper and crickets eat up the stem and leaves. Also, goats on ranges eat up the plant (mostly in the farms that are closer to the villages).

Sorghum

Post-harvest losses occur in the sorghum ears due to weevil infestation. Grasshopper and crickets eat up the stems and leaves. Also, goats eat up the plants, in the farms that are closer to the village. When the seeds are sown, birds scratch out the seeds to eat them up thus reducing greatly the plant population.

Groundnut

Rodents in the likes of hare, rabbits and rats dig out the seeds and eat them up. Also, the seeds are infested with weevil after harvesting. Leaves are eaten as well by rodents.

SOLUTIONS

The indigenous knowledge options for solving such production problems include:

Cassava

Respondents collected some neem leaves (*Azadirachta indica*), pounded it in the mortar and then had it mixed with water to form a resultant bitter solution. The bitter solution was sprinkled on the cassava plants with the use of a special flexible broom made from raffia palm.

Yam

Tubers harvested are stored in a hut which is clean, cool and well ventilated. Before tubers are stored, they are sprinkled with ash from burnt firewoods to repel termite attacks. Seed yams are wholly immersed in the neem solution and then planted to repel termites and crickets. Also, the solution prepared from the neem plant and water is sprayed on the plants using a special flexible raffia palm broom. The cut surface of seed yams is sprinkled with ash to prevent rot.

Maize

Cobs are stored up in barns which have tiny holes for proper ventilation. Weevils are prevented from attacking the seeds by immersing in neem solution. Maize (cobs) which are to be used as planting materials for the next farming season are hanged above fires in the kitchen to be smoked thus preventing weevil infestation. For maize seeds extracted from the cobs, the seeds are admixed with ground red pepper then bagged to prevent weevil attack. Grasshopper and cricket that eat up stem and leaves of the plant are prevented from doing so by sprinkling the plant with a neem solution with the use of a special flexible broom made from raffia palm. Goats which eat up plant are warded off by collecting the pellets of their droppings and mixing it with water to form a solution and the resultant solution sprinkled on the plant.

Sorghum

The ears are stored in a barn with tiny holes for proper ventilation. Weevils are prevented from attacking the seeds extracted from the ears by mixing it with ground red pepper then bagged. Grasshopper and cricket that eat up the stem and leaves of the plant are prevented from doing so by sprinkling the plant with neem solution with the help of raffia palm broom. Similarly goats, which eat up plant are warded off by sprinkling solution made of their pellets. Traps are used to prevent birds that scratch out seeds to eat them. Also, the seeds that are sown are increased so that a sizable produce is maintained at the end of the day. The use of objects to scare birds away, like polythene bags tied to a twig producing scary sounds when wind is blows is also used.

Groundnut

Traps are used to prevent rodents. Harvested seeds are admixed with ground pepper and stored to prevent weevil attack. (Seeds are first sun dried to reduce the moisture content.)

PROBLEMS IN LIVESTOCK

The major problems associated in livestock production are:

Scabies

This is called "ikwa" by the respondents. They describe the

disease as rashes that appear on the dermis (skin) of goats making the hair to fall off.

Coccidiosis

This is called "Omagogo" by the respondents. They described the disease as loss of weight, blood stained diarrhoea, nervous in co-ordination resulting in the head perpetually bent backwards and then zigzag movement exhibited by the chicken.

Helminthes

This is called "inyilo" by the respondents. They described the disease as low feed conversion efficiency. The animal will eat a lot of food and will not gain weight.

SOLUTIONS TO LIVESTOCKS

The options for solving such problems include:

Scabies

The respondents treat this disease in goats by buying sulphur from the market, had it ground into powder and then mixed with palm oil into a paste. The affected part of the body is scraped with a razor blade or a sharp knife and the preparation applied topically three times every other day until the condition disappears.

Coccidiosis

The respondents treat this diseased condition with the use of the bark of different trees and herbs. The bark of these trees/ herbs are used: *Angessins licarpus* (otra), *Afromonium meguigata* (alligator pepper) (otuta), *Khaye senegalensis* (opi) and *Annon senegalensis* (ukpo). The herbs are boiled in water using a small earthen pot. The water is not allowed to boil and pour into the fire since it implies that the potency of the preparation for treatment will not be lost. The liquid is poured into a bowl and allowed to cool, then the animals (chickens) which were previously starved of water were administered the preparation to drink for 5-7 days.

Helminthes

The respondents treated this disease condition with the use of the bark of different trees and herbs. The bark of these trees/herbs are used; *Cassia occidentalis* (Anyemba), *Erytrina senegalensis* (Ache), *crinium ornatum* (Igbingbi). The herb is boiled in water using an earthen pot. The liquid is prevented from spilling into the fire so that the potency will not be lost. The mixture is poured into a bowl and allowed to cool, then administer to the goats to drink for 3-5 days. Only the mixture will be used as drinking water throughout the duration the medication is to last.

Other indigenous options used in the study area include:

PLANT PROTECTION

a. Neem leaves (*Azadirachta indica*) pounded and mixed with water and sprinkled on cassava with a broom to prevent grasshoppers and crickets from eating the stems and leaves.

b. Seed yams immersed in a solution of neem leaves (*Azadirachta indica*) pounded and mixed with water to prevent being eaten by termites and crickets when planted.

c. Neem leaves (*Azadirachta indica*) pounded and mixed with water and sprinkled on yam vine and leaves with a broom to prevent being eaten by crickets and grasshopper.

d. The cut surface of a seed yam is covered with wood ash to prevent infections which will lead to rotten conditions.

e. Sprinkle maize and sorghum plants with a solution of neem leaves (Azadirachta indica) and water with a broom to prevent leaves and stem from being eaten by grasshopper and goats and cricket as well.

f. Sprinkling maize and sorghum plants with a solution of goat pellets and water with a broom to prevent being eaten by goats on range.

Post Harvest Prevention and Loss Reduction

a. Tubers of yam harvested from the farm are sprinkled with wood ash and then stored in a clean, cool and well-ventilated hut to prevent termite from attacking them.

b. Maize cobs are stored in barns which have tiny holes at intervals for ventilation.

c. Immersing corn cobs in a solution of neem leaves (*Azadirachta indica*) then dried in the sun, then stored in the barn to prevent weevil attack.

d. Maize seed extracted from the cobs are admixed with red pepper that is ground, then stored in the bag to prevent weevil attack.

e. A special barn with holes for ventilation is employed to store ears of sorghum.

f. Sorghum seeds are admixed with red pepper ground then stored in a bag to prevent weevil attack.

g. Groundnut seeds (dried) are admixed with red pepper that is ground and then stored in a bag to prevent weevil attack.

Seed Sowing/Planting Technique

The seeds of sorghum are planted and covered, then replanted again and covered to ensure that birds that scratch and eat up seeds do not reduce the produce of the plant below expectation.

The respondents were of the opinion that the options (indigenous knowledge system) represents an integral part of their rich cultural heritage and therefore they will continue to try and propagate it amongst the younger generation via their own local means of oral tradition. The elders have made it a point of duty to integrate some of the youths into the elder's council in a bid to work hand in hand with them to ensure that the knowledge system does not go extinct since it is threatened. They try as much as possible to arouse the interest of the youth and especially the younger generation who are still in the formative stage. They were also of the opinion that government should look into the viable knowledge systems and then see how it can help make it complementary with modern science to be scaled up for the benefit of the inhabitants of the study area. The respondents lamented greatly during the interview section about the way the knowledge system has been marginalized and ignored. They were of the opinion that the knowledge system is threatened to a very high degree and is going into extinction. They attributed the reason predominantly to modern science. But they opine that though the modern science has its benefits it does not suit their situation completely.

Conclusion

In a bid to make agriculture self-sustaining, government and researchers are exploring available options. In the face of government's inability to provide modern inputs at affordable rates and in time, the use of indigenous knowledge system became imperative. The generation and utilization of this knowledge system is constrained by the antecedents of colonialism, wars, conflicts, natural disasters and of recent, HIV/AIDS pandemic. It therefore became apt to document proven indigenous knowledge or risk losing the entire indigenous heritage. In the villages of Edikwu, Upu and Obaganya, proven indigenous knowledge in crop production, protection and Animal disease control were verified and documented. The authors recommend that similar studies be carried out in other geo-political zones in order to enrich the data base of IK system in Nigeria.

Abbrevations

BNARDA	—	Benue State Agricultural and Rural Development Authority
FGD	—	Focus Group Discussion
IK	—	Indigenous Knowledge
NACRDB	—	Nigerian Agricultural Co-operative and Rural Development Bank
NGOs	—	Non-Government Organizations
OIs	—	Oral Interviews

References

Abu, G.A. (2005), "The use of indigenous knowledge in crop and livestock production in Benue State, Nigeria," *African Journal of Indigenous Knowledge System*, vol. 4, no. 1, pp. 245-48.

Benue Agricultural and Rural Development Authority (1990), Crop Area Yield Survey, (BNARDA occasional paper, no. 4.)

Cultivating and Industrializing Indigenous Knowledge Tract in Africa, *African Journal of Indigenous Knowledge System*, vol. 4, no. 1, pp. 145-65.

Nel., P.J. (2005), Indigenous knowledge systems: Contestation.

Njoku, C.A. (2005), Wisdom in Re-Inventing the Wheel?

Rhetoric and Space, *African Journal of Indigenous Knowledge Systems*, vol. 4 no. 1, pp. 2-14.

Warren, D.M., L.J. Slikkerveer and S.O. Titilola (1989), "Indigenous Knowledge systems: Implication for Agriculture and International Development", Studies in Technology and Social change, no. 11, Ames, Iowa: Technology and Social Change Programme, Iowa State University.

Part V

Indigenous Rights and Sustainable Development

22

Recognition of Indigenous Rights in Contemporary Mexico
A Historical-Social Approach

José G. Vargas-Hernŏndez

Social Movements for Recognition of Indigenous Rights

THE struggle for the recognition of indigenous rights is one of the most important social movements in Mexico. Before the 1970s, existing peasant organizations did not represent indigenous concerns. Since 1975 there has been a resurgence of indigenous movements and they have raised new demands in defence of their cultural values. However, indigenous social mobilization had been laid in local and regional peasant struggles across the 1970s and 1980s.

Indigenous peoples created and participated in unions, political parties or co-operatives that, until the 1980s, did not articulate their demands in terms of their identity; rather they tended to identify themselves as peasant organizations (Yashar, 1998; Albó, 1999). After 1980, indigenous movements actively participated in the democratization process of Latin America (Van Cott, 1994; Diaz Polanco, 1997; Horst, 1998; Ramos, 1998; Warren, 1998). The renewal for indigenous movements across Mexico began with the 1987 publication of *México Profundo* (*Deep Mexico: A Civilization Denied*).

The indigenous movement is not homogeneous and does not include all ethnic groups in the country, but it has many different expressions, and encompasses different entities at local, regional and national levels. Movements at local levels are based on their ethnicity and community with limited mobilization. At regional level are integrated associations of ethnic groups. At national level the indigenous movement began in 1975 with indigenous organizations, such as the National Council of Indigenous Peoples (CNPI) and the National Association of Bilingual Teachers. According to Estrada (2003) the Indigenous Organizations are mentioned in the following Table:

Table 22.1
Indigenous Organizations

National Indigenous Movement of the National Peasant Confederation	Movimiento Nacional Indígena de la Confederación Nacional Campesina	MINI-CNC
National Confederation of Indigenous People	Confederación Nacional de Pueblos Indígenas	CONAIN
National Union of Autonomous Regional Peasant Organizations	Unión Nacional de Organizaciones Regionales Campesinas Autónomas	UNORCA
Indigenous People Independent Front	Frente Nacional de Pueblos Indígenas	FIPI
National Indigenous Council	Consejo Nacional Indigena	CNI

Source: Estrada (2003)

Indigenous movements are shaped by the struggle for identity and the need to open a space for survival within the national political, economic and social environment. Class and ethnic conflicts are at the base of the struggle for identity of the indigenous movements. This struggle has its roots during the colonial period. Although indigenous movements have an ethnic component, they share common features with other social movements.

Indigenous movements' participation in the democratization movements adopt organizational forms to establish relationships of control and input with the political and judicial processes. The organization affects them in such a way they can further their claims through political parties, NGOs, etc. with direct access to the decision-making processes at different levels of government. The inward strategic orientation of indigenous movements towards the national context depends on the level of control and input. The demographic weight of indigenous movements is nationally and regionally important.

Indigenous movements have recourse to ambiguous norms about human rights, environmental sustainability and cultural diversity. The Mexican environmental and indigenous movements focused on agriculture and the quest for sustainable alternatives, struggle to revalidate, revitalize and integrate traditional ecological knowledge into grass-roots development projects.

The preservation of species diversity is intrinsic to sustainable development and to environmental movements and international indigenous rights movement. Agrarian and ethnic movements are conscious of the struggle for identity and began to state their demands as rights, land rights, labour rights or educational rights. Indigenous movements need to follow more a multi-pronged strategy of lobbying, alliance making, appealing to courts, and public campaigns than a legal alternative which is besieged by traps and counterproductive results.

Carruthers (1995) uses the term "indigenous political ecology" to refer to the consolidation of social movement alliances based in an effort to preserve, defend, apply and integrate traditional ecological knowledge (TEK) embedded in indigenous and peasant culture and practice into grass-roots development efforts. Indigenous ecology refers to alliances between environmental and indigenous social movement organizations. Internationalization of the indigenous ecology movement reveals ongoing tension between two contending social movement visions, one of which is the own social movement activity.

Carruthers (1996) analyses cross-movement alliance formation between contemporary environmental groups, formed by the urban, educated middle class, which have found a convergence of interest with existing peasant and indigenous organizations of the most marginalized segment of Mexico's rural poor.

A multi-pronged strategy includes alliances with other social movements depending upon the existence of points of common interest. Indigenous communities ally with environmental and human rights movements to lobby and exert pressures on national governments. Alliance of indigenous movements and alliances may have some possibilities of reshaping the current structures of governance.

Agroecology, as a social movement, seeks to rescue traditional practices, to protect biological and cultural diversity and to bring together First World and Third World forms of environmentalism. The emerging agroecology movement in Mexico is fuelled by high ecological costs of industrial agriculture. Agroecological experimentation is fostered by state agencies that maintain linkages with activists in the peasant or environmental movements.

Alliances of environmental, agroecology and indigenous social movements foster and strengthen linkages between grass-roots organizations (GROs) that represent existing indigenous, peasant, and smallholders' organizations, and Grass-roots Support Organizations (GRSOs) which represent the applied face of the Mexican environmental and agroecology movements. A GRSO "is a developmental civic entity that provides services for and channels resources to local groups of disadvantaged rural or urban households and individuals" (Bendahmane, 1991, 31).

The indigenous communities are cohesively responding to the ethnic conflict as one of the most significant social movements in Mexico's history to the surprise of other social actors, such as government, politicians, analysts and academics. Mejía Pineros and Sarmiento Silva (1987), Moguel, Botey, and Hernández, eds. (1992), and Warman and Argueta, eds. (1993) have researched regional indigenous movements in Mexico, as well as the journals *Ojarasca* and *Cuadernos Agrarios*. The priority of the indigenous movement is the bilingual educational programmes or recovery of traditional cultures.

The 1980s was a time of social mobilization and expansion in Mexican social indigenous and peasant movements. Indigenous civil society, in some regions richly textured and thin, heavily structured by clienteles in others, reflect the historical legacies of both past movements from below and openings from above (Fox, 1997). Some local movements are defections from the ruling corporatist party while others emerged from an opening within the ruling political class in the early 1970s and have independently promoted bottom-up strong ethnic identity-based mobilization, as in the case of the democratization of Oaxaca's Zapotec market town of Juchitán.

The local movement development increased with mobilization from below, from political alliances and from reform-oriented elites-controlled state politics. Social movements often attempt to occupy the cracks in the system from below, demanding access to the state while articulating their own interests.

Different positions about the new relation between developmental and environmental concerns become more visible as different organizations, institutions and movements established connections with each other. Indigenous communities and their alliances with non-Indigenous communities and wider movements have transformative effects on the structures of governance. The contradiction between the growing pressures on international financial institutions and the state widened with the consolidation in the 1990s of the transnational environmentalist movement, and the indigenous communities' rights to sustain their own life projects were legitimated and the international indigenous movement and environmentalism was consolidated.

Several factors have raised the consciousness of the new indigenous movement. American indigenous movements started in 1992 with the legitimacy to the heightened indigenous issues and international awareness coming out from the boost of the 500th Anniversary of Columbus's "discovery" of the Americas. The 1992 has been a time of renewal for indigenous movements when Rigoberta Menchú, a Mayan woman was awarded the 1992 Nobel Peace Prize for her role as a symbol of the rising consciousness of the new indigenous movement.

The celebrations reinvigorated organizations and Indian movement ties, creating new alliances between indigenous groups, pan-Indian movements, NGOs, environmental groups and others. This and other events created an environment in Mexico for the formation of new indigenous movement organizations and new alliances between indigenous movements.

The indigenous social movements gain access to the political sphere based on solidarity among members and the capacity to create new forms of social relations and practice, like shared antagonism towards others. Power is not central, defined as a "continuing overt relationship of conflict between collective actors and authorities" (Evers, 1985). However, collective actors are prone to disperse, fragmented and atomized, into networks, which quickly disappear from political relevance into sects, emotional support circles and therapy groups.

The struggle of indigenous peoples of Chihuahua, the Taraumaras is articulated against illegal forestry practices, in particular, water and biodiversity. An indigenous, religious and social movement, the Civil Society Las Abejas, emerged in 1992 as a coalition of local indigenous Maya-Tzotzil communities who united to solve land conflicts. The Land Research Action Network was launched in Chiapas to mobilize people in support of popular movements who are struggling for access to land. Identity among communities provides emotional involvement in collective action.

In January of 1994, the Zapatista uprising of Mayan indigenous communities in Chiapas received solidarity from indigenous and peasant movement organizations, networks, alliances, and coalitions. The Zapatista guerrilla movement that emerged in Chiapas in 1994 has triggered social movements in Mexico and abroad, to emphasize the increasing levels of poverty under the neo-liberal economic policy and demanding a more equitable income distribution.

As a resistance movement, the Zapatista uprising in Chiapas has been successful using the slogan — Basta ya! (enough!) and presenting their 11-word programme to the

Mexican Government: "Trabajo, Tierra, Techo, Pan, Salud, Educación, Democracia, Libertad, Paz, Independencia y Justica" (work, land, shelter, bread, health, education, democracy, liberty, peace, independence and justice).

Local indigenous and environmental movements are peaceful and unarmed, and draw on legal instruments, build ties with NGOs, churches and the scientific community. The Zapatista movement represents grass-roots organizations, which can broaden and deepen without external alliances. In 1994, diverse local civic movements that included human rights movements, co-operatives, and ethnic rights emerged throughout the region in conflict in Chiapaz, ejected most of the ruling party mayors of municipalities and installed instead pluralistic town councils. The strategy designed to pursue their demands and management of relationship with state institutions are two factors for indigenous movements to succeed.

Las Abejas movement is an expression of the "civil society" movement comprising of several peasant, indigenous and local non-governmental organizations. Since 1997, when 45 members were massacred in Acteal, human rights organizations supported the use of non-violent methods of conflict resolution. The interactions among members form a unique "global syncretic identity," which inspires the movement in its collective action of resistance against displacement and military land invasion.

As a social movement, the EZLN is distinguishable from other popular movements in Mexico having actively mobilized not only the indigenous groups but also other large groups of economic, social and political actors. Indigenous communities re-focus on traditional values and transform old meanings in order to continue with their land struggle. The EZLN can strategically develop either into a new political movement or into an indigenous autonomy movement.

The Zapatista movement is considered a transnational rhizomes or social network weaving a global electronic fabric of struggle and mounting a social network against a state lagging at democratization. The Zapatista rebellion is a prototype for social network in the 21st century, in which almost every aspect of modern computer communications have been used.

There is new capacity for this and other social movements to communicate across borders and to operate at a transnational level. The analyses of this movement have recognized how the content of the rhizomatic or networking forms of social mobilization, pulling together grass-roots movements against the current political and economic order in Mexico and the world and of facilitating alternative approaches to social organization. Governments should learn to counter such social movements and have to improve its ability to wage counter-netwar.

The unprecedented success of EZLN as a new social movement has been attributed to its postmodernity. The EZLN as a new social movement has been characterized as the first "postmodern" peasant rebellion because of the sophisticated communication techniques. A Mexican analyst, Gustavo Esteva, posed the question, "Is ours the last Central American guerrilla war, or has the new postmodern revolutionary era begun?" (Cockburn, 1994: 404).

Through creative use of images and information, indigenous people have turned marginality and poverty into their greatest strength on the emergence of "internationalized" identity-based movements. Kelley (2002: 9) states that "how oppressed we are or that merely chronicles the [follies] of radical movements doesn't seem very useful . . . Progressive social movements do not simply produce statistics and narratives of oppression; rather, the best ones do what great poetry always does: transport us to another place, compel us to relive horrors and, more importantly, enable us to imagine a new society."

Chiapas revolt remains an indigenous revolt because it's the EZLN revolt supported by the rest of social movements in Mexico. It is still early to evaluate the extent to which the EZLN movement is achieving change of cultural politics through elements that are part of the movement's history, such as radical democratic and autonomy practices, claims to indigenous identity, traditions and dignity. The indigenous movement maintains some levels of autonomy and has increased its capacity to bargain with the state.

The Zapatistas have positioned themselves in dialogue with anti-neoliberal social movements in Mexico and around the world. The EZLN offers a coherent alternative to social movements in Mexico. The National Indigenous Congress (CNI) began in 1996 to bring together the indigenous movements aligned with the Zapatistas under the assumption of creating an understanding of a collective sense of self in movement. This was in contrast to homogenizing mestizaje (mixed-race) and identity categories so as to gain recognition as citizens (Rosaldo, 2000).

Sustained indigenous social movements in Mexico and indigenous peoples have an important role to achieve resolutions and demands of the National Indigenous Congress and social movements in Mexico aimed at nurturing and conserving natural and cultural biodiversity. An environmental movement in Southern Mexico and Central America pretends to preserve the wealth of biodiversity. Social movements in

Mexico and around the world have raised the issues to control seeds and medicinal plants at different international conventions.

Internationalization of the Mexican indigenous social movement finds support around the world. The Bi-national Mixtec-Zapotec Front, (FM-ZB) based in California, organizes migrant farmworkers of Oaxacan origin and promotes indigenous resistance and worker and human rights and sustainable agricultural development projects.

There are other bi-national movements, such as the Frente Indigena Oaxaqueno Binacional, which is comprised of Mexican and U.S. based indigenous and migrant workers' organizations. These migrant organizations include the CCPM (Popular Mixtec Civic Committee), the ORO (Oaxacan Regional Organization), the COTLA (Tlacolulense Community in Los Angeles), the OPEO (Organization of Exploited and Oppressed Peoples), etc.

Some of these movements maintain affiliations with the César Chávez's United Farmworkers of America, and the San Francisco-based NGO AT-Work (The Appropriate Technology Working Group, of the Earth Island Institute). Neither the indigenous movement, nor other social movements in Mexico, has an ideological support for drug prohibition.

Abbrevations

AT-Work — Appropriate Technology Working Group
CCPM — Popular Mixtec Civic Committee
CNPI — National Council of Indigenous Peoples
COTLA — Tlacolulense Community in Los Angeles
FM-ZB — Mixtec-Zapotec Front
GROs — Grass-Roots Organizations
GRSOs — Grass-roots Support Organizations

OPEO — Organization of Exploited and Oppressed Peoples
ORO — Oaxacan Regional Organization
TEK — Traditional Ecological Knowledge

References

Albó, X. (1999), "Andean people in the twentieth century," in F. Salomon and S. Schwartz (eds.), *The Cambridge History of the Native Peoples of the Americas*, vol. 3: South America — Part 2, Cambridge: Cambridge University Press, pp. 765–869.

Bendahmane, Diane B. (1991), Performance review for NGOs, *Grass-roots Development* 15, no. 2: pp. 31-37.

Carruthers, David (1995), "The Political Ecology of Indigenous Mexico: Social Mobilization and State Reform," PhD diss., University of Oregon, Eugene, Oregon, USA.

Carruthers, D.V. (1996), "Indigenous ecology and the politics of linkage in Mexican social movements," *Third World Quarterly*, vol. 17, no. 5, pp. 1007-28.

Cockburn, Alexander (1994), "Chiapas and the Americas," *Nation*, 28 March 1994, p. 404.

Diaz Polanco, H. (1997), *Indigenous Peoples in Latin America: The Quest for Self-Determination*, Boulder, CO: Westview Press.

Estrada, German (2003), Profile of the Indigenous People of Mexico Political Movements and Indigenous Organizations, Chapter 9 — Parts 4-5, Forest Resources.

Evers, Tilman (1985), "Identity: The Hidden Side of New Social Movements in Latin America," In David Slater, ed., *New Social Movements and the State in Latin America*, Amsterdam: CEDLA, 1985.

Fox, Jonathan (1997), "The difficult transition from clientelism to citizenship: Lessons from Mexico," in Chalmers, Douglas A. Vilas, Carlos M. Hite, Katherine, Martin, B. Scott, Piester, Kerianne Segarra, Monique (1997), *The new politics of inequality in Latin America — Rethinking participation and representation*, Oxford University Press.

Horst, Rene (1998), "Authoritarianism, Indigenous resistance and religious missions: Paraguay, 1958–1992," PhD thesis, Department of History, Indiana University.

Kelley, Robin D.G. (2002), *Freedom Dreams : The Black Radical Imagination*, Boston: Beacon Press.

Mejía Pineros, María Consuelo, and Sergio Sarmiento Silva (1987), *La lucha indígena : Un reto a la ortodoxia*, Mexico City: IIS/Siglo XXI.

Moguel, Julio, Carlota Botey, and Luis Hernández, eds. (1992). *Autonomía y nuevos sujetos sociales en el desarrollo rural*, Mexico City: Siglo XXI/CEHAM.

Ramos, A.R. (1998), *Indigenism : Ethnic Politics in Brazil*, Madison: University of Wisconsin Press.

Silva, Eduardo (1994), "Thinking politically about sustainable development in the tropical forests of Latin America," *Development and Change*, 25: 697-721.

Van Cott, D. (ed. 1994), *Indigenous Peoples and Democracy in Latin America*, New York: St Martin's Press.

Warman, Arturo, and Arturo Argueta (eds. 1993), *Movimientos indígenas contemporáneos en México*, Mexico City: CIIH/UNAM/Miguel Angel Porrúa.

Warren, Kay B. (1998), *Indigenous Movements and Their Critics : Pan-Maya Activism in Guatemala*, Princeton: Princeton University Press.

Yashar, D. (1998), "Indigenous movements and democracy in Latin America," *Comparative Politics*, vol. 31, no. 1, pp. 23-43.

23

Sustainable Development
Looking Through the Eyes of Indigenous Communities

Odile Schwarz-Herion

> Only when the last tree is rooted out, the last lake is poisoned and the last fish is catched you will realize that money cannot be eaten. (Prophecy of the Cree[1])

Introduction

"How can one buy or sell the sky or the heath from the earth. The thought is unknown to us. . . . We know that the white man doesn't understand our way of thinking. . . . Because he is a stranger coming at night and steals from the land everything he needs. The earth is not his brother, but his enemy, and when he has impoverished it, he moved on. . . . He plunders the earth from his children. . . . His greed will one day swallow up the earth and leave it just like a desert. . . . What was man without the animals? If all the animals were gone, man would die of spiritual loneliness, because all that happens to the animals will also happen to man. Everything is connected. . . . This we know: The earth doesn't belong to man — man belongs to the earth" (from the speech of the

1. Indigenous (Indian) people of North America.

Indian Chief Seattle; cited after: Kidforum. Blue Print Earth 1997, pp. 2-3).

Relationship with Nature in Indigenous Cultures and in Western Civilization

These phrases from the appealing speech of the Indian Chief Seattle (original name: *See-at-la*) in 1854 show a wisdom, understanding, and respect of nature which the majority of people in Western societies seem to have lost to a growing extent within the last two centuries. Profit maximization is considered more important than anything else in most of the countries in Western civilized societies today — ignoring the fact that natural resources are limited and sinks cannot be overstained without minimizing or destroying quality of life for future generations.

In contrast there are still several indigenous communities in the world who think and live in a similar way as the Indian Chief Seattle. Let us take, for example, the indigenous people from the Indian isle groups Andamans and Nicobars who have guarded their original culture which is 30,000 years old and who still live in accordance with nature. When South and South-East Asia was struck by the Tsunami catastrophe in December 2005 thousands of dead bodies were found — mostly of Asian people living in civilized regions as well as of tourists. Nevertheless among the dead bodies which were identified one did not find any wild animals or any persons from the Indigenous people, living in the Andamans and Nicobars. Later on it turned out that these indigenous people for whom rescue teams had searched desperately in their relief campaigns actually had survived the catastrophe without any help. How can this phenomenon be explained?

Researchers found out that the indigenous people, living in the isle groups mentioned above, used their ancient knowledge how to interpret gestures and sounds of wild animals — knowledge which had been transferred from generation to generation. This knowledge allowed them to receive warning signals from the wild animals living with them in time and to flee to higher regions. This way their traditional way of living had saved their lives while many people in the civilized regions of South and South-East Asia were killed by the high tide in December 2005.

The tendency of people in Western cultures to exploit natural resources and overuse sinks in an almost unlimited way seems to be deeply rooted in the way of thinking of the Christian Occident which — to a large extent — might be due to the following sentence in Genesis 1, verse 28: ". . . Fill the earth and subdue it." This frequently quoted phrase, a literal English translation from the Latin "Vulgata," which is distorting the original Hebrew and Greek version of the Old Testament, had often served as justification for unsustainable behaviour of people from Western civilized societies. The correct translation of the word *kyrieuein* in the Greek original text is not "subdue" but "dominate" or "rule over" and therefore gives this phrase a quite different meaning. While "subdue" is usually rather understood as a violent action of gaining power the verbs *rule over* or *dominate* — apart from having power — additionally include responsibility for and protection of the dominated subject. This interpretation of the phrase in question is underlined by Genesis 2, verse 15: "God took the man and put him into the Garden of Eden to till it and to care for it." You see from the items mentioned above that a right translation and interpretation of Genesis 1 and 2 shows that the old Jewish religion which had also been adopted by the Christian religion later on does not legitimize unlimited exploitation of the earth and therefore is not that different from the cultures of indigenous people as described in the speech of Chief Seattle.

Apart from the wrong and misleading translation and interpretation of some parts of the Bible another reason for the unsustainable conduct of the white conquerers and colonialists towards nature who see the earth rather as enemy than as brother, as addressed in the speech of Chief Seattle, might be the fear for nature which is intrinsic to the culture and mentality of the white race. This fear of white people might come from travelling to unknown regions of the world where the colonialists were suddenly confronted with the wild and untamed nature — a difficult situation, created by themselves.

The German scientist E.U. von Weizsäcker who deals intensively with problems of sustainability writes in context with the questions mentioned above: "Critical Christian people know that the biblical saying "Subdue the Earth" in the Christian area had a disastrous impact for centuries whereas the Indigenous North American cultures seemed to live in accord with the nature" (v. Weizsäcker, 2005, p.1; translation by the author of this chapter). Furthermore v. Weizsäcker points out that the legendary Chief Seattle had done an unusually wise speech in front of the European intruders and their president. According to v. Weizsäcker this civilization of sustainability, addressed in Seattle's speech, had already been established throughout North America before the Vikings and Columbus discovered the "New World" (see v. Weizsäcker, 2005, p. 1). Nevertheless in v. Weizsäcker's opinion the respect for the creation is also possible for Christians if you flatly reject each irreversible destruction of nature.

One typical example for a common ground between Western culture and the North American indigenous culture, as depicted in the speech of the Chief Seattle, is shown in the world-famous definition of sustainability which we can find in the report of the so-called Brundtland Commission[2] (World Commission on Environment and Development = WCED): "Sustainable development is a development that meets the needs of the present without compromising the ability of future generations to meet their own needs" (*Our Common Future,* 1998, p. 43).

In the so-called "Rio Declaration" which was worked out in the frame of the United Nations Conference on Environment and Development (UNCED) in Rio de Janeiro (1992) for the first time the term "Sustainable Development" encompassed explicitly the integration of *ecological, social* and *economic* sustainability (cf. Burschel et al. 2004, p. 23). Here should be stressed that all three dimensions are closely tied to each other and interact permanently.

The Brundtland Report *Our Common Future* from 1987 "was among the first international reports to recognize the sustainable ways of indigenous and tribal communities and the role of indigenous and tribal institutions and ideas in envisioning more sustainable future for everybody on the planet" (Kuokkanen, 2000, p. 2).

Sustainable Development and Indigenous Communities

INDIGENOUS PEOPLE'S PLAN OF IMPLEMENTATION (2002)

The most impressive document concerning the importance of indigenous knowledge for the implementation of Sustainable Development, as seen by indigenous people themselves, is the "Indigenous People's Plan of Implementation on

2. Called after the Chairwoman of this commission, the then Norwegian Minister for the Environment and the future prime minister of Norway, Gro Harlem Brundtland.

Sustainable Development," presented to the United Nations World Summit on Sustainable Development in Johannesburg, South Africa, 2 September 2002 (cf. Dialogue between Nations, 2002). This "Plan of Implementation" (in the following briefly: "Plan"), based on the *Kimberley Declaration* from 2002,[3] summarizes all kinds of contribution to Sustainable Development that indigenous people have made for a long time and can make in the future.

This general tendency is made clear by the following statement as part of the Introduction: "The Plan of implementation reflects the heart and mind of Indigenous Peoples as traditional caretakers of Mother Earth who, for many millennia, has developed and refined our sustainable societies (Dialogue between Nations, 2002, p.1). Points 1 to 3 (Cosmovision and Spirituality) make clear that the indigenous peoples' understanding of Sustainable Development deeply roots in cosmological and spiritual ideas and dimensions. The "interrelation of the different forms of life in Nature" is seen as the origin of culture and spirituality (see point 1 of the "Plan"). Furthermore "elders" and "wise authorities" play an important role as the keepers of our traditional wisdom which embodies our spirituality and cosmovision as an alternative to the existing unsustainable cultural models" (point 2 of the "Plan"). Here implicitly is pointed out the fundamental difference to the mainly economy-oriented line of thought of the First World. Logically indigenous people object, for example, to energy, mega projects, mining, and tourism, i.e. activities which in general are described as "unsustainable" (see point 3 of the "Plan").

3. The Kimberley Declaration International Indigenous Peoples' summit on Sustainable Development, KHOL-San Territory, Kimberley, South Africa, 20-23 August, 2002.

Within the paragraph "Self-Determination and Territory" e.g. there is articulated the willingness to "share experiences about our use and management systems of natural resources with other indigenous people" (see point 7 of the "Plan"), furthermore the determination to protect and to strengthen "institutions, safeguarding customary laws and practices" as "bases of sound sustainable management of our environment and territories" (see point 9 of the "Plan"). Equally for the purpose of Sustainable Development governments are urged "to initiate a process of restitution of indigenous People's ancestral lands and territories, as a concrete way of furthering human and environmental sustainability" (point 11 of the "Plan"). Here the social and the ecological dimensions of Sustainable Development are addressed quite bluntly.

The paragraph "Children and Youth" contains remarkable thoughts concerning the idea of *intergenerational justice* in the sense of the famous Brundtland definition of Sustainable Development (see above). In this context the aim of nurturing "an environment of intergenerational support, thereby laying strong foundation for future generations" is declared (point 13 of the "Plan"). Since indigenous peoples' future and the survival of their knowledge and their sustainable way of life depend on their children and youth, the latter need protection from the well-known widespread dangers in developing countries, as for example child labour, sexual exploitation of children, child trafficking and in general "injustices against indigenous children" (see point 16 of the "Plan").

In the same way the rights of indigenous women are reaffirmed mainly with regard to their "vital role in human, cultural and environmental sustainability" (see point 17 of the "Plan"). Indigenous women are seen as "custodians of traditional knowledge, culture and the sustainable use of biological diversity" (see point 19 of the "Plan"). Furthermore the Plan claims not only for women's "fair and equitable access to land, resources, education, and other social and welfare services," but also for indigenous women's right to "participate in all levels of governance and leadership both locally, nationally and internationally" (point 17 of the "Plan"). You can see that, concerning equal rights for women which also form an important part of sustainability, indigenous people defend an opinion which is significantly more advanced than that of several civilized nations in the Middle East.

With regard to Sustainable Development the claims concerning "Food Security" play a pivotal role in the "Indigenous People's Plan of Implementation on Sustainability" (see points 21 to 26 of the "Plan"). The promotion of "conservation, sustainable use and management of . . . traditional foods," strengthening the indigenous "models, systems, and networks of production and trade" are of immediate importance here. States should be urged "to guarantee the integrity of . . . biological habitats for this purpose" (point 21 of the "Plan"). Point 22 of the "Plan" announces resistance against "technologies, policies, and legal regimes that violate indigenous peoples' rights to maintain our traditional knowledge practices, seeds, and other food-related genetic resources." Governmental and international institutions are exhorted to support these traditional practices and indigenous people's institutions in order to ensure their "food sovereignty" (see point 23 of the "Plan"). Therefore it is logical that indigenous people demand an immediate stop of the "development, cultivation, and use of genetically modified seeds, plants, fish and other organisms." In the sense of Sustainable Development, governments are urged to declare a respective "immediate moratorium . . . in order to protect human health, native seeds, and other food-related genetic resources" (point 24 of the "Plan"). Traditional practices like gathering, pastoralism, expressly described as "viable and sustainable economic systems that ensure food sovereignty" should be strengthened (see point 25 of the "Plan"). Beyond refusing the use of genetic modified organisms governments shall be urged in co-operation with indigenous peoples "to stop the introduction of alien or invasive species which threaten the health of our traditional territories and food sources" (point 26 of the "Plan").

The paragraph "Indigenous Knowledge and Intellectual Property Rights (IPR)" mainly deals with the protection of indigenous knowledge and the guarantee of the IPR. Indigenous knowledge is among other things seen as bound up with biological and cultural diversity and diversity of life in general (see points 27 and 28 of the "Plan"). This makes clear that indigenous peoples themselves regard indigenous knowledge as totally different from Western scientific knowledge. There are several authors who argue in a similar way (see e.g. Wolfe et al., 1991; Lalonde, 1993, p. 3; Gorjestani, 2000). In contrast, Agrawal underlines the similarity between indigenous knowledge and scientific knowledge and denies considerable differences between them (see Agrawal, 1995, 2004). Indigenous peoples turn against "any IPR regime that attempts to assert patents, copyrights, or trademark monopolies for products, data, or processes derived or originating from our knowledge"(see point 28 of the "Plan"). In consequence, indigenous people demand that "genetic material, isolated genes, life forms, or other natural processes must be excluded from IPR regimes" (point 28 of the "Plan") and that all biopiracy[4] activities must be stopped immediately (see point 29 of the "Plan"). According to these demands States and governments are urged "to respect the spirit of Article 8 (j) of the Convention on Biological Diversity," including the "right to full and effective participation in the national and international decision-making arenas on biodiversity and traditional knowledge such as Convention on Biological Diversity (CBD)" (see points 30 and 31 of the "Plan").

The next paragraph explains some specific problems around biodiversity such as a demand of a moratorium on "all activities related to human genetic diversity (see point 32 of the "Plan"), the demand for disclosing "all human, botanical and genome collections" (point 33 of the "Plan"), and for "the establishment of an international code of ethics on bioprospecting[5] to avoid biopiracy" (see point 34 of the "Plan"). Furthermore indigenous people stress the importance to play an active role "in the full process of the Convention on Biological Diversity, through the International Indigenous Forum on Biodiversity." The main goal here is to "defend and safeguard" the biodiversity of their lands and territories (see point 35 of the "Plan"). To be consistent, the opposition against biopiracy and "the patenting of all life forms" is pointed

4. The American Heritage Dictionary of the English Language (2000) gives the following definition of the term *biopiracy:* "The commercial development of naturally occurring biological materials, such as plant substances or genetic cell lines, by a technologically advanced country or organization in whose territory the materials were originally discovered. Because biopiracy was often connected with colonialism some authors speak about "biocolonialism" (see e.g. Rifkin, 1998, p. 88).

5. Bioprospecting is a somewhat neutral term and can be understood as "legalized or ethical biopiracy" (Wikipedia, 2006, p. 1).

out (see point 36 of the "Plan"), equally the demand for "constitutional and legislative recognition of our conservation and management of biodiversity" which are regarded as "inherent to the sovereignty of indigenous people" (see point 37 of the "Plan").

Fastening to these statements and demands concerning biodiversity the following paragraph deals with indigenous peoples' rights concerning "Forests and Protected Areas." The demands formulated here refer — among other things — to the guarantee of indigenous peoples' full rights to manage and control their forests (see point 38 of the "Plan") and to the defence of all economic activities which could be harmful for the cultural value and the material integrity of their forests including the granting of concessions for oil and timber exploitation or mining (see point 39 of the "Plan"). In the same way States are urged to transfer the control over protected areas within indigenous lands and territories (inclusive of wetlands, coasts, and seas) to indigenous people (see point 40 of the "Plan").

In the next paragraph "Mining," the governments and corporations are exhorted to recognize and respect indigenous peoples' fundamental rights "to self-determination and to free, prior, and informed consent on all forms on mining" (see point 41 of the "Plan"). Mining activities must undergo a multi-criteria assessment, including environmental, social, cultural and health impact assessments (see point 42 of the "Plan"). Here at least two fundamental dimensions of Sustainable Development are explicitly touched upon: the environmental and the social aspects. Furthermore indigenous people underline the necessity that governments prohibit the confiscation of indigenous lands for mining activities by establishing appropriate laws and that indigenous lands and territories "must not be included in the planning zones for mining" (see point 43 of the "Plan").

Especially in view of Sustainable Development the following paragraph "Energy" plays a pivotal role. In point 44 of the "Plan," indigenous people demand the declaration of governmental moratoria on the following four groups of activities:

- Expansion of and new exploration for the extraction of oil, natural gas and/or uranium and coal mining within or near environmentally, socially, culturally and historically sensitive indigenous land and territories.
- Construction of large dams according to the framework, proposed by the World Commission on Dams.
- Erections of new nuclear power plants. Instead indigenous people demand the "phase out and decommission of all nuclear power plants."
- Transportation and storage of radioactive waste on indigenous peoples' land and territories, but rather "containment and monitoring of nuclear waste on-site."

You can see that indigenous peoples' critical view especially of atomic energy coincides to a large extent with the opinions of Western anti-nuclear activists, mainly represented by the European Green Parties. The rejection of large dam-projects are of high topicality in the face of the current events around the protests against the Chinese "Three-Valleys-Dam."

In conformity with the idea of sustainable energy industry, evolved from Western industrial nations, the representatives of indigenous people support the promotion of renewable energy sources to meet the energy needs of indigenous communities; at this the indigenous traditional knowledge should be encompassed (see point 45 of the "Plan"). "Government subsidies of unsustainable energy" must be "phased out under a five-year time-frame" (point 48 of the "Plan").

Tourism activities within indigenous lands and territories will be only accepted on condition that indigenous communities' "rights, cultures and integrity of ecosystems" are respected (see points 49 and 50 of the "Plan").

Equally with regard to fisheries, marine and coastal resources the indigenous peoples' principles of sustainability should be observed. This includes sustainable harvesting, avoidance of overfishing and waste and toxic dumping in order to maintain indigenous communities' marine and freshwater resources (see point 51 and 52 of the "Plan").

One of the most vital ecological problems is pointed out in points 55 to 57 of the "Plan": Protection of water in general, tracking the trade of water, preventing the privatization of water and the diversion of water which could be harmful to the integrity of water and ecosystems within indigenous peoples' lands and territories.

The great significance which indigenous people contribute to the Climate Change is already indicated by the size of the paragraph concerning this issue which encompasses nine points (i.e. points 58 to 66 of the "Plan"). In the following only the most important aspects will be considered: All States which have not yet done so (for example US) are urged to sign the Kyoto Protocol to reduce the greenhouse gas emissions in general. In this context indigenous people demand an economic mitigation of natural disasters and damages, caused by Climate Change, because they don't feel responsible for this phenomenon. Moreover indigenous people demand equal participation by bringing in their traditional knowledge and practice to stop greenhouse effect.

Within the paragraph "Health and Toxics," indigenous communities demand the protection of indigenous plants, animals and men from harmful environmental pollutants. Furthermore industrial nations are called to account for pollution and contamination they have caused in the indigenous lands and territories (see points 72 to 74 of the "Plan").

With regard to "Sustainable Livelihoods" States and international communities are exhorted to further the protection of "natural, cultural, social and technological capital" which indigenous peoples and communities see as basis for the economy (see point 87 of the "Plan"). Here for the first time in the "Plan" all dimensions of Sustainable Development (ecological, social and cultural, and economic) and their interaction are emphasized, particularly focusing on economy.

The last two paragraphs ("Governance" and "Human Rights") contain claims for indigenous peoples' full participation at decision-making on promoting Sustainable Development (see point 90 of the "Plan"), especially with regard to chapters 20 and 26 of the Agenda 21, which refer to the participation of indigenous peoples and local communities (Local Agenda 21). Furthermore remarkable is point 93 of the "Plan" where indigenous peoples declare the rejection of any kind of so-called "indigenous authorities, imposed . . . by the Government" and the implementation of "development models, whether sustainable or not."

The finishing paragraph ("Human Rights," points 94 to 100 of the "Plan") deals with the promotion of human rights, especially referring to indigenous people's issues in connection with Sustainable Development. The last point of the "Plan" (point 100) summarizes the main intention of the whole "Plan of Implementation" with the following statement: "We support the UN Permanent Forum on Indigenous Issues as a global focal point for promoting co-operation among States and indigenous people in the implementation of international policies, commitments and action plans on indigenous people and sustainable development."

Conclusion

The fact that indigenous peoples or rather communities consider many practices of Western civilization in general as *unsustainable* can, by inversion of an argument, lead to the conclusion that they regard their own practices, their cultures, and their way of life in sum as *sustainable*. This follows, e.g. from point 2 of the indigenous peoples' "Plan of Implementation on Sustainable Development" where, among other things, indigenous peoples' "spirituality and cosmovision" are seen "as an alternative to the existing unsustainable cultural models." Without naming explicitly the representatives of these *unsustainable cultural models,* it is quite clear that there is talk of "Western" culture or rather "civilization." More unambiguous here is point 3 of the "Plan" where indigenous peoples speak about "safeguarding" their cultural integrity "against energy mega projects, mining, tourism, logging" which expressly are named as *unsustainable activities* among others. These are obvious activities which, in sum, can be considered as typical for (western) industrial nations — activities which are mainly characterized by more or less strong interventions in the nature. Such impacts evidently are considered by indigenous communities not only as superfluous but also as harmful.

It is evident that renouncing such activities means doing without much comfort of daily life: *without* mining no metals and therefore no machines of any kind, no railway, no cars, no aeroplanes, etc.; *without* drilling for oil no plastics, no synthetic fibres, a lack of a large part of drugs, etc.; *without* tourism the cessation of important sources of income for little developed regions, etc.; *without* dams in many cases no electricity for industry, traffic, private households, etc. In consequence, refusing the activities in question (mining, drilling for oil, tourism, dams, etc.) indigenous people have to relinquish the advantages of technical progress mentioned above.

On the other hand you must take into consideration that not only in countries like USA, Canada, Japan or China but also in many developing countries the majority of people prefer a modern way of life by using TV, public transport, cars, refrigerator, etc. including the use of electricity, of public roads and of modern infrastructure in general. Many passages of the "Plan" clearly show that indigenous people are aware of the fact that comfort, made by technical progress is to be paid by destroying nature. Therefore weighing up between Western belief in progress and protection of the nature and indigenous culture is unavoidable.

In any case indigenous people should not be enticed to take over Western ways of life which seem to be so "propitious" but which — without "countersteering" by Sustainable Development — would probably lead to an ecological catastrophe. In contrast indigenous people could teach industrial countries all over the world to live in a way which takes to heart the words of Chief Seattle: "Earth doesn't belong to man — man belongs to the earth."

Abbrevations

CBD — Convention on Biological Diversity

IPR — Intellectual Property Rights

UNCED — United Nations Conference on Environment and Development

WCED — World Commission on Environment and Development

References

Agrawal, A. (1995), Dismantling the divide between Indigenous and Scientific Knowledge, In *Development and Change*, pp. 413-39.

——— (2004), Indigenous and Scientific Knowledge: Some critical comments. URL: http://www.nuffic.nl/ciran/ikdm/3-3/articles/agrawal.html.

Andamanen und Nikobaren: Wie die Natur die Eingeborenen rettete. URL: http://www.stern.de/wissenschaft/natur/534509.html?nv=cb.

Burschel, C., D. Losen and A. Wiendl (2004), Betriebswirtschaftslehre der Nachhaltigen Unternehmung, München.

Chief Seattle (1854), Speech "How could he know. . . ." In: KIDFORUM: *Blue Print, Earth* 1997. URL: http://www.kidlink.org/KIDFORUM/Blue-97/BluePrint_report.html.

Dialogue Between Nations (2002), Indigenous People's Plan of Implementation on Sustainable Development, Johannesburg (South Africa). URL: http://www.dialoguebetweennations.com/IR/englisch/KariOcaKimberley/Indigenous People.

Gorjestani, N. (2000), Indigenous Knowledge for Development. Opportunities and Challenges, Geneva.

Kuokkanen, R. (2000), Indigenous Knowledge. URL: http://www.globalautonomy.ca/global1/glossary_entry.jsp?id=CO.0056.

Lalonde, A. (1993), African Indigenous Knowledge and its Relevance to Sustainable Development. URL: http://www.idre.ca/en/ev-84408-201-DO_TOPIC.html.

Rifkin, J. (1998), *The Biotech Century*, New York.

The Kimberley Declaration (2002), International Indigenous Peoples Summit on Sustainable Development. URL: http://www.quechanetwork.org/yachaywasi/The_Kimberley_Declaration.htm.

V. Weizsäcker, E.U. (2005), Schöpfung bewahren- Leitlinien für eine Politik des schöpferischen Fortschritts. URL: http://weizsaecker.bawue.spd.de/main.php?dociel=0004000201id=94

Wolfe, J., C. Bechard, P. Cizek and D. Cole (1991): *Indigenous and Western Knowledge and Resource Management Systems*. Report based on passed and continuing research of the faculty and graduate students of USRPD, Guelph, Ontario.

24

Sustainable Development in Mexico
How the Indigenous Communities View it

Dra. María de Lourdes Cárcamo Solís

Introduction

THE environmental crisis began with the Industrial Revolution in the nineteenth century, but it dramatically increased after the second half of the twentieth century until it achieved its global dimension.

In 1972, The Roman Club published that the unlimited económical development has a high price: the damaging pollution and destruction of natural resources. This warning was not rapidly included in the international agenda until the sustainable development concept was implemented; it meant that each society, country, region and the whole world can have a better life without scarifying the environment.

Nowadays, the unstoppable expansion of the modern capitalism has developed certain structures, like geographic dispersion of productive forces, integrated by labour, technology and capital, the international social division and the market promotion, and finally, the probable domain of an economy articulated by the global economic system.

The Report Bruntland made by the World Commission on Environment and Development in 1987, played its maybe most important role in clearly establishing the link between environment and development. The development creates impacts: the destruction of environment and the damage to social conditions of indigenous communities. The sustainable development was described in this way: "Humanity has the ability to make development sustainable to ensure that it meets the needs of the present without compromising the ability of future generations to meet their own needs" (Our common future, 1987). The main worry of society is not only the constant damage to environment but also the socio-economic conditions under which many indigenous communities live, which depend ever more in the use and making the most of the natural resources. Because of that, a series of measures have been proposed by government, non-governmental organizations, indigenous people, community leaders, educational institutions, firms and other interested parties, to compensate for the social damage by promoting the Global Economy of Mexico. This is the case of productive alternatives to improve the living conditions of indigenous communities that lack income that may allow them to cover their basic needs.

Methodology

In the present cases of study of the natural protected areas, the methodological approach was based on the analysis of natural, physical and visual components, with emphasis on the dynamic relations established between them.

In a theory basis, we can analyse that the practical cases of the environmental issues of natural protected areas, is the result of what Habermas defines as a proof of the vital world. First, we should try to apply this concept to indigenous communities. The vital world means a set of living systems based on the promotion of traditional local economies, like self-consumption agriculture and cattle, and as a complement to these rooted activities, development of informal economies, when they dedicate themselves to services and commerce done incompletely. And their ideas and common experiences involving the use and taking advantage of natural resources commonly shared daily, which are derived particularly because of their poor life conditions, defined as behaviour patterns. Nevertheless, this vital world is affected by disturbances and hardships caused by systematic logic (formed by sub-systems of the State and the Economy), defining as a proof of the structures of a vital world.

To be precise, this vital world has been highly affected by rationalization imposed by the economy, which is explained by globalization. Specifically, the global system has changed as a determinant fact in the sharpness of the vital conditions, which are based on the small fragile economies, which tend to disappear against the competitive process of capital mobilization, finding their place as self consumption forms.

In Mexico, during the last three decades, the production system has been based on the development of globalization, which has accelerated the weakening of the local economies based on primary activities; extremely restrictive handling of the economic policies, increasing unemployment, poverty, a general deterioration in the standard of living, and a well known polarization process, which destroys the most unpredictable and basic ways of social organization because of the lack of the right conditions, being capable of joining the economic model. This is the reason why, frequently, the possible finding of solutions represented by its policies and environmental laws has not been achieved. The State has caused environmental issues, by accelerating poverty in the indigenous communities, which is one of the main causes of the environmental devastation, stopping with it, the efficiency of policies and environmental laws.

Social Conditions of Indigenous Communities

Particularly, indigenous communities are very poor. The available information revealed that poverty and extreme poverty affected indigenous people more severely than the rest of population, both in their communities of origin and in urban areas. In the case of Mexico, 80 per cent of the population is poor, of which 30 per cent comprises indigenous people. Generally, the voices of indigenous peoples were not taken into account. Millennium target processes might lead to accelerated assimilation, thus prolonging and even worsening their marginalization, discrimination and poverty. It also stressed that education should take into account the identities, languages, cultural and traditional knowledge of indigenous communities. This implies that indigenous peoples must be studied holistically: thus the policymakers have to promote non-discriminatory laws, policies, resources and programmes, promoting full participation of indigenous groups in decisions that affect their lifestyles, traditional lands and territories and cultural integrity, particularly women, children and youth; furthermore, implementing legal, policy and operational frameworks for protecting indigenous peoples and improving their lives (United Nations, 2005).

Now, we evaluate if the indigenous initiatives are defined for sustainable development principles. In Mexico, there are indigenous communities, such as "Matlazincas," "Otomies," "Tarahumaras" and "Mayas"; who have developed many sustainable productive projects.

Ecotourism Projects of Communities

The economic and social impact of ecotourism depends on various factors, specially, the level of participation and the benefits of the local population. To promote the participation of the different communities, it is necessary to inform them about these ecotourism projects because most of these communities, socially disorganized, ignore what ecotourism would mean for the preservation of many ecosystems.

In the context of the globalization impact in Mexico, the forest problem of the natural protected area of Monte Alto (Valle de Bravo, Mexico) is a fundamental result of the rationalization that has imposed the economy by spoiling the conditions of life in the towns of Valle de Bravo, San Mateo Acatitlán, Tres Puentes, and the cushioning area of Monte Alto, la Loma de Chihuahua, La Loma de Rodriguez and Rincon de Estradas (these communities are constituted by "Matlazincas" and "Otomies" peoples) which are all adjacent to this natural protected area. On the other hand, the disorders that the State has caused by not curbing the irregular settlements and the clandestine felling, in addition to the inefficiency and ineffectiveness of the implementation of the forest legal system and the political practice, have provoked Monte Alto to be the subject of complete squandering of forest resources. This problem, generalized everywhere through Valle de Bravo, is the main reason for the emergence of the environmental organizations with their reforestation and protection actions towards the forest wealth of Monte Alto.

Generally speaking, the population in the municipality of Valle de Bravo lacks the capacity for self-organization to solve the problems of the natural protected area. Due to this, it hasn't become a social actor, and we cannot say that it is just because it participates in tasks of forest preservation and protection promoted by the environmental organizations. On the other hand, these are parts of a social actor that promotes a new logic about how to make sustainable use of the natural resources, boosting a series of solutions that have contributed to gradually resolve the problems of political origin.

The environmental organizations define themselves as voluntary associations united by bonds of friendship and co-operation to solve the forest problems, that worsen every day. They have been moved by a series of values, demands and rights, all of which assume a transition towards a more supportive and democratic society where decisions are no longer taken only by the omnipresent and omnipotent States, but by new actors participating with a new proactive attitude; an attitude that no longer has revolutionary dreams to change the economic system and the political regime that governs society. Their main worry is not only the constant damage to the environment but also the socio-economic conditions under which many indigenous communities live, which depend ever more in the use and making the most of the natural resources. Because of that, a series of measures have been proposed to compensate for the social damage by promoting the Global Economy of Mexico. The results of these organizations can be appreciated in the progress achieved in different confines, which include human rights, organic agriculture, health, community development and local and regional development. With this, they search for new forms of social organization based on sustainable development.

To improve the living standards, in the case of the rural and indigenous communities dedicated to primary activities, it is important to consider the analysis of elasticity of soil demand. It is demonstrated that an increase of one per cent in the real salaries reduces cultivated surface by 1.17 per cent[1].

1. On the contrary, if the real salaries continue to show a decreasing tendency, this will provoke an increase in the cultivable land demand and will increase the felling of trees. As a result of this, we can deduce that the demand for land is elastic (the change for the amount of land demanded is greater than that of the real salaries).

An increase in real income for field workers decreases deforestation since labour is the major productive factor in the agricultural livestock sector as well as in the forestry. Therefore, land demand is very sensible before perceived real salaries variation in the primary activity or any other productive task. But, why the need in Valle de Bravo to improve real salaries?

The macroeconomic conditions should be landed to the local scope. In the case of Valle de Bravo, in the short run it is necessary to generate productive projects which can be translated in the improvement of life conditions of the majorities in the communities that survive with scarce real income. Productive projects that are being generated in Monte Alto, with the kick-off of the Project for the Implementation of a Self-sustainable Recreation Natural Park, obey properly to ecotourism which is considered an important element in the sustainable development principle that links economic development to the preservation and protection of natural resources. There are different types of ecotourism such as archaeo-tourism, ethno-tourism, nature and adventure tourism.

If this project falls within purely economic logic, we will obtain as a result a greater damage of the forest wealth of Monte Alto. It requires that income coming from the park's entrance, cabin's rentals, and other services charges be used for the protection and preservation of the existing forest resources in this natural protected area. In that respect, it is recommended to set adequate prices to the tourism services offered. Consider that these services are scarce and extremely appreciated by the many national and foreign visitors who live in huge cities and whose need is the contact with nature, and for that reason, it would be reasonable to raise the service's prices in order to obtain greater incomes and to preserve and conserve the forest of the natural protected area of Monte Alto.

Ecotourism services and tasks of forest preservation and protection should be carried on by individuals hired (belonging to the scarce resources towns surrounding Monte Alto), who must receive a payment financed from the very income from the park or from resources from State Commission for Parks and Fauna (while ecotourism becomes profitable by itself). In a few words, the ecotourism project in order to be sustainable must yield environmental and social results. The economic and social impact of ecotourism depends on various factors, but specially, the level of participation and the benefits to the local population. To promote the participation of the different communities, it is necessary to inform them about these ecotourism projects because most of these communities, socially disorganized, ignore what ecotourism would mean for Monte Alto (Carcamo, 2003).

The "Sontecomapan" (state of Veracruz, Mexico) community, a group of families, has organized to offer ecotourism services without destroying the environment and the lagoon resources. These services offer boat travels to the Island of Birds and the Crabs' River; travels to Sontecomapan Bar, travel to "Poza de los Enanos," among others. The travels are part of the tours organized by the community ecotourism network. These forms of co-operation must result in social and environmental benefits to avoid socio-environmental tensions. The area is free of oil exploitation complexes, chemical plants or industrial operations. In the seventies, the Sontecomapan was considered one of the richest mangrove vegetation zones in the country and a highly productive lagoon. However, now this area lives with a terrible destruction of its forests. Deforestation has caused the running down of sand from the hills to the bottom of the lagoon dangerously reducing its depth. For this reason, and concerned about the situation, the community has looked forward to the reversal of these processes through people awareness and best use of our resources. Thus, we have considered ecotourism as a feasible and long-lasting alternative for the development of Sontecomapan.

Social and Economic Projects

The Centre of Indigenous Development is civil society's[2] organization, that works in the communities of Sierra Tarahumara in State of Chihuahua, Mexico, exchanging food for native handicrafts. This organization promotes the initiatives of help for those communities developed in sustainable framework, avoiding traditional model of social assistance. It is very important to provide adequate protection of the rights, livehoods and culture of "Tarahumara" communities. This civil organization has obtained an initial investment, which has been donated by private sector, beginning to operate in January 2002. This investment translates into social welfare. The programme has six centres in Guillochi Guajurana, San Luis Majimachi, Creel municipality, Norogachi and Guachochi municipality exchanging basic foods for work of indigenous art. Furthermore, this organization helps the welfare of 1200 indigenous families of the region.

From a sustainable development perspective, there is a place called El Tomatal," Oaxaca, where a group of thirty

---

2. Civil society is seen as the space of social experimentation for the development of new forms of life, new types of solidarity, and social relations of co-operation and work, (Cohen and Arato, 1990, p. 38).

women began to organize themselves to work with environmental health topics. They conclude that peanuts and sesame both are foods with high nutritive value, with this knowledge they were determined to manufacture products with peanuts and sesame. Contact with organizations like "Cosmeticos Naturales de Mazunte," "Ecosta Yutu Cii" and "Ecosolar" brought awareness to their environment and quality of life. They looked for the improvement of their permaculture, green manure sowing and soil improvement with organic manure, planting trees to protect crops and using hand selected creole seeds. All of these practices have increased soil efficiency without contaminating it. All of the raw material to manufacture food products are obtained in the region, which comprises 50 hectares in seasonal and virtually flat fields of sandy texture used specially for these crops. The workers sow with seed drills and harvest with combines. They have harvested up to 75 tonnes of peanuts and 10 tonnes of sesame that, although not yet certified, can be classified as ecological crops since neither agrochemicals nor pesticides are used during the production process and the lands are under soil improvement practices. In 2000, they opened a small factory with all sanitary requirements involved in the production, packaging and labelling processes. This factory was constructed by women using their own savings and financial support.

Kabi'tah is an organization of peasants dedicated for some years to the production of organic honey in the municipality of Holpechen, State of Campeche, Mexico. This organization always has promoted the importance of working united since this organization has allowed us to maintain stable prices for our products and make our partners more conscious about the importance of cultivated products free of pesticides and chemicals fertilizers harmful to our land. Mainly, fifteen Mayas communities constitute the Kabi'tah. There are 220 beekeepers, 180 women working in horticulture and 40 in agroindustrial activities, 200 comrades dedicated to agroforest labour, as well as eight groups incharge of health, education and communication in our communities. Kabi'tah is working in a biosphere reserve called Calakmul; this natural protected area has a large tropical forest that deserves all our care and attention.

In a field research done in Temascaltepec, in the State of Mexico,[3] we visited a ranch producer of lettuce, fine herbs, flowers, cheeses, marmalade, natural sweets, white fish, bottled spring water among other products, whose characteristic is the simplicity of its manufacturing methods and techniques. The facilities for the production of these goods consist of steel sheets, doors, aluminium structures, cardboard, plastic, pipes, panoramic advertisement boards (formerly set in big avenues of Mexico City) which are not needed by others anymore, and so they are used with no cost by the owners of this ranch.

To start these small businesses, financial support is needed as subjects of credit which may potentially contribute to the economic and social development of the country; preferring

---

3. On March 23, 2002, we made a field visit to these producer ranchs located in la Cuadrilla de Dolores, 2.5 km. on the highway to Valle de Bravo, Temascaltepec, State of Mexico. These companies are named "Impulsora Agropecuaria de Valle de Bravo, S.A. de C.V. ; Avandaro Industrias, S.A. y Manantiles Bios, S.A. We were personally greeted by Mr Alejandro Alvarez de la Peza and some of the indigenous employees who gave us a tour of the companies showing us all the productive work they have been carrying on. On March 12, 2002, we interviewed Mr Alvarez de la Peza, member of Biocenosis, A.C. who talked to us about the projects that are being carried on at Rancho Nuevo.

instead a debtor-consumer market (which among other things, causes inflation) in a market of payer-producers (measure that generates more production, employment and well-being, that, along with the implementation of measures of productivity, generates no risk of high inflation rates). In spite of this, many micro entrepreneurs have used their credit cards or have searched for personal credits to finance their fixed assets or working capital when starting a business or financing an existing one.

Conclusion and Proposals

With the aim of assuring a more rational management of natural resources that will allow compliance with the sustainable development project, required at first instance is a set of incentives directed to the user of natural resources such as greater security regarding the possession of the land, clarification of the rights of the resources, access to financing, which can be done through a government trust managed by the banking developing system and/or the injection of micro credits at low rates or by saving banks whose financing must be assured by a set of standards and laws to prevent corruption.

Furthermore, at an economic level, the State through its economic policies, is the one with the political capacity to mitigate in the long run, social backwardness in the subject of poverty. Mexico must not only strive for achieving macroeconomic stability, but also be conducive to change focusing towards the microeconomic scope, that may mean greater linking of the microeconomic achievements with the development and the internal market strengthened through greater liquidity, that permit finance for the sustainable economic growth, with a strong investment in education, generation of employment and social well-being, along with fiscal discipline, where government directs its expenditure exclusively towards strategic segments to enable the Mexican economy to raise its productivity and efficiency, such as education, deregulation of the productive apparatus, fiscal reform, (the increase in the taxable base thereby eliminating fiscal evasion), labour law reforms, and the total liberation of the economy and a greater attention to public safety. With these, in the long run, we truly will begin to solve the environmental problems of many ecosystems with which we will start introducing the famous principle of sustainable development in the handling of natural resources.

According to Samuelson and Nordhaus, in order to promote economic growth in the open and emerging economies, as in the case of Mexico, it is vital to maintain the relation of savings-investment; for that, we must maintain certain conditions, such as, a predictable and stable micro economic climate, which presupposes a low inflation rate, stable exchange rate, that will assure the coming and going of resources, reasonably low and predictable taxes; reliable rights of property, and predictable and attractive investment climate, an institutional framework attractive to national and foreign investment, joint technological projects with other countries, a strong investment in human capital, a more just income distribution, a greater generation of employment, education and production opportunities; eliminating corruption, that translates into a tributary system, which raises production costs of firms, generating uncertainty and distrust to national and foreign companies.

This restates, once the macro economic stability has taken place, that the monetary expansion promoted by the Bank of Mexico should also impact positively the undertaking of small producers through bank micro credits at comfortable interest rates direct to small rate production of agriculture livestock and forestry, industrial, commercial and other services which can potentially mean a solution to poverty for many excluded indigenous communities. In addition, a greater investment in training in sustainable management of natural resources, strong investment in education, technical assistance for producing and exporting; aspects that as a set contribute to a rise in productivity without sacrificing labour. In this way, the improvement of the living conditions, and in particular of the indigenous communities, does not translate into inflation since this monetary expansion is being linked to training and to education, and with the increase of production that small and micro enterprises in this municipality will generate. Improving with this the present conditions of the internal market on the side of the supply, more production; on the side of the demand, more employment and improvement of the purchasing power; having as a precedent the control of inflation.

At the social level, the implementation of a formal education programme (for students) and one informal (for communities without academic preparation and visitors) is important in many places in Mexico; these programmes designed by public and private education institutions counting on the support of environmental organizations to promote different education topics such as ecology, use and conservation of natural resources, and botany, using as a model the natural protected area, that offers a diversity of biotic and abiotic elements that can potentially be the subject of research for schools and research centres. Also, in the ecosystems, courses of art, crafts, gastronomy, history, culture, language, organic agriculture can be implemented; trying to use them as additional points of interest for people to visit these places and feel part of them.

In the same way, to search for coherence and integration in the environmental policies with economic programmes that the municipal governments may be developing, as well as, social participation (environmental organizations, indigenous communities and producers) in the process of planning of this policy, which may permit the creation of a vigilance committee, that would be in charge of making sure and monitoring that the environment is not translated into mere statistical *figs.* This measure obviously means the democratization of the environmental policies of the natural protected areas, which in the long run, will allow the efficient and rational management of public and private resources applied to these areas (Carcamo, 2003).

References

Carcamo Solis, Lourdes (2003), Thesis: "*The forest problems of Monte Alto, Valle de Bravo (1994–2004): A case of reconstruction of the civil society,*" pp. 195-98, Iberoamericana, A.C. University, D.F. Mexico.

Cohen, Jean and Andrew Arato (1990), *Civil Society and Political Theory* (the MIT press, Cambridge, Massachusetts), pp. VII-X.

Guiddens, Anthony, Jürgen Habermas (et al. 1988), *Habermas and modernity*, (Class, Theorem Collection, Madrid, Spain), p. 95.

Lara Bulcao, Luis Ribeiro and Pedro Arsenio (2004), The protection of landscape as a resource, case study- Monte da Guia protected area (Faial-Azores), *Management of Environmental Quality: An International Journal*, vol. 15, no. 1, 2004, pp. 48-54.

Leff, Enrique, 1998, *Environmental Knowledge*, (century XXI editors, Mexico), pp. 119-35.

Merino Pérez, Leticia, 1999, Collective management of the forest resources (*External Commerce Magazine*, vol. 49, no. 12, Mexico, D.F.), p. 1121.

Samir, Amin (1998), *Capitalism in the globalization era,* (Paidos Iberica Edition, Spain), pp. 11-13.

25

Global Sustainable Development and Significance of Indigenous Locality

Mert Bilgin

Introduction

The significance of indigenous locality is increasing in conformity with the rising consciousness on sustainable development which aims to attain a balance among social, economic and environmental needs through a desirable compromise between global pressures and local systems. "Current interest in indigenous knowledge is overwhelmingly driven by research into sustainable development practices in developing countries and the scientific community's concern about loss of biodiversity of species and ecosystems, and the future implications of that for the whole planet."[1] This is why indigenous people, along with their traditional ways of life, have become a central concern as indigenousness represents disconnected spaces, which contribute to sustainable development both at local, domestic and global levels.

Today it is estimated that 370 million indigenous people, descendants of those who lived in an area at a time when those from a different culture arrived on their land, spread

1. B. Sen, "Indigenous Knowledge for Development: Bringing Research and Practice Together," *The International Information & Library Review*, vol. 37, no. 4, December 2005, p. 376.

across 70 countries, making up about 6 per cent of the world's population in around 5000 separate groupings.[2] However, most of the indigenous peoples are in danger because of being cut from their traditional production systems, which exacerbate their life conditions by putting indigenous knowledge in oblivion. Problems worsen for those who somehow migrate to cities.

Improvement of life standards of indigenous people is considered to be among urgent issues. UN Permanent Forum on Indigenous Issues (UNPFII) declared 2005 to 2015 as second International Decade of the World's Indigenous Peoples by putting main objectives as follows:[3]

- Promoting non-discrimination and inclusion of indigenous peoples in the design, implementation and evaluation of international, regional and national processes regarding laws, policies, resources, programmes and projects;
- Promoting full and effective participation of indigenous peoples in decisions which directly or indirectly affect their lifestyles, traditional lands and territories, their cultural integrity as indigenous peoples with collective rights or any other aspect of their lives, considering the principle of free, prior and informed consent;
- Redefining development policies that depart from a vision of equity and that are culturally appropriate,

2. R. Horton, "Indigenous Peoples: Time to Act Now for Equity and Health," *The Lancet*, vol. 367, no. 9524, 27 May 2006–2 June 2006, p. 1705.
3. UNPFII, "Second International Decade of the World's Indigenous People," (Adopted by the UN General Assembly, 22 December 2004). http://www.un.org/esa/socdev/unpfii/en/second.html

including respect for the cultural and linguistic diversity of indigenous peoples;

- Adopting targeted policies, programmes, projects and budgets for the development of indigenous peoples, including concrete benchmarks, and particular emphasis on indigenous women, children and youth;
- Developing strong monitoring mechanisms and enhancing accountability at the international, regional and particularly the national level, regarding the implementation of legal, policy and operational frameworks for the protection of indigenous peoples and the improvement of their lives.

Even though these measures are indispensable for revitalizing indigenous cultures in order to support global sustainability, they may not be adequate even in the best case scenario. In other words, enumerating indigenous population and then helping them to improve their life standards can be sufficient neither for multiculturalism nor for global sustainability. Revitalization of indigenous ways of life shall constitute one of the most significant sustainability criteria, regarding economic, ecological and socio-cultural concerns. This is why indigenousness shall go beyond being a mere understanding of ethnic culturalism and embrace indigenous knowledge of production within an idiosyncratic way of life.

Yet, there is one issue that deserves further elaboration: conceptualization of indigenousness does not seem adequate for sustaining a sound reciprocal integration between local, domestic and global levels. Indigenousness cannot be identified by closed communities, nor can the value of indigenous peoples be liberated from their production systems. Within this context, this article puts a special emphasis on the concept of indigenous locality, (locality from now on) as a notion, which promises to contribute sustainability by integrating traditional production with domestic and global systems while sustaining idiosyncratic ways of life.

Locality promises to be a solution which comprises sustainability and the need for multiple trajectories for development with the need for a lifestyle based on less consumptive balance of work and leisure without hampering being free to choose. This hypothesis comes along with certain issues which need to be clarified. Firstly, the meaning of locality for domestic economic growth shall be clarified. Secondly, indicating the difference between community and locality is a must not only for avoiding conceptual misuses, but also for showing how these concepts may contribute to sustainability by emancipating multiplicity of development trajectories. Thirdly, it is of utmost significance to explain the reason which makes indigenous knowledge worthy of care. This care shall not be an outcome of causal relationship, or a sort of over-valued nostalgia. Following this perspective, this article starts its analysis by elaborating to what extent locality promises contribution during integration of domestic economies with global systems. Then it involves in a conceptual clarification of community and locality, all by referring to reasons which increase the role and significance of locality for sustainable development.

Localities and Multiple Development Trajectories under Single Sustainability

Three reasons increase the significance of localities drastically. First of all, national economies cannot prove a success as far as they ignore local idiosyncrasies and adopt global pressures as if they are the formula of a universal modernization project. Secondly, localities not only offer premises to develop one's own paths of development, but also contribute to economic growth by directly integrating with the global market. Thirdly, localities along with their traditional production and culture are indispensable for sustainability with regard to economic, environmental, social and cultural aspects. The significance of locality for attaining multiple development trajectories under single sustainability can be analyzed under two subtitles: (1) "Locality as a lever of economic growth," embraces the first two reasons, and (2) "Locality as a lever of global sustainability," elaborates the third one.

LOCALITY AS A LEVER OF ECONOMIC GROWTH

To start with the first reason, it should be emphasized that although integration with the world economy is inevitable, this process tends to create negative effects as far as it neglects local production and puts over-emphasis on global demands. The last four decades in the development history of East and South-East Asia have proven that conventional methods to overcome poverty such as high tariffs, quantitative trade restrictions, over-valued exchange rates, subsidized credit, under-priced energy, water, and other publicly provided inputs, low prices of food for the urban poor etc. have been counter-productive in terms of efficiency and equity.[4] Consequently, most of the developing countries prefer to involve in integration with the world economy. However, integration of national economies with the global system brings structural infects. Once the integration starts, the exogenous changes in the environment such as market prices, costs or regulations and/or in the opportunities such as the appearance of a cost-saving innovation or changes in the prices of inputs or outputs, etc. create immediate direct effect of the change and the full effect after organizational structure has had time

4. P. Bardhan, "Efficiency, Equity and Poverty Alleviation: Policy Issues in Less Developed Countries," *The Economic Journal*, vol. 106, no. 438, 1996, pp. 1344-56.

to adjust.[5] Meanwhile this process imposes vicious circles, which make integration characterized by unavoidable infects. Governments stumble between choosing fixed exchange rates and capital mobility at the cost of losing monetary autonomy, and combining fixed exchange rates with monetary autonomy (at least in the short run), at the cost of restricting capital mobility.[6] Besides many others, this simple vicious circle imposes financial burdens, which force the developing nations to seek credits, loans and other sorts of financing. In most of the cases, global capital market is segmented, and developing countries face credit-rationing rules set by official (governments) and private creditors (banks) in the industrialized countries, thus incorporating theories of international lending under sovereign risk and oligopolistic behaviour of the international bank firm.[7] Consequently international financing brings other measures concerning not only macro-economic indicators but also institutional behaviours and market characteristics. This kind of integration creates a sort of harmonization effect in which the concerned economy ignores its local idiosyncrasies. "Integration means not only increased market-based trade and financial flows, but also institutional harmonization with regard to trade policy, legal codes, tax systems, ownership patterns, and other

---

5. S.J. Decanio, C. Dibble and K. Amir-Atefi, "The Importance of Organizational Structure for the Adoption of Innovations," *Management Science*, vol. 46, no. 10, 2000, pp. 1285-99.
6. D. Rodrik, "How Far Will International Economic Integration Go?," *The Journal of Economic Perspectives*, vol. 14, no. 1, 2000, p. 180.
7. R. Vos, "Aid Flows and the International Transfer Problem in a Structuralist North-South Model," *The Economic Journal*, vol. 103, no. 417, 1993, pp. 494-508.

regulatory arrangements."[8] This harmonization limits the capacities of the concerned country because local production networks, which could function well under certain circumstances, cannot maintain their economic activities and lose their cultural idiosyncrasies. As a result, their ability to contribute to sustainability at regional and global scales extensively vanishes.

Even though generalization of this picture may lead to wrong analyses, there are two significant facts that deserve to be mentioned here. It is not possible to identify development as if it is only a monetary issue, and it is not possible to consider development as if it is a universal modernization project. Therefore, multiple trajectories for development are necessary to transform geographic and cultural idiosyncrasies into advantages. Amongst many other factors the role locality for multiple trajectories of development should be attributed a special attention. "Together, localization and globalization-driven progress have not translated into a particular path of development; rather localities have demonstrated contextually specific paths."[9] Indeed, localities are important for at least they offer premises for customization of development projects. Furthermore, localities promise to contribute to economic growth by directly integrating with the market without changing their indigenous essentials. "Territories where indigenous peoples live often have considerable economic potential as sources of water, timber and high-value niche products such as medicinal plants, organic

---

8. J.D. Sachs, A. Warner, A. Aslund and S. Fischer, "Economic Reform and the Process of Global Integration," *Brookings Papers on Economic Activity*, 1995, no. 1, 25th Anniversary Issue, 1995, p. 2.

9. P.J. Marcotullio, "Asian Urban Sustainability in the Era of Globalization," *Habitat International*, vol. 25, no. 4, December 2001, p. 578.

foods and other products."[10] In fact "more than 100 pharmaceutical companies are currently funding projects to study indigenous plant knowledge and specific plants used by native healers," yet with unfair returns to indigenous people.[11]

Even though current figures indicate unfair returns to indigenous people, it must be mentioned that locality is becoming more important within the global context as it started to constitute a lever of branding.[12] Environmental and health concerns, farm animal welfare, safety, quality and taste make the locality a promising milieu of production and a tool of value adding.[13] Recent studies indicate that "in managing the political bottom line, managers must adopt a deeper notion of corporate citizenship and address the systemic problems of the global economy and the compromised independence of communities and governments."[14]

Localities promise to contribute to development by the help of recent progress in the phases of logistics and marketing.

---

10. *IFAD, Indigenous Peoples, International Fund for Agricultural Development*, Rome, p. 4. http://www.ifad.org/pub/factsheet/ip/e.pdf
11. Ibid, p. 2.
12. T. Marsden and E. Smith, "Ecological Entrepreneurship: Sustainable Development in Local Communities Through Quality Food Production and Local Branding," *Geoforum*, vol. 36, no. 4, 2005, pp. 440-51.
13. M. Winter, "Embeddedness: The New Food Economy and Defensive Localism," *Journal of Rural Studies*, vol. 19, no. 1, 2003, pp. 23-32.
14. J. Bendell and K. Kearins, "The Political Bottom Line: The Emerging Dimension to Corporate Responsibility for Sustainable Development," *Business Strategy and the Environment*, vol. 14, no. 6, November/December 2005, p. 381.

Empirical evidence obtained from certain Southern countries, which are above poverty line, indicates that local manufacturers prefer to involve in interaction with broader markets on their own. "Local/urban, national, and international product and capital supply links incorporate small, informal vendors into economic systems that operate not only at the micro level but also at the meso- and macro-level.[15] This ability is an implicit indicator of the advantage acquired from globalization and challenges the commonly accepted assumption that most manufacturers in local areas operate without direct linkages to broader economic processes. Above all, it shows that local producers may meet the global markets by keeping their traditional production systems. As a matter of fact, local producers and local networks will be more integrated with the domestic and global systems as far as they manage to keep their idiosyncratic ways of life.

LOCALITY AS A LEVER OF GLOBAL SUSTAINABILITY

The first two reasons show the significance of localities as a lever of economic growth and multiculturalism. In fact, these reasons mainly contribute to the concerned actors at local and domestic levels. The third reason indicates the important role of locality for global sustainability, which therefore shall be a concern of everybody. The link between locality and sustainability promises to increase multiculturalism as it has already become clear that the Earth needs more disconnected spaces in order to sustain the livelihoods of today's and future's generations.

This necessity shall be elaborated with regard to two aspects. Firstly; as mentioned above, general projects of

15. S. Teltscher, "Small Trade and the World Economy: Informal Vendors in Quito, Ecuador," *Economic Geography*, vol. 70, no. 2, 1994, p. 183.

development lead to negative consequences when they undermine local idiosyncrasies. Secondly; the problem persists, and even worsens, under the assumption that all the modernization projects may work well and create a harmonized world population living in Western standards. "This expansion of the human species and Western culture at the expense of all other species and cultures is suggesting the existence of Pareto optimality at the system level."[16] Global system needs more disconnected localities in order to sustain this optimality. The 1997 UNDP Human Development Report clearly urges that popularization of Western lifestyles has limits beneath the capacities of the planet Earth.[17] This is why "sustainable consumption" is gaining interest as a key factor of sustainable development which reminds of the contradiction between over-emphasis on continued economic growth and the need to change in lifestyle towards a less consumptive balance of work and leisure.[18] Hence, multiple trajectories for development are necessary for global sustainability, which shall embrace local modes of life based on less consumptive balances.[19]

Another sustainability reason which makes indigenous knowledge indispensable for locality arises from concern for ecology. Localities as spaces for indigenous way of life promise to contribute to sustainability not only in terms of economic growth and socio-cultural aspects mentioned hitherto, but also

16. I. Matutinovic, "The Aspects and the Role of Diversity in Socio-economic Systems: An Evolutionary Perspective," *Ecological Economics*, vol. 39, no. 2, November 2001, p. 253.

17. UNDP, *Human Development Report 1997*, Oxford: Oxford University Press, p. 19.

18. C. Sanne, "The Consumption of Our Discontent," *Business Strategy and the Environment*, vol. 14, no. 5, 2005. pp. 315-23.

19. Ibid.

regarding environment. "The widespread replacement of native plant species with engineered high-yielding varieties, abandonment of traditional agricultural practices, destruction of habitat and the ways of life of the remaining hunting and gathering tribes, mass resettlement of people caused by large dam projects, and in the fast pace of industrialization and urbanization in the Southern countries over the past forty years are among the major threats that destroy the local cultures."[20] Though they may not have a deep knowledge on sustainability, *primitive ecological wisdom* of local cultures, so to state in Milton's words, indicates extensive compatibility with the notion of sustainable development.[21] This explanation may be found pervasive as "link between ecosystemicness and sustainability has come to be associated either — (1) with anti-industrial sentiments and feelings of sympathy for "backward" indigenous populations under pressure from more "advanced" majorities, or (2) with the casual observation that "ecosystemic" populations do not radically modify their environments over the time, and of the desire for model solutions to sustainability problems."[22] The causality between locality and sustainability cannot be stated pervasive or accidental to the extent that traditional cultures are by definition long standing systemic structures that have harmonized their lifestyles with their environment. Locality takes place at the heart of the natural component of indigenous cultures, which by definition indicates a certain level of harmony with nature and ongoing

20. Matutinovic, p. 253.

21. K. Milton, *Environmentalism and Cultural Theory*, London: Routledge and Kegan Paul, 1996.

22. T.N. Jenkins, "Putting Postmodernity into Practice: Endogenous Development and the Role of Traditional Cultures in the Rural Development of Marginal Regions," *Ecological Economics*, vol. 34, no. 3, September 2000, pp. 303-04.

socio-economic activities. As a matter of fact, sustaining a balance between economic growth, measures to overcome poverty[23] and the need for multiculturalism[24] all in harmony with environment, appears to be the reality of nowadays for which indigenous locality offers significant highlights. At this point an accurate conceptualization regarding locality is necessary as to show how indigenous locality may help to overcome these concerns by keeping traditional patterns of production and idiosyncratic cultures.

Localities for Multicultural Development

Analyses on locality necessitates a reciprocal interaction between global to local as top-bottom level, and from local to global as bottom-top level. Having put forward the economic connotation of locality as a lever of development and sustainability, it is now necessary to make a conceptual clarification which may activate the interaction between two levels of analyses by referring to socio-cultural aspects. Every local way of production takes place with an idiosyncratic culture that leads to an idiosyncratic way of life. What makes locality to be of utmost significance arises from the way of life, comprising with indigenous knowledge. To the extent that global knowledge and culture shall be open to everybody, so shall the local knowledge and culture be. This openness is necessary in order to allow people to choose the life they want. To exemplify, an indigenous Indian shall be offered the chance of social upward mobility through more accessible education and less discrimination. In fact, this is exactly what the

23. UNDP, *Human Development Report 2003, Millennium Development Goals: A compact among nations to end human poverty,* Oxford: Oxford University Press.

24. UNDP, *Human Development Report 2004, Cultural Liberty in Today's Diverse World,* New York: UNDP Publications.

institutions such as UNPFII are attempting to do.[25] However, to be forced to live within a local way of life may also appeal a sort of compulsory backwardness, if this life is not a free choice. Reciprocally, there are many other people, raised in the cities with global culture, but search for indigenous ways of life. Therefore, locality shall be open to people who want to live within indigenous knowledge. This is why a conceptualization of locality beyond ethnic, religious and other similar specificities is necessary. This conceptualization also promises to solve problems which are upsetting either in terms of ethnic and religious clashes or identity politics in terms of competition within the public sphere. This section will first elaborate the link between economic concerns and cultural liberties. Then it will put emphasis on organic understanding of locality as a way of life that is open to everybody regardless of ethnic, religious, sexual and other factors *by birth*.

Economic Aspect of Cultural Liberty

Cultural liberty is becoming a significant sustainability determinant both in regional and global scales, and increases the role of localities as disconnected spaces. Even though the word "culture" has a variety of meanings from associations with fine arts, opera and corporate attitudes to slimy things on microscope slides; within the context of sustainable development it is to do with "received beliefs," "predominant attitudes and behaviours that characterize the functions of a group or organization" as well as "the totality of socially transmitted behaviour patterns."[26] "A further dimension of

25. UNPFII.

26. F. Birkin, P. Edwards and D. Woodward, "Accounting's Contribution to a Conscious Cultural Evolution: An End to Sustainable Development," *Critical Perspectives on Accounting*, vol. 16, no. 3, April 2005, p. 186.

human development, difficult to measure and even to define, is vitally important: cultural liberty is central to the capability of people to live as they would like to."[27] Nevertheless, as mentioned above, social, political and economic opportunities do not guarantee cultural liberty, and in most of the cases they distort indigenous cultures when there are quite differences in between the existing structures and the pressures imposed upon them.

Firstly, countries that attract foreign capital due to their natural resources express grief about investments in extractive sectors and misappropriations of traditional knowledge that threaten their livelihoods. Secondly, countries that are already involved in integration process cannot find any solution to resist against losing their culture other than demanding that cultural goods (mainly cinema and audio-visual products) not be treated as any other goods in international trade since they weaken national cultural industries on behalf of global values. Thirdly, migrants ask to sustain their way of life and respect for the multiple identities they have in both the local community and their country of origin. Meanwhile, the fear of local communities grow because they think that their societies are becoming divided in coincidence with the erosion of national values and indigenous identities.[28]

These findings, which indicate that integration of the local with the domestic and global takes place within a difficult process, are not better for those people who have already migrated to cities. "Indigenous people often form an integral part of a city's history, cultural heritage, and diversity, and are forming an increasing proportion of urban communities through high fertility rates and migration from rural areas,

27. UNDP, 2004, p. 6.

28. UNDP, 2004, p. 11.

spurred by socio-economic opportunities or family ties, or due to a loss of traditional land, resources or housing."[29] Yet, most of these people confront difficulties just because of their particular interest in keeping their idiosyncrasies. Darity and Nembhard identifies Australia, Belize, Brazil, Canada, India, Israel, Japan, Malaysia, New Zealand, South Africa, Trinidad and Tobago, and the United States as countries with data of reasonable quality that measure the gap between economically subaltern and dominant groups (Darity and Nembhard, 2000, pp. 308-11). The results are interesting in the sense that inter-group inequality occurs: (1) in countries with both large populations (India, US, Brazil and Japan) and small populations (Belize, Trinidad and Tobago, Israel and New Zealand; (2) in higher income countries (Australia, Canada, Japan and the US); (3) in lower income countries (India, Belize, South Africa); (4) countries with high growth rates (Malaysia, Japan, Belize and India); (5) in countries with low or negative growth rates (South Africa and New Zealand); (6) in countries characterized by high levels of general inequality (Brazil, South Africa and Malaysia); and (7) in countries with low levels of general inequality. (Canada, India, Australia and Israel).

These inequalities make people, who feel suppressed because of their idiosyncrasies, involve in identity politics through affirmative actions. Identity politics not only leads to political confrontations, especially in the case of ethnic minorities who have to live within a country where a dominant national identity is articulated, but also creates a competition among various identity groups. Consequently, identity politics leads to another level of inequality between those who are

---

29. N. Cardinal, "The Exclusive City: Identifying, Measuring, and Drawing Attention to Aboriginal and Indigenous Experiences in an Urban Context," *Cities*, vol. 23, no. 3, June 2006, p. 218.

well acculturated with the domestic and global systems, and therefore may manifest their idiosyncrasies through affirmative actions, and the rest, who are either unable or unwilling to involve in identity politics. This vicious circle may be solved, to a certain extent, by privileging indigenous production methods and the way of life, rather than promoting differences in terms of ethnicity, religion and language as a means of identity politics. Therefore, in addition to language, folklore, historicity and anthropological idiosyncrasies, traditional production and traditional goods constitute the cultural markers, which differentiate indigenous locality from the global as well as from the other kinds of localities.[30]

These findings offer highlights for understanding the difficulties arising from integration of indigenous people with domestic and global systems and lead to a final remark. When traditional ways of life are annihilated, new problems not only jeopardize indigenous people but also spread out menacing global sustainability. Integration of indigenous economic activities with domestic and global levels through an unyielding way of life may: (1) allow alleviation of tough conditions regarding indigenous people; and (2) contribute to economic growth and global sustainability. This is why the term locality should replace community understanding of certain indigenous populations, as it envisages interaction with domestic and global systems while sustaining idiosyncratic characteristics of concerned groups.

Moving from Community to Locality

Although the difference between community and locality has been a debatable issue, differentiation of locality from community may help to resolve the problems mentioned above.

---

30. C. Ray, "Culture, Intellectual Property and Territorial Rural Development," *Sociologia Ruralis*, vol. 38, no. 1, 1998, pp. 3-20.

Some suggest that community has a relation to a relatively small local area, for others the community is as large as the nation state and the small local area is not to be considered.[31] Conventionally community studies focus on distinctive parts of society, mainly in terms of culture and what this culture shapes, which has remained unchanged, or relatively less changed, throughout time. Within this sense, community is composed of sets of values that prevail in harmony with reproduction of culture corresponding to strong ties of kinship and/or solidarity. This conceptualization puts emphasis on stable, unchanging characteristic of a certain amount of population. This stability nowadays is unique to certain intact groups or societies. For most of the places it is almost impossible to remain outside of the change notion, as penetration of global values leave aside very few spaces. "If we are thus to move beyond "community" to a theoretical understanding of change rather than stability, and, in particular context it is important to consider the possibility that "locality is the more appropriate theoretical concept."[32]

Meanwhile, the term locality has become significant locus of interest within sustainability context because both endogenous and exogenous development necessitate change at least in the form of better socio-economic indicators when compared with the previous situation. The emphasis to sustain is apparent with regard to high care for keeping certain economic, environmental, social and cultural elements as they are. The contradiction, which was apparent between community based on "sustain and never change" and locality

31. M. Stacey, "The Myth of Community Studies," *The British Journal of Sociology*, vol. 20, no. 2, June 1969, p. 135.

32. P. Cooke, "Locality, Structure and Agency: A Theoretical Analysis," *Cultural Anthropology*, vol. 5, no. 1, February 1990, p. 5.

based on "change and sustain," is also inherent within the context of sustainability or sustainable development. In fact, in their quintessential connotation, the term "sustainability" focuses on continuity of something or somebody while changing something or somebody; in contrast to "sustainable development" which emphasizes the change of something or somebody while preserving something or somebody. The point where sustainability matches locality necessitates a care for certain aspects of the local, which by definition contribute to sustainable development. Within this perspective, sustainable development (or sustainability) may be defined as a continuing process of mediation among social, economic and environmental needs leading to a positive socio-economic change which does not hamper the essential ecological and social systems of communities.[33]

The significance of locality arises from the ability of this concept to stress "both the external determining forces which contribute to the nature of specific localities and the internal agency effects of which individuals and social groups are capable, acting within localities by using locality as a basis for social mobilization."[34] The social change should be under the control of local actors and structures if this change is related to the notion of sustainable development.[35] "The challenge is therefore not to resist modernization, but to control it and take it further, increasing indigenous people's abilities to negotiate market relationships, administer rural enterprises

33. M. Carley and J. Christie *Managing Sustainable Development*, Minneapolis: University of Minnesota Press, 1993, p. 48.

34. Cooke, p. 14.

35. W. Adams, *Green Development: Environment and Sustainability in the Third World*, London: Routledge 2001.

and agro-industry, and compete in a hostile market."[36] Therefore, communities may continue their idiosyncratic ways of life, as this may be of their choice, which may also correspond to the logic of sustainable development in certain circumstances. If interaction between internal and external factors of development is inevitable, then a shift from community to locality is necessary as this concept embraces indigenous knowledge and represents a better milieu of articulation between what is regional and what is global.

Conceptualization of locality as the good, which confronts the bad global as its constitutive outside, may lead to misinterpretations and wrong analyses. For instance global (multinational) firms prove better results regarding environmental sustainability when compared with their local (regional) counter parts in industry.[37] Therefore, neither globalization nor traditional production, but rather awkward, obsessive or ignorant industry jeopardizes sustainability. This finding puts forward a necessity of going beyond a simple confrontation between the good local and the bad global.

As a matter of fact, locality shall refer not to local industry and local trade with regional attributes, but rather to indigenous ways of life that comprise indigenous production and articulate with the global market. Indigenous locality shall embrace a sort of intactness, almost as a place to share some form of disconnection, which keeps conventional production systems.[38] Yet this intactness should go beyond being closed

36. A. Bebbington, "Modernization From Below: An Alternative Indigenous Development?," *Economic Geography: Environment and Development, Part 1*, vol. 69, no. 3, July 1993, p. 289.

37. D. Webster, "The Urban Environment in South-East Asia: Challenges and Opportunities," *South-East Asian Affairs*, Singapore: Institute of South-East Asian Studies, 1995, pp. 89–107.

38. Marsden and Smith, pp. 440-451.

communities. Therefore, integration with the global system is another must, as otherwise, it would be oppressive for the members of the community, for at least closed communities, do not allow their members alternatives to choose from.

Furthermore, indigenous way of life is the indispensable condition of locality beyond mere regionalism or identity politics. Though distinct ethnic groups and aborigines may be important for identifying thc local, as they may be representatives of idiosyncratic cultures, this conceptualization may create unexpected negative consequences. These communities may articulate with the national and global systems, by promoting idiosyncratic cultural imprints as privileges, which is in fact nothing less than micro-nationalism or in certain cases micro-chauvinism. Therefore, locality shall represent interaction with national and global systems through indigenous way of life, which in turn creates a space that favours essential ecological and social systems. Putting indigenous way of life as an essential criterion of sustainability promises contributions both at global, domestic and local levels.

Conclusion

Locality offers significant contribution for resolving the difficulty to attain compromise between global restraints, domestic demands and the need for single sustainability. In fact, locality emancipates multiple trajectories for development and embraces economic, ecological, social and cultural aspects of sustainability.

With regard to economic aspect, this article showed that, domestic economies should not underestimate the significance of local production throughout their integration with the global market. Local producers have the opportunity to benefit from globalization as the mode of production controversy lost its pre-eminence because it is nowadays possible to reach markets for all kinds of goods and services regardless of how and where they are being produced. Consequently, localities are apposite for vitalizing multiple trajectories of development.

With regard to sustainability, this article brought out the significance of local spaces, which represent idiosyncratic lifestyles, for sustainability both at domestic and global levels. Regarding domestic level; ecology appears to be amongst important contributions of locality as indigenous knowledge is an outcome of harmony with the nature; the broader use of which promises less degradation. Regarding global level; the vital significance of idiosyncratic lifestyles became apparent because it is not possible to supply the consumption of a world population based on Western consumptive modes.

Meanwhile, the concept of locality assured better consequences than communitarian or ethnic approaches. In fact, conceptualization of indigenousness based on ethnic, religious and similar specificities may provoke either upsetting clashes or competitive identity politics among different groups. This is why locality shall be based on the way of production that comprises an idiosyncratic mode of life. This conceptualization emancipates, and appeals, a reciprocal mobility between global and local systemic levels, which may contribute to sustainable development in terms of perpetuating disconnected spaces, and of cultural freedom in terms of being free to choose.

References

Adams, W. (2001), *Green Development: Environment and Sustainability in the Third World*, London: Routledge.

Bardhan, P. (1996), "Efficiency, Equity and Poverty Alleviation: Policy Issues in Less Developed Countries," *The Economic Journal*, vol. 106, no. 438, pp. 1344-56.

Bebbington, A. (1993), "Modernization From Below: An Alternative Indigenous Development?," *Economic Geography: Environment and Development*, Part I, vol. 69, no. 3, July 1993, pp. 274-92.

Bendell, J. and K. Kearins (2005), "The Political Bottom line: The Emerging Dimension to Corporate Responsibility for Sustainable Development," *Business Strategy and the Environment*, vol. 14, no. 6, November/December 2005, pp. 372-83.

Birkin, F., P. Edwards and D. Woodward (2005), "Accounting's contribution to a conscious cultural evolution: An end to sustainable development," *Critical Perspectives on Accounting*, vol. 16, no. 3, April 2005, pp. 185-208.

Cardinal, N. (2006), "The Exclusive City: Identifying, Measuring, and Drawing Attention to Aboriginal and Indigenous Experiences In an Urban Context," *Cities*, vol. 23, no. 3, June 2006, pp. 217-28.

Carley, M. and J. Christie (1993), *Managing Sustainable Development*, Minneapolis: University of Minnesota Press.

Cooke, P. (1990), "Locality, Structure, and Agency: A Theoretical Analysis," *Cultural Anthropology*, vol. 5, no. 1, February 1990, pp. 3-15.

Decanio, S.J., C. Dibble and K. Amir-Atefi (2000), "The Importance of Organizational Structure for the Adoption of Innovations," *Management Science*, vol. 46, no. 10, pp. 1285-99.

Horton, R. (2006), "Indigenous Peoples: Time to Act Now for Equity and Health," *The Lancet*, vol. 367, Issue 9524, 27 May 2006–02 June 2006, pp. 1705-07.

IFAD (2006), *Indigenous Peoples, International Fund for Agricultural Development, Rome*. http://www.ifad.org/pub/factsheet/ip/e.pdf

Jenkins, T.N. (2000), "Putting Postmodernity into Practice: Endogenous Development and the Role of Traditional Cultures in the Rural Development of Marginal Regions," *Ecological Economics*, vol. 34, no. 3, September 2000, pp. 301-13.

Marsden, T. and E. Smith (2005), "Ecological Entrepreneurship: Sustainable Development in Local Communities Through Quality Food Production and Local Branding," *Geoforum*, vol. 36, no. 4, pp. 440-51.

Matutinovic, I. (2001), "The Aspects and the Role of Diversity in Socio-economic Systems: An Evolutionary Perspective," *Ecological Economics*, vol. 39, no. 2, November 2001, pp. 239-56.

Marcotullio, P.J. (2001), "Asian Urban Ssustainability in the Era of Globalization," *Habitat International*, vol. 25, no. 4, December 2001, pp. 577-98.

Milton, K. (1996), *Environmentalism and Cultural Theory*, London: Routledge and Kegan Paul.

Ray, C. (1998), "Culture, Intellectual Property and Territorial Rural Development," *Sociologia Ruralis*, vol. 38, no. 1, pp. 3-20.

Rodrik, D. (2000), "How Far Will International Economic Integration Go?," *The Journal of Economic Perspectives*, vol. 14, no. 1, pp. 177-86.

Sachs, J.D., A. Warner, A. Aslund and S. Fischer (1995), "Economic Reform and the Process of Global Integration," *Brookings Papers on Economic Activity*, 1995, no. 1, 25th Anniversary Issue.

Sanne, C. (2005), "The Consumption of our Discontent," *Business Strategy and the Environment*, vol. 14, no. 5, pp. 315-23.

Sen, B. (2005), "Indigenous Knowledge for Development: Bringing Research and Practice Together," *The International Information and Library Review*, vol. 37, no. 4, December 2005, pp. 375-82.

Stacey, M. (1969), "The Myth of Community Studies," *The British Journal of Sociology*, vol. 20, no. 2, June 1969, pp. 134-47.

Teltscher, S. (1994), "Small Trade and the World Economy: Informal Vendors in Quito, Ecuador," *Economic Geography*, vol. 70, no. 2, pp. 167-88.

UNDP (1997), *Human Development Report 1997*, Oxford: Oxford University Press.

UNDP (2003), *Human Development Report: Millennium Development Goals: A Compact Among Nations to End Human Poverty*, Oxford: Oxford University Press.

UNDP (2004), *Human Development Report: Cultural Liberty in Today's Diverse World*, New York: UNDP Publications.

UNPFII (2006), *Second International Decade of the World's Indigenous People*, (Adopted by the UN General Assembly, 22 December 2004), http://www.un.org/esa/socdev/unpfii/en/second.html.

Vos, R. (1993), "Aid Flows and the International Transfer Problem in a Structuralist North-South Model," *The Economic Journal*, vol. 103, no. 417, pp. 494-508.

Webster, D. (1995), "The Urban Environment in South-East Asia: Challenges and Opportunities," *South-East Asian Affairs*, Singapore: Institute of South-East Asian Studies, pp. 89–107.

Winter, M. (2003), "Embeddedness: The New Food Economy and Defensive Localism," *Journal of Rural Studies*, vol. 19, no. 1, pp. 23–32.

26

On the Threshold of Change in Rural Belize

Indigenous Knowledge of Rural Women

Francis Higdon,
Lori Zimmaro and *Ashley Frost*

Introduction

RURAL villages along the southern coast of Belize have been described as resting on the "cusp of development" as foreign investors flood into the region in hopes of developing the region's pristine beaches and lagoons for international tourism. While the increasing levels of international investment will be a boon to some residents near these developments, we often know very little about how these same residents understand the changes facing them and their families. This study examines how rural residents, specifically women in one remote fishing village, understand their life situation and how change will impact their lives in the future. In March 2005, a team of Penn State faculty and students visited Monkey River Village in the southern part of Belize in order to attempt to explore how rural residents see change in their community due to development pressures brought on by increased foreign investment. Through interviews and observation, our team attempted to create a portrait of life in

Monkey River Village in order to estimate what kind of changes "development" might bring, especially with respect to women's roles within the community.

Development is a nebulous theoretical concept — and using the term "sustainable" to describe a "better" development can add to the conceptual ambiguity. Sustainable development suggests multiple connotations of wise resource use, increased equity, higher levels of social justice, and a cleaner environment. However, the meaning of sustainable development varies widely among audiences, especially between industrialized and non-industrialized nations. In this case study, let us supplement our conventional understanding of sustainable development with two main development priorities identified by Monkey River Villagers — the establishment of a locally controlled "ecotourism" within their community, and a significant expansion of their community infrastructure (i.e. electricity and roads) in order to improve their basic living standards and to help stem the migration of youth out of the community. This may seem like conventional goals, but unlike many goals that are foisted upon rural people by outside agencies — these goals have been established by indigenous voices.

With less than 200 residents, Monkey River Village is a very rural hamlet that is as diverse in its opinions, ambitions, and visions of the future as many larger population centres. The following personal profiles serve as representative vignettes of the women of Monkey River Village. They are field interviews conducted by our team during a week of field research in the community. The individuals selected do not represent one overall trend in opinion among the women of Monkey River Village. Rather, the following interviews were selected in order to demonstrate the diverse perspectives found in a relatively small village. Interestingly, the first two personal profiles with older members of the community represent more "progressive" attitudes, while the later profiles with younger women may be described as showcasing more "traditional" opinions. These younger village women may have been expressing more traditional attitudes in regard to women's opportunities, rights, and liberties because of their more limited life experiences outside the village. The older women in this study were better educated and had lived outside the village for many years. We have changed our informants' identities in this report in order to help protect their privacy.

Ms Jones: Primary School Director

Family life is central to the people living in Monkey River Village. Children remain close to their siblings and parents throughout adulthood; many sons and daughters give up economic opportunity elsewhere to live with their aging parents in the village and raise children of their own. In a community of tightly woven extended families, traditional values and attitudes are passed through mothers and fathers, and very little seems to change with the passage of time. When women in the community were asked whether the traditional division of labour frustrated them, they asserted that "women have always cared for the house and the children, and men have earned money outside the home, and this is the way it has always been." The lives led by parents and grandparents are looked at as examples, and parental influence on children continues throughout adulthood.

Life circumstances can dramatically shift an individual's opportunity structures and traditional viewpoints. For Ms Jones, the school director of Monkey River Village, a chance circumstance in childhood dramatically changed the course of her life. In 1943, at the age of 9, she was sent to live with an Aunt in a nearby town.

> My going to Placencia was an accident actually. I had an Aunt who needed somebody to help her, and she asked for my older sister. But my mother needed my older sister's help more, and I was a sickly child, and so she sent me. It was a good accident, but I didn't see it that way then, of course. It wasn't easy moving out of a family of eight of us to a place where I didn't know anybody and the household was run very strictly. But I adjusted.

The move to Placencia shaped the rest of her life; Ms Jones continued her schooling there, and later moved to Belize City to get her diploma, which at that time was the only city in the country with public high schools. She continued on to college, earning her associate's degree in teaching, and began her career as a teacher in the late 1950s. Ms Jones was very unique in her accomplishments: not one of her seven siblings had the opportunity to finish high school. By attending school in Placencia and experiencing the world outside of Monkey River Village, Ms Jones's perspective began to diverge from that of her mother, who lived a life close to home, keeping house and raising eight children. Like Ms Jones's father, who worked as a carpenter, her mother did not have a desire to see the world outside of Monkey River Village.

> I think my outlook on life is different from my mother's. I think she was generally satisfied with the life she led with my father, but I desired more. I think it's because I moved out of Monkey River and saw a different kind of life.

In addition to shaping her own life, the opportunities that Ms Jones experienced also had a significant impact on the attitudes and aspirations of the children she raised. After marrying a husband who valued girls' education as much as she, Ms Jones had four children, and worked hard to teach them the way she thought best:

> We gave them a lot of attention, saw that they had a proper high school education, we tried to inculcate Christian values in them, and gave them whatever opportunity we could.

The emphasis she placed on education with her own children resulted in significantly different career outcomes from those of her siblings, who became farmers, traders, fishermen, and tour guides. Her eldest son became a senior customs officer, her middle son moved to the United States, her youngest son works as a consultant for the ministry of works, and her daughter works for the Peace Corps. When asked whether her own parents valued education the way in which she does, Ms Jones exclaimed:

> Now that is something I wonder because they themselves were pretty literate; we used to read quite a lot, and in those days, a primary school education was almost like a high school education. But I don't think they tried hard enough for us, and especially for the girls. I think they still had that policy that girls did not need an education.

Ms Jones clearly demonstrates her commitment to education and gender equality by supporting the development of her daughter's career. Traditionally, educational and job opportunities in Belize are more limited for young women than those for young men, and Ms Jones's unique opportunity to pursue both a college education and a career in her own life led her to raise her sons and daughter with the expectation that all her children would finish school and start a career. Often the challenges were greater for her daughter; at times Ms Jones had to speak with her daughter's teachers to ensure that she was being treated fairly in the classroom. Ms Jones's emphatic support of her daughter's education marked not only a schism with the attitudes that marked her own upbringing, but also with traditional cultural attitudes. Ms Jones is a woman who experienced unique life circumstances, earned a degree and started a career against many odds, successfully raised children with uniquely gender-equal perspectives. Fortunately, for the community of Monkey River Village, her work does not stop there.

As an educator, Ms Jones has the opportunity to influence and shape the ideas and perspectives of her students. Each day, she combats the gender-biased beliefs that her students, both girls and boys, bring into the classroom:

> The girls' outlook from the beginning is that when they reach a certain age they will take somebody [to marry] and the boys will go out to sea. I have a hard time convincing some of the boys here to continue on with their high school education.

In other communities in Belize, traditional gender roles discourage girls and encourage boys to go to school, creating a gender bias in favour of boys. But in Monkey River Village, traditional gender roles manage to discourage both boys and girls from pursuing an education, and sometimes more seriously hamper the ambitions of boys:

> I wish I could change the attitude of some of the boys, away from just fishing, the feeling that because their father succeeded without an education that they can do the same. We have tried to train them to remember that this is a changing world, and no matter how we would want to keep the rest of the world out, the changes will come to Monkey River. And unless they are equipped they will find themselves left behind.

Because boys want to follow closely in the footsteps of their fathers, and they see that their fathers succeed without formal education, they have little motivation to continue on in school.

For the girls of Monkey River Village, attitudes are changing slowly. There are many positive female role models in the community, such as Ms. Jones, the three female school teachers, and the Village Chairperson, Ms. Smith. Monkey River Village is unique in the amount of female leadership it has, and this has led to an increasing interest in girls' education. High school education has become significantly more accessible in recent years. Students can travel to the town of Independence each day to attend school and return to Monkey River Village in the evening, instead of boarding there during the week, which was previously required of high school students.

Ms Jones is pragmatic in her hopes for her students. She wants as many of her students as possible to continue on to high school, but she also sees the need for providing skills-based training to children who are less academically inclined. She hopes the girls of Monkey River Village have the opportunity to get a job and be independent, something that she believes is too infrequent in Monkey River Village. She cares deeply for the children of Monkey River Village. At the age of 71, she works extremely long hours, waking up at 4:00 am each day to begin her preparations for school. She sees so much that could be done to improve the lives of children in the community and the school itself, but as one individual, she knows she cannot do it all. Ms Jones recognizes that she had more opportunities than her mother, and her children had more opportunities than her. She sees progress occurring in Belize, and her hopes are high for the coming generations.

Yet progress in Monkey River Village is tinged with ambivalence; the more education children receive, the less job opportunity they will have as adults in the community. Ironically, as opportunities open up to the community, more people are forced to move out for greater job prospects. Ms Jones understands that if people need jobs they will leave the village, but her hope is that more will return to Monkey River to raise children, and give back to the community as she has done in her later years.

Ms Eleanor Smith: Village Council

> I always believed that the community supports you and you support the community.

Community is a concept which Eleanor Smith, Village Chairperson, has valued in her entire adult life and professional career. Monkey River Village is a tiny seaside village whose tranquil life mimics the lazy rhythm of the sea, which in all senses serves as the livelihood of the village. The sea provides food, jobs, and represents the village's principle connection to the outside world. However, unlike the sea, whose vastness conveys a sense of eternity, Monkey River Village is dying. Just a couple of years ago, it was designated as a town, but due to out-migration of its youth, the community is now viewed as merely a village. If the population decline continues, even the official designation of village may be an over-statement.

There are a host of new problems and opportunities choking off this rural village. One could argue that economic progress and changing expectations among the younger residents represent the best hopes, and worst fears for the future. While the tidal rhythms yield a laid-back lifestyle, there are differing indigenous viewpoints on the importance of personal ambition, and a varied understanding of how traditional work ethics prepare younger residents to succeed in a competitive, ever-globalizing world. As Ms Smith observed, "I always believed that the community supports you and you support the community. That idea just doesn't sit with many people though. They lack the work ethic. They just sit around, doing nothing." After returning to the small town in which she was born following twenty years of residence in the United States and limited contact with Monkey River Village, Ms Smith observed, "I saw the problem Monkey River had: low education." Although Ms Smith explains her return to Monkey River Village as an accident, she affirms that her staying was completely by choice. She has set lofty goals for herself and her community.

Upon returning to Monkey River Village in the late 1980s, Ms. Smith began initiating change in the local community. Channeling her efforts through the school and church, her primary targets were the children. Paying out of her own pocket, she hired a young woman, a recent high school graduate to teach elementary school classes. She also convinced a retired teacher to reassume her position. Quickly, Ms Smith had doubled the teachers and classroom in the village. Education was and is Ms Smith's primary focus. She has pushed for earlier education and, even more important, more fervent support on the part of the family:

> I'd like to see younger education. They should put kids in school at four. There is a big difference between those who start at four and five. There is little support from parents, both from lack of interest and lack of ability. I would like to at least see parents emphasize the importance of learning. If I win one child every year, I think that I have accomplished something. Have the education so that if you want to use it,

> you have it. I have always loved people. I work because I want a better life. I saw my mother as dependent on my father. I didn't want that.

This emphasis on education comes from a woman who herself did not finish high school. Rather, at sixteen she dropped out and started working, occasionally taking free courses offered either in Belize City or New York, her two residences after leaving Monkey River, and trying to self-educate through constantly reading. Despite her lack of education, Ms Smith has led a successful life. She credits this success to a strong work ethic, recalling how she often worked two jobs while in New York City and lamenting on how this affected her family. Thirty years ago, Ms Smith explains, one could get by with limited education, but today things are changing. In reference to her world with the local school, "I try to emphasize reading, and not only reading, but reading comprehension with the children. The world is changing. You have to be able to survive. Even fishing requires filling out forms."

Despite her good intentions and dedication to improving education in Monkey River Village, Ms Smith met disconcerting opposition during the early years of her work: "Not everyone was happy. Monkey River needed help, and people recognized that, but they didn't want me to do it. They said that I was this American who wanted to change everything. They slowly came around though once they started seeing their kids go to high school." Eventually, attitudes began to change, and they continue to change. Changing attitudes toward life and education are contributing to the exodus of young adults from the community.

Young people with a high school degree and career ambitions are leaving Monkey River in search of employment, higher education and basic amenities. It creates a difficult dilemma: How can Monkey River encourage education and professional ambition, while maintaining a vibrant community? Ms Smith struggles in particular with this conflict,

> I just wish that Monkey River had the professional and intellectual opportunities to attract young, educated people. It kills a town when all of the educated people leave to find work. Kids don't have anyone to look up to. This is why Monkey River is no longer a town. Not it is just a village. I want the children to continue their education and use it. Maybe, you know with the internet, they can work for larger companies from the village. Now you can work from your computer anywhere. Maybe that is a solution.

While it is difficult, if not impossible, for local leaders to know exactly how to proceed, no one would challenge the benefits of increased education, especially for women.

As a small, traditional village, Monkey River is typical with respect to rural society's traditional viewpoints concerning women and their roles within the family and community. "There's this idea that *men are men*," explains Ms Smith. This idea has been perpetuated across generations. Traditional ideas are slow to change, especially when women do not have equal access to the economic market. Ms Smith is hoping to change that through increased education. As she says, "I would like to see less dependency among women. That is hard to change though because women don't have paying jobs. Opportunities are so limited, but these women know nothing else. When you get married you take not only a husband to care for, but you also inherit your father-in-law and any sons that you might have." Ms Smith credits her own mother's dependence on her father as inspiration for her to gain economic independence as a young woman. As much as Ms Smith values community support, she places more value upon individual independence. When Ms Smith was asked about the most important qualities "for a woman" in Monkey River Village to possess, she answered:

> Independence. She should be able to take care of children and family if husband were to die. She should have the self-confidence to go after something that she wants. There is nothing to say that you can't. Granted, you may not get something when you want it. But there is nothing to say that you can't get it eventually if you work hard enough.

Danette Brown: Cook/Waitress/Housekeeper

"That's why Dandrea so close to my mother, not me anymore. She doesn't love me much," responded Danette Brown when asked about her 7-year-old daughter Dandrea. Danette's eyes and the solemn tone testify to the difficulties faced by young Belizean women. Despite its location along the beautiful Caribbean Sea, life in the village falls far short of paradise.

Danette Brown is a 24-year-old single mother who has lived in the village her entire life, excepting brief stints in nearby towns trying to secure work. During each of these trips, which lasted several weeks, she had to leave her daughter behind. The separation has obviously put a strain on her relationship with her daughter, who according to Danette, looks to Danette's mother rather than to herself for maternal affection. Unfortunately, Dannette's case is not unusual within this small town. Many women, abandoned by the fathers of their children, have to travel throughout Belize in order to find work, work that usually consists of waiting tables or cleaning rooms in a tourist hotel. With high rates of extra-marital births and generally low parental participation among single men, women must rely on their sisters, aunts, mothers, and grandmothers in order to raise their children. As Danette explains, "A lot of the women wouldn't mind working, but they don't want to leave home." Unfortunately, in the attempt to earn extra money and improve the quality of life for their families, many women ultimately sacrifice the close bond normally shared between a mother and her children. This is Danette's chief regret. As she relates, Dandrea seemed somewhat detached from Danette when she returned to Monkey River Village. Her sorrow is obvious, conveyed openly in her voice as she admits that Dandrea would rather be with her grandmother than with her mom. This is just one of the struggles that a woman must face if she decides to leave Monkey River Village in search of jobs.

Another problem facing the women in the village is that there is little expectation that they will pursue higher education. When asked about high school, Danette responded, "I had to finish early because my brother was graduating and my mother could only afford one." Funding for high school is difficult to secure, especially in a town with such a limited cash flow. While scholarships are available, not everyone qualifies, leaving many children with no other option than to drop out before completing the mandatory twelve years. Generations of uneducated women have created misconceptions among today's young adults; they do not see the need for higher education. Despite increases in funding and support for a high school education, the younger girls continue to demonstrate scant interest in furthering their education beyond primary school. Danette is an example of this trend, dropping out simply because she did not like going to school. She has made no attempt to return to school. She does, however, stress the importance of education to her daughter. When we asked her what she wanted for her daughter, she said, "I want her to leave and get a better opportunity." Danette equated this opportunity with higher education. Although as a young girl Danette did not herself highly value education, as a mom, she now recognizes its importance, especially for women.

Like in other rural villages, antiquated gender roles often prevail: women are expected to stay home and do all the housework and care for the children, while men get formal jobs and earn the family income. Most mothers don't like their girls playing sports because they feel that it is only something that little boys should do. She wished that she could do some of the men's work and that is why she decided to become part of the tour guide association. When we asked what her biggest accomplishment was, she responded by saying, "probably when I helped my mother to build her house and to pay for supplies. I did more than my brother." It was hard work and she was extremely proud to show everyone that she was capable of doing a man's job and more. She helped lay cement, put up boards, and paint the house. It gave her a sense of accomplishment to be able to repay her mother for all the help that she had provided her raising Dandrea.

With time and across generations, thought and opinions evolve. There are marked differences between how children were raised ten or fifteen years ago in comparison to today. Certainly, children are granted more freedom and afforded better access to a primary school education. For example, Danette confesses that as a girl, she was not even allowed to walk around the village without parental supervision. A more relaxed parenting approach is obviously visible now. According to Danette, "there is less discipline, the kids have grown up faster. A lot of stuff I didn't know at that age the kids know now, like where babies come from. You just ask and they tell you." The emergence of more open parenting styles is not unique to Monkey River Village — it is clearly a global trend manifest at the local level. Children are afforded more opportunities and learn more than their parents were taught, but through this increased exposure, they are learning about the realities of sex and violence at younger ages. Within Monkey River Village, increased exposure has also opened their eyes to the increased opportunities that lie beyond their small rural village.

Malvary Hall: Tour Guide

"It's tradition." As Malvary Hall explains, it is because of tradition that things remain the same in this small village. It is the main reason why men and women differ in behaviour, opportunity, and quality of life. It is because of tradition that the women of Monkey River Village engage almost solely in domestic work. They complete daily household chores such as cooking, cleaning, washing, and tending to the children. Traditionally, limited income was brought into the family by women. When asked if she was bothered by the marked distinction between men and women related to work, Malvary responded, "No, they (men) go out and bring the money home." Despite this seemingly second-class citizenship awarded to women, it is the women who constitute the backbone of the Monkey River Village community. As a result of Hurricane Ivan, which devastated the village in 1998, there has been a great loss in family income and job opportunity in Monkey River Village. Many families moved away when their homes were destroyed by the hurricane, and as a result, their jobs and businesses were lost. The loss of jobs and population is now seen as the biggest threat to the community's future. In her interview, Malvary identified increased job opportunities as the number one thing that would improve lives of women in Monkey River Village. Families continue to leave the village in search of employment. As more families leave, the needs and responsibilities for those remaining become more difficult and complex.

Local culture and "tradition" dictate that men remain the primary income earners within families; however, all traditions evolve, and the devastation wrought by Hurricane Ivan has initiated some recent changes. Malvary, for instance, is a local tour guide, a position previously held solely by men. She is one of three women in Monkey River Village to have earned tour guide certification. Unfortunately, however, she has yet to give a tour on her own. As all tours require boat transportation, she will need to earn her Motor Craft certification first. Currently, she simply assists her father as he leads local groups. Her brother has shown little support for Malvary's interest in becoming a tour guide.

Women seeking jobs outside the home have become more typical. One of the reasons for this change is due to the education that the children are receiving in Monkey River Village. "Schooling is much easier [to access] and better than when I went to school." When Malvary was in school there was not a nice school house, supplies, textbooks, and there were more students and less teachers. Children in Monkey River Village are now starting school when they are 3 or 4 years old. She expressed her joy that her son would have a better education and schooling. When asked why it's important for her son to have an education and her response was, "I want him to get the best education. If they don't have an education then he can't get a job." Malvary emphasized how important it was for him to receive a higher education, stating that she wanted him to go as far academically as he could and that she would have to make sacrifices in order for him to do that. Although finding a good job might require her son to leave Monkey River Village, Malvary was fine with him leaving. She said, "if he wants to move it's okay. I love it here. I will stay here." Many children have the opportunity to continue their education even though finances and attitudes still prevent many from moving forward with their plans.

Malvary felt that the children today in Monkey River Village are much different from when she was a child. Beyond the better education that the children were receiving, she felt that the children have less restrictions and more freedom. Malvary and other women in the community expressed how the kids aren't kept at home and in sight as much as they used to be. Malvary explained that Monkey River Village is a very quiet place without any crime, "it's a good place to raise children." However with the idea of the community being safe, the children are allowed to wander more and end up causing more mischief themselves. When asked what she would do when she saw another young boy being mischievous she replied that she would scold them or spank them. She stated that the children had more opportunities (such as schooling) but also had more stuff (such as toys) that she never had as a child.

Monkey River Village appears quite traditional to visitors, although like many Belizean communities, the indigenous culture is being inundated by North American consumerism and values. Transcultural and global exchanges have led to a mutually beneficial evolution of indigenous values and perspectives. Young women such as Malvary are the leading edge of a wave of expanded aspirations washing over Monkey River Village. Most women long to see more local jobs and also hope to eventually see their children go to high school or college. The irony is that the reason they want their children to seek higher education is to find a high-paying job, but the majority of these "better" jobs are located far from the village. If the educated students could return to the village and start their own jobs and businesses, then the community's employment issues could slowly be improved. Until then, there will remain a lack of jobs, family income, and a continuing decline in the number of families remaining in the village. While traditional values among local residents appear to decline, many of those who grew up in this remote rural hamlet do not want to leave their homes, families, and friends. They want to improve their lives in this particular place.

Conclusion

A small community, with limited access to jobs and infrastructure, Monkey River Village remains a quiet, safe, and in some respects, bucolic community. Just as these rural qualities constitute the core characteristics valued by its residents, they also threaten to undermine the village's future prosperity. Increased emphasis on education, especially among young women, juxtaposed with decreased job opportunities has created a schism within the community. The more progressive individuals, those who aspire to a high school education and beyond, are leaving the village in search of jobs and higher education. Those who stay behind carry the burden of maintaining community traditions, traditions that must evolve in the face of new economic and social realities.

The indigenous viewpoints of the rural women in this study serves to illustrate the growing tension found in other rural villages facing rapid economic, social and environmental changes. Although one would hesitate to draw too many conclusions regarding community dynamics and opinions from the opinions expressed, these participants were selected with the intention of demonstrating the diversity of indigenous viewpoints about the future of Monkey River Village and specifically with respect to transitioning gender roles. Monkey River Village stands upon a threshold, straddling tradition and social change. Traditional stereotypes and gender roles have typically limited women's opportunities in education and employment. As women venture into new endeavours beyond the domestic, the community dynamic will undoubtedly change. The ability of local residents to embrace this change while holding firm to their own sense of what constitutes "the good life" will ultimately determine the cultural and economic sustainability of the community. Teetering on the "cusp of development," it is difficult for residents or outside observers to predict what lies in the future for this small community, and more importantly, how development pressures will continue to shape indigenous viewpoints and perspectives.

27

Sustainable Development in Serbia

Slobodan Milutinovic

Introduction

SUSTAINABLE development is a phrase increasingly used by policy makers and academics, yet what it means in practice can be frustratingly difficult to pin down. Perhaps the most well-known definition of sustainable development is that of the World Commission on Environment and Development (WCED) which identified it as "development that meets the needs of the present without compromising the ability of future generations to meet their own needs." (WCED, 1987). This seems like a straightforward idea, at the heart of which lies connections between economic development, environmental protection and social inclusion; each element reinforcing the other. In May 2001, the European Commission had developed a new consulting strategy for sustainable development: Sustainable Europe for a Better World — European Strategy of Sustainable Development [COM (2001) 264 final]. The strategy was adopted at the Goteborg European Council (held on June 15-16, 2001).

Agenda 21 set out a global action plan for sustainable development. While there have been successes on some of the issues, on many there has been little progress and indicators show that things have got worse. These major issues include tackling poverty, finance for development, and the need to transform unsustainable patterns of production and consumption, especially in the richer nations. Local sustainable development has been one of the areas of success. Several researchers have suggested that this work, led in many nations by the Local Agenda 21 process, is the most successful outcome of the 1992 Earth Summit. This new focus was primarily the result of one sentence in one Chapter of Agenda 21. Chapter 28: "By 1996, most local authorities in each country should have undertaken a consultative process with their populations and achieved a consensus on *a local Agenda 21* for the community." It has also been pointed out that over half the action points within Agenda 21 need action at a local level.

But awareness of sustainable development is still low both amongst the public and those working in national and local government. There is a need for a new internationally-guided information and awareness initiative to promote and support local action. The single biggest barrier to sustainable development in Serbia, nationally and locally, is the failure of national governments to implement the international agreements they have signed up to, most notably those arising from the 1992 UN Earth Summit. Also, national governments should work with local authorities and NGOs to identify priorities within these plans and to agree how these can be helped by co-ordinated actions at a local level.

Serbia at the Beginning of Third Millennium

Serbia is facing large problems and challenges not only in the environmental, but also in the social, economic, scientific, educational, legislative, institutional, and other areas of life. Unfortunately, the concept of sustainable development is neither sufficiently developed, nor implemented in Serbia. The reasons for such state of affairs are numerous, but are primarily to be looked for in economic and other forms of stagnation in the past 10-15 years. Overcoming these problems presents an enormous obligation for the Government of the Republic of Serbia.

Historically Serbia was the constitutional part of various West Balkan States (Yugoslavia, Federal Republic of Yugoslavia, State Union of Serbia and Montenegro). Recently Serbia became an independent State, due to the referendum decision of Montenegro to break down the State Union. The decade of mismanagement of the economy, an extended period of economic sanctions, and the damage to Yugoslavia's infrastructure and industry during the NATO airstrikes in 1999 have left the economy only half the size it was in 1990. After the ousting of former Federal Yugoslav President Milosevic in October 2000, the Democratic Opposition of Serbia (DOS) coalition government implemented stabilization measures and embarked on an aggressive market reform programme. After renewing its membership in the IMF in December 2000, Yugoslavia continued to reintegrate into the international community by rejoining the World Bank (IBRD) and the European Bank for Reconstruction and Development (EBRD). An agreement rescheduling the country's $4.5 billion Paris Club government debts was concluded in November 2001; it wrote off 66 per cent of the debt. The complexity of Serbia and Montenegro political relationships, slow progress in privatization, legal uncertainty over property rights, and scarcity of foreign investment are holding back Serbia and Montenegro's economy. Arrangements with the IMF, especially requirements for fiscal discipline, are an important element in policy formation. Severe unemployment remains a key political economic problem.

Table 27.1
Some economic indicators of Serbia

GDP:	purchasing power parity - $24.01 billion (2003 est.)
GDP - real growth rate:	2% (2003 est.)
GDP - per capita:	purchasing power parity - $2,300 (2003 est.)
GDP - composition by sector:	*agriculture:* 26% *industry:* 36% *services:* 38% (2001 est.)
Population below poverty line:	30% (1999 est.), 10.4% (2004)
Inflation rate (consumer prices):	11.6% (2003), 16.7% (2004)
Labour force:	3 million (2001 est.)
Unemployment rate:	34.5% (2003 est.)
Budget:	*revenues:* $3.9 billion *expenditures:* $4.3 billion, including capital
Industries:	machine building (aircraft, trucks, and automobiles; tanks and weapons; electrical equipment; agricultural machinery); metallurgy (steel, aluminium, copper, lead, zinc, chromium, antimony, bismuth, cadmium); mining (coal, bauxite, nonferrous ore, iron ore, limestone); consumer goods (textiles, footwear, foodstuffs, appliances); electronics; petroleum products; chemicals; and pharmaceuticals
Industrial production growth rate:	1.7% (2002), over 3% (2005)
Electricity - production:	31.71 billion kWh (2001)
Electricity - production by source:	*fossil fuel:* 62.9% *hydro:* 37.1% *nuclear:* 0% *other:* 0% (2001)

Electricity - consumption:	32.37 billion kWh (2001)
Agriculture - products:	cereals, fruits, vegetables, tobacco, olives; cattle, sheep, goats
Exports:	\$2.667 billion f.o.b. (2003 est.)
Exports - commodities:	manufactured goods, food and live animals, raw materials
Imports:	\$7.144 billion f.o.b. (2003 est.)
Imports - commodities:	machinery and transport equipment, fuels and lubricants, manufactured goods, chemicals, food and live animals, raw materials
Debt - external:	\$12.8 billion (2003 est.)
Economic aid - recipient:	\$2 billion pledged in 2001 (disbursements to follow for several years)

Sources: The CIA World Factbook, U.S. Department of State, Area Handbook of the US Library of Congress

Overall environmental situation in Serbia is unsatisfactory. This statement signifies equally on the water and water resources, air, biodiversity, forests and land conditions. The approach to waste management and dangerous chemicals management seems to be poor and high risks of chemical accidents, as well as high noise levels exist. The analyses of environmental policies indicate weak links between environmental policies and other sectoral policies, lack of necessary institutional capacity to respond to existing problems, inefficient environmental monitoring and reporting system, insufficient and inadequate legislative system, low investments and the lack of economic incentives, as well as low environmental awareness level. According to the preliminary cost assessment in national environmental action programme, environmental degradation causes annual costs for Serbian economy between 4.4 per cent GDP (the conservative scenario) and 13.1 per cent GDP (the maximal scenario) (Jantzen and Pesic, 2004). It is estimated that 53 per cent of overall environmental costs are caused by air pollution, 22 per cent by water pollution, and 11 per cent by weak waste management. In addition, following the anticipated 5 per cent annual GDP growth in coming years, the portion of environmental investments should increase from 0.1 per cent in 2005 to 1.2 per cent in 2009 and 2.4 per cent in 2014.

Recent political changes in Serbia and lifting of the sanctions imposed by the international community, mandated new activities/obligations/objectives: preparation of Serbia for accession to the European Union; active participation in various international conferences, as well as obligations arising from international agreements signed (international conventions and documents adopted in the world and European conferences, etc.).

Historically, the Serbian State in its various forms has employed centralization as an avenue of modernization, assuming an ever-greater role in communal affairs. Before 2000, legal and fiscal arrangements were specifically designed to weaken local government. In early 2002, the Serbian Parliament began to reconsider decentralization, passing a new Law on Local Self-government. The legal framework prior to February 2002, however, contributes to the extremely limited responsibilities and powers to municipalities. Former practices remain; the endurance of these practices requires investigation. The 29 districts (*okrug*) of Serbia function as extensions of the central government. While major changes have recently taken place at the federal, republican and local level, there has been very little political or structural change at the district level (Milutinovic, 2003).

Presently, each district contains several municipalities (*opstina*) – 167 in Serbia. The 2002 Law on Local Self-Government has divested a municipality of its definition of a territorial unit. Municipalities, rather, can organize "local communities" (*mesne zajednice*), and exist as corporate entities encompassing towns, villages and rural areas. While a municipal government is normally situated in the largest town, it is responsible for the entire district.

The new law signifies innovations in sub-national governance, with refined aims including functionality, professionalism, efficacy and personal responsibility in administrative execution. The actors of local government have also transformed: formerly appointed by a Municipal Assembly, mayors are now to be directly elected by citizens. The new law has also expanded the scope of the competences of the local government. Consequently, the following areas currently fall under the responsibility of the municipalities: provision of utility services such as supply of water and gas, sewage, sanitation, collecting and disposing of garbage, as well as certain parts of the traffic infrastructure and the road network, in addition to the areas of elementary education and primary health care, cultural institutions and activities, social services, sports, recreation, ecology and environmental protection and finally, stimulating the economic development. Certain competencies in social care have been transferred from the national to the municipal level, but these are still out under the auspices of the State bodies. To some extent the financial autonomy of the municipalities has been strengthened, giving them the right to raise loans, collect several republican taxes, and a portion of receipts is re-distributed back to them. But the new law, importantly, has not solved the problem of ownership. Municipalities possess the right to manage ownership, the right to possess land, business facilities and assets possessed by the Republic. Finally, accountability and reporting were neither explicitly mentioned in this law, nor are they addressed in the 2002 revision. The reporting system has historically been hierarchical — information flows from the bottom to the top — and generally concerns annual reports, and little more (Milutinovic, 2004a).

Sustainable Development: Approaches and Initiatives

NATIONAL SUSTAINABLE DEVELOPMENT STRATEGY

The project on Sustainable Development Strategy for Serbia was initiated as a response to the World Summit on Sustainable Development and its call for National Sustainable Development Strategies. Pursuant to the plan adopted at the 2002 Johannesburg Sustainable Development Summit, which specifies that the implementation of national strategies on sustainable development is to be implemented by 2005, the Government of the Republic of Serbia has constituted a Council for Sustainable Development and started drafting its National Strategy for Sustainable Development. In 2004, a project document "Development of Strategies for Sustainable Development in Serbia and Montenegro through co-operation between countries was prepared." The Government of Sweden, through its Agency for International Development (SIDA) has allocated significant funds for the implementation of this project, which is co-ordinated through UNDP. The project objective is to produce a Sustainable Development Strategy for the Republic of Serbia and it is being managed by the Office of the Deputy Prime Minister. The project will be closely co-ordinated with the implementation process of the Poverty Reduction Strategy (PRS), and it will be implemented in co-operation with the academic community and with the participation of country stakeholders in Serbia. It will build upon the work done for the PRS and initially focus on adding an environmental dimension that is expected to use inputs from the still ongoing work on the National Environmental Action Plan. The European Integration Strategy will provide an input into the Sustainable Development Strategy for Serbia and align with the local sustainable development strategy prepared by the Standing Conference of Towns and Municipalities and a variety of existing sector strategies.

Drafting of the Sustainable Development Strategy for Serbia will be conducted through three major Working Groups, each covering one of the identified three pillars for Sustainable Development in Serbia: Knowledge-based economy; Economic and social development; and Environment and public health. Outputs of these three Working Groups are intended to fill in the gaps in the existing sectoral and cross-sectoral strategies, as well as to prepare the ground for an umbrella project of assistance to the Government of Serbia in implementation of the pool of strategies and development objectives.

POLICY-MAKING

In December 2004, the National Assembly of the Republic of Serbia adopted a set of environmental protection laws: The Law on Environmental Protection; The Law on Evaluation of Environmental Impact; The Law on Strategic Evaluation of Environmental Impact; and The Law on Integrated Prevention and Control of Pollution of the Environment. These laws are in line with the EU Directives and their adoption is a significant step forward to harmonizing with the European Standards regulating environmental protection.

NEAP

NEAP (National Environmental Action Programme) is a part of the process "Environment for Europe" initiated in Central and Eastern Europe. The Action Programme of Environmental

Protection for Central and Eastern Europe, adopted at the "Environment for Europe" conference in Lucerne in 1993, provided a set of methodological guidelines for the development of NEAP.

The NEAP process in Serbia has been under way since 2003, as a part of "Strengthening Environmental Capacity" funded by EAR. The goal of this project is the development of recommendations of National Policies of Environmental Protection and the development of the National Ecology Action Plan, through detailed identification of environmentally related issues, in order to subsequently set priorities and goals of environmental protection policy and define the package of measures of the action plan.

SUSTAINABLE DEVELOPMENT INDICATORS

In 2003, the Ministry in charge of environmental protection has initiated the project called "Defining the Sustainable Development Indicators." The project was due to end early in 2005. Based on this project and other activities undertaken in co-operation with relevant bodies and organizations, the defined plan is to generate a set of indicators for the sustainable development of Serbia, by applying the internationally accepted methodologies and withstanding the national idiosyncrasies.

THE LOCAL SUSTAINABLE DEVELOPMENT STRATEGY

Strategic planning is a new tool for post-communist municipalities. It fosters innovative, co-operative approaches to urban governance that involves business, government, academics and other partners in the process. It also allows responsiveness and selective intervention. The experience so far indicates that cities have identified similar strategic directions, but different priorities and operational instruments, depending on the level of political commitment and institutional capacities.

The primary focus of strategic planning in post-communist cities and municipalities is the institutional strengthening of local government units through the creation of locally-owned municipal strategy development processes that are participatory, integrated and holistic (Tsenkova 2004). While different contexts produce different methodologies, most strategy development processes are cyclical and involve a number of basic components, namely purpose and approach search, contextual analysis and strategy development (visioning, strategic directions — goals and mission statement, objectives for each strategic direction — prioritised targets and milestones, actions).

Although some efforts have recently been made, Serbian municipalities still suffer from the lack of contemporary strategic planning mechanisms. There is a considerable gap between long-term plans (obligatory by the law) and the short-term "project documentation" and annual investment programmes prepared by the municipalities; the crucial intermediary phase of medium-term strategic planning is missing.

In such circumstances, decision-makers lack the capacity to compare investment options across different sectors. Also, the potential of community participation in planning and decision-making processes is not adequately realized. Although no institutional assessments were made in this study, the degree of co-operation and consensus among various local government bodies and agencies appears to be less than satisfactory in some cases. To a certain degree, the previous, highly centralized system, the "external" relationship between local central agencies perseveres, to the detriment of "internal" co-operation and policy coherence at the municipal level.

Programme for Environmental Protection and Sustainable Development in Serbian Towns and Municipalities 2004–2006, developed by Serbian Association of Towns and Municipalities (Standing Conference of Towns and Municipalities — SKGO) and supported by Norwegian Association of Local and Regional Authorities — KS), is created with overall goal to

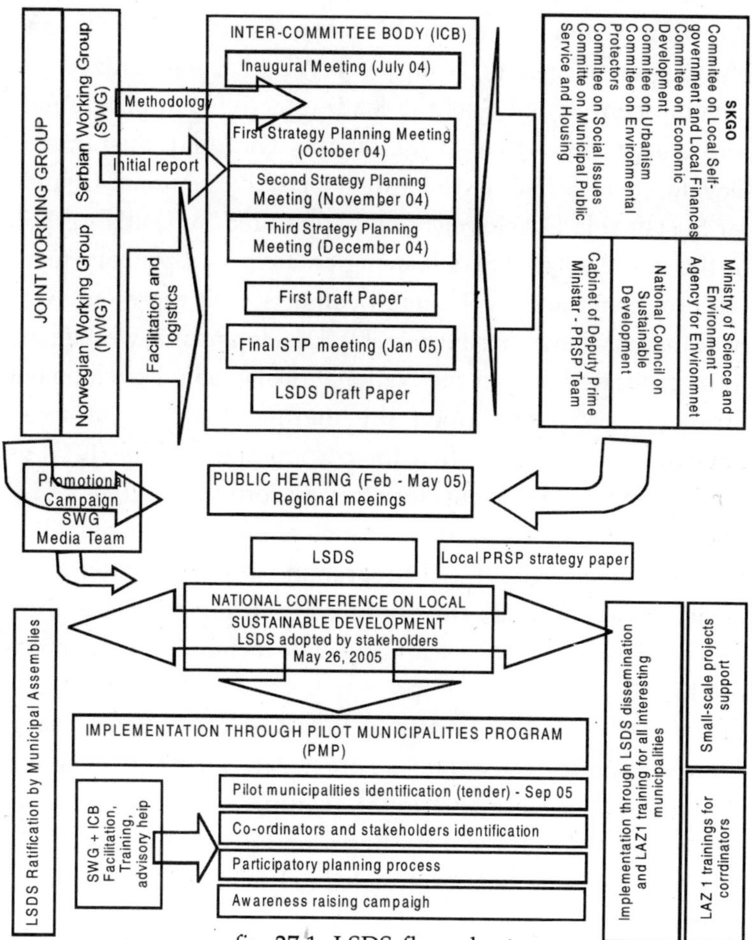

fig. 27.1. LSDS flow chart

improve quality of life in Serbian local communities, by obtaining better environmental conditions and enabling local governments, as well as national government, to define and pursue policies of sustainability in the future development of Serbian towns and municipalities. Carrying activity for the first year of programme implementation was development of Local Sustainable Development Strategy Paper (LSDS).

Immediately after programme initiation in May 2004, Joint Working Group (Serbian Working Group — SWG and Norwegian Working Group — NWG) has recognized the development of LSDS as the leading activity in programme implementation. Even though the National Sustainable Development Strategy (to be developed by National Council for Sustainable Development and sponsored by UNDP) is still in the initial stage, LSDS is being created with primary focus on local communities. Through contacts with representatives of National Council for Sustainable Development it was agreed to incorporate LSDS in the National Sustainable Development Strategy. SWG developed the methodology for strategy development and identified Inter-Committee Group (ICG) as a main stakeholder group for strategy formulation (*fig*. 27.1.). The methodology engaged was nominal group technique. SWG from the very beginning of programme implementation made efforts to include all stakeholders in strategy formulation processes. In that respect ICG did not include only members of SKGO Committees — representatives of local governments, but also the representatives of the Ministry of Science and Environmental Protection — Directorate for Environmental Protection, of the National Council for Sustainable Development and NGOs. Representatives from various Ministries, slowly but surely, pledged their full commitment toward the programme.

After the initial inaugural ICG meeting in July 2004, SWG had performed a field work study in August of same year, aimed to collect data for an initial assessment of environment and sustainable development situation in Serbian cities and municipalities. According to the gathered data the initial report was prepared in September 2004 both as the basis for further ICG strategy formulation and as information gathered to create specialized SKGO database (Kaludjerovic et al., 2004). ICG held three workshops on strategy formulation (in October, November and December). Based on the ICG recommendations, SWG prepared the draft of Local Sustainable Development Strategy in December 2004.

Draft of Local Sustainable Development Strategy was completed in final ICG workshop in January 2005. LSDS Draft Paper was ready to undertake adjustments and corrections from participation through public discussions.

A set of public discussion about LSDS draft had been organized in March and April 2004. Ten regional meetings were organized in regional centres (Pirot, Leskovac, Kragujevac, Bor, Čačak, Valjevo, Pančevo, Novi Sad, Subotica and Beograd). Almost half of 167 Serbian municipalities and the members of business and civil society participated and made a significant input.

LSDS was adopted at the National Conference of Local Sustainable Development in Belgrade, May 26th 2005. Immediately after that implementation phase began through ratification by each municipal assembly, pilot LA21 projects in seven Serbian municipalities and capacity building activities, organized by SKGO.

According to the LSDS, the local governments in Serbia agreed to join their efforts in order to attain the following vision.

Cities and municipalities of Serbia develop in accordance with the principles of sustainable development, through:

Development of participative democracy;

Efficient and effective management;

Taking over the responsibility for protection, preservation and ensuring equal approach to the common natural resources;

Rational management of resources, whereby a sustainable production and consumption is achieved;

Creation of positive economic environment and employment capacity, in accordance with the environmental protection principles;

Urban planning that meets the needs of creation of social, economic and environmental standards;

Promoting sustainable patterns of life, health, and benefit to the citizens, inclusive of all community processes.

In order to attain the vision projected thus, it is necessary for the local governments and their associations to achieve specific **goals**, as follows:

I. In the area of **infrastructure**

A. Development, quality and continuous improvement of infrastructure by hiring the most skilled professional staff available; implementation of transparent processes; utilization of all the available sources of funding; and development of standards regulating the management of infrastructure systems.

B. Protection and utilization of natural resources in accordance with the principles of sustainable development by applying the appropriate economic instruments.

II. In the area of **space and urban planning**

A. Creation of a better organized and co-ordinated planning at local government-level; local administration; and public enterprises in order to improve the development of the urban planning documentation.

B. Intensive public education activities in order to include the general public.

C. Incorporating the principles of best practices of sustainable development into the urban planning documentation.

III. In the area of **economic development and employment**

A. Development and adoption of local strategies for economic development and employment, accompanied with municipal decisions, and building or strengthening of the local government institutions, in order to facilitate development and implementation of the strategies.

B. Initiate adoption of legal regulations defining the rights and obligations of local governments in the area of support to the local economic development and employment incentives.

C. Introduction and promotion of incentives in local economic development and employment.

D. Development of local economies based on available natural resources with the development of systems supporting the promotion of sustainable resource utilization.

E. Regional networking.

F. Improvement of local government inspection services, through providing equipment, education, and incentives to preventive action.

IV. In the area of **social development**

A. Institutional strengthening of local governments.

B. Raising the level of knowledge of the elected and appointed officials in the municipal administration, as well as of the general public, about the sustainable development concept, and the methods and techniques this concept encompasses.

C. Promotion of health in the broadest sense, in all the spheres of social development and for all population groups.

D. Appraisal of traditional values through economic activities.

E. Facilitating more accessible and equal exercising of health and social welfare benefits, on a local level.

F. Exchange of "best practices" and experiences among municipalities in order to reduce the differences in social development capacities.

G. Encouraging the participation of the media in social development programmes.

H. Initialising the changes in legislation, towards providing tax incentives for investing in social development

V. In the area of **environmental protection**

A. Development of strategic documents and improving the environmental protection on a local level.

B. Introduction of economic instruments to facilitate more cost-effective resource management.

C. Promoting rationalization of spending.

D. Introduction of the monitoring system and measures for protection and improvement of the environment.

E. Promoting the transparency of work and participation of general public in the decision-making process.

VI. In the area of **poverty reduction**

A. Creation of local strategies (action plans) for poverty reduction and creation of institutional framework in the local government to facilitate poverty reduction goals.

B. Promoting municipalities to attract potential interested investors.

C. Creating incentives for development of entrepreneurship and self-employment.

D. Achieving a bilateral dialogue with the socially excluded groups.

ICG developed more specific activities to be undertaken to achieve those goals, delegate responsibilities and set time-frame (short, medium and long-term activities).

Local Sustainable Development Strategy Paper has been harmonized with the Consultative Strategy of Sustainable Development of the European Union: "Sustainable Europe for a Better World — the European Strategy for Sustainable Development" (COM (2001) 264 final), the 1994 Charter of European Cities and Municipalities towards Sustainability — (Aalborg Charter), the 1996 Lisbon action plan: "From Charter to Action," the 2000 "Invitation from Hanover to the European

Municipal Leaders at the Turn of the Twenty-first Century," the 2002 "Invitation from Johannesburg," the final document of the +10 Aalborg Conference: "Aalborg Commitments" and "Fano Guidelines" — the final document of the "Managing Sustainable Cities" conference.

Conclusion

The achievement of sustainability in national development requires a strategic approach, which is both long-term in its perspective and integrated or "joined-up" in linking various development processes so that they are as sophisticated as the challenges are complex. A strategic approach at the national level implies:

- Linking long-term vision to medium-term targets and short-term action;
- "Horizontal" linkages across sectors, so that there is a co-ordinated approach to development;
- "Vertical" spatial linkages, so that local, national and global policy, development efforts and governance are all mutually supportive; and
- Genuine partnership between government, business, and community and voluntary organizations, since the problems are too complex to be resolved by any group acting alone.

In accordance with the conclusions of the Johannesburg Conference, local governments implementing the sustainable development are bound to enter a decade of increasingly effective action towards creation of sustainable communities, and protection of common world goods. Adhering to these facts, but also having in mind the efforts that Republic of Serbia is undertaking in implementation of improved living conditions for its citizens in all segments of economic and social development, as well as implementation of environmental protection, the local governments in Serbia agreed to join their efforts in order to attain the sustainability vision. The Law on Local Self-Government from 2002 has just initiated the decentralization, while the forthcoming constitutional reform is to create the normative basis for a further decentralization and a functional reform of all the governmental levels. The process of modernization and strengthening of the status and functional capacities of the local government implies a new distribution of competence, and a new type of partnership relations among the various levels of government, the new forms of co-ordination and establishing of new financial arrangements, together with strengthening of the local government autonomy (fiscal federalism). Regulations on municipalities and other types of territorial organization, public administration, property, local finances, etc. are a precondition of reform in this area.

Abbrevations

DOS	—	Democratic Opposition of Serbia
EAR	—	European Agency for Reconstruction
EBRD	—	European Bank for Reconstruction and Development
ICG	—	Inter-Committee Group
LSDS	—	Local Sustainable Development Strategy
NEAP	—	National Environmental Action Programme
NWG	—	Norwegian Working Group
PRS	—	Poverty Reduction Strategy
SIDA	—	Sweden International Development Agency
SKGO	—	Standing Conference of Towns and Municipalities
SWG	—	Serbian Working Group
WCED	—	World Commission on Environment and Development

References

Jantzen, J. and R. Pesic (2004). *Assessment of the Economic Value of Environmental Degradation in Serbia.* Environmental Capacity Building Program. An EU-funded project managed by the European Agency for Reconstruction (personal communication).

Kaludjerovic, L.J., S. Milutinovic, A. Popovic and M. Milenkovic (2004), *Programme for Environment and Sustainable Development for Serbian Towns and Municipalities: A Preliminary Analysis,* Belgrade: Standing Conference of Towns and Municipalities, (mimeo).

Milutinovic, S. (2006), Country to Country Co-operation in LSD Strategic Planning: The Strategy for Local Sustainable Development in Serbia. Abstracts. *ICLEI World Congress 2006,* Cape Town, South Africa, March 27th-April 3rd, 2006, http://www.iclei-europe.org/fileadmin/user_upload/ITC/worldcongress2006/LA2_Milutinovic_Slobodan.pdf

——— (2005), Transition in Serbia and the challenge of local sustainable development, Proceedings of Abstracts, *International Conference Sustainable Construction: Action for Sustainability in the Mediterranean,* Athens, June 9th-11th 2005.

——— (2004), *Local Agenda 21: The Introduction in Sustainable Development Planning,* Belgrade: Standing Conference of Towns and Municipalities of Yugoslavia (in Serbian).

——— (2004), Performance Measurement in Serbian Local Government: Future Improvements or Another Urban Government Fiction. In *Winds of Societal Change* (eds.), Z. Nedovic-Budic and S. Tsenkova, Urbana-Champaign: University of Illinois, pp.181-96.

——— (2004), *Urbanization and Sustainable Development,* Nis: Faculty of Occupational Safety (in Serbian).

——— (2003), Introducing Performance Measurement to Local Administration in Serbia: Options and Possibilities, In *Gauging Success: Performance Measurement in South Eastern Europe* (ed.), Zeljko Sevic, Budapest: Local Government and Public Service Reform Initiative, pp. 119-48.

Milutinovic, S. and L.J. Kaludjerovic (2005), Local Support for Global Citizenship — Transition in Serbia and the Challenge of Local Sustainable Development, *International Sustainability Conference ISC 2005,* Basel, Switzerland, October 13th-14th 2005.

Milutinovic, S., L.J. Kaludjerovic, M. Milenkovic and A. Popovic (2005), Local sustainable development strategy in Serbia, *Proceedings of the Conference, "Environment for Europe,"* Belgrade, June 2005 (contributed for publishing).

Ševic, Ž. (2003), Performance Measurement in the (Western) Balkans: Regional Experience and International Perspective. In *Gauging Success: Performance Measurement in South Eastern Europe* (ed.) Z. Sevic, Budapest: Local Government and Public Service Reform Initiative, pp. 149-60.

———, (2001), Local Government in Yugoslavia. In *Stabilization of Local Government* (ed.) Emilia Kandeva. Budapest: Local Government and Public Service Reform Initiative.

Tsenkova, S. (2004), Managing Change in Post-Communist Cities, In *Winds of Societal Change* (eds.), Z. Nedovic-Budic and S. Tsenkova, Urbana-Champaign: University of Illinois, pp. 3-20.

White Paper (1994), *Preparation of the Associated Countries of Central and Eastern Europe for Integration into the Internal Market of the Union.* Brussels: Commission of the European Communities.

———, *The Strategy for Local Sustainable Development*, Belgrade, 26 May 2005.

———, *The CIA World Factbook,* U.S. Department of State, Area Handbook of the US Library of Congress.

The Contributors

1. **G.A. Abu**
   Lecturer and Research Fellow
   Department of Agricultural Economics
   University of Agriculture
   MAKURDI (Nigeria)
   E-mail: <goddy_master@yahoo.co.uk>

2. **Dr Salei'a Afele-Fa'amuli** (PhD, M.P.H.)
   National Program Leader, Multicultural Alliances
   Science & Education Resources Development Unit
   Cooperative State Research Education and Extension Service (CSREES)
   USDA
   1400 Independence Ave, S.W., Mail Stop 2251
   WASHINGTON, DC 20250-2251 (USA)

   Express Mail:
   Waterfront Centre, Room 3103
   800 9th St. S.W.
   WASHINGTON, DC 20024 (USA)
   E-mail: sfaamuli@csrees.usda.gov

3. **Dr Wolfgang Amann**
   Executive Director MBA-HSG
   Blumenbergplatz 9
   9000 ST. GALLEN (Switzerland)
   E-mail: <wolfgang.amann@unisg.ch>

4. **F. Antunes**
Assistant Professor
Dept. of Mechanical Engineering
Rua Luis Reis Santos
Pólo II da Universidade de Coimbra
3030-788 COIMBRA (Portugal)
E-mail: <fernando.ventura@dem.uc.pt>

5. **Hamidi Abdul Aziz**
Associate Professor (Environmental Engineering)
School of Civil Engineering
Nibong Tebal, Seberang Selatan, USM
14300 NIBONG TEBAL (Malaysia)
E-mail: <cehamidi@eng.usm.my>

6. **Dr Mert Bilgin**
Associate Professor
Department of International Relations
Faculty of Economics and Administrative Sciences
Dogus University
Ac½badem
34722 ISTANBUL (Turkey)
E-mail: mbilgin@dogus.edu.tr

7. **Dr Adela Coman** (PhD)
Assistant Professor
The North University of Baia Mare
62A/Dr. Victor Babes St.
12A/23 Unirii Blv.
430272 BAIA MARE (Romania)
E-mail: <adela_coman2003@yahoo.com>

8. **Prof. E.P. Ejembi**
Lecturer and Research Fellow
Department of Agricultural Extension and Communication
University of Agriculture

MAKURDI (Nigeria)
E-mail: <egragaba@yahoo.com>

9. Ashley Frost
Docotral Candidate
Sociology and Demography
Pennsylvania State University
211, Oswald Tower
UNIVERSITY PARK, PA 16802 (USA)
E-mail: <afrost@pop.psu.edu>

10. Dr Grace Hampton
Department of African and African American Studies
The Pennsylvania Sate University
214 Willard Building
STATE COLLEGE, Pennsylvania, 16802 (USA)

11. Dr Francis X. Higdon
Senior Lecturer in Community Development
361, Selders Circle
STATE COLLEGE, PA 16801 (USA)
E-mail: <frankxhigdon@yahoo.com>

12. Kendal Hodgman
Doctor of Philosophy Candidate
Institute for Sustainability and Technology Policy
Murdoch University
PERTH, Western Australia, 6150 (Australia)
E-mail: <K.Hodgman@murdoch.edu.au>
Wedsite: http://www.sustainability.murdoch.edu.au

13. Dr Chandra Prakash Kala
Consultant
National Medicinal Plants Board
36 Janpath, Chandralok Building
NEW DELHI- 110 001
E-mail: <cpkala@yahoo.co.uk>, <cpkala@rediffmail.com>

14. Dr Prafulla Kumar Kara
Reader in Geography
Utkal University
Vani Vihar
BHUBANESWAR – 751 004
Orissa (India)

15. Shiban Khan
University of St. Gallen
Blumenbergplatz 9
9000 ST. GALLEN (Switzerland)
E-mail: <shiban.khan@student.unisg.ch>

16. Dr Benjamin Levy
School of International Training
P.O. Box 1313
I Kipling Road
BRATTLEBORO VT 05302 (USA)
E-mail: <donmincho@gmail.com>

17. Dr Leslie Sue Lieberman (PhD)
Director
Women's Research Center
University of Central Florida
P.O. Box 160955 (USA)
ORLANDO, FL 32816-0955 (USA)
Wedsite: <www.womens.research.ucf.edu>

18. Abdullah Mahmood
Associate Professor (Project & Construction Management)
School of Housing, Building and Planning
Minden, USM
11800 PULAU PENANG (Malaysia)
E-mail: <mabdull@usm.my>

19. J. Malça
Adjoint Professor
Dept. of Mechanical Engineering
Instituto Superior de Engenharia de Coimbra
Rua Pedro Nunes
3030-199 COIMBRA (Portugal)
E-mail: <jmalca@isec.pt>

20. Dr Wolfgang Meyer
Centre for Evaluation (CEval)
Saarland University
Box 151 150
66041 SAARBR (Cken)
E-mail: <w.meyer@mx.uni-saarland.de>

21. Dr Slobodan Milutinovic
(Professor of the University of Nis, Serbia and Visiting Professor of the Central European University, Budapest)
Bulevar Nikole Tesle 19/4,
18000 NIS, (Serbia)
E-mail: <boban40@yahoo.com>
Website: http://www.freewebs.com/boban40/

22. Mohammed Nadhir Ibn Muntaka
2005 Graduate of the Pennsylvania Sate University in Integrative Arts
861 Oak Ridge Ave.
STATE COLLEGE, Pennsylvania 16801 (USA)

23. O.G.Okpachu
Graduate Student
Department of Agricultural Economics
University of Agriculture
MAKURDI (Nigeria)
E-mail: <avange04@yahoo.com>

24. Dr Abdelnaser Omran Ali (PhD)
(Environmental Management and Engineering)
School of Housing, Building and Planning
Minden, USM
11800 PULAU PENANG (Malaysia)
E-mail: <naser_elamroni@yahoo.co.uk>

25. Dr R.N. Pati (PhD)
Senior Social Anthropologist
IK Foundation of India
Mahamaya Bhawan
HIG-101, Kanan Vihar
Phase-I, P.O. Patia
BHUBANESWAR – 751031, Orissa (India)
E-mail: <pati_rabindranath@yahoo.com>

26. C. Pereira
Adjoint Professor
Dept. of Mechanical Engineering
Instituto Superior de Engenharia de Coimbra
Rua Pedro Nunes
3030-199 COIMBRA (Portugal)
E-mail: <candida@isec.pt>

27. Bikram Singh Sajwan
National Medicinal Plants Board
Department of Ayush
Ministry of Health & Family Welfare
36 Janpath, Chandralok Building
NEW DELHI – 110 001 (India)

28. Dr Odile Schwarz-Herion (MBA)
Department of Environmental Management
University of Hohenheim
Schwarzwaldring 39
D-76275 ETTLINGEN (Germany)
E-mail: <EOKK.Black@t-online.de>

29. Dr Shailesh R Shukla
Post Doctoral Fellow
Natural Resources Institute
University of Manitoba
WINNIPEG, MB, R3T 2N2 (USA)
E-mail: <shaileshshukla@yahoo.com>

30. Dr María de Lourdes Cŏarcamo Solís
Professor of Social Sciences Department, ITESM.
Eduardo Monroy Cárdenas 2000
San Antonio Buenavista
TOLUCA, c.p. 50110 (México)
E-mail: <lulu.carcamo@itesm.mx>
<carcamo.lulu@gmail.com>

31. Dr Markus Thüer
Head of Environmental Technology
Ciba®Expert Services
P.O.Box
CH 4002 BASEL (Switzerland)
E-mail: <markus.thueer@cibasc.com>

32. Dr José G. Vargas-Hernŏndez (M.B.A., PhD)
Research Professor
National System of Researchers, México
Instituto Tecnològico de Cd. Guzmàn
Ave. Tecnològico 100
Cd. Guzmàn
JALISCO, 49100 (México)
Private: Cerrada Petronilo Lòpez 31
Cd. Guzmàn
JALISCO, 49000 (México)
E-mail: <jgvh0811@yahoo.com>

33. Dr Glenda Verrinder
Senior Lecturer
Department of Health & Environment
School Public Health

La Trobe University
PO Box, 199
BENDIGO, 3552 (Australia)
E-mail: <g.verrinder@latrobe.edu.au>

34. Lori Zimmaro
Graduate Student in Community Economic Development
Pennsylvania State University
Armsby Building
UNIVERSITY PARK, PA 16803 (USA)
Private: 1300, Osbourne Ave
ROSLYN, PA 19001 (USA)
E-mail: <lzimmaro@verizon.net>

35. Dr Elayne Zorn (PhD)
Associate Professor of Anthropology
Anthropology Undergraduate Coordinator
Department of Anthropology
University of Central Florida
Phillips Hall 309
ORLANDO, Florida 32816-1361 (USA)
E-Mail: <ezorn@mail.ucf.edu>

Index